THEORY OF GROUND VEHICLES

THEORY OF GROUND VEHICLES

Second Edition

J. Y. WONG, Ph.D., D.Sc.
Department of Mechanical and Aerospace Engineering
Carleton University
Ottawa, Canada

A Wiley-Interscience Publication
JOHN WILEY & SONS, INC.
New York / Chichester / Brisbane / Toronto / Singapore

Copyright © 1993 by John Wiley & Sons, Inc.

All rights reserved. Published simultaneously in Canada.

Library of Congress Cataloging in Publication Data:
Wong, J. Y. (Jo Yung)
    Theory of ground vehicles/J. Y. Wong. — 2nd ed.
      p. cm.
    Includes bibliographical references and index.
    ISBN 0-471-52496-4 (acid-free paper)
    1. Motor vehicles—Design and construction. 2. Ground-effect
  machines—Design and construction. I. Title.
  TL240.W66 1993
  629.23—dc20   92-21523

Printed in the United States of America

10 9 8 7

To May
Chak
Ben
Jing
Kay
Leo
Sang
Loretta
San
Nicholas
and the memory of my parents

CONTENTS

3 PERFORMANCE CHARACTERISTICS OF ROAD VEHICLES   168

PREFACE

Since the first edition of this book was published in 1978, it has gone through ten printings. A number of engineering schools in North America, Europe, Asia, and elsewhere have adopted it as a text for courses in automotive engineering, vehicle dynamics, off-road vehicle engineering, agricultural engineering, etc. It was translated into Russian and published in Moscow, Russia, in 1982, and into Chinese and published in Beijing, China, in 1985. Meanwhile, significant technological developments in the field have taken place. To reflect these new developments and to serve the changing needs of the educational and professional communities, the time is ripe for the second edition of this book.

With the growing emphasis being placed by society on energy conservation, environmental protection, and safety, transportation technology is under greater challenge than ever before. To improve fuel economy and to reduce undesirable exhaust emission, in addition to improvements in power plant design, measures such as improving vehicle aerodynamic performance, better matching of transmission with engine, and optimizing power requirements have received intense attention. To improve driving safety, antilock brake systems and traction control systems have been introduced. To provide better ride comfort while maintaining good road-holding capability, active and semi-active suspension systems have attracted considerable interest. To expedite the development of new products, computer-aided methods for vehicle performance and design optimization have been developed. Discussions of these and other technological developments in the field have been included in this second edition. Furthermore, data on various topics have been updated.

As with the first edition, this second edition of *Theory of Ground Vehicles* is written with the same philosophy of emphasizing the fundamental engineering principles underlying the rational development and design of nonguided ground vehicles, including road vehicles, off-road vehicles, and air-cushion vehicles. Analysis and evaluation of performance characteristics, handling behavior, and ride comfort of these vehicles are covered. A unified method of approach to the analysis of the characteristics of various types of ground vehicle is again stressed. This book is intended primarily to introduce senior undergraduate and beginning graduate students to the study of ground vehicle engineering. However, it should also be of interest to engineers and researchers in the vehicle industry.

Similar to the first edition, this second edition consists of eight chapters. Chapter 1 discusses the mechanics of pneumatic tires. Practical methods for predicting the behavior of tires subject to longitudinal or side force, as well as under their combined action, are included. New experimental data on tire performance are added. Chapter 2 examines the mechanics of vehicle–terrain interaction, which has become known as "terramechanics." Computer-aided methods for the design and performance evaluation of off-road vehicles are included. Experimental data on the mechanical properties of various types of terrain are updated. Chapter 3 deals with the analysis and prediction of road vehicle performance. Included is updated information on the aerodynamic performance of passenger cars and articulated heavy commercial vehicles. Procedures for matching transmission with engine to achieve improved fuel economy while maintaining adequate performance are outlined. Characteristics of continuously variable transmissions and their effects on fuel economy and performance are examined. The operating principles of antilock brake systems and traction control systems and their effects on performance and handling are presented in some detail. The performance of off-road vehicles is the subject of Chapter 4. Discussions on the optimization of the performance of all-wheel-drive off-road vehicles are expanded. In addition, various criteria for evaluating military vehicles are included. Chapter 5 examines the handling behavior of road vehicles. In addition to discussions of the steady-state and transient handling behavior of passenger cars, the handling characteristics of tractor-semitrailers are examined. The handling diagram for evaluating directional response is included. The steering of tracked vehicles is the topic of Chapter 6. In addition to skid-steering, articulated steering for tracked vehicles is examined. Chapter 7 deals with vehicle ride comfort. Human tolerance to vibration, vehicle ride models, and applications of the random vibration theory to the evaluation of ride comfort are covered. Furthermore, the effects of suspension spring stiffness, damping, and unsprung mass on vibration isolation characteristics, road holding, and suspension travel are examined. The principles of active and semi-active suspensions are also discussed. In addition to conventional road vehicles and off-road vehicles, air-cushion vehicles have found applications in ground transportation. The basic principles of air-cushion systems and the unique characteristics of air-cushion vehicles for overland and overwater operations are treated in Chapter 8. New data on the mechanics of skirt–terrain interaction are included.

The material included in this book has been used in the undergraduate and graduate courses in ground transportation technology that I have been teaching at Carleton for some years. It has also been presented, in part, at seminars and in professional development programs in Canada, China, Finland, Germany, Italy, Singapore, Spain, Sweden, Taiwan, the United Kingdom, and the United States.

In preparing the second edition of this book, I have drawn much on my experience acquired from collaboration with many of my colleagues in industry, research organizations, and universities in North America, Europe, Asia, and elsewhere. The encouragement, inspiration, suggestions, and comments that I have received from Dr. A. R. Reece, formerly of the University of Newcastle-upon-Tyne, and currently Managing Director, Soil Machine Dynamics Limited, England; Professor L. Segel, Professor Emeritus, University of Michigan; and Professor E. H. Law, Clemson University, are particularly appreciated. I would also like to record my gratitude to the late Dr. M. G. Bekker, with whom I had the good fortune to collaborate in research projects and in joint offerings of professional development programs, upon which some of the material included in this book was developed.

The typing of the manuscript by D. Dodds and the preparation of additional illustrations by J. Brzezina for this second edition are appreciated.

Jo Yung Wong

Ottawa, Canada

CONVERSION FACTORS

Quantity	U.S. Customary Unit	SI Equivalent
Acceleration	ft/s^2	$0.3048 \ m/s^2$
Area	ft^2	$0.0929 \ m^2$
	$in.^2$	$645.2 \ mm^2$
Energy	$ft \cdot lb$	$1.356 \ J$
Force	lb	$4.448 \ N$
Length	ft	$0.3048 \ m$
	$in.$	$25.4 \ mm$
	$mile$	$1.609 \ km$
Mass	$slug$	$14.59 \ kg$
	ton	$907.2 \ kg$
Moment of a force	$lb \cdot ft$	$1.356 \ N \cdot m$
Power	hp	$745.7 \ W$
Pressure or stress	lb/ft^2	$47.88 \ Pa$
	$lb/in.^2 \ (psi)$	$6.895 \ kPa$
Speed	ft/s	$0.3048 \ m/s$
	mph	$1.609 \ km/h$
Volume	ft^3	$0.02832 \ m^3$
	$in.^3$	$16.39 \ cm^3$
	$gal \ (liquids)$	$3.785 \ liter$

NOMENCLATURE

A	area, contact area
A_c	cushion area
A_f	frontal area
A_u	parameter characterizing terrain response to repetitive loading
a	acceleration
a_x	acceleration component along the x axis
a_y	acceleration component along the y axis
a_z	acceleration component along the z axis
B	tread of the vehicle
B_a	barometric pressure
B_m	working width of machinery
B_o	barometric pressure under standard atmospheric conditions
B_v	vapor pressure
b	width
C, CI	cone index
C_D	aerodynamic resistance coefficient
C_f	ratio of braking effort to normal load of vehicle front axle
C_i	longitudinal stiffness of tire subject to a driving torque
C_L	aerodynamic lift coefficient
C_{ld}	lift/drag ratio
C_M	aerodynamic pitching moment coefficient

C_r	ratio of braking effort to normal load of vehicle rear axle
C_{ro}	restoring moment coefficient
C_s	longitudinal stiffness of tire during braking
C_{se}	ratio of braking effort to normal load of semitrailer axle
C_{sk}	coefficient of skirt contact drag
C_{sp}	coefficient of power spectral density function
C_{sr}	speed ratio of torque converter
C_{tr}	torque ratio of torque converter
C_α	cornering stiffness of tire
$C_{\alpha f}$	cornering stiffness of front tire
$C_{\alpha r}$	cornering stiffness of rear tire
$C_{\alpha s}$	cornering stiffness of semitrailer tire
C_γ	camber stiffness of tire
c	cohesion
c_a	adhesion
c_{eq}	equivalent damping coefficient
c_{sh}	damping coefficient of shock absorber
c_t	damping coefficient of tire
D	diameter
D_c	discharge coefficient
D_h	hydraulic diameter
E	energy
E_d	energy available at vehicle drawbar
F	force, thrust
F_b	braking force
F_{bf}	braking force of vehicle front axle
F_{br}	braking force of vehicle rear axle
F_{bs}	braking force of semitrailer axle
F_{cu}	lift generated by air cushion
F_d	drawbar pull
F_f	thrust of vehicle front axle
F_h	hydrodynamic force acting on a tire over flooded surfaces
F_{hi}	horizontal force acting at the hitch point of a tractor–semitrailer
F_i	thrust of the inside track of a tracked vehicle
F_l	lift generated by the change of momentum of an air jet
F_{net}	net thrust
F_o	thrust of the outside track of a tracked vehicle

F_p	resultant force due to passive earth pressure
F_{pn}	normal component of the resultant force due to passive earth pressure
F_r	thrust of vehicle rear axle
F_s	side force
F_x	force component along the x axis
F_y	force component along the y axis
F_{yf}	cornering force of front tire
F_{yr}	cornering force of rear tire
$F_{y\alpha}$	cornering force of tire
$F_{y\gamma}$	camber thrust of tire
F_z	force component along the z axis
f	frequency
f_c	center frequency
f_{eq}	equivalent coefficient of motion resistance
f_{n-s}	natural frequency of sprung mass
f_{n-us}	natural frequency of unsprung mass
f_r	coefficient of rolling resistance
G	grade, sand penetration resistance gradient
G_{acc}	lateral acceleration gain
G_{yaw}	yaw velocity gain
g	acceleration due to gravity
h	height of center of gravity of the vehicle
h_a	height of the point of application of aerodynamic resistance above ground level
h_b	depth
h_c	clearance height
h_d	height of drawbar
I	mass moment of inertia
I_w	mass moment of inertia of wheels
I_y	mass moment of inertia of the vehicle about the y axis
I_z	mass moment of inertia of the vehicle about the z axis
i	slip
i_f	slip of front tire
i_i	slip of the inside track of a tracked vehicle
i_o	slip of the outside track of a tracked vehicle
i_r	slip of rear tire
i_s	skid

J_j	momentum flux of an air jet
j	shear displacement
K	shear deformation modulus
K_a	augmentation factor
K_{bf}	proportion of total braking force placed on vehicle front axle
K_{br}	proportion of total braking force placed on vehicle rear axle
K_{bs}	proportion of total braking force placed on semitrailer axle
K_d	coefficient of thrust distribution
K_{di}	gear ratio of a controlled differential
K_e	engine capacity factor
K_p	passive earth pressure coefficient
K_{por}	coefficient taking into account the effect of ground porosity on the flow and power requirement of an air-cushion vehicle
K_s	ratio of the angular speed of the outside track sprocket to that of the inside track sprocket
K_{tc}	torque converter capacity factor
K_{us}	understeer coefficient
$K_{us.s}$	understeer coefficient of semitrailer
$K_{us.t}$	understeer coefficient of tractor
K_v	ratio of the theoretical speed of the front tire to that of the rear tire
K_{we}	weight utilization factor
k_c	cohesive modulus of terrain deformation
k_f	front suspension spring stiffness
k_p	stiffness of underlying peat for organic terrain (muskeg)
k_r	rear suspension spring stiffness
k_s	stiffness of suspension spring
k_{tr}	equivalent spring stiffness of tire
k_u	parameter characterizing terrain response to repetitive loading
k_ϕ	frictional modulus of terrain deformation
k_0	parameter characterizing terrain response to repetitive loading
L	wheelbase
L_c	characteristic length
L_s	wheelbase of semitrailer
L_t	wheelbase of tractor
l	length
l_{cu}	cushion perimeter
l_j	nozzle perimeter
l_o	distance between oscillation center and center of gravity of the vehicle
l_t	contact length

l_1	distance between front axle and center of gravity of the vehicle
l_2	distance between rear axle and center of gravity of the vehicle
M_a	aerodynamic pitching moment
M_b	braking torque
M_e	engine output torque
M_r	moment of turning resistance
M_{ro}	restoring moment in roll
M_{tc}	torque converter output torque
M_w	wheel torque
M_x	moment about the x axis
M_y	moment about the y axis
M_z	moment about the z axis
MI	mobility index
m	vehicle mass
m_m	pressure–sinkage parameter for organic terrain (muskeg)
m_s	sprung mass
m_{us}	unsprung mass
N	exponent of power spectral density function
N_c, N_q, N_γ	bearing capacity factors
N_ϕ	flow value for soils
n	exponent of terrain deformation
n_e	engine speed
n_g	number of speeds in a gearbox
n_{tc}	torque converter output speed
P	engine power
P_a	power required to sustain the air cushion
P_d	drawbar power
P_m	power required to overcome momentum drag
P_o	engine power under standard atmospheric conditions
P_{st}	power consumption of a tracked vehicle in straight line motion
P_t	power consumption of a tracked vehicle during a turn
p	pressure
p_c	pressure exerted by tire carcass
p_{cr}	critical pressure
p_{cu}	cushion pressure
p_d	dynamic pressure
p_g	ground pressure at the lowest point of contact
p_{gcr}	critical ground pressure

p_i	inflation pressure
p_j	total jet pressure
Q	volume flow
q	surcharge
R	turning radius
R_a	aerodynamic resistance
R_c	motion resistance due to terrain compaction
R_d	drawbar load
R_g	grade resistance
R_h	motion resistance of tire due to hysteresis and other internal losses
R_i	motion resistance of the inside track of a tracked vehicle
R_{in}	internal resistance of track system
R_L	aerodynamic lift
R_l	lateral resistance of track
R_m	momentum drag
R_o	motion resistance of the outside track of a tracked vehicle
R_r	rolling resistance
R_{rf}	rolling resistance of front tire
R_{rr}	rolling resistance of rear tire
R_{rs}	rolling resistance of semitrailer tire
R_{sk}	skirt contact drag
R_{tot}	total motion resistance
R_w	wave-making drag
R_{wave}	drag due to wave
R_{wet}	wetting drag
r	radius of wheel or sprocket
r_e	effective rolling radius of tire
r_y	radius of gyration of the vehicle about the y axis
S	distance
$S_g(f)$	power spectral density function of terrain profile (temporal frequency)
$S_g(\Omega)$	power spectral density function of terrain profile (spatial frequency)
$S_v(f)$	power spectral density function of vehicle response (temporal frequency)
s	displacement
T	temperature, tension
T_b	breaking torque on a tire
T_o	temperature under standard atmospheric conditions

t	time
t_j	thickness of air jet
t_p	pneumatic trail of tire
t_t	track pitch
U	energy dissipation
u_a	fuel consumed for work performed per unit area
u_e	energy obtained at the drawbar per unit volume of fuel spent
u_h	fuel consumed per hour
u_s	specific fuel consumption
u_t	fuel consumed during time t
u_{tr}	fuel consumed per unit payload for unit distance
V	speed
V_a	speed of wind relative to vehicle
V_c	speed of air escaping from cushion
V_i	speed of the inside track of a tracked vehicle
V_j	slip speed
V_{jc}	jet speed
V_m	average operating speed
V_o	speed of the outside track of a tracked vehicle
V_p	hydroplaning speed of tire
V_t	theoretical speed
V_{tf}	theoretical speed of front tire
V_{tr}	theoretical speed of rear tire
W	normal load, weight
W_a	load supported by air cushion
W_c	critical load
W_d	proportion of vehicle weight applied to driven wheels
W_f	load on vehicle front axle
W_{hi}	normal load at the hitch point of a tractor–semitrailer
W_p	payload
W_r	load on vehicle rear axle
W_s	load on semitrailer axle
z	depth, penetration
z_{cr}	critical sinkage
z_w	pressure–sinkage parameter for snow cover

α	slip angle of tire, angle
α_a	angle of attack
α_{an}	angular acceleration
α_b	inclination angle
α_f	slip angle of front tire
α_r	slip angle of rear tire
β_b	inclination angle of blade
Γ	articulation angle
γ	camber angle of tire
γ_m	vehicle mass factor
γ_s	specific weight of terrain
δ	angle of interface friction
δ_f	steer angle of front tire
δ_i	steer angle of inside front tire
δ_o	steer angle of outside front tire
δ_t	tire deflection
ϵ	strain
ζ	damping ratio
η_b	braking efficiency
η_c	torque converter efficiency
η_{cu}	cushion intake efficiency
η_d	tractive efficiency, drawbar efficiency
η_m	efficiency of motion
η_p	propulsive efficiency
η_s	slip efficiency
η_{st}	structural efficiency
η_t	transmission efficiency
η_{tr}	transport efficiency
θ	angular displacement
θ_c	cushion wall angle
θ_j	nozzle angle
θ_s	slope angle
θ_t	trim angle

μ	coefficient of road adhesion
μ_p	peak value of coefficient of road adhesion
μ_s	sliding value of coefficient of road adhesion
μ_t	coefficient of lateral resistance
μ_{tr}	coefficient of traction
ν	concentration factor
ξ	gear ratio
ξ_o	overall reduction ratio
ξ_s	steering gear ratio
ρ	air density
ρ_f	density of fluid
ρ_w	density of water
σ	normal stress
σ_a	active earth pressure
σ_p	passive earth pressure
σ_r	radial stress
σ_z	vertical stress
τ	shear stress
$\tau_{\max}$	maximum shear stress
τ_r	residual shear stress
ϕ	angle of internal shearing resistance
Ω	spatial frequency
Ω_x	angular speed about the x axis
Ω_y	angular speed about the y axis
Ω_z	angular speed about the z axis
ω	angular speed
ω_i	angular speed of the sprocket of the inside track of a tracked vehicle
ω_n	circular natural frequency
ω_o	angular speed of the sprocket of the outside track of a tracked vehicle

INTRODUCTION

Ground vehicles are those vehicles that are supported by the ground, in contrast to aircraft and marinecraft that in operation are supported by air and water, respectively.

Ground vehicles may be broadly classified as guided and nonguided. Guided ground vehicles are constrained to move along a fixed path (guideway), such as railway vehicles and tracked levitated vehicles. Nonguided ground vehicles can move, by choice, in various directions on the ground, such as road and off-road vehicles. The mechanics of nonguided ground vehicles is the subject of this book.

The prime objective of the study of the mechanics of ground vehicles is to establish guiding principles for the rational development, design, and selection of vehicles to meet various operational requirements.

In general, the characteristics of a ground vehicle may be described in terms of its performance, handling, and ride. Performance characteristics include the ability of the vehicle to accelerate, to develop drawbar pull, to overcome obstacles, and to decelerate. Handling qualities of interest are the response of the vehicle to the driver's commands and its ability to stabilize its motion against external disturbances. Ride characteristics are related to the vibration of the vehicle excited by surface irregularities and its effects on passengers and goods. The theory of ground vehicles is concerned with the study of the performance, handling, and ride and their relationships with the design of ground vehicles under various operating conditions.

The behavior of a ground vehicle represents the results of the interactions among the driver, the vehicle, and the environment, as illustrated in Fig. 1. An understanding of the behavior of the human driver, the characteristics of the vehicle, and the physical and geometric properties of the ground is, therefore, essential to the design and evaluation of ground vehicle systems.

1

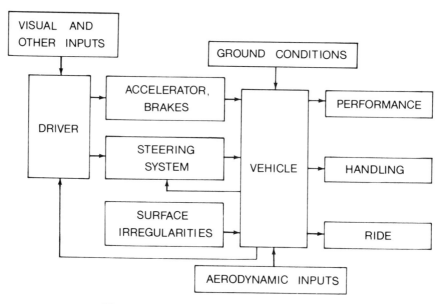

Fig. 1   The driver–vehicle–ground system.

CHAPTER 1

MECHANICS OF PNEUMATIC TIRES

Aside from aerodynamic and gravitational forces, almost all other forces and moments affecting the motion of a ground vehicle are applied through the running gear–ground contact. An understanding of the basic characteristics of the interaction between the running gear and the ground is, therefore, essential to the study of the performance characteristics, ride quality, and handling behavior of ground vehicles.

The running gear of a ground vehicle is generally required to fulfill the following functions:

- to support the weight of the vehicle
- to cushion the vehicle over surface irregularities
- to provide sufficient traction for driving and braking
- to provide adequate steering control and directional stability.

Pneumatic tires can perform these functions effectively and efficiently; thus, they are universally used in road vehicles, and are also widely used in off-road vehicles. The study of the mechanics of pneumatic tires therefore is of fundamental importance to the understanding of the performance and characteristics of ground vehicles. Two basic types of problem in the mechanics of tires are of special interest to vehicle engineers. One is the mechanics of tires on hard surfaces, which is essential to the study of the characteristics of road vehicles. The other is the mechanics of tires on deformable surfaces (unprepared terrain), which is of prime importance to the study of off-road vehicle performance.

The mechanics of tires on hard surfaces is discussed in this chapter, whereas the behavior of tires over unprepared terrain will be discussed in Chapter 2.

3

A pneumatic tire is a flexible structure of the shape of a toroid filled with compressed air. The most important structural element of the tire is the carcass. It is made up of a number of layers of flexible cords of high modulus of elasticity encased in a matrix of low modulus rubber compounds, as shown in Fig. 1.1. The cords are made of fabrics of natural, synthetic, or metallic composition, and are anchored around the beads made of high tensile strength steel wires. The beads serve as the ''foundations'' for the carcass and provide adequate seating of the tire on the rim. The ingredients of the rubber compounds are selected to provide the

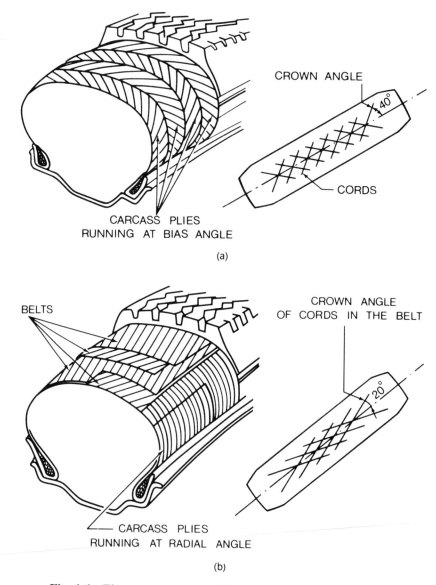

CROWN ANGLE

40°

CORDS

CARCASS PLIES
RUNNING AT BIAS ANGLE

(a)

BELTS

CROWN ANGLE
OF CORDS IN THE BELT

20°

CARCASS PLIES
RUNNING AT RADIAL ANGLE

(b)

Fig. 1.1   Tire construction. (a) Bias-ply tire. (b) Radial-ply tire.

tire with specific properties. The rubber compounds for the sidewall are generally required to be highly resistant to fatigue and scuffing, and styrene–butadiene compounds are widely used [1.1].[1] The rubber compounds for the tread vary with the type of tire. For instance, for heavy truck tires, the high load intensities necessitate the use of tread compounds with high resistance to abrasion, tearing, and crack growth, and with low hysteresis to reduce internal heat generation and rolling resistance. Consequently, natural rubber compounds are widely used for truck tires, although they intrinsically provide lower values of coefficient of road adhesion, particularly on wet surfaces, than various synthetic rubber compounds universally used for passenger car and racing car tires [1.1]. For tubeless tires, which have become dominant, a thin layer of rubber with high impermeability to air (such as butyl rubber compounds) is attached to the inner surface of the carcass.

The load transmission of a pneumatic tire is analogous to that of a bicycle wheel, where the hub hangs by the spokes from the upper part of the rim, which in turn is supported at its lower part by the ground. For an inflated pneumatic tire, the inflation pressure causes tension to be developed in the cords comprising the carcass. The load applied through the rim of the wheel hangs primarily by the cords in the sidewalls through the beads.

The design and construction of the carcass determine, to a great extent, the characteristics of the tire. Among the various design parameters, the geometric dispositions of layers of rubber-coated cords (plies), particularly their directions, play a significant role in the behavior of the tire. The direction of the cords is usually defined by the crown angle, which is the angle between the cord and the circumferential center line of the tire, as shown in Fig. 1.1. When the cords have a low crown angle, the tire will have good cornering characteristics, but a harsh ride. On the other hand, if the cords are at right angle to the centerline of the tread, the tire will be capable of providing a comfortable ride, but poor handling performance.

A compromise is adopted in a bias-ply tire, in which the cords extend diagonally across the carcass from bead to bead with a crown angle of approximately 40°, as shown in Fig. 1.1(a). A bias-ply tire has two plies (for light-load tires) or more (up to 20 plies for heavy-load tires). The cords in adjacent plies run in opposite directions. Thus, the cords overlap in a diamond-shaped (criss-cross) pattern. In operation, the diagonal plies flex and rub, thus elongating the diamond-shaped elements and the rubber-filler. This flexing action produces a wiping motion between the tread and the road, which is one of the main causes of tire wear and high rolling resistance [1.2, 1.3].

The radial-ply tire, on the other hand, is constructed very differently from the bias-ply tire. It was first introduced by Michelin in 1948, and has now become dominant for passenger cars and trucks and increasingly for heavy-duty earth-moving machinery. However, the bias-ply tire is still in use in particular fields, such as cycles, motorcycles, agricultural machinery, and some military equipment. The radial-ply tire has one or more layers of cords in the carcass extending radially

---

[1]Numbers in brackets designate references at the end of the chapter.

from bead to bead, resulting in a crown angle of 90°, as shown in Fig. 1.1(b). A belt of several layers of cords of high modulus of elasticity (usually steel or other high strength materials) is fitted under the tread, as shown in Fig. 1.1(b). The cords in the belt are laid at a low crown angle of approximately 20°. The belt is essential to the proper functioning of the radial-ply tire. Without it, a radial-ply carcass can become unstable since the tire periphery may develop into a series of buckles due to the irregularities in cord spacing when inflated. For passenger car tires, usually there are two radial plies in the carcass made of synthetic material, such as rayon or polyester, and two plies of steel cords and two plies of cords made of synthetic material, such as nylon, in the belt. For truck tires, usually there is one radial steel ply in the carcass and four steel plies in the belt. For the radial-ply tire, flexing of the carcass involves very little relative movement of the cords forming the belt. In the absence of a wiping motion between the tire and the road, the power dissipation of the radial-ply tire could be as low as 60% of that of the bias-ply tire under similar conditions, and the life of the radial-ply tire could be as long as twice that of the equivalent bias-ply tire [1.3]. For a radial-ply tire, there is a relatively uniform ground pressure over the entire contact area. In contrast, the ground pressure for a bias-ply tire varies greatly from point to point as tread elements passing through the contact area undergo complex localized wiping motion.

There are also tires built with belts in the tread on bias-ply construction. This type of tire is usually called the bias-belted tire. The cords in the belt are of materials with a higher modulus of elasticity than those in the bias-plies. The belt provides high rigidity to the tread against distortion, and reduces tread wear and rolling resistance in comparison with the conventional bias-ply tire. Generally, the bias-belted tire has characteristics midway between those of the bias-ply and the radial-ply tire.

Although the construction of pneumatic tires differs from one type to another, the basic problems involved are not dissimilar. In the following sections, the mechanics fundamental to all types of tire will be discussed. The characteristics peculiar to a particular kind of tire will also be described.

1.1 TIRE FORCES AND MOMENTS

To describe the characteristics of a tire and the forces and moments acting on it, it is necessary to define an axis system that serves as a reference for the definition of various parameters. One of the commonly used axis systems recommended by the Society of Automotive Engineers is shown in Fig. 1.2 [1.4]. The origin of the axis system is the center of tire contact. The X axis is the intersection of the wheel plane and the ground plane with a positive direction forward. The Z axis is perpendicular to the ground plane with a positive direction downward. The Y axis is in the ground plane, and its direction is chosen to make the axis system orthogonal and right hand.

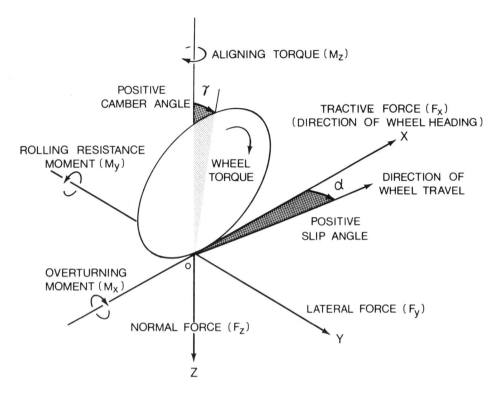

Fig. 1.2 Tire axis system.

There are three forces and three moments acting on the tire from the ground. Tractive force (or longitudinal force) F_x is the component in the X direction of the resultant force exerted on the tire by the road. Lateral force F_y is the component in the Y direction, and normal force F_z is the component in the Z direction. Overturning moment M_x is the moment about the X axis exerted on the tire by the road. Rolling resistance moment M_y is the moment about the Y axis, and aligning torque M_z is the moment about the Z axis.

With this axis system, many performance parameters of the tire can be conveniently defined. For instance, the longitudinal shift of the center of normal pressure is determined by the ratio of the rolling resistance moment to the normal load. The lateral shift of the center of normal pressure is defined by the ratio of the overturning moment to the normal load. The integration of longitudinal shear stresses over the entire contact patch represents the tractive or braking force. A driving torque about the axis of rotation of the tire produces a force for accelerating the vehicle, and a braking torque produces a force for decelerating the vehicle.

There are two important angles associated with a rolling tire: the slip angle and the camber angle. Slip angle α is the angle formed between the direction of wheel travel and the line of intersection of the wheel plane with the road surface. Camber angle γ is the angle formed between the XZ plane and the wheel plane. The lateral force at the tire–ground contact patch is a function of both the slip angle and the camber angle.

1.2 ROLLING RESISTANCE OF TIRES

The rolling resistance of tires on hard surfaces is primarily caused by the hysteresis in tire materials due to the deflection of the carcass while rolling. Friction between the tire and the road caused by sliding, the resistance due to air circulating inside the tire, and the fan effect of the rotating tire on the surrounding air also contribute to the rolling resistance of the tire, but they are of secondary importance. Available experimental results give a breakdown of tire losses in the speed range 128–152 km/h (80–95 mph) as 90–95% due to internal hysteresis losses in the tire, 2–10% due to friction between the tire and the ground, and 1.5–3.5% due to air resistance [1.5, 1.6]. Of the total energy losses within the tire structure, it is found that for a radial truck tire, hysteresis in the tread region, including the belt, contributes 73%, the sidewall 13%, the region between the tread and the sidewall, commonly known as the shoulder region, 12%, and the beads 2%.

When a tire is rolling, the carcass is deflected in the area of ground contact. As a result of tire distortion, the normal pressure in the leading half of the contact patch is higher than that in the trailing half. The center of normal pressure is shifted in the direction of rolling. This shift produces a moment about the axis of rotation of the tire, which is the rolling resistance moment. In a free-rolling tire, the applied wheel torque is zero; therefore, a horizontal force at the tire–ground contact patch must exist to maintain equilibrium. This resultant horizontal force is generally known as the rolling resistance. The ratio of the rolling resistance to the normal load on the tire is defined as the coefficient of rolling resistance.

A number of factors affect the rolling resistance of a pneumatic tire. They include the structure of the tire (construction and materials) and its operating conditions (surface conditions, inflation pressure, speed, temperature, etc.). Tire construction has a significant influence on its rolling resistance. Figure 1.3 shows the rolling resistance coefficient at various speeds of a range of bias-ply and radial-ply passenger car tires at rated loads and inflation pressures on a smooth road [1.7]. The difference in rolling resistance coefficient between a bias-ply and a radial-ply truck tire of the same size under rated conditions is shown in Fig. 1.4 [1.8]. Thicker treads and sidewalls and an increased number of carcass plies tend to increase the rolling resistance because of greater hysteresis losses. Tires made of synthetic rubber compounds generally have higher rolling resistance than those made of natural rubber. Tires made of butyl rubber compounds, which are shown to have better traction and road-holding properties, have an even higher rolling resistance than those made of conventional synthetic rubber. It is found that the rolling resistance of tires with tread made of synthetic rubber compounds and that made of butyl rubber compounds are approximately 1.06 and 1.35 times that made of natural rubber compounds, respectively [1.9].

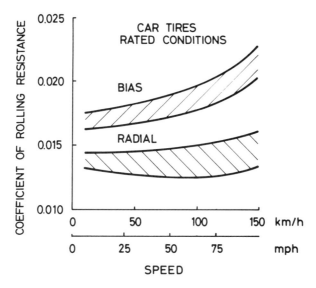

Fig. 1.3 Variation of rolling resistance coefficient of radial-ply and bias-ply car tires with speed on a smooth, flat road surface under rated load and inflation pressure. (Reproduced with permission from *Automotive Handbook*, 2nd edition, Robert Bosch GmbH, Germany.)

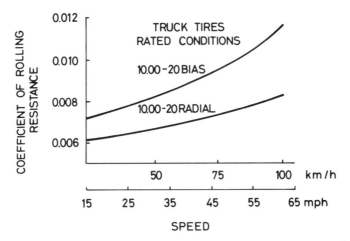

Fig. 1.4 Variation of rolling resistance coefficient of radial-ply and bias-ply truck tires with speed under rated load and inflation pressure. (Reproduced with permission from reference 1.8.)

Surface conditions also affect the rolling resistance. On hard, smooth surfaces, the rolling resistance is considerably lower than that on a rough road. On wet surfaces, a higher rolling resistance than on dry surfaces is usually observed. Figure 1.5 shows a comparison of the rolling resistance of passenger car tires over six road surfaces with different textures, ranging from polished concrete to coarse asphalt [1.10]. The profiles of these six surfaces are shown in Fig. 1.6. It can be seen that on the asphalt surface with coarse seal-coat (surface no. 6) the rolling

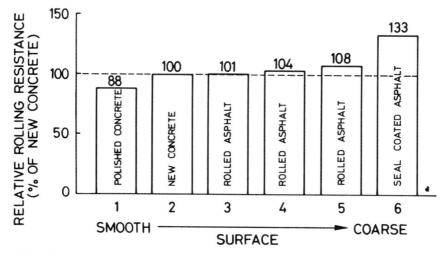

Fig. 1.5 Variation of tire rolling resistance with pavement surface texture. (Reproduced with permission of the Society of Automotive Engineers from reference 1.10.)

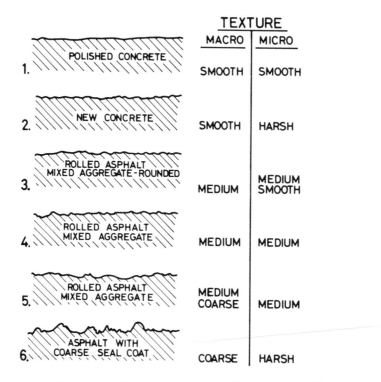

Fig. 1.6 Texture of various types of pavement surface. (Reproduced with permission of the Society of Automotive Engineers from reference 1.10.)

resistance is 33% higher than that on a new concrete surface (surface no. 2), while on the polished concrete (surface no. 1), it shows a 12% reduction in comparison with that on the new concrete surface.

Inflation pressure affects the flexibility of the tire. Depending on the deformability of the ground, the inflation pressure affects the rolling resistance of the tire in different manners. On hard surfaces, the rolling resistance generally decreases with the increase in inflation pressure. This is because, with higher inflation pressure, the deflection of the tire decreases, with consequent lower hysteresis losses. Figure 1.7 shows the effects of inflation pressure on the rolling resistance of a radial-ply tire (GR78-15), a bias-ply tire, and a bias-belted tire (both G78-15) under various normal loads, expressed in terms of the percentage of the rated load at an inflation pressure of 165 kPa (24 psi) [1.11]. The results were obtained with the inflation pressure being regulated, that is, the pressure was maintained at a specific level throughout the tests. It can be seen that inflation pressure has a much more significant effect on the rolling resistance of the bias and bias-belted tires than the radial-ply tire. On deformable surfaces, such as sand, high inflation pressure results in increased ground penetration work, and therefore higher rolling resistance, as shown in Fig. 1.8 [1.12]. Conversely, lower inflation pressure, while decreasing ground penetration, increases the deflection of the tire and hence internal hysteresis losses. Therefore, an optimum inflation pressure exists for a particular tire on a given deformable surface, which minimizes the sum of ground penetration work and internal losses of the tire.

Inflation pressure not only affects the rolling resistance, but also the tread wear of a tire. Figure 1.9 shows the effects of inflation pressure on tread wear of a radial-ply, a bias-ply, and a bias-belted tire [1.11]. The wear rate at 165 kPa (24 psi) is used as a reference for comparison. It can be seen that the effects of inflation pressure on tread wear are more significant for the bias-ply and bias-belted tire than the radial-ply tire.

Rolling resistance is also affected by driving speed because of the increase of work in deforming the tire and of vibrations in the tire structure with the increase in speed. The effects of speed on the rolling resistance of bias-ply and radial-ply passenger car and truck tires are illustrated in Figs. 1.3 and 1.4, respectively. For a given tire under a particular operating condition, there exists a threshold speed above which the phenomenon popularly known as standing waves will be observed, as shown in Fig. 1.10. The approximate value of the threshold speed V_{th} may be determined by the expression $V_{th} = \sqrt{F_t/\rho_t}$, where F_t is the circumferential tension in the tire and ρ_t is the density of tread material per unit area [1.13]. Standing waves are formed because, owing to high speed, the tire tread does not recover immediately from distortion originating from tire deflection after it leaves the contact surface, and the residual deformation initiates a wave. The amplitude of the wave is the greatest immediately on leaving the ground, and is damped out in an exponential manner around the circumference of the tire. The formation of the standing wave greatly increases energy losses, which in turn cause considerable heat generation that could lead to tire failure. This places an upper limit on the safe operating speed of tires.

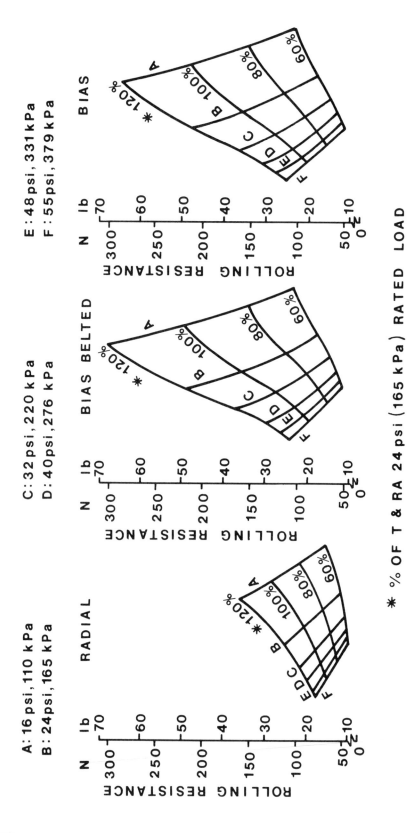

Fig. 1.7 Variation of rolling resistance of radial-ply, bias-belted, and bias-ply car tires with load and inflation pressure. (Reproduced with permission of the Society of Automotive Engineers from reference 1.11.)

A: 16 psi, 110 kPa
B: 24 psi, 165 kPa
C: 32 psi, 220 kPa
D: 40 psi, 276 kPa
E: 48 psi, 331 kPa
F: 55 psi, 379 kPa

* % OF T & RA 24 psi (165 kPa) RATED LOAD

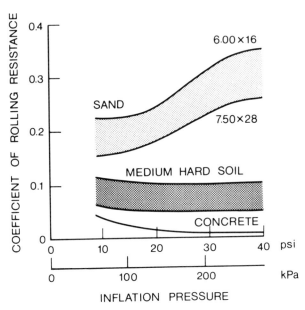

Fig. 1.8 Variation of rolling resistance coefficient with inflation pressure of tires on various surfaces. (Reproduced with permission from reference 1.12.)

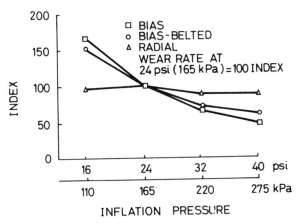

Fig. 1.9 Variation of shoulder-crown wear with inflation pressure for radial-ply, bias-ply, and bias-belted car tires. (Reproduced with permission of the Society of Automotive Engineers from reference 1.11.)

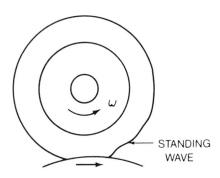

Fig. 1.10 Formation of standing waves of a tire at high speeds.

Operating temperature, tire diameter, and tractive force also have effects on the rolling resistance of a tire. Tire temperature affects the rolling resistance in two ways: one is by changing the temperature of the air in the tire cavity, and thereby changing the operating inflation pressure; and the other is by changing the stiffness and hysteresis of the rubber compounds. Figure 1.11 shows the dependence of the rolling resistance on the internal tire temperature for an automobile tire [1.5]. The variation of rolling resistance coefficient with shoulder temperature of a radial-ply passenger car tire is shown in Fig. 1.12 [1.14]. It can be seen that the rolling resistance at a shoulder temperature of −10°C is approximately 2.3 times that at 60°C for the tire examined. It is also found that the shoulder temperature of the tire, and not the ambient temperature, is a basic determining factor of the tire

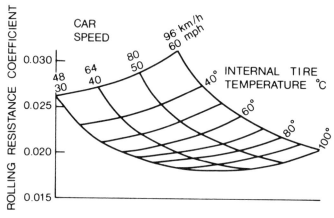

Fig. 1.11   Effect of internal temperature on rolling resistance coefficient of a car tire. (Reproduced with permission of the Council of the Institution of Mechanical Engineers from reference 1.5.)

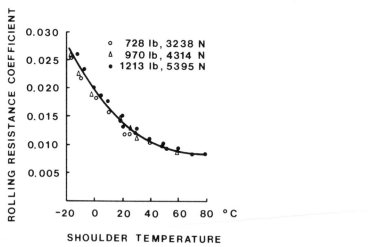

SHOULDER TEMPERATURE

Fig. 1.12   Variation of rolling resistance coefficient with shoulder temperature for a car tire P195/75R14. (Reproduced with permission of the Society of Automotive Engineers from reference 1.14.)

rolling resistance coefficient. The effect of tire diameter on the coefficient of rolling resistance is shown in Fig. 1.13 [1.12]. It can be seen that the effect of tire diameter is negligible on hard surfaces (concrete), but is considerable on deformable or soft ground. Figure 1.14 shows the effects of the braking and tractive effort on the rolling resistance [1.6].

When considering the effects of material, construction, and design parameters of tires on rolling resistance, it is necessary to have a proper perspective of the energy losses in the tire and the characteristics of the tire–vehicle system as a whole. Although it is desirable to keep the rolling resistance as low as possible, it should be judged against other performance parameters, such as tire endurance and life, traction, cornering properties, cushioning effect, cost, etc. For instance, from

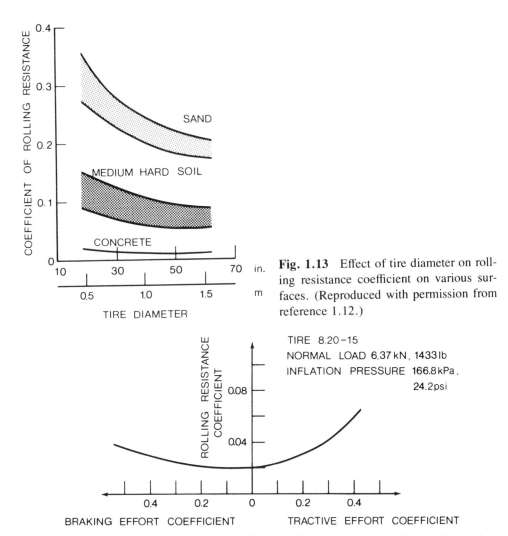

Fig. 1.13 Effect of tire diameter on rolling resistance coefficient on various surfaces. (Reproduced with permission from reference 1.12.)

Fig. 1.14 Effect of tractive and braking effort on rolling resistance coefficient of a car tire. (Reproduced with permission from *Mechanics of Pneumatic Tires*, edited by S. K. Clark, Monograph 122, National Bureau of Standards, 1971.)

the standpoint of rolling resistance, synthetic rubber compounds are less favorable than natural rubber compounds, yet because of significant advantages in cost, tread life, wet-road grip, and tire squeal, they have virtually displaced natural rubber compounds from passenger car tires, particularly for treads. For high-performance vehicles, there may be some advantage for using butyl rubber tires because of the marked gains in traction, road-holding, silence, and comfort, in spite of their poor hysteresis characteristics [1.5].

The complex relationships between the design and operational parameters of the tire and its rolling resistance make it extremely difficult, if not impossible, to develop an analytic method for predicting the rolling resistance. The determination of the rolling resistance, therefore, relies almost entirely on experiments. To provide a uniform basis for collecting experimental data, the Society of Automotive Engineers recommends rolling resistance measurement procedures for various types of tire on different surfaces, which may be found in the *SAE Handbook*.

Based on experimental results, many empirical formulas have been proposed for calculating the rolling resistance of tires on hard surfaces. For instance, based on the experimental data shown in Fig. 1.3, for radial-ply passenger car tires under rated loads and inflation pressures on a smooth road, the relationship between rolling resistance coefficient f_r and speed V (up to 150 km/h or 93 mph) may be expressed by

$$f_r = 0.0136 + 0.40 \times 10^{-7} V^2 \qquad (1.1)$$

and for bias-ply passenger car tires,

$$f_r = 0.0169 + 0.19 \times 10^{-6} V^2 \qquad (1.2)$$

where V is in km/h.

Based on the experimental data shown in Fig. 1.4, for the radial-ply truck tire under rated load and inflation pressure, the relationship between the rolling resistance coefficient f_r and speed V (up to 100 km/h or 62 mph) may be described by

$$f_r = 0.006 + 0.23 \times 10^{-6} V^2 \qquad (1.3)$$

and for the bias-ply truck tire,

$$f_r = 0.007 + 0.45 \times 10^{-6} V^2 \qquad (1.4)$$

where V is in km/h.

The rolling resistance coefficient of truck tires is usually lower than that of passenger car tires on road surfaces. This is primarily due to the higher inflation pressure used in truck tires (typically 620–827 kPa or 90–120 psi as opposed to 193–248 kPa or 28–36 psi for passenger car tires).

In preliminary performance calculations, the effect of speed may be ignored, and the average value of f_r for a particular operating condition may be used. The average values of f_r for various types of tire over different surfaces are summarized in Table 1.1 [1.12].

TABLE 1.1 Coefficient of Rolling Resistance

Tire type	Surface		
	Concrete	Medium Hard Soil	Sand
Passenger car	0.015	0.08	0.30
Truck	0.010	0.06	0.25
Tractor	0.02	0.04	0.20

Source: Adopted from reference 1.12.

1.3 TRACTIVE (BRAKING) EFFORT AND LONGITUDINAL SLIP (SKID)

When a driving torque is applied to a pneumatic tire, a tractive force is developed at the tire–ground contact patch, as shown in Fig. 1.15 [1.6]. At the same time, the tire tread in front of and within the contact patch is subjected to compression. A corresponding shear deformation of the sidewall of the tire is also developed.

As tread elements are compressed before entering the contact region, the distance that the tire travels when subject to a driving torque will be less than that in free rolling. This phenomenon is usually referred to as longitudinal slip. The lon-

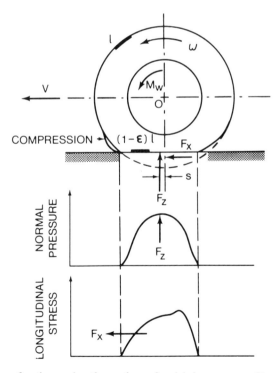

Fig. 1.15 Behavior of a tire under the action of a driving torque. (Reproduced with permission from *Mechanics of Pneumatic Tires*, edited by S. K. Clark, Monograph 122, National Bureau of Standards, 1971.)

gitudinal slip of the vehicle running gear, when a driving torque is applied, is usually defined by

$$i = \left(1 - \frac{V}{r\omega}\right) \times 100\% = \left(1 - \frac{r_e}{r}\right) \times 100\% \qquad (1.5)$$

where V is the linear speed of the tire center, ω is the angular speed of the tire, r is the rolling radius of the free-rolling tire, and r_e is the effective rolling radius of the tire, which is the ratio of the linear speed of the tire center to the angular speed of the tire.

When a driving torque is applied, the tire rotates without the equivalent translatory progression; therefore, $r\omega > V$ and a positive value for slip results. If a tire is rotating at a certain angular speed but the linear speed of the tire center is zero, then in accordance with Eq. 1.5, the longitudinal slip of the tire will be 100%. This is often observed on an icy surface, where the driven tires are spinning at high angular speeds, while the vehicle does not move forward. The definition of longitudinal slip given by Eq. 1.5 is adopted in the analysis of the mechanics of tires in this book.

A definition of longitudinal slip different from that given by Eq. 1.5 appears in some publications. For instance, in the *SAE Handbook Supplement, Vehicle Dynamics Terminology J670e* [1.4], longitudinal slip is defined as "the ratio of the longitudinal slip velocity to the spin velocity of the straight free-rolling tire expressed as a percentage." The longitudinal slip velocity is taken as "the difference between the spin velocity of the driven or braked tire and the spin velocity of the straight free-rolling tire." Both spin velocities are measured at the same linear velocity at the wheel center in the X direction (Fig. 1.2). A positive value of slip results from a driving torque. In essence, the definition of longitudinal slip i' suggested by the SAE can be expressed by

$$i' = \left(\frac{r\omega}{V} - 1\right) \times 100\% = \left(\frac{r}{r_e} - 1\right) \times 100\% \qquad (1.6)$$

where V, ω, r, and r_e are defined in the same way as that for Eq. 1.5.

It should be noted that in accordance with the definition suggested by the SAE, when a tire is rotating at a certain angular speed but the linear speed of the tire center is zero, the longitudinal slip i' of the tire will be denoted as infinite.

As the tractive force developed by a tire is proportional to the applied wheel torque under steady-state conditions, slip is a function of tractive effort. Generally speaking, at first the wheel torque and tractive force increase linearly with slip because, initially, slip is mainly due to elastic deformation of the tire tread. This corresponds to section OA of the curve shown in Fig. 1.16. A further increase of wheel torque and tractive force results in part of the tire tread sliding on the ground. Under these circumstances, the relationship between the tractive force and the slip is nonlinear. This corresponds to section AB of the curve shown in Fig. 1.16. Based on available experimental data, the maximum tractive force of a pneumatic tire on hard surfaces is usually reached somewhere between 15 and 20% slip. Any

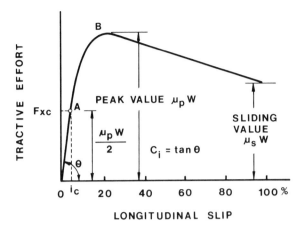

Fig. 1.16 Variation of tractive effort with longitudinal slip of a tire.

further increase of slip beyond that results in an unstable condition, with the tractive effort falling rapidly from the peak value $\mu_p W$ to the pure sliding value $\mu_s W$, as shown in Fig. 1.16, where W is the normal load on the tire and μ_p and μ_s are the peak and sliding values of the coefficient of road adhesion, respectively.

A general theory that can accurately predict the relationship between the tractive effort and the longitudinal slip of pneumatic tires on hard surfaces has yet to be evolved. However, several theories have been proposed that could provide a basic understanding of the physical nature of the processes involved. One of the earliest theoretical treatments on the relationship between the tractive effort and the longitudinal slip of pneumatic tires was made by Julien [1.15].

In Julien's theory, it is assumed that the tire tread can be regarded as an elastic band, and that the contact patch is rectangular and the normal pressure is uniformly distributed [1.15]. It is further assumed that the contact patch can be divided into an adhesion region and a sliding region. In the adhesion region, the interacting forces depend on the elastic properties of the tire, whereas in the sliding region, the interacting forces depend upon the adhesive properties of the tire–ground interface. When a driving torque is applied to a tire, in the region in front of the contact patch, the driving torque produces a longitudinal strain ϵ (in compression) in the tread. It remains constant in the adhesion region of the contact patch, where no sliding between the tire tread and the ground takes place. Let e_0 be the longitudinal deformation of the tire tread in front of the contact patch, and let e be the longitudinal deformation of the tread at a point at a distance x behind the front contact point

$$e = e_0 + x\epsilon \qquad (1.7)$$

Assume that e_0 is proportional to ϵ, and $e_0 = \lambda\epsilon$. Then

$$e = (\lambda + x)\epsilon \qquad (1.8)$$

It is further assumed that, within the adhesion region, where no sliding between the tire tread and the ground takes place, the tractive force per unit contact length is proportional to the deformation of the tread. Thus,

$$\frac{dF_x}{dx} = k_t e = k_t(\lambda + x)\epsilon \tag{1.9}$$

where k_t is the tangential stiffness of the tire tread and F_x is the tractive force. Based on experimental data of a sample of heavy truck tires under rated loads and inflation pressures, it is found that the value of k_t varies in a narrow range from approximately 3930 kN/m² (570 lb/in.²) for a radial-ply tire to 4206 kN/m² (610 lb/in.²) for a bias-ply tire.

$$F_x = \int_0^x k_t(\lambda + x)\epsilon \, dx = k_t \lambda x \epsilon \left(1 + \frac{x}{2\lambda}\right) \tag{1.10}$$

Let p be the normal pressure, b the width of the contact patch, and μ_p the peak value of the coefficient of road adhesion. Then no sliding will take place between the tread and the ground if the following condition is satisfied:

$$\frac{dF_x}{dx} = k_t(\lambda + x)\epsilon \leq \mu_p pb \tag{1.11}$$

This implies that if a point at a distance of x behind the front contact point is in the adhesion region, then x must be less than a characteristic length l_c, which defines the length of the region where no sliding between the tire tread and the ground takes place, that is,

$$x \leq l_c = \frac{\mu_p pb}{k_t \epsilon} - \lambda = \frac{\mu_p W}{l_t k_t \epsilon} - \lambda \tag{1.12}$$

where W is the normal load on the tire and l_t is the contact length of the tire.

If $l_t \leq l_c$, then the entire contact area is an adhesion region. Letting $x = l_t$ in Eq. 1.10, the tractive force becomes

$$F_x = k_t \lambda l_t \epsilon \left(1 + \frac{l_t}{2\lambda}\right) = K_t \epsilon \tag{1.13}$$

where $K_t = k_t \lambda l_t[1 + l_t/2\lambda]$.

Since the longitudinal strain ϵ is a measure of the longitudinal slip i of the tire, it is concluded that if the entire contact patch is an adhesion region, the relationship between the tractive force F_x and the slip i is linear. This corresponds to the region between points O and A on the tractive effort–slip curve shown in Fig. 1.16.

The condition for sliding at the rear edge of the contact area is given by

$$l_t = l_c = \frac{\mu_p W}{l_t k_t i} - \lambda \tag{1.14}$$

This means that, if the slip or tractive force reaches the respective critical value

i_c or F_{xc} given below, sliding in the trailing part of the contact patch begins:

$$i_c = \frac{\mu_p W}{l_t k_t (l_t + \lambda)} \tag{1.15}$$

$$F_{xc} = \frac{\mu_p W [1 + (l_t/2\lambda)]}{1 + (l_t/\lambda)} \tag{1.16}$$

A further increase of slip or tractive force beyond the respective critical value results in the spread of the sliding region from the trailing edge towards the leading part of the contact patch. The tractive force F_{xs} developed in the sliding region is given by

$$F_{xs} = \mu_p W (1 - l_c/l_t) \tag{1.17}$$

and the tractive force F_{xa} developed in the adhesion region is given by

$$F_{xa} = k_t \lambda i l_c \left(1 + \frac{l_c}{2\lambda}\right) \tag{1.18}$$

where l_c is determined by Eq. 1.12.

Hence, the relationship between the total tractive force and the slip when part of the tire tread sliding on the ground is expressed by

$$F_x = F_{xs} + F_{xa} = \mu_p W - \frac{\lambda(\mu_p W - K'i)^2}{2l_t K'i} \tag{1.19}$$

where $K' = l_t k_t \lambda$.

This equation clearly indicates the nonlinear behavior of the tractive effort–longitudinal slip relationship when sliding occurs in part of the contact area. This corresponds to the region beyond point A of the curve shown in Fig. 1.16.

When sliding extends over the entire contact patch, the tractive force F_x is equal to $\mu_p W$. Under this condition, the slip i is obtained by setting l_c to zero in Eq. 1.14. The value of the slip i_m where the maximum tractive effort occurs is equal to $\mu_p W / l_t k_t \lambda$ and corresponds to point B shown in Fig. 1.16. A further increase of tire slip results in an unstable situation, with the coefficient of road adhesion falling rapidly from the peak value μ_p to the pure sliding value μ_s.

In practice, the normal pressure distribution over the tire–ground contact patch is not uniform. There is a gradual drop of pressure near the edges. It is expected, therefore, that a small sliding region will be developed in the trailing part of the contact area, even at low slips.

Using Julien's theory to define the relationship between tractive effort and longitudinal slip, in addition to the parameters μ_p, W, and l_t, the value of λ, which determines the longitudinal deformation of the tire tread prior to entering the contact patch, must be known. To determine the value of λ for a given tire would require considerable effort and elaborate experiments. In view of this, a simplified theory has been developed in which the effect of λ is neglected. From Eq. 1.9, by neglecting the term λ, the tractive force per unit contact length in the adhesion region at a distance of x from the front contact point is given by

$$\frac{dF_x}{dx} = k_t x \epsilon = k_t x i \tag{1.20}$$

If there is no sliding between the tire tread and the ground for the entire contact patch, the relationship between the tractive force and slip can be expressed by

$$F_x = \int_0^{l_t} k_t i x \, dx = (k_t l_t^2 / 2)i \tag{1.21}$$

The term $k_t l_t^2 / 2$ may be taken as the slope C_i of the tractive effort–slip curve at the origin as shown in Fig. 1.16, that is,

$$\frac{k_t l_t^2}{2} = C_i = \tan \theta = \left. \frac{\partial F_x}{\partial i} \right|_{i=0} \tag{1.22}$$

where C_i is usually referred to as the longitudinal stiffness of the tire.

If no sliding takes place on the contact patch, the relationship between the tractive force and the slip will, therefore, be linear:

$$F_x = C_i i \tag{1.23}$$

Equation 1.23 applies to section OA of the curve shown in Fig. 1.16.

With the increase of slip beyond point A shown in Fig. 1.16, the tractive force per unit contact length at the trailing edge of the contact patch reaches the adhesion limit, and sliding between the tread and the ground takes place.

$$\frac{dF_x}{dx} = k_t l_t i = \mu_p pb = \frac{\mu_b W}{l_t} \tag{1.24}$$

This indicates that when the slip or tractive force reaches the respective critical value i_c or F_{xc} given below, sliding in the trailing part of the contact patch begins:

$$i_c = \frac{\mu_p W}{k_t l_t^2} = \frac{\mu_p W}{2C_i} \tag{1.25}$$

$$F_{xc} = \frac{\mu_p W}{2} \tag{1.26}$$

In other words, if slip $i \leq i_c$ or the tractive force $F_x \leq F_{xc}$, the relationship between the tractive force and slip is linear, as shown in Fig. 1.16. Equation 1.26 indicates that the upper limit for the linear range of the tractive force–slip relationship is identified by the tractive force being equal to one half of its maximum value $(\mu_p W / 2)$.

A further increase of slip or tractive force beyond the respective critical value (i.e., $i > i_c$ or $F_x > F_{xc}$) results in the spread of the sliding region from the trailing edge towards the leading part of the contact patch. The tractive force F_{xs} developed in the sliding region is given by

$$F_{xs} = \mu_p W \left(1 - \frac{\mu_p W}{2C_i i}\right) \tag{1.27}$$

and the tractive force F_{xa} developed in the adhesion region is expressed by

$$F_{xa} = \frac{\mu_p^2 W^2}{4C_i i} . \tag{1.28}$$

Hence, the relationship between the total tractive force and the slip when part of the tread is sliding on the ground (i.e., $i > i_c$ or $F_x > F_{xc}$) is given by

$$F_x = F_{xs} + F_{xa} = \mu_p W \left(1 - \frac{\mu_p W}{4C_i i}\right) \tag{1.29}$$

The equation above indicates the nonlinear nature of the tractive effort–longitudinal slip relationship when sliding occurs in part of the contact patch. It is applicable to predicting the tractive effort–slip relation when the tractive effort is lower than its maximum value $\mu_p W$.

In comparison with Julien's theory, the simplified theory described above requires only three parameters, μ_p, W, and C_i, to define the tractive effort–longitudinal slip relationship. As pointed out previously, the value of C_i can easily be identified from the initial slope of the measured tractive effort–slip curve.

When a braking torque is applied to the tire, a stretching of the tread elements occurs prior to entering the contact area, as shown in Fig. 1.17, in contrast with the compression effect for a driven tire. The distance that the tire travels when a braking torque is applied, therefore, will be greater than that in free rolling. The severity of braking is often measured by the skid of the tire i_s, which is defined as

$$i_s = \left(1 - \frac{r\omega}{V}\right) \times 100\%$$

$$= \left(1 - \frac{r}{r_e}\right) \times 100\% \tag{1.30}$$

For a locked wheel, the angular speed ω of the tire is zero, whereas the linear speed of the tire center is not zero. Under this condition, the skid is denoted 100%. It should be noted that using the definition of slip suggested by the SAE and given by Eq. 1.6, for a locked tire, the slip will be -100%.

A simplified theory for the relationship between the braking effort and the skid can also be developed, following an approach similar to that for the relationship between the tractive force and the slip described previously. It should be mentioned that according to the definitions of slip i and skid i_s given by Eqs. 1.5 and 1.30, respectively, the expressions for slip i and skid i_s are related by

$$|i| = |i_s/(1 - i_s)| \tag{1.31}$$

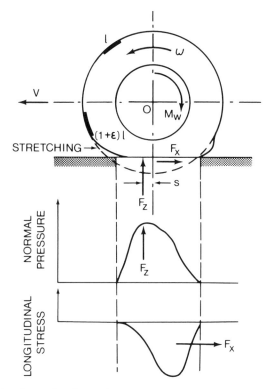

Fig. 1.17 Behavior of a tire under the action of a braking torque. (Reproduced with permission from *Mechanics of Pneumatic Tires*, edited by S. K. Clark, Monograph 122, National Bureau of Standards, 1971.)

If no sliding takes place on the contact patch, the relationship between the braking effort and the skid can be established by replacing C_i and i in Eq. 1.23 with C_s and $i_s/(1 - i_s)$, respectively.

$$F_x = C_s i_s/(1 - i_s) \tag{1.32}$$

where F_x is the braking effort acting in the opposite direction of motion of the tire center, and C_s is the slope of the braking effort–skid curve at the origin, and is given by [1.8]

$$C_s = \left.\frac{\partial F_x}{\partial i_s}\right|_{i_s = 0} \tag{1.33}$$

C_s is referred to as the longitudinal stiffness of the tire during braking. Similar to the parameter C_i, the value of C_s can easily be identified from the initial slope of the measured braking effort–skid curve.

It is interesting to note from Eq. 1.32 that, using the definition of skid given by Eq. 1.30, the relationship between braking effort and skid is nonlinear, even at low skids, where no sliding takes place between the tread and the ground.

The critical value of skid i_{sc}, at which sliding between the tread and the ground begins, can be established by replacing C_i and i in Eq. 1.25 with C_s and $i_s/(1 - i_s)$, respectively.

$$i_{sc} = \frac{\mu_p W}{2C_s + \mu_p W}$$ (1.34)

The corresponding critical value of braking effort F_{xc}, above which sliding between the tread and the ground begins, is given by

$$F_{xc} = \frac{\mu_p W}{2}$$ (1.35)

When sliding takes place in part of the contact patch (i.e., $i_s > i_{sc}$, the relationship between the braking effort and the skid can be established by replacing C_i and i in Eq. 1.29 with C_s and $i_s/(1 - i_s)$, respectively.

$$F_x = \mu_p W \left[1 - \frac{\mu_p W(1 - i_s)}{4C_s i_s} \right]$$ (1.36)

While the theory described above represents a simplified model for the highly complex phenomenon of tire–ground interaction, it has been proven to be useful in representing tire behavior in the simulations of the dynamics of passenger cars [1.8, 1.16].

Figure 1.18 shows the variation of the braking effort coefficient, which is the ratio of the braking effort to the normal load, with skid for a bias-ply passenger car tire over various surfaces [1.17]. The peak and sliding values of the coefficient of road adhesion of a bias-ply, a bias-belted, and a radial-ply passenger car tire of the same size with various inflation pressures at a speed of 64 km/h (40 mph) on

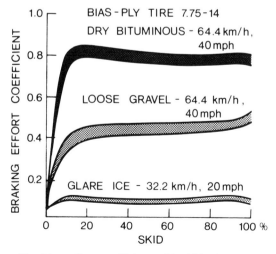

Fig. 1.18 Variation of braking effort coefficient with skid of a car tire on various surfaces. (Reproduced with permission of the Society of Automotive Engineers from reference 1.17.)

a dry, aggregate asphalt surface are shown in Fig. 1.19 [1.11]. It appears that on a dry surface, the coefficient of road adhesion does not vary significantly with tire construction and inflation pressure. Average peak and sliding values of the coefficient of road adhesion μ_p and μ_s on various surfaces are given in Table 1.2 [1.12].

Among the operational parameters, speed and normal load have noticeable effects on the tractive (braking) effort–slip (skid) characteristics. Figure 1.20 shows

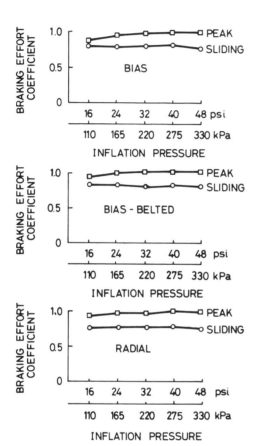

Fig. 1.19 Variation of peak and sliding values of braking effort coefficient with inflation pressure for bias-ply, bias-belted, and radial-ply car tires on dry pavement. (Reproduced with permission of the Society of Automotive Engineers from reference 1.11.)

TABLE 1.2   Average Values of Coefficient of Road Adhesion

Surface	Peak Value μ_p	Sliding Value μ_s
Asphalt and concrete (dry)	0.8–0.9	0.75
Asphalt (wet)	0.5–0.7	0.45–0.6
Concrete (wet)	0.8	0.7
Gravel	0.6	0.55
Earth road (dry)	0.68	0.65
Earth road (wet)	0.55	0.4–0.5
Snow (hard-packed)	0.2	0.15
Ice	0.1	0.07

Source: Reference 1.12.

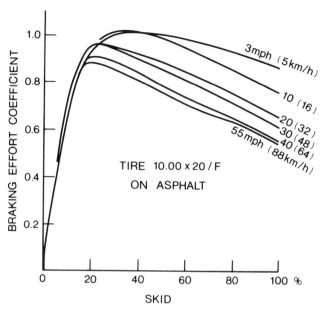

Fig. 1.20 Effect of speed on braking performance of a truck tire on asphalt. (Reproduced with permission from reference 1.18.)

the influence of speed on the braking effort coefficient–skid characteristics of a bias-ply truck tire on a dry asphalt surface [1.18]. As shown in Fig. 1.20, speed appears to have a significant effect on the tractive (braking) performance of a tire. Therefore, it has been suggested that to improve the prediction of the relationship between the tractive (braking) effort and the slip (skid), the effect of the sliding speed between the tire tread and the ground should be incorporated into the theories described previously [1.8]. Figure 1.21 shows the effect of normal load on the braking performance of a bias-ply truck tire on a dry asphalt surface [1.18]. It is noted that the value of the longitudinal stiffness C_s increases noticeably with an increase of the normal load. This is because the tire contact length increases with the normal load for a given inflation pressure. According to Eq. 1.21, to develop a given longitudinal force, the longer tire contact length results in lower longitudinal slip (or skid).

A sample of the peak and sliding values of the coefficient of road adhesion μ_p and μ_s for truck tires at 65 km/h (40 mph) on dry and wet concrete pavements is shown in Table 1.3 [1.19]. The pavements were aggressively textured, like those of relatively new roads meeting the requirements of the U.S. Federal Interstate Highway System.

It can be seen from Table 1.3 that the ratio of the peak value μ_p to the sliding value μ_s for truck tires on dry concrete pavement is around 1.4, whereas on wet concrete pavement, it ranges from approximately 1.3 to 1.6. It is also noted that there appear to be no clear distinctions between the tractive (braking) performance of bias-ply and radial-ply truck tires.

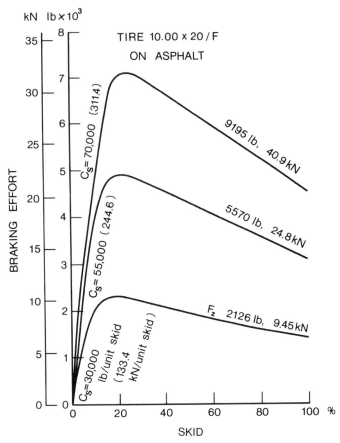

Fig. 1.21 Effect of normal load on braking performance of a truck tire on asphalt. (Reproduced with permission from reference 1.18.)

TABLE 1.3 Values of Coefficient of Road Adhesion for Truck Tires on Dry and Wet Concrete Pavement at 65 km/h (40 mph)

Tire Type	Tire Construction	Dry		Wet	
		μ_p	μ_s	μ_p	μ_s
Goodyear Super Hi Miler (Rib)	Bias-ply	0.850	0.596	0.673	0.458
General GTX (Rib)	Bias-ply	0.826	0.517	0.745	0.530
Firestone Transteel (Rib)	Radial-ply	0.809	0.536	0.655	0.477
Firestone Transport 1 (Rib)	Bias-ply	0.804	0.557	0.825	0.579
Goodyear Unisteel R-1 (Rib)	Radial-ply	0.802	0.506	0.700	0.445
Firestone Transteel Traction (Lug)	Radial-ply	0.800	0.545	0.600	0.476
Goodyear Unisteel L-1 (Lug)	Radial-ply	0.768	0.555	0.566	0.427
Michelin XZA (Rib)	Radial-ply	0.768	0.524	0.573	0.443
Firestone Transport 200 (Lug)	Bias-ply	0.748	0.538	0.625	0.476
Uniroyal Fleet Master Super Lug	Bias-ply	0.739	0.553	0.513	0.376
Goodyear Custom Cross Rib	Bias-ply	0.716	0.546	0.600	0.455
Michelin XZZ (Rib)	Radial-ply	0.715	0.508	0.614	0.459
Average		0.756	0.540	0.641	0.467

Source: UMTRI, reference 1.19.

The significant difference between the peak value μ_p and the sliding value μ_s of the coefficient of road adhesion indicates the importance of avoiding wheel lock-up during braking (skid $i_s = 100\%$) or wheel spinning during acceleration (slip $i = 100\%$).

1.4 CORNERING PROPERTIES OF TIRES

1.4.1 Slip Angle and Cornering Force

When a pneumatic tire is not subject to any force perpendicular to the wheel plane (i.e., side force), it will roll in a direction coinciding with the wheel plane. If, however, a side force F_s is applied to a tire, a lateral force will be developed at the contact patch, and the tire will move along a path at an angle α with the wheel plane, as *OA* shown in Fig. 1.22. The angle α is usually referred to as the slip angle, and the phenomenon of side slip is mainly due to the lateral elasticity of the tire.

The lateral force developed at the tire–ground contact patch is usually called the cornering force $F_{y\alpha}$ when the camber angle of the wheel is zero. The relationship between the cornering force and the slip angle is of fundamental importance to the directional control and stability of road vehicles.

When the tire is moving at a uniform speed in the direction of *OA*, the side force F_s applied at the wheel center and the cornering force $F_{y\alpha}$ developed in the ground plane are usually not collinear, as shown in Fig. 1.22. At small slip angles, the cornering force in the ground plane is normally behind the applied side force, giving rise to a torque (or couple), which tends to align the wheel plane with the direction of motion. This torque is called the aligning or self-aligning torque, and is one of the primary restoring moments which help the steered tire return to the original position after negotiating a turn. The distance t_p between the side force and the cornering force is called the pneumatic trail, and the product of the cornering force and the pneumatic trail determines the self-aligning torque.

The relationships between the slip angle and the cornering force of various types of tire under a variety of operating conditions have been investigated extensively. Typical plots of the cornering force as a function of the slip angle for a bias-ply and a radial-ply passenger car tire are shown in Fig. 1.23 [1.6]. It can be seen that for slip angles below a certain value, such as 4° shown in Fig. 1.23, the cornering force is approximately proportional to the slip angle. Beyond that, the cornering force increases at a lower rate with an increase of the slip angle, and it reaches a maximum value where the tire begins sliding laterally. For passenger car tires, the maximum cornering force may occur at a slip angle of about 18°, while for racing car tires, the cornering force may peak at about 6°. Figure 1.23 shows that the cornering force of a bias-ply tire increases more slowly with an increase of the slip angle than that of a radial-ply tire. These characteristics are considered to be more suited to two-wheeled vehicles, such as motorcycles. A more gradual increase of the cornering force with the slip angle enables the driver to exercise better control over a two-wheeled vehicle. This is one of the reasons why bias-ply tires are used for motorcycles [1.1]. Figure 1.24 shows the variations of the ratio of the corner-

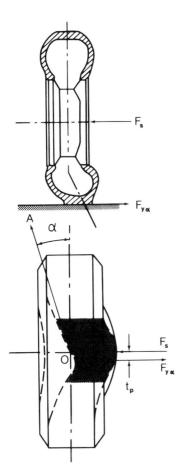

Fig. 1.22 Behavior of a tire subject to a side force. (Reproduced with permission from *Mechanics of Pneumatic Tires*, edited by S. K. Clark, Monograph 122, National Bureau of Standards, 1971.)

ing force to the normal load with the slip angle for radial-ply and bias-ply truck tires of size 10.00–20 with different tread designs (ribbed or lugged) [1.8]. Similar to that shown in Fig. 1.23 for passenger car tires, the cornering force of radial-ply truck tires increases more rapidly with an increase of the slip angle than that of bias-ply truck tires.

A number of factors affect the cornering behavior of pneumatic tires. The normal load on the tire strongly influences the cornering characteristics. Some typical results are shown in Fig. 1.25 [1.6]. It can be seen that for a given slip angle, the cornering force generally increases with an increase of the normal load. However, the relationship between the cornering force and the normal load is nonlinear. Thus, the transfer of load from the inside to the outside tire during a turning maneuver will reduce the total cornering force that a pair of tires can develop. Consider a pair of tires on a beam axle, each with normal load F_z, as shown in Fig. 1.26. The cornering force per tire with normal load F_z is F_y for a given slip angle. If the vehicle undergoes a steady-state turn, owing to lateral load transfer, the normal load on the inside tire will be reduced to F_{zi} and that on the outside tire will be increased to F_{zo}. As a result, the total cornering force of the two tires will

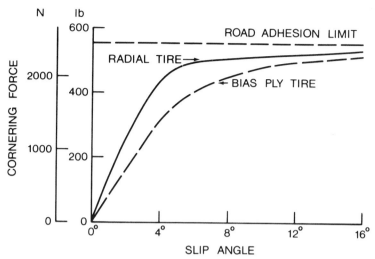

Fig. 1.23 Cornering characteristics of a bias-ply and a radial-ply car tire. (Reproduced with permission from *Mechanics of Pneumatic Tires*, edited by S. K. Clark, Monograph 122, National Bureau of Standards, 1971.)

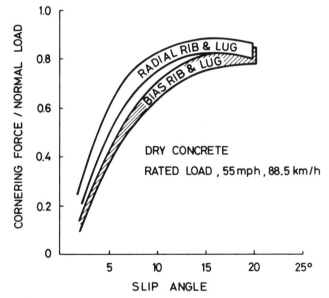

Fig. 1.24 Cornering characteristics of bias-ply and radial-ply truck tires on dry concrete. (Reproduced with permission from reference 1.8.)

be F_{yi} and F_{yo}, which is less than $2F_y$, as shown in Fig. 1.26. This implies that for a pair of tires on a beam axle to develop the required amount of cornering force to balance a given centrifugal force during a turn, the lateral load transfer results in an increase in the slip angle of the tires.

To provide a measure for comparing the cornering behavior of different tires, a parameter called cornering stiffness C_α is used, which is defined as a the derivative of the cornering force $F_{y\alpha}$ with respect to slip angle α evaluated at zero slip angle:

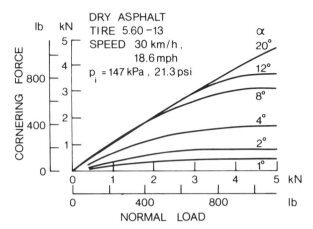

Fig. 1.25 Effect of normal load on the cornering characteristics of a car tire. (Reproduced with permission from *Mechanics of Pneumatic Tires*, edited by S. K. Clark, Monograph 122, National Bureau of Standards, 1971.)

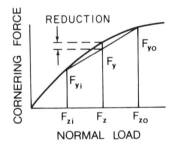

Fig. 1.26 Effect of lateral load transfer on the cornering capability of a pair of tires on an axle.

$$C_\alpha = \frac{\partial F_{y\alpha}}{\partial \alpha}\bigg|_{\alpha = 0} \tag{1.37}$$

Figure 1.27 shows a comparison of the relationships between the cornering stiffness and the normal load for a sample of passenger car, light truck, and heavy truck tires [1.8]. In the figure, RL indicates the rated load for a specific tire. It can be seen that for the three passenger car tires tested, the cornering stiffness reaches a maximum at the rated load, and decreases with a further increase in the normal load. However, for the light truck and heavy truck tires shown, the cornering stiffness keeps increasing beyond the rated load, although at a lower rate.

To evaluate the effect of the normal load on the cornering ability of tires, a parameter called the cornering coefficient, which is defined as the cornering stiffness per unit normal load, is often used. Figure 1.28 shows a typical relationship between the cornering coefficient and the normal load of a tire [1.12]. It shows that the cornering coefficient decreases with an increase in the normal load.

Inflation pressure usually has a moderate effect on the cornering properties of a tire. In general, the cornering stiffness of tires increases with an increase of the

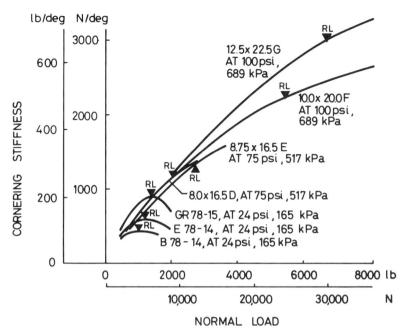

Fig. 1.27 Comparison of cornering stiffness of car, light truck, and heavy truck tires. (Reproduced with permission from reference 1.8.)

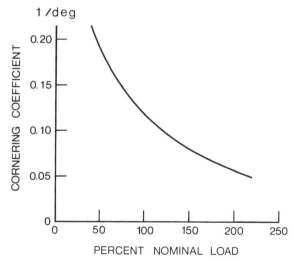

Fig. 1.28 Effect of normal load on the cornering coefficient of a tire. (Reproduced with permission from reference 1.12.)

inflation pressure. Figure 1.29 shows a comparison of the cornering coefficients at different inflation pressures of a radial-ply, a bias-belted, and a bias-ply passenger car tire [1.11]. Table 1.4 shows a sample of the values of the cornering coefficient for truck tires at rated loads and inflation pressures (unless specified) [1.19].

A number of attempts have been made to develop mathematical models for the cornering behavior of pneumatic tires. There are two basic types of model. One is

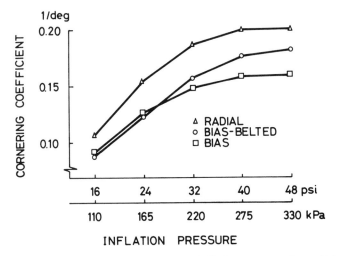

Fig. 1.29 Variation of cornering coefficient with inflation pressure for radial-ply, bias-ply, and bias-belted car tires. (Reproduced with permission of the Society of Automotive Engineers from reference 1.11.)

TABLE 1.4 Cornering Coefficients for Truck Tires at Rated Loads and Inflation Pressures (Unless Specified)

Tire Type	Tire Construction	Cornering Coefficient (deg^{-1})
Michelin Radial XZA (1/3 Tread)	Radial-ply	0.1861
Michelin Radial XZA (1/2 Tread)	Radial-ply	0.1749
Michelin Pilote XZA	Radial-ply	0.1648
Michelin Radial XZA	Radial-ply	0.1472
Goodyear Unisteel G159, 11R22.5 LRF at 655 kPa (95 psi)	Radial-ply	0.1413
Michelin XZZ	Radial-ply	0.1370
Goodyear Unisteel 11, 10R22.5 LRF at 620 kPa (90 psi)	Radial-ply	0.1350
Goodyear Unisteel G159, 11R22.5 LRG at 792 kPa (115 psi)	Radial-ply	0.1348
Goodyear Unisteel 11, 10R22.5 LRF at 758 kPa (110 psi)	Radial-ply	0.1311
Firestone Transteel	Radial-ply	0.1171
Firestone Transteel Traction	Radial-ply	0.1159
Goodyear Unisteel R-1	Radial-ply	0.1159
Goodyear Unisteel L-1	Radial-ply	0.1121
Firestone Transport 1	Bias-ply	0.1039
General GTX	Bias-ply	0.1017
Goodyear Super Hi Miler	Bias-ply	0.0956
Goodyear Custom Cross Rib	Bias-ply	0.0912
Uniroyal Fleet Master Super Lug	Bias-ply	0.0886
Firestone Transport 200	Bias-ply	0.0789

Sources: UMTRI and TRIF, reference 1.19.

based on the assumption that the tread of the tire is equivalent to a stretched string restrained by lateral springs, representative of the sidewall, with the wheel rim acting as the base of the springs, as shown in Fig. 1.30. In the other model, the tread is considered equivalent to an elastic beam with continuous lateral elastic support [1.15, 1.20]

In both models, it is assumed that the cornering behavior of a tire can be deduced from the characteristics of the equatorial line of the tire, which is the intersection of the undeformed tire tread with the wheel plane. The portion of the equatorial line in the contact area is called the contact line. One of the major differences in these two basic models is that in the stretched-string model, discontinuities of the slope of the equatorial line are permissible, whereas for the beam model, that is not the case. It has been shown that for small slip angles, the stretched-string model can provide a basic understanding of the lateral behavior of a pneumatic tire. In the following, the stretched-string model as proposed by Temple and von Schlippe will be discussed [1.15].

Consider a tire in a steady-state motion with a fixed slip angle. The shape of the equatorial line BC in the contact area shown in Fig. 1.31 is the path of the tire,

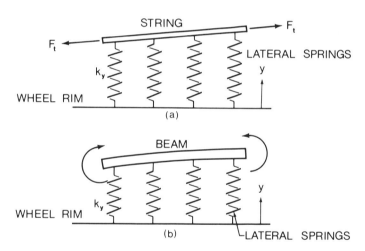

Fig. 1.30 Models for cornering behavior of tires. (a) Stretched string model. (b) Beam on elastic foundation model. (Reproduced with permission from *Vehicle Dynamics* by J. R. Ellis, Business Books, 1969.)

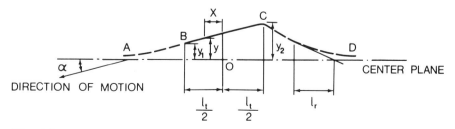

Fig. 1.31 Behavior of the equatorial line of a rolling tire subject to a side force.

and it is immobile relative to the ground when no sliding takes place. Let the dotted line AB in the figure represent the projection of the portion of the equatorial line outside and in front of the contact patch. As the tire rolls forward, points of AB become points of BC. This indicates that AB and BC must have a common tangent at point B. At the rear of the contact patch, such conditions do not hold, and a kink may be present at point C. Thus, it can be stated that for a rolling tire, the slope of the equatorial line is continuous at the front edge of the contact area, but not necessarily at the rear.

Consider an element of the distorted equatorial line shown in Fig. 1.31. Let the lateral deflection from the wheel plane be y, and the distance measured along the undistorted equatorial line be x, with the origin at the center of the contact patch. It is assumed that the lateral force applied to the rim by the element due to lateral deflection y is given, in differential form, by

$$dF_{y1} = k_y y \, dx \tag{1.38}$$

where k_y is the lateral stiffness of the tire. This equation applies at all points of the periphery. Based on experimental data of a sample of bias-ply and radial-ply heavy truck tires under rated loads and inflation pressures, it is found that the value of k_y varies in a narrow range. The average value is approximately 2275 kN/m² (330 lb/in.²).

In an element of the equatorial line, there is another force component acting in the lateral direction, which is due to the tension in the string. This component is proportional to the curvature of the equatorial line, and for small deflection is given, in differential form, by

$$dF_{y2} = -F_t \frac{d^2 y}{dx^2} \, dx \tag{1.39}$$

where F_t represents the tension in the string. It is usually convenient to write $F_t = k_y l_r^2$, where l_r is termed the "relaxation length," in which the lateral deflection, described by an exponential function, decreases to $1/2.718$ of its prior value, as shown in Fig. 1.31.

Let l_t be the contact length with the origin for x at the center, and let y_1 and y_2 be the deflections of the equatorial line at the front and rear ends of the contact patch, as shown in Fig. 1.31. Over that part of the tire not in contact with the ground (i.e., free region) having total length l_h, the tire is not loaded by external means, and therefore from Eqs. 1.38 and 1.39,

$$k_y \left(y - l_r^2 \frac{d^2 y}{dx^2} \right) = 0 \tag{1.40}$$

The solution of this differential equation will yield the deflected shape of the equatorial line in the free region, which is given by

$$y = \frac{y_2 \sinh\,[(x - l_t/2)/l_r] + y_1 \sinh\,[(l_t/2 + l_h - x)/l_r]}{\sinh\,(l_h/l_r)} \qquad (1.41)$$

If r is the tire radius, under normal conditions l_h lies between $4.5r$ and $6r$, whereas l_r is approximately equal to r [1.15]. Hence, Eq. 1.41 may be approximated by an exponential function.

For the free region near the front of the contact area (i.e., $x > l_t/2$),

$$y = y_1 \exp\left[\frac{-(x - l_t/2)}{l_r}\right] \qquad (1.42)$$

For the free region near the rear of the contact area (i.e., $x < l_t/2 + l_h$),

$$y = y_2 \exp\left[\frac{-(l_t/2 + l_h - x)}{l_r}\right] \qquad (1.43)$$

Thus, in the free region not in contact with the ground but near either end of the contact patch, the shape of the equatorial line is an exponential curve.

The expressions for the lateral deflection and the lateral forces acting on an element of the tread described above permit the determination of the cornering force and the aligning torque in terms of constants k_y and l_r and contact length l_t. This can be achieved in two ways:

1. Integrating the lateral force exerted on the tire over the contact length, but including an infinitesimal length of the equatorial line in the free region at either end, as proposed by Temple.
2. Integrating the lateral force exerted on the rim by the tire over the entire circumference, including the contact length, as proposed by von Schlippe. The essence of these two methods is illustrated in Fig. 1.32.

Following Temple's method, and assuming that the equatorial line in the contact region is a straight line, one can obtain the total lateral force F_y by integration.

$$\begin{aligned} F_y &= k_y \int_{-l_t/2}^{l_t/2} \left(y - l_r^2 \frac{d^2 y}{dx^2}\right) dx \\ &= k_y \int_{-l_t/2}^{l_t/2} y\, dx - k_y l_r^2 \left(\frac{dy}{dx}\right)\Bigg]_{l_t/2}^{l_t/2} \\ &= k_y\,(y_1 + y_2)l_t/2 + k_y l_r(y_1 + y_2) \\ &= k_y(y_1 + y_2)(l_r + l_t/2) \qquad (1.44) \end{aligned}$$

For a nonrolling tire subject to a pure side force,

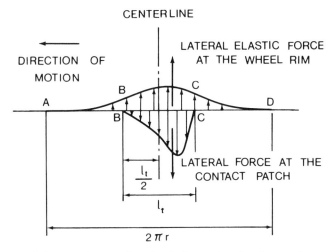

Fig. 1.32   Lateral force acting on the wheel rim and at the tire–road contact patch.

$$y_1 = y_2 = y_0 \text{ and } F_y = 2k_y y_0(l_r + l_t/2) \tag{1.45}$$

The moment of lateral force about a vertical axis through the center of contact (i.e., the aligning torque) is given by

$$M_z = k_y \int_{-l_t/2}^{l_t/2} x\left(y - l_r^2 \frac{d^2y}{dx^2}\right) dx$$

$$= k_y \int_{-l_t/2}^{l_t/2} xy\, dx - k_y l_r^2 \left(x\frac{dy}{dx} - y\right)\Big]_{l_t/2}^{l_t/2}$$

$$= k_y \frac{(l_t/2)^2}{3}(y_1 - y_2) + k_y l_r\left(l_r + \frac{l_t}{2}\right)(y_1 - y_2)$$

$$= k_y(y_1 - y_2)\left[\frac{(l_t/2)^2}{3} + l_r\left(l_r + \frac{l_t}{2}\right)\right] \tag{1.46}$$

Following von Schlippe's approach, one can obtain the same expressions.

For a tire rolling at a slip angle α, the slope of the equatorial line in the contact area is equal to tan α if the tread in the contact patch is not sliding. Thus,

$$\alpha \simeq \tan \alpha = \frac{y_2 - y_1}{l_t} = \frac{y_1}{l_r} \tag{1.47}$$

Substituting the above expression into Eqs. 1.44 and 1.46, the relationships between the lateral force and the self-aligning torque and the slip angle become

$$\frac{F_y}{\alpha} = 2k_y\left(l_r + \frac{l_t}{2}\right)^2 \tag{1.48}$$

$$\frac{M_z}{\alpha} = k_y l_t \left[\frac{(l_t/2)^2}{3} + l_r \left(l_r + \frac{l_t}{2} \right) \right] \qquad (1.49)$$

The pneumatic trail t_p is given by

$$t_p = \frac{M_z}{F_y} = \frac{(l_t/2)\,[(l_t/2)^2/3 + l_r\,(l_r + l_t/2)]}{(l_r + l_t/2)^2} \qquad (1.50)$$

The two basic parameters k_y and l_r, which specify the characteristics of the lateral elasticity of the pneumatic tire, can be measured by suitable tests. It is noted that the ratio of F_y/α to M_z/α is independent of k_y, and therefore l_r can be determined from the measured values of F_y/α and M_z/α (contact length of the tire l_t being known). On the other hand, the ratio of $(F_y/y_0)^2$ of a nonrolling tire to F_y/α is independent of l_r, and therefore k_y can be determined from the measured values of $(F_y/y_0)^2$ and F_y/α. Measurements of k_y and l_r have been carried out by several investigators. Values of l_r for a family of aircraft tires of different sizes but with similar proportion were found by von Schlippe to vary from $0.6r$ to $0.9r$ approximately. Values of k_y measured by von Schlippe were about 90% of the inflation pressure [1.15].

Equations 1.48 and 1.49 indicate that, if no sliding between the tread and the ground occurs, the lateral force and the aligning torque increase linearly with the slip angle. This is the case for small slip angles, as shown in Fig. 1.23. As the slip angle increases, sliding between the tread and the ground occurs. The assumption that the equatorial line in the contact patch is a straight line is no longer valid. Thus, the theory proposed by Temple and von Schlippe is restricted to small slip angles.

As noted above, using Temple's or von Schlippe's theory to define the relationship between the cornering force and the slip angle, the values of k_y and l_r must be known. Their determination is usually quite an involved process. In view of this, a simplified theory has been proposed [1.8]. In the simplified model, it is assumed that if no sliding takes place, the lateral deflection y' of a tread element on the ground at a longitudinal distance of x from the front of the contact patch (along the wheel plane) is proportional to $\tan \alpha$ and is given by

$$y' = x \tan \alpha \qquad (1.51)$$

where the lateral deflection y' is measured with respect to the front contact point and perpendicular to the wheel plane, and α is the slip angle.

If k_y' is the equivalent lateral stiffness of the tire, then when no lateral sliding between the tire tread and the ground takes place, the lateral force per unit contact length is given by

$$\frac{dF_{y\alpha}}{dx} = k_y' x \tan \alpha \qquad (1.52)$$

and the cornering force developed on the entire contact patch is expressed by

$$F_{y\alpha} = \int_0^{l_t} k_y' x \tan \alpha \, dx$$

$$= (k_y' l_t^2 / 2) \tan \alpha \tag{1.53}$$

where l_t is the contact length of the tire.

The term $(k_y' l_t^2 / 2)$ may be taken as the cornering stiffness C_α defined by Eq. 1.37, that is, the slope of the cornering force–slip angle curve at the origin, which can easily be identified:

$$\frac{k_y' l_t^2}{2} = C_\alpha = \left. \frac{\partial F_{y\alpha}}{\partial \alpha} \right|_{\alpha = 0} \tag{1.54}$$

Therefore, when no lateral sliding takes place on the contact patch, the relationship between the cornering force and the slip angle is expressed by

$$F_{y\alpha} = C_\alpha \tan \alpha \tag{1.55}$$

If the slip angle α is small, $\tan \alpha \approx \alpha$, and Eq. 1.55 may be rewritten as

$$F_{y\alpha} = C_\alpha \alpha \tag{1.56}$$

Following an approach similar to that for analyzing the relationship between the tractive effort and the longitudinal slip described in Section 1.3, the critical values of the slip angle α_c and the cornering force $F_{y\alpha c}$, at which lateral sliding in the trailing part of the contact patch begins, can be determined. The critical value of α_c is given by

$$\alpha_c = \frac{\mu_p W}{2 C_\alpha} \tag{1.57}$$

and the critical value of $F_{y\alpha c}$ is given by

$$F_{y\alpha c} = \frac{\mu_p W}{2} \tag{1.58}$$

Similar to the relationship between the tractive effort–longitudinal slip described in Section 1.3, Eq. 1.58 indicates that the relationship between the cornering force and the slip angle will be linear and no lateral sliding will take place, if the cornering force is less than one half of its peak value $(\mu_p W / 2)$.

When lateral sliding between the tire tread and the ground takes place (i.e.,

$\alpha \geq \alpha_c$ or $F_{y\alpha} > F_{y\alpha c}$), the relationship between the cornering force and the slip angle is expressed by

$$F_{y\alpha} = \mu_p W \left(1 - \frac{\mu_p W}{4 C_\alpha \tan \alpha} \right) = \mu_p W \left(1 - \frac{\mu_p W}{4 C_\alpha \alpha} \right) \qquad (1.59)$$

The above equation indicates the nonlinear nature of the cornering force–slip angle relationship when lateral sliding takes place in part of the contact patch.

While the theories described above provide physical insight into certain aspects of the cornering behavior of the pneumatic tire, they are simplified representations of a highly complex process. In the simulations of the lateral dynamic behavior of road vehicles, to more accurately represent tire characteristics, measured tire data, rather than theoretical relationships, are often used. Measured tire data in tabular form or represented by empirical equations may be entered as input to the simulation models. For instance, the following empirical equation has been proposed to represent the relationship between the cornering force $F_{y\alpha}$ and the slip angle α [1.20]:

$$F_{y\alpha} = c_1 \alpha + c_2 \alpha^2 + c_3 \alpha^3 \qquad (1.60)$$

where c_1, c_2, and c_3 are empirical constants derived from fitting Eq. 1.60 to the measured data of a given tire.

As mentioned previously, normal load has a significant influence on the development of cornering force. To take the effects of normal load into account, the coefficients c_1, c_2, and c_3 may be expressed as a quadratic function of normal load [1.20]. This would require an additional curve-fitting exercise.

In the discussion of the cornering behavior of pneumatic tires described above, the effect of the longitudinal force has not been considered. However, quite often both the side force and the longitudinal force are present, such as braking in a turn. In general, tractive (or braking) effort will reduce the cornering force that can be generated for a given slip angle; the cornering force decreases gradually with an increase of the tractive or braking effort. At low values of tractive (or braking) effort, the decrease in the cornering force is mainly caused by the reduction of the cornering stiffness of the tire. A further increase of the tractive (or braking) force results in a pronounced decrease of the cornering force for a given slip angle. This is due to the mobilization of the available local adhesion by the tractive (or braking) effort, which reduces the amount of adhesion available in the lateral direction.

The difference in behavior between a bias-ply and a radial-ply passenger car tire is shown in Fig. 1.33 [1.6]. It is interesting to note that for a radial-ply tire, the cornering force available at a given slip angle is more or less the same for both braking and driving conditions. For a bias-ply tire, however, at a given slip angle, a higher cornering force is obtained during braking than when the tire is driven. The fact that the presence of the tractive (or braking) effort requires a higher slip angle to generate the same cornering force is also illustrated in Fig. 1.33. Figure

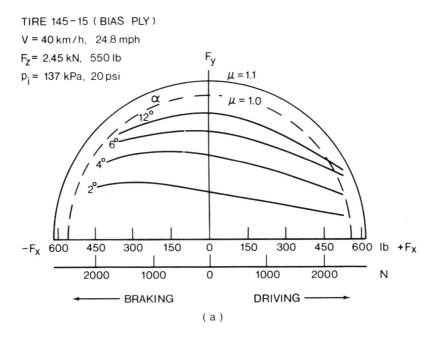

TIRE 145–15 (BIAS PLY)
V = 40 km/h, 24.8 mph
F_z= 2.45 kN, 550 lb
p_i = 137 kPa, 20 psi

(a)

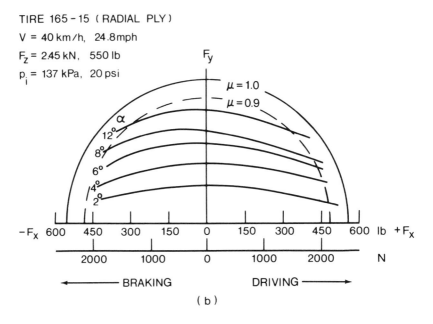

TIRE 165–15 (RADIAL PLY)
V = 40 km/h, 24.8 mph
F_z = 2.45 kN, 550 lb
p_i = 137 kPa, 20 psi

(b)

Fig. 1.33   Effect of tractive and braking effort on the cornering characteristics of (a) a bias-ply and (b) a radial-ply car tire. (Reproduced with permission from *Mechanics of Pneumatic Tires*, edited by S. K. Clark, Monograph 122, National Bureau of Standards, 1971.)

1.34 shows the effects of longitudinal force on the development of cornering force for a truck tire at different slip angles [1.8]. Similar to that shown in Fig. 1.33, for a truck tire, the cornering force available at a given slip angle also decreases with an increase of the longitudinal force.

It is interesting to point out that if an envelope around each family of curves of Fig. 1.33 is drawn, a curve approximately semi-elliptical in shape may be obtained. This enveloping curve is often referred to as the friction ellipse.

The friction ellipse concept is based on the assumption that the tire may slide on the ground in any direction if the resultant of the longitudinal force (either tractive or braking) and lateral (cornering) force reaches the maximum value defined by the coefficient of road adhesion and the normal load on the tire. However, the longitudinal and lateral force components may not exceed their respective maximum values $F_{x\max}$ and $F_{y\max}$, as shown in Fig. 1.35. $F_{x\max}$ and $F_{y\max}$ can be

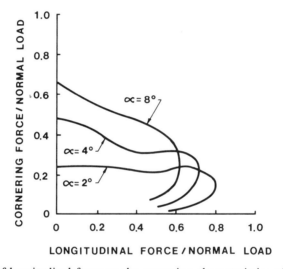

Fig. 1.34 Effect of longitudinal force on the cornering characteristics of truck tires. (Reproduced with permission of the Society of Automotive Engineers from reference 1.34.)

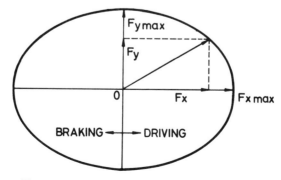

Fig. 1.35 The friction ellipse concept relating the maximum cornering force to a given longitudinal force.

identified from measured tire data, and constitute the major and minor axis of the friction ellipse, respectively, as shown in Fig. 1.35.

Based on the experimental observations described above, attempts have been made to formulate a general theory for predicting the longitudinal force and cornering force as functions of combined longitudinal slip (or skid) and slip angle.

One of the simplest theories for predicting the cornering force available at a specific slip angle in the presence of a tractive or braking force is based on the friction ellipse concept described above. The procedure for determining the available cornering force based on this simple theory is outlined below.

1) From measured tire data, the relationship between the cornering force and the slip angle under free rolling conditions (i.e., in the absence of tractive or braking effort) is first plotted, as shown in Fig. 1.36 (a).

2) The cornering forces at various slip angles under free rolling conditions are then marked on the vertical axis of Fig. 1.36 (b), as shown. For instance, the cornering force developed at a slip angle of 4° is identified as F_{y4} on the vertical axis, which constitutes the minor axis of an ellipse to be established.

3) From measured tire data, the maximum tractive or braking force, $F_{x\max}$, in the absence of lateral force, is marked on the horizontal axis in Fig. 1.36 (b) as shown, which constitutes the major axis of the ellipse.

4) The available cornering force F_y at a given slip angle, such as the 4° angle shown in Fig. 1.36 (b), for any given tractive or braking force F_x is then determined from the following equation:

$$(F_y/F_{y4})^2 + (F_x/F_{x\max})^2 = 1 \tag{1.61}$$

It is noted that the above equation describes an ellipse with the measured values of $F_{x\max}$ and F_{y4} as the major and minor axis, respectively.

Following the procedure outlined above, the available cornering force at any slip angle in the presence of any given tractive or braking force can be determined,

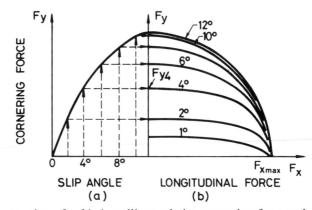

Fig. 1.36 Construction of a friction ellipse relating cornering force to longitudinal force for a given slip angle.

and a set of curves illustrating the relationships between the cornering force and the tractive (or braking) force at various slip angles can be plotted, as shown in Fig. 1.36 (b). It is noted that for a given slip angle, the cornering force is reduced as a tractive (or braking) force is applied to the tire. This is consistent with the trends of the measured data shown in Figs. 1.33 and 1.34.

Based on the simplified theory for the relationship between the braking force and the longitudinal skid described in Section 1.3 and that between the cornering force and the slip angle described earlier in this section, another semi-empirical method for predicting the braking force and cornering force in the presence of both the longitudinal skid and slip angle has been proposed [1.8].

In this method, it is assumed that when no sliding takes place, the braking force per unit contact length at a distance of x from the front contact point is given by (see Eqs. 1.20 and 1.31)

$$\frac{dF_x}{dx} = k_t x i_s / (1 - i_s) \tag{1.62}$$

where i_s is the longitudinal skid, as defined by Eq. 1.30.

If, at the same time, the tire develops a slip angle α, then due to the longitudinal skid, the tread in contact with the ground will be elongated at a rate equal to $1/(1 - i_s)$. As a result, the lateral deflection y' of a point on the tread in contact with the ground is given by (see Eq. 1.51)

$$y' = x \tan \alpha / (1 - i_s) \tag{1.63}$$

The corresponding lateral force per unit contact length is, therefore, expressed by (see Eq. 1.52)

$$\frac{dF_{y\alpha}}{dx} = k'_y x \tan \alpha / (1 - i_s) \tag{1.64}$$

Let p be the uniform normal pressure on the contact patch, b the contact width, and μ the coefficient of road adhesion. Then, based on the concept of friction ellipse described above, no sliding will take place at a point located at a distance of x from the front contact point if the resultant of the braking force and lateral force per unit contact length is less than a maximum value defined by the coefficient of road adhesion μ and the normal pressure p, that is,

$$\sqrt{[k_t x i_s / (1 - i_s)]^2 + [k'_y x \tan \alpha / (1 - i_s)]^2} = \mu p b = \frac{\mu W}{l_t} \tag{1.65}$$

where W is the normal load and l_t is the contact length of the tire.

This implies that if a point at a distance x from the front contact point is in the adhesion region, then x must be less than a characteristic length l_c, which defines the length of the adhesion region where no sliding between the tire tread and the ground takes place. The value of l_c in relation to the contact length l_t can be derived from Eq. 1.65, and is given by

$$\frac{l_c}{l_t} = \frac{\mu W (1 - i_s)}{2 \sqrt{(k_t l_t^2 i_s / 2)^2 + (k_y' l_t^2 \tan \alpha / 2)^2}}$$

$$= \frac{\mu W (1 - i_s)}{2 \sqrt{(C_s i_s)^2 + (C_\alpha \tan \alpha)^2}} \tag{1.66}$$

where $k_t l_t^2 / 2 = C_s$ and $k_y' l_t^2 / 2 = C_\alpha$, as described by Eqs. 1.33 and 1.54, respectively.

If $l_c / l_t \geq 1$, the entire contact patch is an adhesion region. The braking force is given by

$$F_x = \int_0^{l_t} [k_t x i_s / (1 - i_s)] \, dx = k_t l_t^2 i_s / 2(1 - i_s)$$

$$= C_s i_s / (1 - i_s) \tag{1.67}$$

and the cornering force $F_{y\alpha}$ as a function of slip angle α and skid i_s is expressed by

$$F_{y\alpha} = \int_0^{l_t} [k_y' x \tan \alpha / (1 - i_s)] \, dx$$

$$= k_y' l_t^2 \tan \alpha / 2(1 - i_s)$$

$$= C_\alpha \tan \alpha / (1 - i_s) \tag{1.68}$$

If $l_c / l_t < 1$, then sliding between the tread and the ground will take place. The braking force developed on the adhesion region F_{xa} is given by

$$F_{xa} = \int_0^{l_c} [k_t x i_s / (1 - i_s)] \, dx$$

$$= \frac{\mu^2 W^2 C_s i_s (1 - i_s)}{4 [(C_s i_s)^2 + (C_\alpha \tan \alpha)^2]} \tag{1.69}$$

and the braking force developed on the sliding region F_{xs} is expressed by

$$F_{xs} = \frac{\mu W C_s i_s}{\sqrt{(C_s i_s)^2 + (C_\alpha \tan \alpha)^2}} \left[1 - \frac{\mu W (1 - i_s)}{2 \sqrt{(C_s i_s)^2 + (C_\alpha \tan \alpha)^2}} \right] \tag{1.70}$$

The total braking force F_x is given by

$$F_x = F_{xa} + F_{xs}$$

$$= \frac{\mu W C_s i_s}{\sqrt{(C_s i_s)^2 + (C_\alpha \tan \alpha)^2}} \left[1 - \frac{\mu W (1 - i_s)}{4 \sqrt{(C_s i_s)^2 + (C_\alpha \tan \alpha)^2}} \right] \tag{1.71}$$

Similarly, if sliding between the tread and the ground takes place, then the cornering force developed on the adhesion region is given by

$$F_{y\alpha a} = \int_0^{l_c} [k_y' x \tan \alpha / (1 - i_s)] \, dx$$

$$= \frac{\mu^2 W^2 C_\alpha \tan \alpha \, (1 - i_s)}{4[(C_s i_s)^2 + (C_\alpha \tan \alpha)^2]} \tag{1.72}$$

and the cornering force developed on the sliding region is expressed by

$$F_{y\alpha s} = \frac{\mu W C_\alpha \tan \alpha}{\sqrt{(C_s i_s)^2 + (C_\alpha \tan \alpha)^2}} \left[1 - \frac{\mu W (1 - i_s)}{2\sqrt{(C_s i_s)^2 + (C_\alpha \tan \alpha)^2}} \right] \tag{1.73}$$

The total cornering force $F_{y\alpha}$ is given by

$$F_{y\alpha} = F_{y\alpha a} + F_{y\alpha s}$$

$$= \frac{\mu W C_\alpha \tan \alpha}{\sqrt{(C_s i_s)^2 + (C_\alpha \tan \alpha)^2}} \left[1 - \frac{\mu W (1 - i_s)}{4\sqrt{(C_s i_s)^2 + (C_\alpha \tan \alpha)^2}} \right] \tag{1.74}$$

It should be noted that the parameters μ, W, C_s, and C_α may change with operating conditions. For instance, it has been found that on a given surface, the values of μ, C_s, and C_α are functions of the normal load and operating speed of the tire. In a dynamic maneuver involving both braking and steering, the normal load and speed of the tires on a vehicle change as the maneuver proceeds. To achieve more accurate predictions, the effects of normal load and speed on the values of μ, C_s, C_α, and other tire parameters should be properly taken into account [1.8].

The semi-empirical method for modeling tire behavior described above has been incorporated into a computer model for simulating the directional response and braking performance of commercial vehicles [1.8]. It should be noted that the method presented above is for predicting the braking force and cornering force of a tire during combined braking and cornering. Following the same approach, however, a method for predicting the tractive force and cornering force as functions of combined longitudinal slip and slip angle can be formulated.

In addition to the methods described above, a number of other tire models have been developed or proposed for use in vehicle dynamics studies [1.21–1.23].

Example 1.1. A truck tire $10 \times 20/F$ with a normal load of 24.15 kN (5430 lb) is traveling on a dry asphalt pavement with a coefficient of road adhesion $\mu = 0.85$. The cornering stiffness of the tire C_α is 133.30 kN/rad (523 lb/deg) and the longitudinal stiffness C_s is 186.82 kN/unit skid (42,000 lb/unit skid).

Estimate the braking force and the cornering force that the tire can develop at a slip angle $\alpha = 4°$ and a longitudinal skid of 10%.

Solution. To determine whether sliding takes place on the tire contact patch under the given operating conditions, the ratio l_c/l_t is calculated using Eq. 1.66:

$$\frac{l_c}{l_t} = \frac{\mu W (1 - i_s)}{2\sqrt{(C_s i_s)^2 + (C_\alpha \tan \alpha)^2}}$$

$$= \frac{0.85 \times 24.15 \times (1 - 0.1)}{2\sqrt{(186.82 \times 0.1)^2 + (133.30 \times 0.0699)^2}} = 0.442$$

Since $l_c/l_t < 1$, sliding takes place in part of the contact patch.

The braking force can be predicted using Eq. 1.71:

$$F_x = F_{xa} + F_{xs}$$

$$= \frac{\mu W C_s i_s}{\sqrt{(C_s i_s)^2 + (C_\alpha \tan \alpha)^2}}\left[1 - \frac{\mu W (1 - i_s)}{4\sqrt{(C_s i_s)^2 + (C_\alpha \tan \alpha)^2}}\right]$$

$$= \frac{0.85 \times 24.15 \times 186.82 \times 0.1}{\sqrt{(186.82 \times 0.1)^2 + (133.30 \times 0.0699)^2}}$$

$$\cdot \left[1 - \frac{0.85 \times 24.15 \times (1 - 0.1)}{4\sqrt{(186.82 \times 0.1)^2 + (133.30 \times 0.0699)^2}}\right]$$

$$= 14.30 \text{ kN (3215 lb)}$$

The cornering force can be predicted using Eq. 1.74:

$$F_{y\alpha} = F_{y\alpha a} + F_{y\alpha s}$$

$$= \frac{\mu W C_\alpha \tan \alpha}{\sqrt{(C_s i_s)^2 + (C_\alpha \tan \alpha)^2}}\left[1 - \frac{\mu W (1 - i_s)}{4\sqrt{(C_s i_s)^2 + (C_\alpha \tan \alpha)^2}}\right]$$

$$= \frac{0.85 \times 24.15 \times 133.30 \times 0.0699}{\sqrt{(186.82 \times 0.1)^2 + (133.30 \times 0.0699)^2}}$$

$$\cdot \left[1 - \frac{0.85 \times 24.15 \times (1 - 0.1)}{4\sqrt{(186.82 \times 0.1)^2 + (133.30 \times 0.0699)^2}}\right]$$

$$= 7.14 \text{ kN (1605 lb)}$$

1.4.2 Slip Angle and Aligning Torque

As mentioned in Section 1.4.1, the side force F_s applied at the wheel center and the cornering force $F_{y\alpha}$ developed in the ground plane are usually not collinear, as shown in Fig. 1.22. This gives rise to a torque commonly known as the aligning or self-aligning torque. Figure 1.37 shows a plot of the cornering force versus the aligning torque for a passenger car tire at various slip angles and under different normal loads [1.24]. Figures 1.38 and 1.39 show the variations of the aligning torque with the slip angle and the normal load for a bias-ply truck tire (10.00–20/F) and for a radial-ply truck tire (10.00–20/G), respectively [1.8]. It is interesting to note that with a given normal load, the aligning torque first increases with an increase of the slip angle. It reaches a maximum at a particular slip angle, and then decreases with a further increase of the slip angle. This is mainly caused by the sliding of the tread in the trailing part of the contact patch at high slip angles, which results in shifting the point of application of the cornering force forward. Table 1.5 shows a sample of measured values of pneumatic trail for truck tires at a slip angle of 1° and under rated loads and inflation pressures (unless specified) [1.19]. It is shown that the pneumatic trail for truck tires varies in the range from 4.6 cm (1.8 in.) to 7.1 cm (2.8 in.). A typical value for a new bias-ply truck tire is 5.8 cm (2.3 in.), while that for a new radial-ply tire is 5.3 cm (2.1 in.).

Longitudinal force affects the aligning torque significantly. Generally speaking, the effect of a driving torque is to increase the aligning torque for a given slip angle, while a braking torque has the opposite effect. Inflation pressure and normal

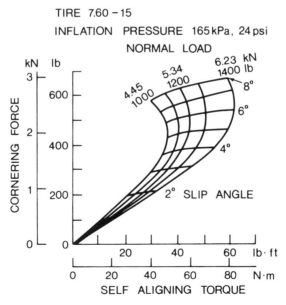

Fig. 1.37 Variation of self-aligning torque with cornering force of a car tire under various normal loads. (Reproduced with permission of the Society of Automotive Engineers from reference 1.24.)

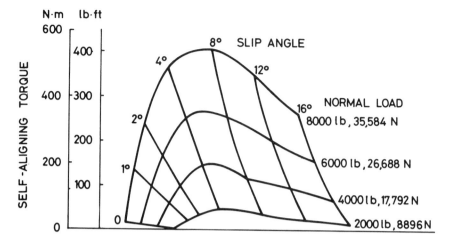

Fig. 1.38 Variation of self-aligning torque with normal load and slip angle for a bias-ply truck tire, 10.00–20/F. (Reproduced with permission from reference 1.8.)

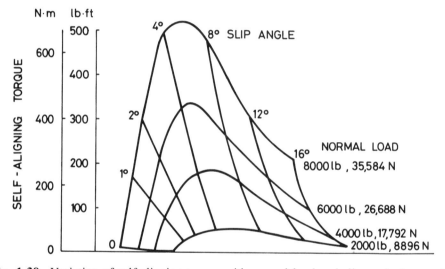

Fig. 1.39 Variation of self-aligning torque with normal load and slip angle for a radial-ply truck tire, 10.00–20/G. (Reproduced with permission from reference 1.8.)

load also have noticeable effects on the aligning torque because they affect the size of the tire contact patch. Higher normal load and lower inflation pressure result in longer tire contact length, and hence pneumatic trail. This causes an increase in the aligning torque.

1.4.3 Camber and Camber Thrust

Camber is the inclination of the wheel plane from a plane perpendicular to the road surface when viewed from the fore and aft directions of the vehicle, as shown in Fig. 1.40. Its main purpose is to achieve axial bearing pressure and to decrease

TABLE 1.5 Pneumatic Trails for Truck Tires at a Slip Angle of 1° Under Rated Loads and Inflation Pressures (Unless Specified)

Tire Type	Tire Construction	Pneumatic Trails	
		cm	in.
Michelin Radial 11R22.5XZA (1/3 Tread)	Radial-ply	6.17	2.43
Goodyear Unisteel II, 10R22.5LRF at 620 kPa (90 psi)	Radial-ply	6.15	2.42
Michelin Radial 11R22.5XZA (1/2 Tread)	Radial-ply	5.89	2.32
Goodyear Unisteel G159, 11R22.5LRG at 655 kPa (95 psi)	Radial-ply	5.87	2.31
Michelin Radial 11R22.5XZA	Radial-ply	5.51	2.17
Goodyear Unisteel G159, 11R22.5LRG at 792 kPa (115 psi)	Radial-ply	5.46	2.15
Goodyear Unisteel II, 10R22.5LRF at 758 kPa (110 psi)	Radial-ply	5.41	2.13
Michelin Radial 11R22.5XZA	Radial-ply	5.38	2.12
Michelin Pilote 11/80R22.5XZA	Radial-ply	4.62	1.82
New Unspecified Model 10.00-20/F	Bias-ply	5.89	2.32
Half-Worn Unspecified Model 10.00-20/F	Bias-ply	7.14	2.81
Fully-Worn Unspecified Model 10.00-20/F	Bias-ply	6.55	2.58

Source: UMTRI, reference 1.19.

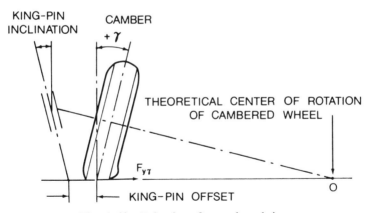

Fig. 1.40 Behavior of a cambered tire.

the king-pin offset. Camber on passenger cars is between 1/2 and 1°. High camber angles promote excessive tire wear [1.12].

Camber causes a lateral force developed on the contact patch. This lateral force is usually referred to as camber thrust $F_{y\gamma}$, and the development of this thrust may be explained in the following way. A free rolling tire with a camber angle would revolve about point O, as shown in Fig. 1.40. However, the cambered tire in a vehicle is constrained to move in a straight line. A lateral force in the direction of the camber is, therefore, developed in the ground plane. It is interesting to note that the camber thrust acts ahead of the wheel center, and therefore forms a small camber torque. The relationship between the camber thrust and the camber angle (at zero slip angle) for a bias-ply passenger car tire is illustrated in Fig. 1.41 [1.25]. It has been shown that the camber thrust is approximately one-fifth the value of the cornering force obtained from an equivalent slip angle for a bias-ply tire and somewhat less for a radial-ply tire. To provide a measure for comparing the camber characteristics of different tires, a parameter called ''camber stiffness'' is often used. It is defined as the derivative of the camber thrust with respect to the camber angle evaluated at zero camber angle.

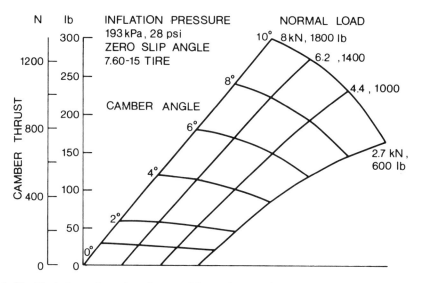

Fig. 1.41 Variation of camber thrust with camber angle and normal load for a car tire. (Reproduced with permission of the Society of Automotive Engineers from reference 1.25.)

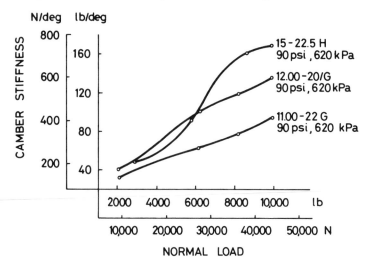

Fig. 1.42 Variation of camber stiffness with normal load for heavy truck tires. (Reproduced with permission from reference 1.8.)

$$C_\gamma = \left.\frac{\partial F_{y\gamma}}{\partial \gamma}\right|_{\gamma = 0} \tag{1.75}$$

Similar to the cornering stiffness, the normal load and inflation pressure have an influence on the camber stiffness. Figure 1.42 shows the variations of the camber stiffness with normal load for three truck tires at an inflation pressure of 620 kPa (90 psi) [1.8]. It is found that for truck tires, the value of the camber stiffness is approximately one-tenth to one-fifth of that of the cornering stiffness under similar operating conditions.

The total lateral force of a cambered tire operating at a slip angle is the sum of the cornering force $F_{y\alpha}$ and the camber thrust $F_{y\gamma}$:

$$F_y = F_{y\alpha} \pm F_{y\gamma} \tag{1.76}$$

If the cornering force and the camber thrust are in the same direction, the positive sign should be used in the above equation. For small slip and camber angles, the relationship between the cornering force and the slip angle and that between the camber thrust and the camber angle are essentially linear; the total lateral force of a cambered tire at a slip angle can, therefore, be determined by

$$F_y = C_\alpha \alpha \pm C_\gamma \gamma \tag{1.77}$$

As discussed previously, the lateral forces due to slip angle and camber angle produce an aligning torque. The aligning torque due to slip angle, however, is usually much greater.

1.5 PERFORMANCE OF TIRES ON WET SURFACES

The behavior of tires on wet surfaces is of considerable interest from a vehicle safety point of view, as many accidents occur on slippery roads. The performance of tires on wet surfaces depends on the surface texture, water depth, tread pattern, tread depth, tread material, and operating mode of the tire (i.e., free-rolling, braking, accelerating, or cornering). To achieve acceptable performance on wet surfaces, maintaining effective contact between the tire tread and the road is of importance, and there is no doubt about the necessity of removing water from the contact area as much as possible.

To maintain effective contact between the tire and the road, the tire tread should have a suitable pattern to facilitate the flow of fluid from the contact area, and the surface of the pavement should have an appropriate texture to facilitate drainage as well. To provide good skid resistance, road surfaces must fulfill two requirements: an open macrotexture to facilitate gross draining, and microharshness to produce sharp points that can penetrate the remaining water film [1.26].

The effects of tread pattern and speed on the braking performance of tires on various wet surfaces have been studied experimentally by a number of investigators. Figures 1.43 and 1.44 show the variations of the peak values μ_p and the sliding values μ_s of the coefficient of road adhesion with speed for a smooth tire, a tire with ribs, and a tire with ribs and sipes on wet quartzite, asphalt, gravel, and concrete [1.26]. It can be seen that there is a marked difference in the coefficient of road adhesion between patterned tires, including the ribbed and siped tires, and smooth tires on wet asphalt and concrete surfaces. The tread pattern increases the value of the coefficient of road adhesion and reduces its speed dependency. In contrast, there is little pattern effect on wet quartzite surfaces, and a high level of road adhesion is maintained over the entire speed range. Thus, it can be concluded

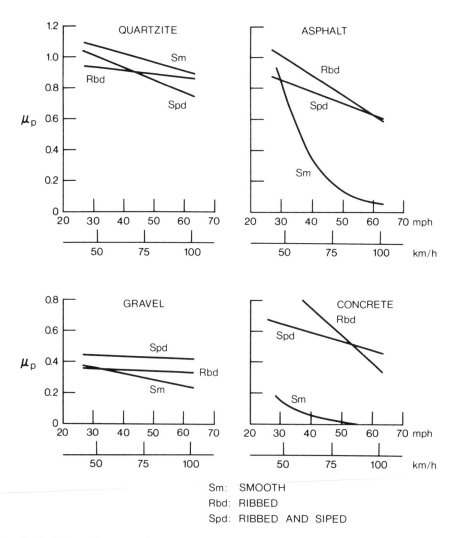

Sm: SMOOTH
Rbd: RIBBED
Spd: RIBBED AND SIPED

Fig. 1.43 Effect of tread design on the peak value of road adhesion coefficient μ_p over wet surfaces. (Reproduced with permission from *Mechanics of Pneumatic Tires*, edited by S. K. Clark, Monograph 122, National Bureau of Standards, 1971.)

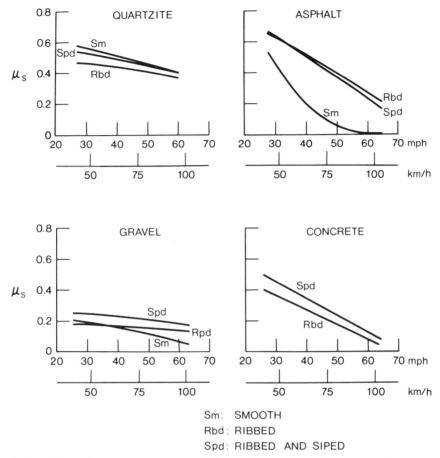

Sm: SMOOTH
Rbd: RIBBED
Spd: RIBBED AND SIPED

Fig. 1.44 Effect of tread design on the sliding value of road adhesion coefficient μ_s over wet surfaces. (Reproduced with permission from *Mechanics of Pneumatic Tires*, edited by S. K. Clark, Monograph 122, National Bureau of Standards, 1971.)

that the advantages of a patterned tire over a smooth tire are pronounced only on badly drained surfaces.

It should be pointed out that tread pattern can function satisfactorily on a wet road only when the grooves and sipes constitute a reservoir of sufficient capacity, and that its effectiveness decreases with the wear of the tread or the tread depth. The decline in value of the coefficient of road adhesion with the decrease of tread depth is more pronounced on smooth than on rough roads, as rough roads can provide better drainage.

When a pneumatic tire is braked over a flooded surface, the motion of the tire creates hydrodynamic pressure in the fluid. The hydrodynamic pressure acting on the tire builds up as the square of speed of the tire, and tends to separate the tire from the ground. At low speeds, the front part of the tire rides on a wedge or a film of fluid. This fluid film extends backward into the contact area as the speed of the tire increases. At a particular speed, the hydrodynamic lift developed under the tire equals the vertical load, the tire rides completely on the fluid, and all contact with the ground is lost. This phenomenon is usually referred to as "hydroplaning," and is illustrated in Fig. 1.45 [1.27].

For smooth or close-patterned tires that do not allow escape paths for water and for patterned tires on flooded surfaces with a fluid depth exceeding the groove depth in the tread, the speed at which hydroplaning occurs may be determined based on the theory of hydrodynamics. It can be assumed that the lift component of the hydrodynamic force F_h is proportional to the tire–ground contact area A, fluid density ρ_f, and the square of the vehicle speed V [1.28, 1.29]:

$$F_h \propto \rho_f A V^2 \tag{1.78}$$

When hydroplaning occurs, the lift component of the hydrodynamic force is equal to the vertical load acting on the tire. The speed at which hydroplaning begins, therefore, is proportional to the square root of the nominal ground contact pressure W/A, which is proportional to the inflation pressure of the tire p_i. Based on this reasoning and on experimental data shown in Fig. 1.46 [1.29], the following formula was proposed by Horne and Joyner for predicting the hydroplaning speed V_p:

$$V_p = 10.35 \sqrt{p_i} \text{ mph} \tag{1.79}$$

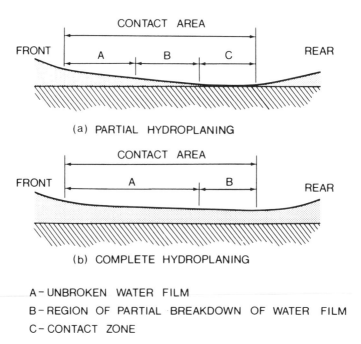

(a) PARTIAL HYDROPLANING

(b) COMPLETE HYDROPLANING

A – UNBROKEN WATER FILM
B – REGION OF PARTIAL BREAKDOWN OF WATER FILM
C – CONTACT ZONE

Fig. 1.45 Hydroplaning of a tire on flooded surfaces. (Reproduced with permission from *Mechanics of Pneumatic Tires*, edited by S. K. Clark, Monograph 122, National Bureau of Standards, 1971.)

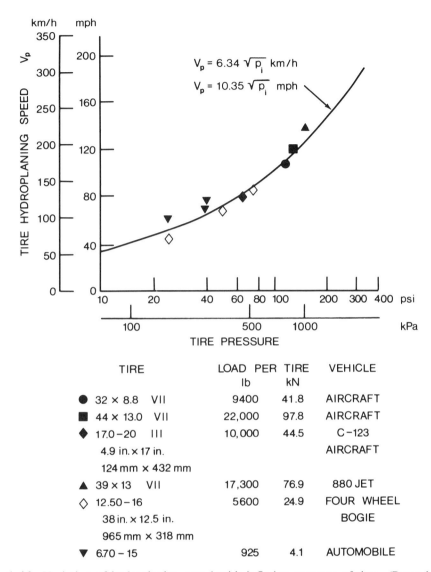

Fig. 1.46 Variation of hydroplaning speed with inflation pressure of tires. (Reproduced with permission of the Society of Automotive Engineers from reference 1.29.)

or

$$V_p = 6.34 \sqrt{p_i} \text{ km/h} \qquad (1.80)$$

where p_i is the inflation pressure of the tire in psi for Eq. 1.79 and in kPa for Eq. 1.80.

For passenger car tires, the inflation pressure is usually in the range 193–248 kPa (28–36 psi). According to Eq. 1.80, the hydroplaning speed V_p for a tire at an inflation pressure of 193 kPa (28 psi) is approximately 88 km/h (54.7 mph), which is well within the normal operating range for passenger cars. For heavy trucks, the inflation pressure is usually in the range 620–827 kPa (90–120 psi). From Eq. 1.80, the hydroplaning speed V_p for a tire at an inflation pressure of 620 kPa (90 psi) is approximately 158 km/h (98 mph), which is beyond the normal range of operating speed for heavy trucks. This would suggest that hydroplaning may not be possible for heavy truck tires under normal circumstances. However, the tractive performance of truck tires is still significantly influenced by the presence of fluid on wet pavements.

For patterned tires on wet surfaces where the fluid depth is less than the groove depth of the tread, the prediction of the hydroplaning speed is more complex, and a generally accepted theory has yet to be evolved. The parameters found to be of significance to hydroplaning are pavement surface texture, pavement fluid depth, fluid viscosity, fluid density, tire inflation pressure, tire normal load, tire tread pattern, and tire tread depth.

The most important effect of hydroplaning is the reduction in the coefficient of road adhesion between the tire and the ground. This affects braking, steering control, and directional stability. Figure 1.47 shows the degradation of the cornering force of passenger car tires on two different wet surfaces at various speeds [1.28].

It should be mentioned that because of the difference in design priorities, a noticeable difference in traction on wet pavements between truck and passenger car tires is observed. Figure 1.48 shows a comparison of the peak value μ_p and sliding value μ_s of the coefficient of road adhesion on wet pavements of a sample of three radial-ply truck tires and a corresponding sample of radial-ply passenger car tires with different tread depths [1.8]. It can be seen that the tractive performance of the truck tires tested is substantially poorer than that of the passenger car tires.

In the design of heavy truck tires, greater emphasis is placed on tread life. As a result, tread patterns and tread compounds for truck tires are different from those for passenger car tires. For instance, natural rubber as the base polymer for the tread is widely used for truck tires, whereas synthetic-rubber based compounds are universally adopted for passenger car tires. As mentioned previously, while natural rubber compounds offer higher abrasion resistance and lower hysteresis losses, synthetic rubber compounds provide a fundamentally higher value of coefficient of road adhesion, particularly on wet pavements. The substantial difference in tractive performance between car and truck tires results in a significant difference in stopping distance. For instance, it has been reported that on a wet, slippery road, the stopping distance for a heavy truck with tires ranging from the best available to the worst, but of a fairly typical type could be 1.65–2.65 times longer than that of a passenger car with normal high grip tires [1.1].

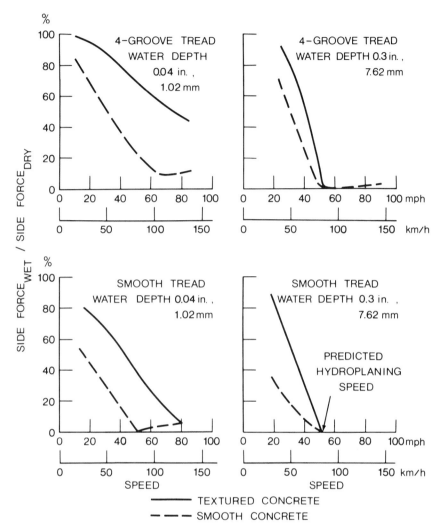

Fig. 1.47 Effect of tread design and surface conditions on the degradation of cornering capability of tires on wet surfaces. (Reproduced with permission of the Society of Automotive Engineers from reference 1.29.)

1.6   RIDE PROPERTIES OF TIRES

Supporting the weight of the vehicle and cushioning it over surface irregularities are two of the basic functions of a pneumatic tire. When a normal load is applied to an inflated tire, the tire progressively deflects as the load increases. Figure 1.49 shows the static load–deflection relationship for a 5.60×13 bias-ply tire at various inflation pressures [1.30]. The type of diagram shown in Fig. 1.49 is usually referred to as a lattice plot, in which the origin of each load–deflection curve is displaced along the deflection axis by an amount proportional to the inflation pres-

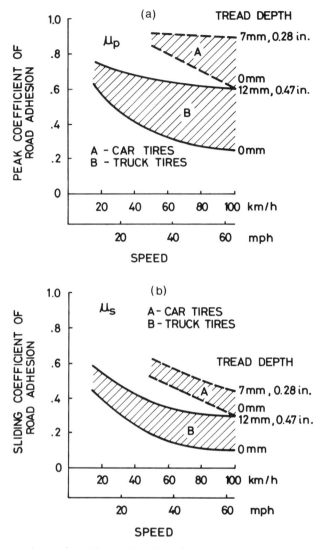

Fig. 1.48 Comparison of (a) the peak value of road adhesion coefficient μ_p and (b) the sliding value of road adhesion coefficient μ_s of car and truck tires on wet surfaces. (Reproduced with permission from reference 1.8.)

sure. The relationship between the load and the inflation pressure for constant deflection can also be shown in the lattice plot. Figure 1.50 shows the interrelationship among the static load, inflation pressure, and deflection for a 165 × 13 radial-ply passenger car tire. The lattice plots of the load–deflection data at various inflation pressures for tractor tires 11–36 and 7.50–16 are shown in Figs. 1.51 and 1.52, respectively [1.31]. The load–deflection curves at various inflation pressures for a terra tire 26 × 12.00–12 are shown in Fig. 1.53. The vertical load–deflection curves are useful in estimating the static vertical stiffness of tires.

In vehicle vibration analysis and ride simulation, the cushioning characteristics of a pneumatic tire may be represented by various mathematical models. The most

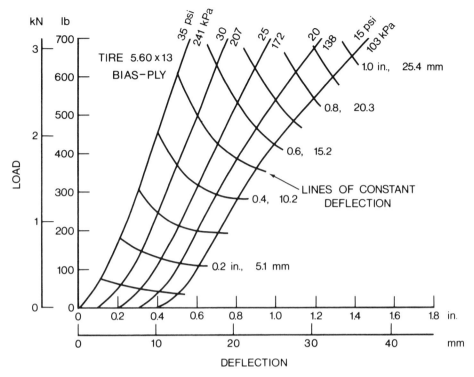

Fig. 1.49 Static load–deflection relationship of a bias-ply car tire. (Reproduced with permission of the Council of the Institution of Mechanical Engineers from reference 1.30.)

widely used and the simplest model representing the fundamental mode of vibration of the pneumatic tire consists of a mass element and a linear spring in parallel with a viscous damping element, as shown in Fig. 1.54. Other models, such as the so-called "viscoelastic" model shown in Fig. 1.54, have also been proposed.

Depending upon the test conditions, three distinct types of tire vertical stiffness may be defined: static, nonrolling dynamic, and rolling dynamic stiffness.

Static Stiffness   The static vertical stiffness of a tire is determined by the slope of the static load–deflection curves, such as those shown in Figs. 1.49–1.53. It has been found that for a given inflation pressure, the load–deflection characteristics for both radial- and bias-ply tires are more or less linear, except at relatively low values of load. Consequently, it can be assumed that the tire vertical stiffness is independent of load in the range of practical interest. Figure 1.55 shows the variation of the stiffness with inflation pressure for the 165 × 13 radial-ply tire. The values of stiffness shown are derived from the load–deflection curves shown in Fig. 1.50 [1.30]. The values of the static vertical stiffness of the tractor tires 11–36 and 7.5–16, and those of the terra tire 26 × 12.00–12 at various inflation pressures are given in Table 1.6.

Nonrolling Dynamic Stiffness   The dynamic stiffness of a nonrolling tire may be obtained using various methods. One of the simplest is the so-called "drop

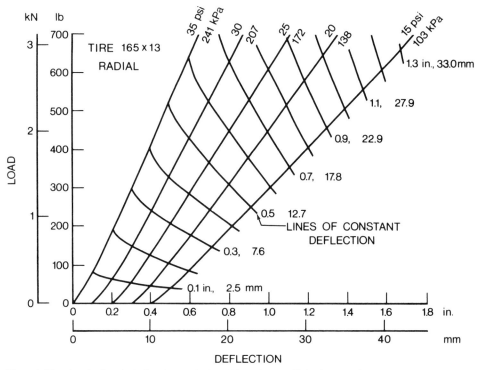

Fig. 1.50 Static load–deflection relationship of a radial-ply car tire. (Reproduced with permission of the Council of the Institution of Mechanical Engineers from reference 1.30.)

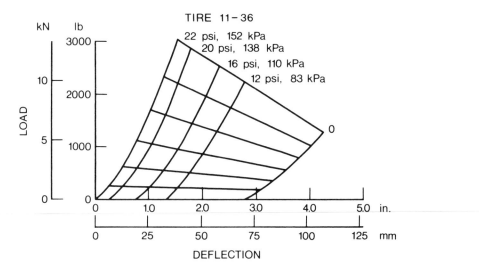

Fig. 1.51 Static load–deflection relationship of a tractor tire 11–36. (Reproduced with permission of the *Journal of Agricultural Engineering Research* from reference 1.31.)

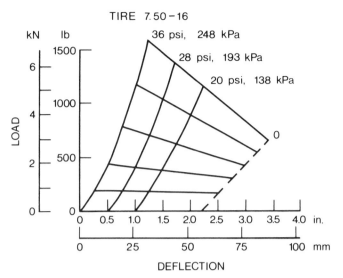

Fig. 1.52 Static load–deflection relationship of a tractor tire 7.50–16. (Reproduced with permission of the *Journal of Agricultural Engineering Research* from reference 1.31.)

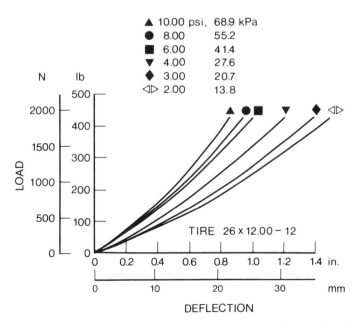

Fig. 1.53 Static load–deflection relationship of a terra tire 26 × 12.00–12 for all-terrain vehicles.

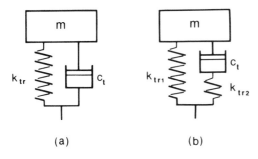

Fig. 1.54 (a) A linear model and (b) a viscoelastic model for tire vibration analysis.

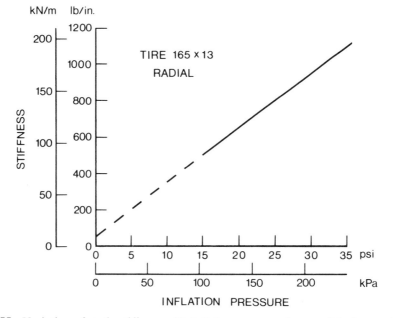

Fig. 1.55 Variation of static stiffness with inflation pressure for a radial-ply car tire. (Reproduced with permission of the Council of the Institution of Mechanical Engineers from reference 1.30.)

test.'' In this test, the tire with a certain load is allowed to fall freely from a height at which the tire is just in contact with the ground. Consequently, the tire remains in contact with the ground throughout the test. The transient response of the tire is recorded. A typical amplitude decay trace is shown in Fig. 1.56. The values of the equivalent viscous damping coefficient c_{eq} and the dynamic stiffness k_z of the tire can then be determined from the decay trace using the well-established theory of free vibration for a single-degree-of-freedom system:

$$c_{eq} = \sqrt{\frac{4m^2\omega_d^2\delta^2/(\delta^2 + 4\pi^2)}{1 - [\delta^2/(\delta^2 + 4\pi^2)]}} \qquad (1.81)$$

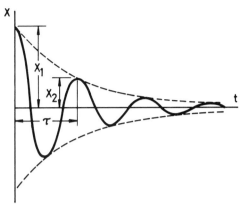

Fig. 1.56 An amplitude decay record of a nonrolling tire obtained from a "drop test."

and

$$k_z = \frac{m\omega_d^2}{1 - \delta^2/(\delta^2 + 4\pi^2)} \qquad (1.82)$$

ω_d is the damped natural frequency of the tire with mass m, and can be identified from the amplitude decay trace shown in Fig. 1.56.

$$\omega_d = 2\pi/\tau \qquad (1.83)$$

where τ is the period of damped oscillation shown in Fig. 1.56.

δ is the logarithmic decrement, which is defined as the natural logarithm of the ratio of any two successive amplitudes, such as x_1 and x_2, shown in Fig. 1.56.

$$\delta = \ln(x_1/x_2) \qquad (1.84)$$

The "drop test" may also be performed utilizing a tire endurance testing machine consisting of a beam pivoted at one end, which carries the test tire loaded against a drum. To initiate the test, the beam is displaced and the system is set in angular oscillation about the pivot of the beam. A decay trace for the amplitude of angular displacement is recorded. A set of equations for this torsional system, similar to that for a single-degree-of-freedom linear system described above, can be derived for determining the equivalent damping coefficient and nonrolling dynamic stiffness for the tire from the decay trace.

Table 1.6 shows the values of the nonrolling dynamic stiffness and the damping coefficient for the tractor tires 11–36 and 7.5–16 [1.31], and the damping coefficient for the terra tire 26 × 12.00–12. The values of the damping coefficient for the 5.60 × 13 bias-ply and the 165 × 13 radial-ply car tire are given in Table 1.7 [1.30].

Rolling Dynamic Stiffness The rolling dynamic stiffness is usually determined by measuring the response of a rolling tire to a known harmonic excitation.

TABLE 1.6 Vertical Stiffness of Tires

Tire	Inflation Pressure	Load	Static Stiffness	Nonrolling Dynamic Stiffness (Average)	Damping Coefficient
11–36 (4-ply)	82.7 kPa (12 psi)	6.67 kN (1500 lb)	357.5 kN/m (24,500 lb/ft)	379.4 kN/m (26,000 lb/ft)	2.4 kN · s/m (165 lb · s/ft)
		8.0 kN (1800 lb)	357.5 kN/m (24,500 lb/ft)	394.0 kN/m (27,000 lb/ft)	2.6 kN · s/m (180 lb · s/ft)
		9.34 kN (2100 lb)	—	423.2 kN/m (29,000 lb/ft)	3.4 kN · s/m (230 lb · s/ft)
	110.3 kPa (16 psi)	6.67 kN (1500 lb)	379.4 kN/m (26,000 lb/ft)	394.0 kN/m (27,000 lb/ft)	2.1 kN · s/m (145 lb · s/ft)
		8.0 kN (1800 lb)	386.7 kN/m (26,500 lb/ft)	437.8 kN/m (30,000 lb/ft)	2.5 kN · s/m (175 lb · s/ft)
		9.34 kN (2100 lb)	394.0 kN/m (27,000 lb/ft)	423.2 kN/m (29,000 lb/ft)	2.5 kN · s/m (175 lb · s/ft)
7.5–16 (6-ply)	138 kPa (20 psi)	3.56 kN (800 lb)	175.1 kN/m (12,000 lb/ft)	218.9 kN/m (15,000 lb/ft)	0.58 kN · s/m (40 lb · s/ft)
		4.45 kN (1000 lb)	175.1 kN/m (12,000 lb/ft)	233.5 kN/m (16,000 lb/ft)	0.66 kN · s/m (45 lb · s/ft)
		4.89 kN (1100 lb)	182.4 kN/m (12,500 lb/ft)	248.1 kN/m (17,000 lb/ft)	0.80 kN · s/m (55 lb · s/ft)
	193 kPa (28 psi)	3.56 kN (800 lb)	218.9 kN/m (15,000 lb/ft)	233.5 kN/m (16,000 lb/ft)	0.36 kN · s/m (25 lb · s/ft)
		4.45 kN (1100 lb)	226.2 kN/m (15,500 lb/ft)	262.7 kN/m (18,000 lb/ft)	0.66 kN · s/m (45 lb · s/ft)
		4.89 kN (1300 lb)	255.4 kN/m (17,500 lb/ft)	277.3 kN/m (19,000 lb/ft)	0.73 kN · s/m (50 lb · s/ft)
26 × 12.00–12 (2-ply)	15.5 kPa (2.25 psi)	1.78 kN (400 lb)	51.1 kN/m (3500 lb/ft)	—	0.47 kN · s/m (32 lb · s/ft)
	27.6 kPa (4 psi)	1.78 kN (400 lb)	68.6 kN/m (4700 lb/ft)	—	0.49 kN · s/m (34 lb · s/ft)

Source: Reference 1.20.

TABLE 1.7 Damping Coefficient of Tires

Tire	Inflation Pressure	Damping Coefficient
Bias-ply	103.4 kPa (15 psi)	4.59 kN · s/m (315 lb · s/ft)
5.60 × 13	137.9 kPa (20 psi)	4.89 kN · s/m (335 lb · s/ft)
	172.4 kPa (25 psi)	4.52 kN · s/m (310 lb · s/ft)
	206.9 kPa (30 psi)	4.09 kN · s/m (280 lb · s/ft)
	241.3 kPa (35 psi)	4.09 kN · s/m (280 lb · s/ft)
Radial-ply	103.4 kPa (15 psi)	4.45 kN · s/m (305 lb · s/ft)
165 × 13	137.9 kPa (20 psi)	3.68 kN · s/m (252 lb · s/ft)
	172.4 kPa (25 psi)	3.44 kN · s/m (236 lb · s/ft)
	206.9 kPa (30 psi)	3.43 kN · s/m (235 lb · s/ft)
	241.3 kPa (35 psi)	2.86 kN · s/m (196 lb · s/ft)

Source: Reference 1.19.

The response is normally measured at the hub, and the excitation is given at the tread. By examining the ratio of output to input and the phase angle, it is possible to determine the dynamic stiffness and the damping coefficient of a rolling tire.

An alternative method for determining the dynamic stiffness of a tire is to measure its resonant frequency when rolling on a drum or belt. Figure 1.57 shows the values of the dynamic stiffness for various types of car tire obtained using this method [1.6]. It is shown that the dynamic stiffness of car tires decreases sharply as soon as the tire is rolling. However, beyond a speed of approximately 20 km/h (12 mph), the influence of speed becomes less important.

Table 1.8 shows the values of vertical stiffness of a sample of truck tires at rated loads and inflation pressures [1.19]. They were obtained when the tires were rolling at a relatively low speed.

It can be seen from Table 1.8 that values of the vertical stiffness for the truck tires tested range from 764 to 1024 kN/m (4363 to 5850 lb/in.), and that the vertical stiffness of radial-ply truck tires is generally lower than that of bias-ply tires of similar size.

Figure 1.58 shows the variation of the dynamic stiffness of a 13.6 × 38 radial tractor tire with speed [1.32]. The static load on the tire was 18.25 kN (4092 lb), and the inflation pressure was 138 kPa (20 psi). It can be seen that the dynamic stiffness of the tractor tire decreases sharply as soon as the tire begins rolling, similar to that for passenger car tires shown in Fig. 1.57. The effects of inflation pressure on the dynamic stiffness of the same tire are shown in Fig. 1.59. The variation of the damping coefficient with speed for the tractor tire is shown in Fig. 1.60. It can be seen that beyond a speed of 1 km/h (0.6 mph), the damping coefficient drops rapidly until a speed of 5 km/h (3.1 mph) is reached, and then approaches an asymptote. The effects of inflation pressure on the damping coefficient are shown in Fig. 1.61.

Attempts to determine the relationship between the static and dynamic stiffness of tires have been made. However, no general conclusions have been reached.

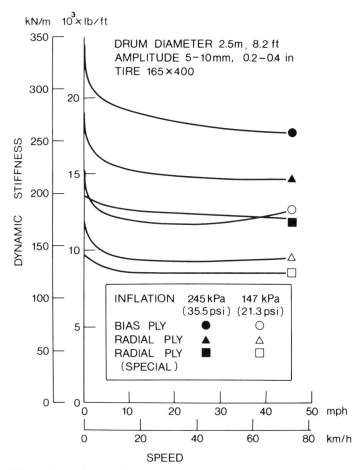

Fig. 1.57 Effect of speed on rolling dynamic stiffness of car tires. (Reproduced with permission from *Mechanics of Pneumatic Tires*, edited by S. K. Clark, Monograph 122, National Bureau of Standards, 1971.)

Some reports indicate that for passenger car tires, the rolling dynamic stiffness may be 10–15% less than the stiffness derived from static load–deflection curves, whereas for heavy truck tires, the dynamic stiffness is approximately 5% less than the static value. For tractor tires, it has been reported that the dynamic stiffness may be 26% lower than the static value. In simulation studies of vehicle ride, the use of the rolling dynamic stiffness is preferred.

It has been shown that among various operational parameters, inflation pressure, speed, normal load, and wear have a noticeable influence on tire stiffness. Tire design parameters, such as the crown angle of the cords, tread width, tread depth, number of plies, and tire material, also affect the stiffness.

The damping of a pneumatic tire is mainly due to the hysteresis of tire materials. Generally speaking, it is neither Coulomb-type nor viscous-type damping, and it appears to be a combination of both. However, an equivalent viscous damping

TABLE 1.8 Vertical Stiffness of Truck Tires at Rated Loads and Inflation Pressures

Tire Type	Tire Construction	Vertical Stiffness kN/m	Vertical Stiffness lb/in.
Unspecified 11.00-22/G	Bias-ply	1024	5850
Unspecified 11.00-22/F	Bias-ply	977	5578
Unspecified 15.00 × 22.5/H	Bias-ply	949	5420
Unspecified 11.00-20/F	Bias-ply	881	5032
Michelin Radial 11R22.5XZA (1/3 Tread)	Radial-ply	874	4992
Michelin Radial 11R22.5XZA (1/2 Tread)	Radial-ply	864	4935
Michelin Radial 11R22.5XZA	Radial-ply	831	4744
Unspecified 10.00-20/F	Bias-ply	823	4700
Michelin Radial 11R22.5XZA	Radial-ply	809	4622
Michelin Pilote 11/80R22.5XZA	Radial-ply	808	4614
Unspecified 10.00-20/F	Bias-ply	788	4500
Michelin Pilote 11/80R22.5XZA	Radial-ply	774	4418
Unspecified 10.00-20/G	Bias-ply	764	4363

Source: UMTRI, reference 1.19.

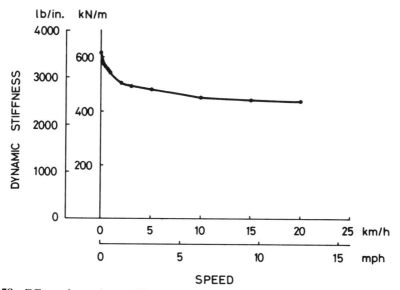

Fig. 1.58 Effect of speed on rolling dynamic stiffness of a radial-ply tractor tire 13.6 × 38. (Reproduced with permission from reference 1.32.)

coefficient can usually be derived from the dynamic tests mentioned previously. Its value is subject to variation, depending on the design and construction of the tire, as well as operating conditions. It has been shown that the damping of pneumatic tires made of synthetic rubber compounds is considerably less than that provided by a shock absorber.

To evaluate the overall vibrational characteristics of tires, tests may be carried

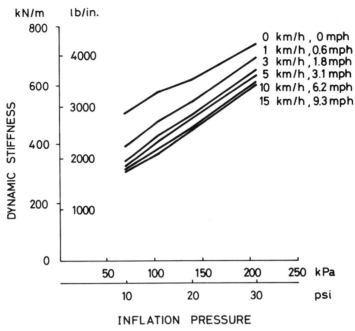

Fig. 1.59 Effect of inflation pressure on rolling dynamic stiffness at various speeds of a radial-ply tractor tire 13.6 × 38. (Reproduced with permission from reference 1.32.)

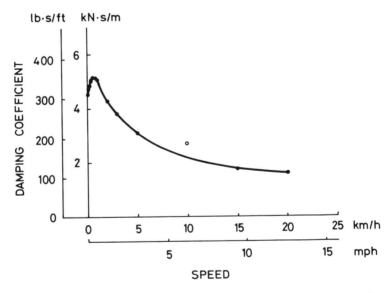

Fig. 1.60 Effect of speed on damping coefficient of a radial-ply tractor tire 13.6 × 38. (Reproduced with permission from reference 1.32.)

out on a variable-speed rotating drum. The profile of the drum may be random, sinusoidal, square, or triangular. Experience has shown that the use of a periodic type of excitation enables rapid assessments to be made. Figure 1.62 shows the wheel hub acceleration as a function of frequency for a radial-ply and a bias-ply

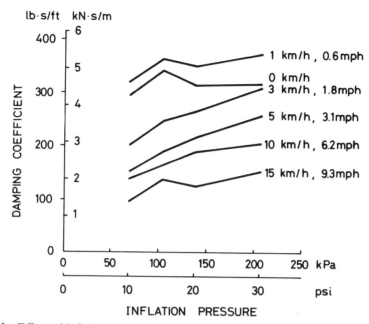

Fig. 1.61   Effect of inflation pressure on damping coefficient at various speeds of a radial-ply tractor tire 13.6 × 38. (Reproduced with permission from reference 1.32.)

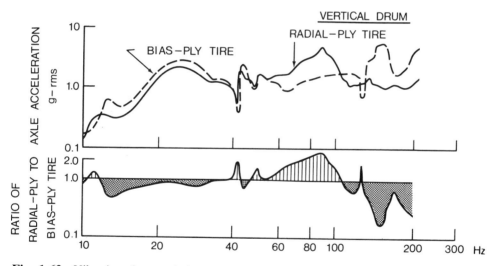

Fig. 1.62   Vibration characteristics of a bias-ply and a radial-ply car tire subject to sinusoidal excitation. (Reproduced with permission of the Council of the Institution of Mechanical Engineers from reference 1.33.)

tire over a sinusoidal profile with 133 mm (5.25 in.) pitch and 6 mm (0.25 in.) peak-to-peak amplitude [1.33]. The transmissibility ratios in the vertical direction over a wide frequency range of a radial-ply and a bias-ply tire are shown in Fig. 1.63 [1.33]. This set of results has been obtained using a vibration exciter. The vibration input is imparted to the tread of a nonrolling tire through a platform mounted on the vibration exciter.

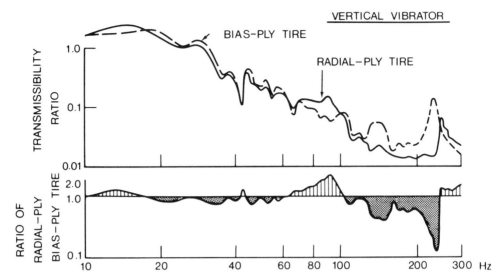

Fig. 1.63 Transmissibility ratio of a bias-ply and a radial-ply car tire. (Reproduced with permission of the Council of the Institution of Mechanical Engineers from reference 1.33.)

It can be seen from Figs. 1.62 and 1.63 that the transmissibility ratio for vertical excitation of the radial-ply tire is noticeably higher than that of the bias-ply tire in the frequency range of 60–100 Hz. Vibrations in this frequency range contribute to the passenger's sensation of "harshness." On the other hand, the bias-ply tire is significantly worse than the radial-ply tire in the frequency range of approximately 150–200 Hz. In this frequency range, vibrations contribute to induced tire noise, commonly known as "road roar" [1.1].

Tire noise is generated by the following major mechanisms [1.34]:

1) Air pumping effect—As the tire rolls, air is trapped and compressed in the voids between the tread and the pavement. Noise is generated when the compressed air is released at high speed to the atmosphere at the exit of the contact patch.

2) Tread element vibrations—Tread elements impact the pavement as the tire rolls. When the elements leave the contact patch, they are released from a highly stressed state. These induce vibrations of the tread, which form a major source of tire noise. Carcass vibrations and the grooves and lug voids in the tread acting like resonating pipes also contribute to noise radiation from the tire.

Since the air pumping effect, the vibrations of tread elements and carcass, etc., are related to speed, the noise level generated by a tire is a function of operating speed. Figure 1.64 shows the variations of noise level with speed for various types of truck tire on a smooth pavement [1.34]. The results were obtained following the SAE J57 test procedure.

The effect of pavement texture on the noise level generated by a bias-ply, ribbed truck tire at 80 km/h (50 mph) is shown in Table 1.9 [1.34].

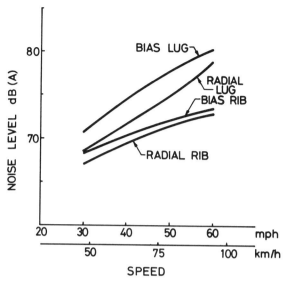

Fig. 1.64 Effect of speed on noise generated by bias-ply and radial-ply truck tires. (Reproduced with permission of the Society of Automotive Engineers from reference 1.34.)

TABLE 1.9   Effect of Pavement Texture on Noise Level Generated by a Bias-Ply Truck Tire

Road Surface	Noise Level dB (A)
Moderately smooth concrete	70
Smooth asphalt	72
Worn concrete (exposed aggregate)	72
Brushed concrete	78

Source: Reference 1.34.

REFERENCES

1.1   T. French, *Tire Technology.*   Bristol and New York: Adam Hilger, 1989.

1.2   V.E. Gough, "Structure of the Tire," in S.K. Clark, Ed., *Mechanics of Pneumatic Tires*, Monograph 122.   Washington, DC: National Bureau of Standards, 1971.

1.3   D.F. Moore, *The Friction of Pneumatic Tyres.*   Amsterdam: Elsevier, 1975.

1.4   *Vehicle Dynamics Terminology*, SAE J670e, Society of Automotive Engineers, 1978.

1.5   T. French, "Construction and Behaviour Characteristics of Tyres," *Proc. of the Institution of Mechanical Engineers, Automobile Division*, AD 14/59, 1959.

1.6   H.C.A. van Eldik Thieme and H.B. Pacejka, "The Tire as a Vehicle Component," in S.K. Clark, Ed., *Mechanics of Pneumatic Tires*, Monograph 122.   Washington, DC: National Bureau of Standards, 1971.

1.7   *Automotive Handbook*, 2nd ed.   Robert Bosch GmbH, 1986.

1.8   L. Segel, "The Mechanics of Heavy-Duty Trucks and Truck Combinations," presented at the Engineering Summer Conferences, University of Michigan, Ann Arbor, 1984.

1.9   J.D. Hunt, J.D. Walter, and G.L. Hall, "The Effect of Tread Polymer Variations on Radial Tire Rolling Resistance," Society of Automotive Engineers, Special Publications, P-74, *Tire Rolling Losses and Fuel Economy—An R&D Planning Workshop*, 1977.

1.10 L.W. DeRaad, "The Influence of Road Surface Texture on Tire Rolling Resistance," Society of Automotive Engineers, Special Publication P-74, *Tire Rolling Losses and Fuel Economy—An R&D Planning Workshop*, 1977.

1.11 B.L. Collier and J.T. Warchol, "The Effect of Inflation Pressure on Bias, Bias-Belted and Radial Tire Performance," Society of Automotive Engineers, paper 800087, 1980.

1.12 J.J. Taborek, "Mechanics of Vehicles," *Machine Design*, May 30–Dec. 26, 1975.

1.13 J.D.C. Hartley and D.M. Turner, "Tires for High-Performance Cars," *SAE Transactions*, vol. 64, 1956.

1.14 M. L. Janssen and G.L. Hall, "Effect of Ambient Temperature on Radial Tire Rolling Resistance," Society of Automotive Engineers, paper 800090, 1980.

1.15 R. Hadekel, "The Mechanical Characteristics of Pneumatic Tyres," S.& T Memo No. 10/52, Ministry of Supply, London, England, 1952.

1.16 P.S. Fancher and P. Grote, "Development of a Hybrid Simulation for Extreme Automobile Maneuvers," in *Proc. 1971 Summer Computer Simulation Conf.*, Boston, MA, 1971.

1.17 J.L. Harned, L.E. Johnston, and G. Sharpf, "Measurement of Tire Brake Force Characteristics as Related to Wheel Slip (Antilock) Control System Design," *SAE Transactions*, vol. 78, paper 690214, 1969.

1.18 R.D. Ervin, "Mobile Measurement of Truck Tire Traction," in *Proc. Symposium on Commercial Vehicle Braking and Handling*, Highway Safety Research Institute, University of Michigan, Ann Arbor, 1975.

1.19 P.S. Fancher, R.D. Ervin, C.B. Winkler, and T.D. Gillespie, "A Fact Book of the Mechanical Properties of the Components for Single-Unit and Articulated Heavy Trucks," Report No. DOT HS 807 125, National Highway Traffic Safety Administration, U.S. Department of Transportation, 1986.

1.20 J.R. Ellis, *Road Vehicle Dynamics*, 1989.

1.21 H. Dugoff, P.S. Fancher, and L. Segel, "Tire Performance Characteristics Affecting Vehicle Response to Steering and Braking Control Inputs," Final Report for Contract No. CST-460, Office of Vehicle Systems Research, National Bureau of Standards, Washington, DC, Aug. 1969.

1.22 E. Bakker, L. Nyborg, and H.B. Pacejka, "Tyre Modelling for Use in Vehicle Dynamic Studies," Society of Automotive Engineers, paper 870421, 1987.

1.23 A. van Zanten, W.D. Ruf, and A. Lutz, "Measurement and Simulation of Transient Tire Forces," Society of Automotive Engineers, paper 890640, 1989.

1.24 V.E. Gough, "Practical Tire Research," *SAE Transactions*, vol. 64, 1956.

1.25 D.L. Nordeen and A.D. Cortese, "Force and Moment Characteristics of Rolling Tires," Society of Automotive Engineers, paper 713A, 1963.

1.26   A. Schallamach, "Skid Resistance and Directional Control," in S.K. Clark, Ed., *Mechanics of Pneumatic Tires*, Monograph 112.   Washington, DC: National Bureau of Standards, 1971.

1.27   S.K. Clark, "The Contact Between Tire and Roadway," in S.K. Clark, Ed., *Mechanics of Pneumatic Tires*, Monograph 122.   Washington, DC: National Bureau of Standards, 1971.

1.28   W.B. Horne and R.C. Dreher, "Phenomena of Pneumatic Tire Hydroplaning," NASA TND-2056, Nov. 1963.

1.29   W.B. Horne and U.T. Joyner, "Pneumatic Tire Hydroplaning and Some Effects on Vehicle Performance," Society of Automotive Engineers, paper 650145, 1965.

1.30   J.A. Overton, B. Mills, and C. Ashley, "The Vertical Response Characteristics of the Non-Rolling Tire," *Proc. Institution of Mechanical Engineers*, vol. 184, part 2A, no. 2, 1969–1970.

1.31   J. Matthews and J.D.C. Talamo, "Ride Comfort for Tractor Operators, III. Investigation of Tractor Dynamics by Analogue Computer Simulation," *Journal of Agricultural Engineering Research*, vol. 10, no. 2, 1965.

1.32   J.A. Lines and N.A. Young, "A Machine for Measuring the Suspension Characteristics of Agriculture Tyre," *Journal of Terramechanics*, vol. 26, no. 3/4, 1989.

1.33   C.W. Barson, D.H. James, and A.W. Morcombe, "Some Aspects of Tire and Vehicle Vibration Testing," *Proc. Institution of Mechanical Engineers*, vol. 182, part 3B, 1967–1968.

1.34   T.L. Ford and F.S. Charles, "Heavy Duty Truck Tire Engineering," *The Thirty-Fourth L. Ray Buckendale Lecture*, Society of Automotive Engineers, SP-729, 1988.

PROBLEMS

1.1   Compare the power required to overcome the rolling resistance of a passenger car weighing 15.57 kN (3500 lb) and having radial-ply tires with that of the same vehicle, but having bias-ply tires in the speed range 40–100 km/h (25–62 mph). The variations of the coefficient of rolling resistance of the radial-ply and bias-ply passenger car tire with speed are described by Eqs. 1.1 and 1.2, respectively.

1.2   A truck tire with vertical load of 24.78 kN (5570 lb) travels on a dry concrete pavement with a peak value of coefficient of road adhesion $\mu_p = 0.80$. The longitudinal stiffness of the tire during braking C_s is 224.64 kN/unit skid (55,000 lb/unit skid). Using the simplified theory described in Section 1.3, plot the relationship between the braking force and the skid of the tire up to skid $i_s = 20\%$.

1.3   Using the simplified theory described in Section 1.4, determine the relationship between the cornering force and the slip angle in the range 0–16° of the truck tire described in Problem 1.2. The cornering stiffness of the tire C_α is 132.53 kN/rad (520 lb/deg). Assume that there is no braking torque applied to the tire.

1.4 Determine the available cornering force of the truck tire described in Problems 1.2 and 1.3 as a function of longitudinal skid at a slip angle of 4°, using the simplified theory described in Section 1.4. Plot the cornering force of the tire at a slip angle of 4° versus skid in the range 0–40%. The coefficient of road adhesion is 0.8.

1.5 A passenger car travels over a flooded pavement. The inflation pressure of the tires is 179.27 kPa (26 psi). If the initial speed of the car is 100 km/h (62 mph) and brakes are then applied, determine whether or not the vehicle will be hydroplaning.

1.6 An all-terrain vehicle weighs 3.56 kN (800 lb) and has four terra tires, each of which has a vertical stiffness of 52.54 kN/m (300 lb/in.) at an inflation pressure of 27.6 kPa (4 psi), and a stiffness of 96.32 kN/m (550 lb/in.) at a pressure of 68.9 kPa (10 psi). Estimate the fundamental natural frequencies of the vehicle in the vertical direction at the two inflation pressures. The vehicle has no spring suspension.

CHAPTER 2

MECHANICS OF VEHICLE–TERRAIN INTERACTION—TERRAMECHANICS

While transporting passengers and goods by vehicles on paved roads constitutes a significant part of the overall transportation activities in a modern society, a wide range of human endeavors in such fields as agriculture, logging, construction, mining, exploration, recreation, and military operations still involves locomotion over unprepared terrain using specialized off-road vehicles. Systematic studies of the principles underlying the rational development and design of off-road vehicles, therefore, have attracted considerable interest, particularly since World War II. The study of the performance of an off-road vehicle in relation to its operating environment (the terrain) has now become known as "terramechanics" [2.1–2.4].

In off-road operations, various types of terrain with differing behavior, ranging from desert sand through soft mud to fresh snow, may be encountered. The properties of the terrain quite often impose severe limitations to the mobility of off-road vehicles. An adequate knowledge of the mechanical properties of the terrain and its response to vehicular loading—terramechanics—is, therefore, essential to the proper development and design of off-road vehicles for a given mission and environment. This is, perhaps, analogous to the role of aerodynamics in the development of aircraft and spacecraft and to that of hydrodynamics in the design of marinecraft. In this chapter, the measurement and characterization of the behavior of the terrain will be discussed.

On a given terrain, the performance of an off-road vehicle is, to a great extent, dependent upon the manner in which the vehicle interacts with the terrain. Consequently, an understanding of the mechanics of vehicle–terrain interaction is of importance to the proper selection of vehicle configuration and design parameters to meet specific operational requirements. A central issue in terramechanics is to establish quantitative relationships between the performance and design of an off-road vehicle for a given operating environment. Over the years, a variety of methods, ranging from empirical to theoretical, for predicting the performance of tracked and wheeled vehicles over unprepared terrain have been developed or proposed. Some of the representative ones will be presented in this chapter.

2.1   DISTRIBUTION OF STRESSES IN THE TERRAIN UNDER VEHICULAR LOADS

Certain types of terrain, such as saturated clay and compact sand, which cover part of the trafficable earth surface, may be compared to an ideal elastoplastic material with the stress–strain relationship shown in Fig. 2.1. When the stress level in the terrain does not exceed a certain limit, such as that denoted by "*a*" in Fig. 2.1, the terrain may exhibit elastic behavior. The idealization of the terrain as an elastic medium has found applications in the prediction of stress distribution in the soil, in connection with the study of soil compaction due to vehicular loads [2.5].

The prediction of stress distribution in an elastic medium subject to any specific load may be based on the analysis of the distribution of stresses under a point load. The method for calculating the stress distribution in a semi-infinite, homogeneous, isotropic, elastic medium subject to a vertical point load applied on the surface was first developed by Boussinesq. His solutions give the following expressions for the vertical stress σ_z at a point in the elastic medium defined by the coordinates shown in Fig. 2.2:

$$\sigma_z = \frac{3W}{2\pi} z^3 (x^2 + y^2 + z^2)^{-5/2}$$

$$= \frac{3}{2\pi} \frac{1}{[1 + (r/z)^2]^{5/2}} \frac{W}{z^2}$$

or

$$\sigma_z = \frac{3W}{2\pi R^2}\left(\frac{z}{R}\right)^3 = \frac{3W}{2\pi R^2} \cos^3 \theta \qquad (2.1)$$

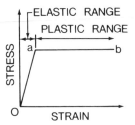

Fig. 2.1   Behavior of an idealized elastoplastic material.

where

$$r = \sqrt{x^2 + y^2} \text{ and } R = \sqrt{z^2 + r^2}$$

When polar coordinates are used, the radial stress σ_r (Fig. 2.2) is given by

$$\sigma_r = \frac{3W}{2\pi R^2} \cos \theta \tag{2.2}$$

It is interesting to note that the stresses are independent of the modulus of elasticity of the material, and that they are only functions of the load applied and the distance from the point of application of the load. It should be mentioned that Eqs. 2.1 and 2.2 are only valid for calculating stresses at points not too close to the point of application of the load. The material in the immediate vicinity of the point load does not behave elastically.

Based on the analysis of stress distribution beneath a point load, the distribution of stresses in an elastic medium under a variety of loading conditions may be predicted using the principle of superposition. For instance, for a circular contact area having a radius r_0 and with a uniform pressure p_0 (Fig. 2.3), the vertical stress at a depth z below the center of the contact area may be determined in the following way [2.1]. The load acting upon the contact area may be represented by a number

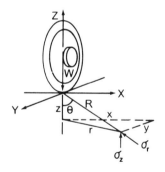

Fig. 2.2 Stresses at a point in a semi-infinite elastic medium subject to a point load. (From *Theory of Land Locomotion* by M.G. Bekker, copyright © by the University of Michigan, 1956, reproduced with permission of the University of Michigan Press.)

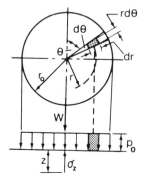

Fig. 2.3 Vertical stresses in a semi-infinite elastic medium below the center of a circular loading area. (From *Theory of Land Locomotion* by M.G. Bekker, copyright © by the University of Michigan, 1956, reproduced with permission of the University of Michigan Press.)

of discrete point loads, $dW = p_0 dA = p_0 r dr d\theta$. Hence, in accordance with Eq. 2.1,

$$d\sigma_z = \frac{3}{2\pi} \frac{p_0 r dr d\theta}{[1 + (r/z)^2]^{5/2} z^2} \tag{2.3}$$

The resultant vertical stress σ_z at a depth z below the center of the contact area is then equal to the sum of the stresses produced by point loads of $p_0 r dr d\theta$, and can be computed by a double integration [2.1]:

$$\sigma_z = \frac{3}{2\pi} p_0 \int_0^{r_0} \int_0^{2\pi} \frac{r dr d\theta}{[1 + (r/z)^2]^{5/2} z^2} = 3 p_0 \int_0^{r_0} \frac{r dr}{[1 + (r/z)^2]^{5/2} z^2}$$

By substituting $(r/z)^2 = u^2$, it is found that

$$\sigma_z = 3 p_0 \int_0^{r_0/z} \frac{u du}{[1 + u^2]^{5/2}} = p_0 \left[1 - \frac{z^3}{(z^2 + r_0^2)^{3/2}} \right] \tag{2.4}$$

The computation of the stresses at points other than those below the center of the contact area is rather involved, and cannot be generalized by a simple set of equations. The stress distribution in an elastic medium under distributed loads over an elliptic area, similar to that applied by a tire, can be determined in a similar way.

Another case of interest from the vehicle viewpoint is the distribution of stresses in the elastic medium under the action of a strip load (Fig. 2.4). Such a strip load may be considered as an idealization of that applied by a tracked vehicle. It can be shown that the stresses in an elastic medium due to a uniform pressure p_0 applied over a strip of infinite length and of constant width b (Fig. 2.5) can be computed by the following equations [2.1]:

$$\sigma_x = \frac{p_0}{\pi} [\theta_2 - \theta_1 + \sin \theta_1 \cos \theta_1 - \sin \theta_2 \cos \theta_2] \tag{2.5}$$

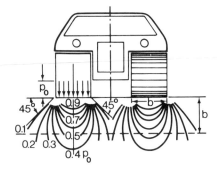

Fig. 2.4 Distribution of vertical stresses in a semi-infinite elastic medium under a tracked vehicle. (From *Theory of Land Locomotion* by M.G. Bekker, copyright © by the University of Michigan, 1956, reproduced with permission of the University of Michigan Press.)

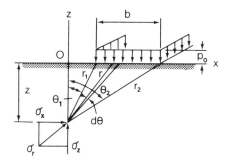

Fig. 2.5 Stresses at a point in a semi-infinite elastic medium subject to a uniform strip load. (From *Theory of Land Locomotion* by M.G. Bekker, copyright © by the University of Michigan, 1956, reproduced with permission of the University of Michigan Press.)

$$\sigma_z = \frac{p_0}{\pi} [\theta_2 - \theta_1 - \sin \theta_1 \cos \theta_1 + \sin \theta_2 \cos \theta_2] \qquad (2.6)$$

$$\tau_{xz} = \frac{p_0}{\pi} (\sin^2 \theta_2 - \sin^2 \theta_1) \qquad (2.7)$$

The points in the medium that experience the same level of stress form a family of isostress surfaces commonly known as pressure bulbs. The general characteristics of the bulbs of vertical pressure under a uniform strip load are illustrated in Fig. 2.4. It is interesting to note that at a depth equal to the width of the strip, the vertical stress under the center of the loading area is approximately 50% of the applied pressure, and it practically vanishes at a depth equal to twice the width of the strip. The boundaries of the bulbs of vertical pressure, for all practical purposes, may be assumed as being sloped at an angle of 45° with the horizontal shown in Fig. 2.4 [2.1].

It should be pointed out that the use of the theory of elasticity for predicting stresses in a real soil produces approximate results only. Measurements have shown that the stress distribution in a real soil deviates from that computed using Boussinesq's equations [2.5]. There is a tendency for the compressive stress in the soil to concentrate around the loading axis. This tendency becomes greater when the soil becomes more plastic due to increased moisture content or when the soil is less cohesive, such as sand. In view of this, various semi-empirical equations have been developed to account for the different behavior of various types of soil. Fröhlich introduced a concentration factor ν to Boussinesq's equations. The factor ν reflects the behavior of various types of soil in different conditions. Introducing the concentration factor, the expressions for the vertical and radial stress in the soil subject to a point load on the surface take the following forms:

$$\sigma_z = \frac{\nu W}{2 \pi R^2} \cos^\nu \theta = \frac{\nu W}{2 \pi z^2} \cos^{\nu + 2} \theta \qquad (2.8)$$

$$\sigma_r = \frac{\nu W}{2 \pi R^2} \cos^{\nu - 2} \theta = \frac{\nu W}{2 \pi z^2} \cos^\nu \theta \qquad (2.9)$$

Equations 2.8 and 2.9 are identical to Eqs. 2.1 and 2.2, respectively, if ν is equal to 3. The value of the concentration factor depends on the type of soil and its moisture content. Figure 2.6 shows the bulbs of radial stress σ_r under a point load in soils with different concentration factors [2.5].

A tire transfers its load to the soil surface usually not at one point, but through a finite area of contact. To determine the stress distribution in the soil due to tire loading, the actual size of the contact area and the pressure distribution over the contact patch must be known. Figure 2.7 shows the measured contact areas of a tire under different soil conditions [2.5]. The rut becomes deeper with increasing porosity and moisture content of the soil. An approximately uniform pressure over the entire contact area may be assumed for tires without lugs in hard, dry soil. In soft soils, the pressure over the contact area varies with the depth of the rut. Usu-

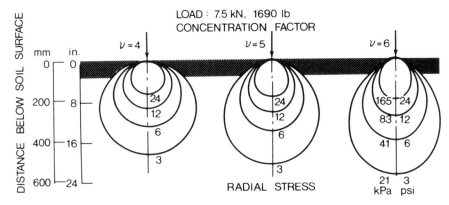

Fig. 2.6 Distribution of radial stresses under a point load in soils with different concentration factors. (Reproduced with permission from reference 2.5.)

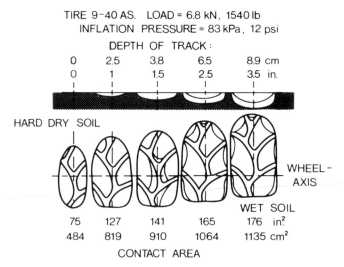

Fig. 2.7 Contact area of a tire under different soil conditions. (Reproduced with permission from reference 2.5.)

ally, the contact pressure decreases towards the outside of the contact area, and is more concentrated towards the center of the loading area. Representative pressure distributions over the contact area in hard, dry soil, in fairly moist, relatively dense soil, and in wet soil are shown in Fig. 2.8(a), (b), and (c), respectively [2.5].

Knowing the shape of the contact area and pressure distribution over the contact patch, it is possible to predict the distribution of stresses in a soil by employing Eqs. 2.8 and 2.9, as proposed by Fröhlich. It has been reported by Söhne that the difference between the measured values and calculated ones obtained using Fröhlich's equations is approximately 25%, which may be regarded as reasonable for this type of problem [2.6]. Figure 2.9 shows the distributions of the major prin-

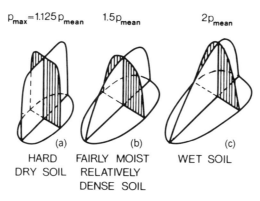

Fig. 2.8 Pressure distribution on the tire contact area under different soil conditions. (Reproduced with permission from reference 2.5.)

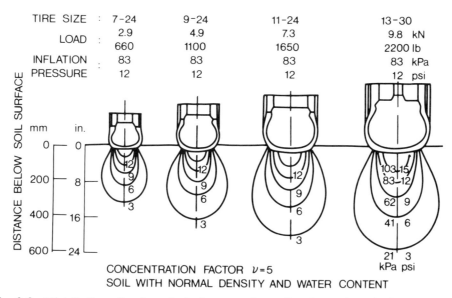

Fig. 2.9 Distribution of major principal stresses in a soil under various tire loads. (Reproduced with permission from reference 2.5.)

cipal stress in a soil having normal field density and moisture under tires of different sizes and carrying different normal loads, but with the same inflation pressure [2.5]. In the calculations, it is assumed that the concentration factor v is 5, and that the pressure distribution over the contact area is similar to that shown in Fig. 2.8(b). It shows that for the same inflation pressure, the stress can penetrate much deeper with larger tires carrying higher loads. This is because the larger tire has a larger contact area. As a result, the stress at the same depth beneath the center of the contact patch increases as indicated by Eq. 2.4, although the pressure applied on the soil surface remains the same. This indicates that the stress distribution in a soil is a function of not only contact pressure, but also contact area. It should also be mentioned that soil compaction is more closely related to the major principal stress than the vertical stress.

Figure 2.10 shows the effects of soil conditions on the shape of the pressure bulbs [2.5]. In hard, dry, and dense soil, the lines of equal major principal stress are approximately circular. The softer the soil, the narrower the pressure bulbs become. This is because in soft soil, the soil can flow sideways so that the stress is more concentrated towards the center of the loading area.

For tires with lugs, such as tractor tires, the pressure distribution over the contact area differs from that shown in Fig. 2.8. In hard, dry soil, the lugs of the tire carry the entire load. The pressure over the contact area of the lugs is three to four times higher than that of an equivalent tire without lugs. In a wet soil, because of the sinkage of the tire, there may be hardly any difference between the contact pressure under the lugs and that under the carcass. In this case, the distribution of contact pressure may be similar to that shown in Fig. 2.8(c). In principle, the stress distribution in the soil under tires with lugs may be estimated following an approach similar to that described above. However, the computation will be more involved.

Example 2.1. The contact patch of a tire on a hard and dry soil may be approximated by a circular area of radius of 20 cm (7.9 in.). The contact pressure is assumed to be a uniform 68.95 kPa (10 psi). For this type of soil, the concentration factor v is assumed to be 4. Calculate the vertical stress σ_z in the soil at a depth of 20 cm below the center of the contact area.

Solution. When the concentration factor v is 4, the vertical stress σ_z at a point in the soil due to a point load W applied on the soil surface is expressed by

$$\sigma_z = \frac{4W}{2\pi R^2} \cos^4 \theta = \frac{4W}{2\pi} \frac{z^4}{(z^2 + r^2)^3}$$

$$= \frac{4W}{2\pi} \frac{1}{z^2[1 + (r/z)^2]^3}$$

The vertical stress σ_z at a depth z below the center of a circular contact area of radius r_0 and with a uniform contact pressure p_0 is given by

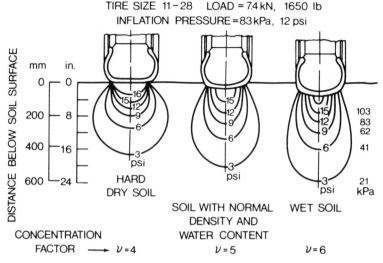

Fig. 2.10 Distribution of major principal stresses under a tire for different soil conditions. (Reproduced with permission from reference 2.5.)

$$\sigma_z = \frac{4p_0}{2\pi} \int_0^{r_0} \int_0^{2\pi} \frac{r\,dr\,d\theta}{z^2\,[1 + (r/z)^2]^3}$$

$$= 4p_0 \int_0^{r_0/z} \frac{u\,du}{[1 + u^2]^3}$$

$$= p_0 \left[1 - \frac{1}{[1 + (r_0/z)^2]^2} \right]$$

where $u^2 = r^2/z^2$. For $p_0 = 68.95$ kPa, $r_0 = 20$ cm, and $z = 20$ cm,

$$\sigma_z = 68.95 \left[1 - \frac{1}{[1 + (20/20)^2]^2} \right]$$

$$= 51.7 \text{ kPa } (7.5 \text{ psi})$$

2.2 APPLICATIONS OF THE THEORY OF PLASTIC EQUILIBRIUM TO THE MECHANICS OF VEHICLE–TERRAIN INTERACTION

When the vehicular load applied to the terrain surface exceeds a certain limit, the stress level within a certain boundary of the terrain may reach that denoted by "*a*" on the idealized stress–strain curve shown in Fig. 2.1. An infinitely small increase of stress beyond point "*a*" produces a rapid increase of strain, which constitutes plastic flow. The state that precedes plastic flow is usually referred to as plastic equilibrium. The transition from the state of plastic equilibrium to that of plastic flow represents the failure of the mass.

There are a number of criteria proposed for the failure of soils and other similar materials. One of the widely used and the simplest criterion is that due to Mohr–Coulomb. It postulates that the material at a point will fail if the shear stress at that point in the medium satisfies the following condition:

$$\tau = c + \sigma \tan \phi \tag{2.10}$$

where τ is the shear strength of the material, c is the apparent cohesion of the material, σ is the normal stress on the sheared surface, and ϕ is the angle of internal shearing resistance of the material.

Cohesion of the material is the bond that cements particles together irrespective of the normal pressure exerted by one particle upon the other. On the other hand, particles of frictional masses can be held together only when a normal pressure exists between them. Thus, theoretically, the shear strength of saturated clay and the like does not depend on the normal load, whereas the shear strength of dry sand increases with an increase of the normal load. For dry sand, therefore, the shear strength may be expressed by

$$\tau = \sigma \tan \phi \tag{2.11}$$

and for saturated clay and the like, it may take the form

$$\tau = c \tag{2.12}$$

Granular masses that cover most of the trafficable earth surface, however, usually have both cohesive and frictional properties.

The meaning of the Mohr–Coulomb criterion may be illustrated with the aid of the Mohr circle of stress. If specimens of a soil are subject to different states of stress, for each mode of failure a Mohr circle can be constructed (Fig. 2.11). If a straight line envelope is drawn to the set of Mohr circles so obtained, it will be of the form of Eq. 2.10, with the cohesion of the soil being given by the intercept of the envelope with the shear stress axis, and the angle of internal shearing resistance being determined by its slope. The Mohr–Coulomb criterion is simply that if a

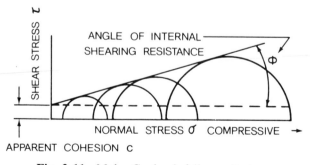

Fig. 2.11 Mohr–Coulomb failure criterion.

Mohr circle representing the state of stress at a point in the soil touches the envelope, failure will take place at that point.

The shear strength parameters c and ϕ in Eq. 2.10 may be measured by a variety of devices [2.4, 2.7]. The triaxial apparatus and the translational shear box are the most commonly used in civil engineering. For vehicle mobility study, however, rectangular or annular shear plates shown in Fig. 2.12 are usually employed to simulate the shearing action of the vehicle running gear and to obtain the shear strength parameters of the terrain. This will be discussed further later in this chapter.

To illustrate the application of the Mohr–Coulomb criterion, let us consider the problem of plastic equilibrium of a prism in a semi-infinite mass (Fig. 2.13). The prism of soil with unit weight γ_s, having depth z and width equal to unity, is in a state of incipient plastic failure due to lateral pressure, as shown in Fig. 2.13. There are no shear stresses on the vertical sides of the prism; the normal stress on the base of the prism and that on the vertical sides are therefore the principal stresses. The prism may be set into a state of plastic equilibrium by two different operations: one is to stretch it, and the other is to compress it in the horizontal direction. If the prism is stretched, the normal stress on the vertical sides decreases until the conditions for plastic equilibrium are satisfied, while the normal stress on the bottom remains unchanged. Any further expansion merely causes a plastic flow without changing the state of stress. In this case, the weight of the soil assists in producing an expansion, and this type of failure is called the active failure. On the other hand, if the prism of soil is compressed, the normal stress on the vertical sides increases, while the normal stress at the bottom remains unchanged. In this case, lateral compression of the soil is resisted by its own weight, and the resulting failure is called the passive failure. The two states of stress prior to plastic flow caused by compression and expansion of the soil are often referred to as the Rankine passive and active state, respectively [2.8].

Both types of soil failure may be analyzed quantitatively by means of the Mohr circle, as shown in Fig. 2.13. In the case of active failure, the normal stress σ on the base of the element at depth z ($\sigma = \gamma_s z$) is the major principal stress. Circle

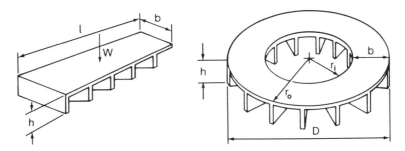

Fig. 2.12 Rectangular and annular shear plates for measuring terrain shear strength parameters. (From *Introduction to Terrain-Vehicle Systems* by M.G. Bekker, copyright © by the University of Michigan, 1969, reproduced with permission of the University of Michigan Press.)

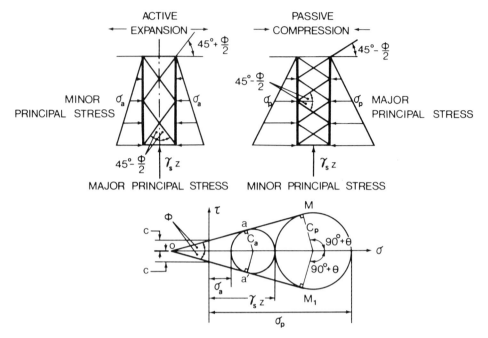

Fig. 2.13 Active and passive failure of soil.

C_a therefore can be traced to represent the state of stress at that point. This circle is tangent to the lines OM and OM_1, which represent the Mohr–Coulomb failure criterion. The point of intersection between the circle and the horizontal axis of the Mohr diagram determines the minor principal stress, which is the normal stress on the vertical sides required to bring the mass at that point into active failure. This normal stress is called the active earth pressure σ_a. From the geometry of the Mohr diagram shown in Fig. 2.13, the expression for the active earth pressure σ_a is given by

$$\sigma_a = \gamma_s z \frac{1}{N_\phi} - 2c \frac{1}{\sqrt{N_\phi}} \tag{2.13}$$

where N_ϕ is equal to $\tan^2 (45° + \phi/2)$ and is called the flow value.

It is interesting to point out that circle C_a touches the boundaries of failure, OM and OM_1, at a and a', as shown in Fig. 2.13. This indicates that there are two planes sloped to the major principal stress plane on either side at an angle of $45° + \phi/2$, on which the shear stress satisfies the Mohr–Coulomb criterion. These planes are called surfaces of sliding, and the intersection between a surface of sliding and the plane of drawing is usually referred to as a shear line or slip line. It follows that there are two sets of slip lines sloped to the major principal stress on either side at an angle of $45° - \phi/2$. In the case of active failure, since the major principal stress is vertical, the slip line field comprises parallel lines sloped to the horizontal at $45° + \phi/2$, as shown in Fig. 2.13.

As passive failure is caused by lateral compression, the normal stress σ acting on the bottom of the element ($\sigma = \gamma_s z$) is the minor principal stress. Circle C_p can, therefore, be drawn to represent the stress conditions of a point in the state of incipient passive failure, as shown in Fig. 2.13. The point of intersection between the circle and the horizontal axis of the Mohr diagram determines the major principal stress, which is also the lateral, compressive stress on the vertical sides required to set the mass at that point into passive failure. This normal stress is referred to as the passive earth pressure σ_p. From the geometric relationships shown in Fig. 2.13, the expression for the passive earth pressure σ_p is given by

$$\sigma_p = \gamma_s z N_\phi + 2c\sqrt{N_\phi} \tag{2.14}$$

For passive failure, since the major principal stress is horizontal, the slip line field is composed of parallel lines sloped to the horizontal at $45° - \phi/2$, as shown in Fig. 2.13.

If a pressure q is applied to the soil surface, usually referred to as the surcharge, then the normal stress at the base of an element at depth z is

$$\sigma = \gamma_s z + q. \tag{2.15}$$

Accordingly, the active and passive pressures are given by

$$\sigma_a = \gamma_s z \, \frac{1}{N_\phi} + q \, \frac{1}{N_\phi} - 2c \, \frac{1}{\sqrt{N_\phi}} \tag{2.16}$$

$$\sigma_p = \gamma_s z N_\phi + q N_\phi + 2c \sqrt{N_\phi} \tag{2.17}$$

The action of the vehicle running gear and other soil-engaging devices generally causes passive failure of the terrain.

The theory of passive earth pressure has found applications in the prediction of the forces acting on a soil cutting blade and in the estimation of the tractive effort developed by a lug (grouser) of a wheel, as shown in Fig. 2.14.

Consider a vertical cutting blade, such as a bulldozer blade, being pushed against the soil. The soil in front of the blade will be brought into a state of passive failure. If the ratio of the width of the blade to the cutting depth is large, the problem may

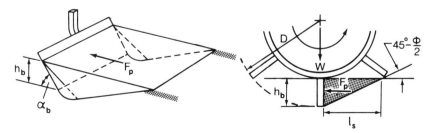

Fig. 2.14 Interaction of a soil cutting blade and a grouser of a wheel with soil.

be considered as two dimensional. Furthermore, if the blade is vertical and its surface is relatively smooth, then the normal pressure exerted by the blade on the soil will be the major principal stress, and will be equal to the passive earth pressure σ_p. If there is no surcharge, the resultant force acting on the blade per unit width F_p may be calculated by integrating the passive earth pressure σ_p over the cutting depth h_b. From Eq. 2.14,

$$F_p = \int_0^{h_b} \sigma_p \, dz = \int_0^{h_b} (\gamma_s z N_\phi + 2c\sqrt{N_\phi}) \, dz$$

$$= \frac{1}{2} \gamma_s h_b^2 N_\phi + 2c h_b \sqrt{N_\phi} \tag{2.18}$$

If there is a surcharge q acting on the soil surface in front of the blade, the resultant force acting on the blade per unit width F_p may be expressed by

$$F_p = \int_0^{h_b} \sigma_p dz = \int_0^{h_b} (\gamma_s z N_\phi + q N_\phi + 2c\sqrt{N_\phi}) \, dz$$

$$= \frac{1}{2} \gamma_s h_b^2 N_\phi + q h_b N_\phi + 2c h_b \sqrt{N_\phi} \tag{2.19}$$

It should be mentioned that for a blade of finite width, end effects would increase the total force acting on the blade.

A similar approach may be followed to estimate the tractive effort developed by the lugs of a cage wheel, such as that used in paddy fields or that attached to a tire as a traction-aid device on wet soils, as shown in Fig. 2.14. In general, the lug may behave in one of two ways. If the spacing between the lugs is too small, the space between them may be filled up with soil, and shearing will occur across the lug tips. Under these conditions, the major effect of the lugs would be the increase of the effective diameter of the wheel. On the other hand, if the spacing between the lugs is large so that the soil fails in a manner shown in Fig. 2.14, then the behavior of the lug will be similar to that of the soil cutting blade. When the ratio of the lug width to the penetrating depth is large and the lug surface is relatively smooth, the tractive effort per unit width developed by the lug in the vertical position can be estimated using Eq. 2.18. If the wheel rim and the lugs are of the same width, there will be a surcharge acting on the soil surface behind the lug due to the vertical load applied through the wheel rim. In this case, Eq. 2.19 is applicable. For cage wheels with lugs attached to tires as traction-aid devices, the wheel rim is relatively narrow, and the vertical load is mainly supported by the tire. Under these circumstances, the benefit of the surcharge would not be obtained. It should be pointed out that the shearing forces developed on the vertical surfaces on both sides of the lug would increase the total tractive effort, and that they should be taken into account when the penetration depth of the lug is relatively large.

Example 2.2. A traction-aid device with 20 lugs on a narrow rim is to be attached to a wheeled vehicle to increase its traction. The outside diameter of the device measured from the lug tips is 1.72 m (5.6 ft). The lugs are 25 cm (10 in.) wide, and penetrate 15 cm (6 in.) into the ground at the vertical position. Estimate the tractive effort that a lug can develop in the vertical position in a clayey soil with $c = 20$ kPa (2.9 psi), $\phi = 6°$, and $\gamma_s = 15.7$ kN/m³ (100 lb/ft³). The surface of the lug is relatively smooth, and the friction and adhesion between the lug and the soil may be neglected.

Solution. The spacing between two lugs at the tip is 27 cm (10.6 in.). The rupture distance l_s shown in Fig. 2.14 with a penetration $h_b = 15$ cm (6 in.) is

$$l_s = \frac{h_b}{\tan (45° - \phi/2)} = 16.7 \text{ cm (6.6 in.)}$$

It indicates that the spacing between two adjacent lugs is large enough to allow the soil to fail, in accordance with the Rankine passive failure. Since the rim of the device is narrow, the effect of surcharge may be ignored. The horizontal force acting on a lug in the vertical position is given by

$$F_p = b \left(\frac{1}{2} \gamma_s h_b^2 N_\phi + 2 c h_b \sqrt{N_\phi} \right)$$

where b is the width of the lug.

Substituting the given data into the above expression, the value of the tractive effort that the lug in the vertical position can develop is

$$F_p = 1.72 \text{ kN (387 lb)}$$

As the wheel rotates, the inclination as well as the penetration of the lug changes. Thus, the tractive effort developed by the lug varies with its angular position. Since more than one lug is in contact with the terrain, the total tractive effort that the traction-aid device can develop is the sum of the horizontal forces acting on all of the lugs in contact with the ground.

There are limitations on the application of the simple earth pressure theory described above to the solutions of practical problems. For instance, the surface of bulldozer blades or lugs is usually not smooth, as assumed in the simple theory. It has been found that the angle of soil–metal friction δ may vary from 11° for a highly polished, chromium-plated steel with dry sand to almost equal to the angle of internal shearing resistance of the soil for very rough steel surfaces [2.7]. Because of the existence of friction and/or adhesion between the soil and the blade (or lug) surface, there will be shear stresses on the soil–blade interface when the soil adjoining the blade is brought into a state of plastic equilibrium. Consequently, the normal pressure on the contact surface will no longer be the principal stress, and the failure pattern of the soil mass will be as that shown in Fig. 2.15(a). The soil mass in zone *ABC* is in the Rankine passive state, which is characterized by straight slip lines inclined to the horizontal at an angle of $45° - \phi/2$. Zone *ABD* adjacent to the blade is characterized by curved and radial slip lines, and is usually called the radial shear zone. The shape of the curved slip lines, such as *DB* in Fig. 2.15(a), can be considered, with sufficient accuracy, as being either a logarithmic spiral (for materials with frictional property) or an arc of a circle (for cohesive materials). In the presence of friction and/or adhesion between the blade and the soil, Eq. 2.14 can no longer be used to predict the passive earth pressure.

Referring to Eq. 2.15(a), the normal component σ_{pn} of the passive earth pressure acting on a vertical rough blade at a depth z below A can be approximately expressed by a linear equation

$$\sigma_{pn} = \gamma_s z K_{p\gamma} + q K_{pq} + c K_{pc} \tag{2.20}$$

where q is the surcharge, and $K_{p\gamma}$, K_{pq}, and K_{pc} are constants and are functions of the angle of internal shearing resistance of the soil and of the friction between the soil and the blade, but do not depend on z and γ_s. They may be computed by

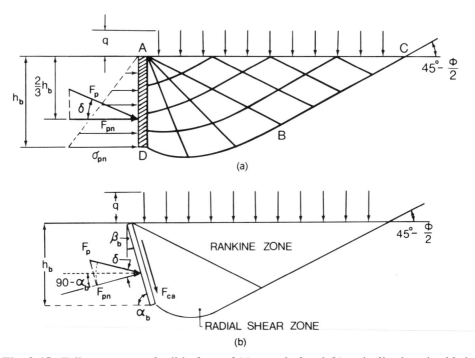

Fig. 2.15 Failure patterns of soil in front of (a) a vertical and (b) an inclined cutting blade with rough surface. (From *Theory of Land Locomotion* by M.G. Bekker, copyright © by the University of Michigan, 1956, reproduced with permission of the University of Michigan Press.)

various methods, including the logarithmic spiral method and the friction circle method [2.8–2.11]. The resultant force F_p will be at an angle δ to the normal of the blade, which is equal to the soil–metal friction angle, as shown in Fig. 2.15(a).

In practice, bulldozer blades are usually not vertical, and the inclination of the lug of a wheel varies as the wheel rotates. If the blade or the lug is sloped to the horizontal at an angle α_b (or to the vertical at an angle $\beta_b = 90° - \alpha_b$), as shown in Fig. 2.15(b), then the resultant force F_{pn} normal to the blade will be

$$F_{pn} = \frac{1}{\sin \alpha_b} \int_0^{h_b} (\gamma_s z K_{p\gamma} + q K_{pq} + c K_{pc})\, dz$$

$$= \frac{1}{2} \gamma_s h_b^2 \frac{K_{p\gamma}}{\sin \alpha_b} + \frac{h_b}{\sin \alpha_b} (q K_{pq} + c K_{pc})$$

or

$$F_{pn} = \frac{1}{2} \gamma_s h_b^2 \frac{K_{p\gamma}}{\cos \beta_b} + \frac{h_b}{\cos \beta_b} (q K_{pq} + c K_{pc}) \tag{2.21}$$

Combining the normal component F_{pn} with the frictional component $F_{pn} \tan \delta$, the resultant force F_p, which acts at an angle δ to the normal on the contact surface, is given by

$$F_p = \frac{F_{pn}}{\cos \delta} = \frac{1}{2} \gamma_s h_b^2 \frac{K_{p\gamma}}{\sin \alpha_b \cos \delta} + \frac{h_b}{\sin \alpha_b \cos \delta} (q K_{pq} + c K_{pc})$$

or

$$F_p = \frac{1}{2} \gamma_s h_b^2 \frac{K_{p\gamma}}{\cos \beta_b \cos \delta} + \frac{h_b}{\cos \beta_b \cos \delta} (q K_{pq} + c K_{pc}) \tag{2.22}$$

In addition to the soil–metal friction, there may be adhesion c_a between the soil and the surface of the blade. The adhesion force F_{ca} is expressed by

$$F_{ca} = \frac{h_b}{\sin \alpha_b} c_a = \frac{h_b}{\cos \beta_b} c_a \tag{2.23}$$

In addition to the methods described above, in recent years, a number of other methods for predicting the passive earth pressure based on a more rigorous application of the theory of plastic equilibrium have been developed [2.9–2.11].

The theory of passive earth pressure also finds application in the prediction of the maximum load of a tracked vehicle that can be supported by a particular type of soil or terrain without causing failure. The vertical load applied by a rigid track to the soil surface may be idealized as a strip load. When the load is light, the soil beneath it may be in a state of elastic equilibrium, as mentioned previously. However, when the load is increased to a certain level, the soil beneath the track will pass into a state of plastic flow, and the sinkage of the track will increase abruptly. This may be illustrated by the load–sinkage curve C_1 shown in Fig. 2.16. The initial part of the curve represents the elastic deformation and compression of the soil. The failure of the soil beneath the track may be identified by the transition of the curve into a steep tangent, such as at W_c of curve C_1 in Fig. 2.16. The load per unit contact area that causes failure is usually called the bearing capacity of the soil.

At the point of failure, the soil beneath the track can be divided into three different zones, as shown in Fig. 2.17(a). When the base of the track is relatively rough, which is usually the case, the existence of friction and adhesion limits the lateral movement of the soil immediately beneath the track. The soil in zone AA_1D

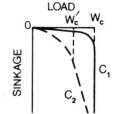

Fig. 2.16 Load–sinkage relationships of a footing under different soil conditions.

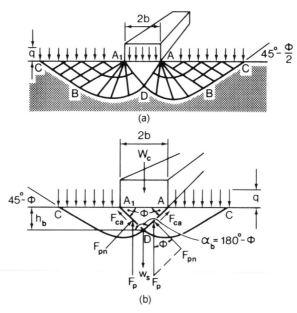

Fig. 2.17 (a) Failure patterns under a strip load and (b) forces acting on a footing. (From *Theory of Land Locomotion* by M.G. Bekker, copyright © by the University of Michigan, 1956, reproduced with permission of the University of Michigan Press.)

is in a state of elastic equilibrium and behaves as if it were rigidly attached to the track. Both boundaries of the wedge-shaped soil body, AD and A_1D, may therefore be identified with the inclined blades discussed previously. However, in this case, the friction angle between the blade and the soil will be equal to the angle of internal shearing resistance of the soil, and the adhesion between the blade and the soil will be the same as the cohesion of the soil. ABD in Fig. 2.17(a) is a radial shear zone, whereas ABC is the Rankine passive zone. As the track sinks, the wedge-shaped soil body AA_1D moves vertically downward. This requires that the slip line DB at point D have a vertical tangent. As mentioned previously, potential slip lines in the soil mass intersect each other at an angle of $90° - \phi$. AD and A_1D therefore must be sloped to the horizontal at an angle of ϕ, as shown in Fig. 2.17(b). In other words, both boundaries AD and A_1D of the wedge-shaped soil body can be considered as inclined blades with an angle $\alpha_b = 180° - \phi$. The problem of determining the bearing capacity of the soil for supporting strip loads can then be solved using the passive earth pressure theory discussed previously [2.8].

The reaction F_p shown in Fig. 2.17(b), which acts at an angle ϕ to the normal on AD and A_1D, will be vertical, as the base angle of the wedge-shaped body AA_1D is equal to ϕ. From Eq. 2.22 and with $\alpha_b = 180 - \phi$, $\delta = \phi$, and $h_b = b \tan \phi$, F_p is expressed by

$$F_p = \frac{1}{2} \gamma_s b^2 K_{p\alpha} \frac{\tan \phi}{\cos^2 \phi} + \frac{b}{\cos^2 \phi} (qK_{pq} + cK_{pc}) \tag{2.24}$$

The adhesion force F_{ca} acting along AD and A_1D is

$$F_{ca} = \frac{b}{\cos \phi} c \tag{2.25}$$

The weight per unit length of the soil in zone AA_1D is

$$w_s = \gamma_s b^2 \tan \phi \tag{2.26}$$

The equilibrium of the soil mass in zone AA_1D requires that the sum of the vertical forces be equal to zero.

$$W_c + w_s - 2F_p - 2F_{ca} \sin \phi = 0 \tag{2.27}$$

where W_c is the critical load per unit length of the track, which causes failure of the soil beneath it.

Substituting Eqs. 2.24, 2.25, and 2.26 into Eq. 2.27, the expression for W_c becomes [2.8]

$$W_c = \gamma_s b^2 K_{p\gamma} \frac{\tan \phi}{\cos^2 \phi} + \frac{2b}{\cos^2 \phi} (qK_{pq} + cK_{pc}) + 2bc \tan \phi - \gamma_s b^2 \tan \phi$$

$$= \gamma_s b^2 \tan \phi \left(\frac{K_{p\gamma}}{\cos^2 \phi} - 1 \right) + 2bq \frac{K_{pq}}{\cos^2 \phi} + 2bc \left(\frac{K_{pc}}{\cos^2 \phi} + \tan \phi \right)$$

$$(2.28)$$

If it is denoted that

$$\frac{1}{2} \tan \phi \left(\frac{K_{p\gamma}}{\cos^2 \phi} - 1 \right) = N_\gamma$$

$$\frac{K_{pq}}{\cos^2 \phi} = N_q$$

and

$$\frac{K_{pc}}{\cos^2 \phi} + \tan \phi = N_c$$

then

$$W_c = 2\gamma_s b^2 N_\gamma + 2bq N_q + 2bc N_c \qquad (2.29)$$

The parameters N_γ, N_q, and N_c, which are usually referred to as Terzaghi's bearing capacity factors, can be determined from $K_{p\gamma}$, K_{pq}, and K_{pc} and the angle of internal shearing resistance ϕ. Since $K_{p\gamma}$, K_{pq}, and K_{pc} in this case are functions of ϕ, the bearing capacity factors N_γ, N_q, and N_c are dependent on ϕ. The variations of the bearing capacity factors with ϕ are shown in Fig. 2.18 [2.8]. It should

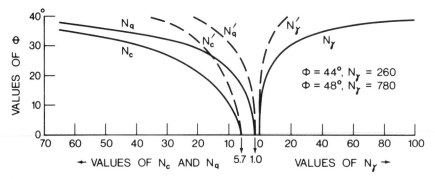

Fig. 2.18 Variation of the Terzaghi bearing capacity factors with the angle of internal shearing resistance of soil. (Reproduced with permission of John Wiley and Sons, Inc., from *Theoretical Soil Mechanics* by K. Terzaghi, 1966.)

be pointed out that Eq. 2.29 and the values of N_γ, N_q, and N_c given in Fig. 2.18 are only applicable to dense soils whose deformation preceding failure is very small. There is no noticeable sinkage of the track until a state of plastic equilibrium is reached. This kind of failure is called general shear failure [2.8]. For loose soils, failure is preceded by considerable deformation, and the relationship between the sinkage and the load is shown by curve C_2 in Fig. 2.16. In this case, the critical load that causes failure of the soil is identified, somewhat arbitrarily, by the point where the curve passes into a steep and fairly straight tangent, as point W'_c in Fig. 2.16. This type of failure is usually referred to as local shear failure [2.8]. Because of the compressibility of the loose soil, the critical load W'_c per unit length for local shear failure is different from that for general shear failure. In the calculation of the critical load for local shear failure, the shear strength parameters c' and ϕ' of the soil are assumed to be smaller than those for general shear failure [2.8]:

$$c' = \frac{2}{3} c$$

and

$$\tan \phi' = \frac{2}{3} \tan \phi$$

Accordingly, the critical load W'_c per unit length of the track for local shear failure is given by

$$W'_c = 2\gamma_s b^2 N'_\gamma + 2bq N'_q + \frac{4}{3} bc N'_c \tag{2.30}$$

The values of N'_γ, N'_q, and N'_c are smaller than those of N_γ, N_q, and N_c, as can be seen from Fig. 2.18.

Based on the theory of bearing capacity, the critical load W_{ct} of a tracked vehicle that may be supported by two tracks without causing failure of the soil can then be estimated by the following equations.

For general shear failure

$$W_{ct} = 2l W_c$$

$$= 4bl \left(\gamma_s b N_\gamma + q N_q + c N_c \right) \tag{2.31}$$

and for local shear failure

$$W'_{ct} = 2l W'_c$$

$$= 4bl \left(\gamma_s b N'_\gamma + q N'_q + \frac{2}{3} c N'_c \right) \tag{2.32}$$

where l is the length of the track in contact with the terrain. Equations 2.31 and 2.32 may shed light on the selection of track configurations from a bearing capacity point of view. Consider the case of general shear failure, and assume that there is no surcharge q. Then in a dry sand (cohesion $c = 0$), the critical load W_{ct} of the vehicle is given by

$$W_{ct} = 4b^2 l\gamma_s N_\gamma \qquad (2.33)$$

This indicates that the load carrying capacity of a track in a frictional soil increases with the square of the track width. To increase the maximum load that the vehicle can carry without causing soil failure, it is, therefore, preferable to increase the track width than to increase the track length. This concept may be illustrated by the following example. Consider two tracked vehicles having the same ground contact area, but the track width of one vehicle is twice that of the other, that is, $b_1 = 2b_2$. Consequently, the contact length of the vehicle with the wider track will be half of that of the other, that is, $l_1 = 0.5l_2$. According to Eq. 2.33, the ratio of the critical loads that the two vehicles can carry is given by

$$\frac{W_{ct1}}{W_{ct2}} = \frac{4b_1^2 l_1 \gamma_s N_\gamma}{4(0.5b_1)^2 \, 2l_1 \gamma_s N_\gamma} = 2$$

This indicates that the critical load that the vehicle with the wider track can support is higher than that of the other, although both vehicles have the same ground contact area.

In cohesive soils, such as saturated clay ($\phi = 0$), the critical load W_{ct} is given by

$$W_{ct} = 4blcN_c \qquad (2.34)$$

This indicates that under these circumstances, the critical load merely depends on the contact area of the track.

It should be emphasized that the use of the bearing capacity theory to predict the critical load that a tracked vehicle can carry without excessive sinkage produces, at best, only approximate results. This is because a number of simplifying assumptions have been made. For instance, the track is simplified as a rigid footing with uniform pressure distribution. In practice, the interaction between the running gear of an off-road vehicle and the terrain is much more complex than the earth pressure theory or the bearing capacity theory assumes. Figures 2.19–2.22 show the flow patterns of sand beneath a wide rigid wheel under various operating conditions [2.4, 2.12, 2.13]. It can be seen that the flow patterns beneath a rigid wheel in the longitudinal plane depend on a number of factors, including wheel slip. There are normally two zones of soil flow beneath a rolling wheel. In one zone, the soil flows forward, and in the other, it flows backward. These two zones degenerate into a single backward zone at 100% slip (Fig. 2.21) and a single forward

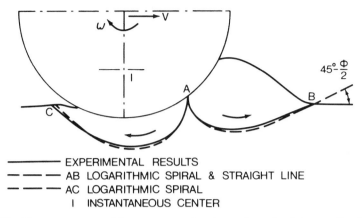

EXPERIMENTAL RESULTS
AB LOGARITHMIC SPIRAL & STRAIGHT LINE
AC LOGARITHMIC SPIRAL
I   INSTANTANEOUS CENTER

Fig. 2.19 Flow patterns and bow wave under the action of a driven roller in sand.

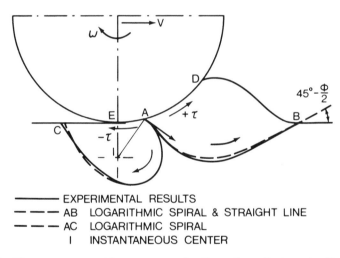

EXPERIMENTAL RESULTS
AB LOGARITHMIC SPIRAL & STRAIGHT LINE
AC LOGARITHMIC SPIRAL
I   INSTANTANEOUS CENTER

Fig. 2.20 Flow patterns and bow wave under the action of a towed roller in sand.

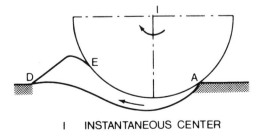

I   INSTANTANEOUS CENTER

Fig. 2.21 Flow patterns beneath a driven roller at 100% slip in sand.

zone for a locked wheel (Fig. 2.22). It is interesting to note that a wedge-shaped soil body is formed in front of a locked wheel, and that it behaves like a bulldozing blade. Figure 2.23 shows the trajectories of clay particles beneath a wide rigid wheel under various operating conditions. The characteristics of the trajectories indicate that the soil is at first in the Rankine passive state when it is in front of an oncoming wheel. As the wheel is advancing, the soil beneath it is driven backward. Under a free-rolling, towed wheel, the final position of a soil particle is in front of its initial position [Fig. 2.23(a)], whereas under a driven wheel, its final position is behind its initial position [Fig. 2.23(b) and (c)]. The characteristics of the trajectories further confirm the existence of two flow zones beneath a rolling wheel. The problem of wheel–soil interaction is complex in that the wheel rim represents a curved boundary, and the interaction is influenced by a variety of design and operational parameters, including wheel slip.

Attempts have been made to apply the theory of plastic equilibrium to the examination of the complex processes of vehicle–terrain interaction, such as the process of wheel–soil interaction described above [2.10]. In the analysis, a set of

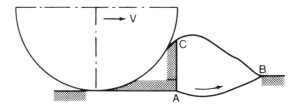

Fig. 2.22   Flow patterns and soil wedge formed in front of a locked wheel with 100% skid in sand.

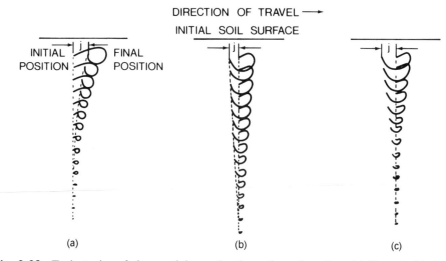

Fig. 2.23   Trajectories of clay particles under the action of a roller. (a) Towed, (b) driven at 37% slip, and (c) driven at 63% slip.

equations that combine the differential equations of equilibrium for the soil mass with the Mohr–Coulomb failure criterion is first established. The boundary conditions, such as the friction angle or, more generally, the direction of the major principal stress on the wheel–soil interface, as well as the contact angles and the separation angle of the front and rear flow zones shown in Figs. 2.19 and 2.20, are then assumed or specified as input. The solution to the set of differential equations with the specified boundary conditions yields the geometry of the slip line field and associated stresses on the wheel–soil interface. As an example, Fig. 2.24 (a) and (b) show the slip line fields in the soil beneath a driven and a towed rigid wheel, respectively [2.14]. Based on the predicted normal and shear stresses on the wheel–soil interface, the motion resistance and the tractive effort developed by the wheel can be predicted.

It should be pointed out that in practice, the boundary conditions on the wheel–soil interface are complex and vary with the design and operational parameters of the wheel, as well as terrain conditions. This makes it very difficult, if not impossible, to assume or specify realistic boundary conditions at the outset. Because of the complexity of the problem, the approach developed so far for specifying the required boundary conditions is primarily empirical in nature [2.10]. This indicates that the elaborate solution procedures based on the theory of plastic equilibrium for predicting the performance of vehicle running gear heavily rely on either empirical inputs or assumed boundary conditions [2.4]. Furthermore, the theory of

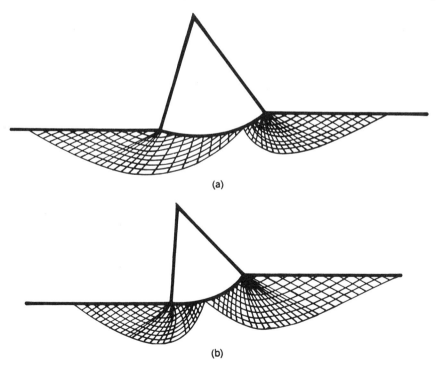

(a)

(b)

Fig. 2.24 Slip line fields in soil beneath (a) a driven rigid wheel and (b) a towed rigid wheel predicted using the theory of plastic equilibrium. (Reproduced with permission from reference 2.14.)

plastic equilibrium is based on the assumption that the terrain behaves like an ideal elastoplastic medium (or a rigid, perfectly plastic material). This means that the terrain does not deform significantly until the stresses within certain boundaries reach the level at which failure occurs. Beyond this point, the strain increases rapidly, while the stress remains essentially constant. Although dense sand and the like may exhibit behavior similar to that of an ideal elastoplastic medium, a wide range of natural terrains encountered in off-road operations, such as snow and organic terrain, have a high degree of compressibility, and their behavior does not conform to that of an idealized material. Failure zones in these natural terrains under vehicular loads, therefore, do not develop in a manner similar to that assumed in the theory of plastic equilibrium, and the sinkage of the vehicle running gear is primarily due to compression and not plastic flow of the terrain material. It should also be mentioned that the theory of plastic equilibrium is mainly concerned with the predicting of the maximum load that causes failure of the soil mass, but does not deal with the deformation of the terrain under load. In many problems in off-road operations, the prediction of terrain deformation under vehicular load, such as vehicle sinkage and slip, is required.

Because of the problems described above, in practice there are severe limitations to the applications of the theory of plastic equilibrium to the evaluation and prediction of off-road vehicle performance in the field [2.4, 2.15].

In recent years, attempts have also been made to apply the finite element method to the analysis of vehicle–terrain interaction [2.16–2.18]. In the analysis, the terrain is represented by a system of elements with specified constitutive relationships and interconnected at nodes to form a mesh. Among the various types of element, the triangular element is the most commonly used. Figure 2.25 shows a mesh of triangular elements developed for the analysis of tire–terrain interaction. The tire is considered as an elastic system, and the terrain as a piecewise linear elastic material. To predict the length of the contact patch between the tire and the terrain, a method originated from the Hertz theory of contact between two elastic bodies,

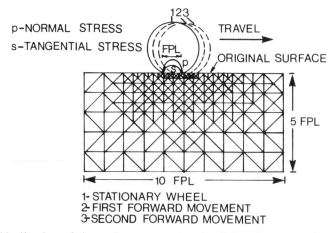

Fig. 2.25 Idealization of tire–soil system using the finite element method. (Reproduced with permission from reference 2.18.)

and modified by Poritsky in 1950 for the study of the contact problems of gears and locomotive wheels, is used [2.18]. To initiate the solution process, the distributions of the normal and shear stresses on the contact patch, as well as the load–unload stress–strain relations for the terrain, are required as input. The output of the analysis is given in terms of stress, strain rate, and velocity fields in the terrain. It should be pointed out that in many cases, it is unrealistic to assume that the terrain is a linear elastic material. Under tire load, natural terrain usually undergoes large yielding and plastic deformation and does not behave elastically. Furthermore, when the normal and shear stresses on the tire–soil interface are specified, the performance of the tire is completely defined. There is no need to use the finite element method to determine the stress, strain rate, and velocity fields in the terrain, as far as the prediction of tire performance is concerned. The finite element method developed so far appears to be suitable only for predicting the response of the terrain to vehicular loading, such as in the study of soil compaction caused by vehicular traffic, when the stress distributions on the vehicle running gear–terrain interface are known or can be realistically defined [2.4, 2.19].

2.3 EMPIRICAL METHODS FOR PREDICTING OFF-ROAD VEHICLE PERFORMANCE

As can be seen from the discussions presented in previous sections, the interaction between an off-road vehicle and the terrain is complex and difficult to model accurately. To circumvent this difficulty, empirical methods for predicting vehicle mobility have been developed.

The general approach to the development of empirical methods for predicting off-road vehicle performance is to conduct tests of a select group of vehicles considered to be representative over a range of terrains of interest. The terrain is identified (or classified) by simple measurements or field observations. The results of vehicle performance testing and the terrain characteristics identified are then empirically correlated. This can lead to the development of empirical relationships for evaluating terrain trafficability on the one hand, and vehicle mobility on the other.

Representative empirical methods for predicting off-road vehicle performance are outlined below.

2.3.1 Empirical Methods Based on the Cone Index

These methods were originally developed during World War II by the U.S. Army Waterways Experiment Station (WES) to provide military intelligence and reconnaissance personnel with a simple means to assess vehicle mobility on a "go/no go" basis in fine- and coarse-grained soils. They form the basis for the subsequent developments of the NATO Reference Mobility Model (NRMM). For these empirical methods, terrain characteristics are identified by a parameter referred to as the cone index, obtained using a cone penetrometer. Vehicle performance is then empirically correlated with the cone index or its derivatives.

The commonly used cone penetrometer consists of a 30° circular cone with a 0.5 in.^{2} (3.23 cm^2) base area, a proving ring, and a dial gauge for indicating the force required to push the cone into the terrain (Fig. 2.26). The recommended rate of penetration is approximately 1.2 in./s (3 cm/s). The force per unit cone base area is called the cone index (CI). Although the CI is commonly used as a parameter with no dimensions, it is, in fact, the penetration force in pounds divided by the area of the cone base in square inches, and thus it has the unit of pressure [2.20]. With recent advances in electronics and computer technology, a variety of cone penetrometers using electronic (or electrical) sensors for monitoring the force and penetration depth, as well as computer technology for storing and processing measured data, have been developed [2.4].

In addition to the cone index, other indices can be obtained using the cone penetrometer. For instance, in fine-grained soils or in poorly drained wet sands, a remolding index (RI) can be obtained to evaluate the change in terrain strength that may occur under repeated vehicular traffic. The RI is the ratio of the cone index of a soil after remolding to that before remolding. Remolding may cause an increase or decrease in the strength of the terrain, depending upon the type and condition of the terrain. The rating cone index (RCI), which is the product of the remolding index (RI) and the cone index (CI) measured before remolding, is used to represent terrain strength under repeated vehicular traffic. For coarse-grained soils, such as sand, in addition to the cone index, the cone penetration resistance gradient with respect to penetration depth is also used for characterizing their strength.

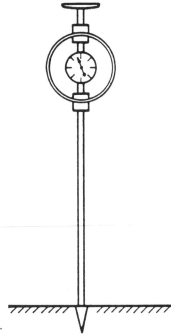

Fig. 2.26 The basic components of a cone penetrometer.

An Empirical Method for Predicting Tracked Vehicle Performance   In the method developed by WES for predicting tracked vehicle performance, an empirical equation is first used to calculate the mobility index (MI) of a given vehicle [2.21]. The mobility index is expressed by

$$\text{Mobility Index} = \left(\frac{\begin{array}{c}\text{contact} \\ \text{pressure} \times \text{weight} \\ \text{factor} \qquad \text{factor}\end{array}}{\begin{array}{c}\text{track} \\ \text{factor}\end{array} \times \begin{array}{c}\text{grouser} \\ \text{factor}\end{array}} + \begin{array}{c}\text{bogie} \\ \text{factor}\end{array} - \begin{array}{c}\text{clearance} \\ \text{factor}\end{array} \right)$$
$$\times \begin{array}{c}\text{engine} \\ \text{factor}\end{array} \times \begin{array}{c}\text{transmission} \\ \text{factor}\end{array} \qquad\qquad (2.35)$$

where

$$\text{Contact pressure factor} = \frac{\text{gross weight, lb}}{\text{area of tracks in contact with ground, in.}^2}$$

Weight factor: less than 50,000 lb (222.4 kN) = 1.0
50,000–69,999 lb (222.4–311.4 kN) = 1.2
70,000–99,999 lb (311.4–444.8 kN) = 1.4
100,000 lb (444.8 kN) or greater = 1.8

$$\text{Track factor} = \frac{\text{track width, in.}}{100}$$

Grouser factor: Grousers less than 1.5 in. (3.8 cm) high = 1.0
Grousers more than 1.5 in. (3.8 cm) high = 1.1

$$\text{Bogie factor} = \frac{\text{gross weight, lb, divided by 10}}{\left(\begin{array}{c}\text{total number of bogies} \\ \text{on tracks in contact} \\ \text{with ground}\end{array}\right) \times \left(\begin{array}{c}\text{area of one track} \\ \text{shoe, in.}^2\end{array}\right)}$$

$$\text{Clearance factor} = \frac{\text{clearance, in.}}{10}$$

Engine factor: $\geq$ 10 hp/ton of vehicle weight = 1.0
$\leq$ 10 hp/ton of vehicle weight = 1.05

Transmission factor: Automatic = 1.0; manual = 1.05

Based on the mobility index (MI), a parameter called the vehicle cone index (VCI) is calculated. The VCI represents the minimum strength of a soil in the critical layer that permits a given vehicle to successfully make a specific number of passes, usually one pass or 50 passes. The values of VCI for one pass and 50 passes, VCI_1 and VCI_{50}, are calculated from the mobility index (MI) using the following empirical equations:

$$\text{VCI}_1 = 7.0 + 0.2\text{MI} - \left(\frac{39.2}{\text{MI} + 5.6}\right) \tag{2.36}$$

$$\text{VCI}_{50} = 19.27 + 0.43\text{MI} - \left(\frac{125.79}{\text{MI} + 7.08}\right) \tag{2.37}$$

The soil strength is described in terms of either the rating cone index (RCI) for fine-grained soils or the cone index (CI) for coarse-grained soils. The critical layer referred to above varies with the type and weight of the vehicle and soil strength profile. For freely draining or clean sands, it is usually the 0–6 in. (0–15 cm) layer. For fine-grained soils and poorly drained sands with fines, it is usually the 0–6 in. (0–15 cm) layer for one pass, and the 6–12 in. (15–30 cm) layer for 50 passes.

After the VCI and soil strength have been determined, the values of the performance parameters of a tracked vehicle, such as the net maximum drawbar pull coefficient (the ratio of drawbar pull to vehicle weight), maximum slope negotiable, and towed motion resistance coefficient (the ratio of towed motion resistance to vehicle weight), are then empirically determined as functions of vehicle type, number of passes to be completed, and the excess of RCI over VCI (i.e., RCI–VCI) for fine-grained soils or CI for coarse-grained soils. Figure 2.27 shows the empirical relations between the net maximum drawbar pull coefficient (or maximum slope negotiatble) and the excess of RCI over VCI for tracked vehicles with different grouser heights over fine-grained soils. The empirical realtions between the first-pass towed motion resistance coefficient and the excess of RCI over VCI for tracked and wheeled vehicles operating on fine-grained soils are shown in Fig. 2.28 [2.21].

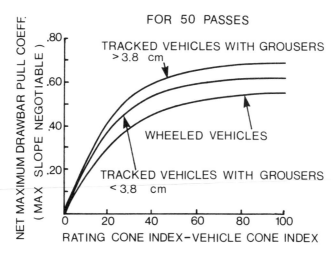

Fig. 2.27 Variation of net maximum drawbar pull coefficient with the excess of RCI over VCI on level, fine-grained soil. (Reproduced from reference 2.21.)

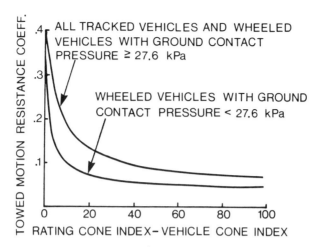

Fig. 2.28 Variation of the first-pass towed motion resistance with the excess of RCI over VCI on level, fine-grained soil. (Reproduced from reference 2.21.)

Empirical Methods for Predicting Wheeled Vehicle Performance
Similar to the empirical method for predicting tracked vehicle performance described above, in this method developed by WES, an empirical equation is used to calculate the mobility index of an off-road wheeled vehicle. The mobility index for a wheeled vehicle is given by

$$
\text{Mobility Index} = \left(\frac{\begin{array}{c}\text{contact} \\ \text{pressure} \times \text{weight} \\ \text{factor} \quad \text{factor}\end{array}}{\begin{array}{c}\text{tire} \\ \text{factor}\end{array} \times \begin{array}{c}\text{grouser} \\ \text{factor}\end{array}} + \begin{array}{c}\text{wheel} \\ \text{load} \\ \text{factor}\end{array} - \begin{array}{c}\text{clearance} \\ \text{factor}\end{array} \right)
$$

$$
\times \begin{array}{c}\text{engine} \\ \text{factor}\end{array} \times \begin{array}{c}\text{transmission} \\ \text{factor}\end{array} \tag{2.38}
$$

where

$$
\begin{array}{c}\text{Contact} \\ \text{pressure} \\ \text{factor}\end{array} = \frac{\text{gross weight, lb}}{\begin{array}{c}\text{nominal} \\ \text{tire width,} \\ \text{in.}\end{array} \times \begin{array}{c}\text{outside} \\ \text{radius of} \\ \text{tire, in.}\end{array} \times \begin{array}{c}\text{no.} \\ \text{of} \\ \text{tires}\end{array}}
$$

Weight factor:

weight range, lb	weight factor equation
< 2000 (8.9 kN)	$\overline{Y} = 0.553\overline{X}$
2000–13,500 (8.9–60 kN)	$\overline{Y} = 0.033\overline{X} + 1.050$
13,501–20,000 (60–88.9 kN)	$\overline{Y} = 0.142\overline{X} - 0.420$
> 20,000 (88.9 kN)	$\overline{Y} = 0.278\overline{X} - 3.115$

where $\overline{Y}$ = weight factor; $\overline{X} = \dfrac{\text{gross weight, kips}}{\text{no. of axles}}$

$$\text{Tire factor} = \frac{10 + \text{tire width, in.}}{100}$$

Grouser factor: with chains = 1.05
without chains = 1.00

$$\text{Wheel load factor} = \frac{\text{gross weight, kips}}{\text{no. of axles} \times 2}$$

$$\text{Clearance factor} = \frac{\text{clearance, in.}}{10}$$

Engine factor: $\geq$ 10 hp/ton of vehicle weight = 1.0
< 10 hp/ton of vehicle weight = 1.05

Transmission factor: automatic = 1.00; manual = 1.05

Similar to the empirical method for predicting tracked vehicle performance described previously, the mobility index of a wheeled vehicle is used to determine a vehicle cone index (VCI). For a self-propelled, wheeled vehicle, the vehicle cone index is related to the mobility index by the following empirical equations.
For one pass,

$$\text{VCI}_1 = 11.48 + 0.2\text{MI} - \left(\frac{39.2}{\text{MI} + 3.74}\right) \tag{2.39}$$

and for 50 passes,

$$\text{VCI}_{50} = 28.23 + 0.43\text{MI} - \left(\frac{92.67}{\text{MI} + 3.67}\right) \tag{2.40}$$

After the VCI of a vehicle and the strength of the soil to be traversed (such as the rating cone index (RCI) for a fine-grained soil) have been determined, the performance parameters of a wheeled vehicle, such as the net maximum drawbar pull coefficient and the towed motion resistance coefficient, can then be predicted using empirical relations such as those shown in Figs. 2.27 and 2.28. The performance parameters are related to the excess of RCI over VCI on fine-grained soils.

For the performance of a single tire, an empirical model based on two dimensionless prediction terms, or soil–tire numerics, was developed at WES [2.22, 2.23]. The clay–tire numeric N_c is for tires operating in purely cohesive soil (near-saturated clay), while the sand–tire numeric N_s is for tires operating in purely frictional soil (air-dry sand). These two numerics are defined as

$$N_c = \frac{Cbd}{W} \times \left(\frac{\delta}{h}\right)^{1/2} \times \frac{1}{1 + (b/2d)} \tag{2.41}$$

and

$$N_s = \frac{G(bd)^{3/2}}{W} \times \frac{\delta}{h} \qquad (2.42)$$

where b is the tire section width, C is the cone index, d is the tire diameter, G is the sand penetration resistance gradient, h is the unloaded tire section height, W is the tire load, and δ is the tire deflection.

For tires operating in soils with both cohesive and frictional properties, a soil–tire numeric N_{cs} was proposed, and is defined as [2.24]

$$N_{cs} = \frac{Cbd}{W} \qquad (2.43)$$

Based on test results obtained primarily in laboratory soil bins, these soil–tire numerics have been empirically correlated with two tire performance parameters: the drawbar coefficient μ, and the drawbar efficiency η at 20% slip. The drawbar coefficient is defined as the ratio of drawbar pull to the normal load on the tire, while the drawbar efficiency is defined as the ratio of the drawbar power (i.e., the product of drawbar pull and forward speed of the tire) to the power input to the tire. Figure 2.29 shows the empirical relations between μ and η at 20% slip and the clay–tire numeric N_c. These relations were obtained on cohesive clays with tires ranging from 4.00–7 to 31 × 15.50–13, with loads from 0.23 to 20 kN (52–4500 lb), and with ratios of tire deflection to section height from 0.08 to 0.35. The cone index values of these clays in the top 15 cm (6 in.) ranged from 55 to 390 kPa (8–56 psi). Figure 2.30 shows the relations between the two tire performance parameters at 20% slip and the sand–tire numeric N_s. These empirical relations were based on test results obtained on a particular type of sand known as desert Yuma sand, with tires similar to those for Fig. 2.29, with loads from 0.19 to 20 kN (42–4500 lb), and with ratios of tire deflection to section height from 0.15 to

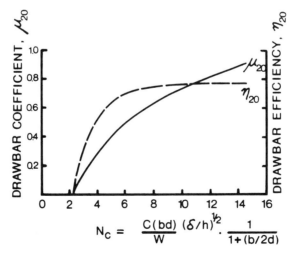

Fig. 2.29 Empirical relations between drawbar coefficient and drawbar efficiency at 20% slip and clay–tire numeric N_c. (Reproduced with permission from reference 2.23.)

0.35. The values of the penetration resistance gradient for the desert Yuma sand ranged from 0.9 to 5.4 MPa/m (3.3–19.8 psi/in.). Figure 2.31 shows the empirical relations between μ and η at 20% slip and the soil–tire numeric N_{cs}. These relations were obtained on cohesive-frictional soils, with tires ranging from 36 to 84 cm (14–33 in.) in width and from 84 to 165 cm (33–65 in.) in diameter, and loads from 2.2 to 28.9 kN (495–6500 lb). These soils ranged from a tilled soil with an average before-traffic cone index value of 130 kPa (19 psi) in a layer of 15 cm (6 in.) deep to an untilled soil with an average cone index value of 3450 kPa (500 psi) [2.23].

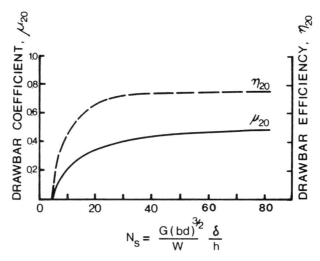

$$N_s = \frac{G(bd)^{3/2}}{W} \frac{\delta}{h}$$

Fig. 2.30 Empirical relations between drawbar coefficient and drawbar efficiency at 20% slip and the sand–tire numeric N_s. (Reproduced with permission from reference 2.23.)

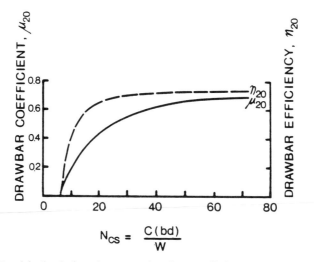

$$N_{cs} = \frac{C(bd)}{W}$$

Fig. 2.31 Empirical relations between drawbar coefficient and drawbar efficiency at 20% slip and the numeric N_{cs} for cohesive-frictional soils. (Reproduced with permission from reference 2.23.)

The empirical relations for predicting tire performance based on soil–tire numerics, particularly the sand–tire numeric, have undergone a number of revisions since they were first proposed as new experimental data emerged [2.4, 2.25].

2.3.2 Empirical Methods Based on the Mean Maximum Pressure

Another empirical method for evaluating the mobility of off-road vehicles is based on the concept of mean maximum pressure (MMP), which is defined as the mean value of the maxima occurring under all of the roadwheel stations [2.26, 2.27].

Empirical equations for predicting the values of MMP of track systems with different design features are given below.

For link and belt tracks on rigid roadwheels,

$$\text{MMP} = \frac{1.26W}{2n_r A_l b \sqrt{t_l D}} \text{ kPa} \qquad (2.44)$$

and for belt tracks on pneumatic tired roadwheels,

$$\text{MMP} = \frac{0.5W}{2n_r b \sqrt{Df_l}} \text{ kPa} \qquad (2.45)$$

where W is the vehicle weight in kN, n_r is the number of wheel stations in one track, A_l is the rigid area of link (or belt track cleat) as a proportion of $b \times t_l$, b is the track or pneumatic tire width in m, t_l is the track pitch in m, D is the outer diameter of the roadwheel or pneumatic tire in m, and f_l is the radial deflection of the pneumatic tire under load in m.

Table 2.1 shows the values of MMP for various types of tracked vehicle calculated using the empirical formulas described above [2.27].

TABLE 2.1 Values of the Mean Maximum Pressure of Some Tracked Vehicles

Vehicle	Track Configuration	Weight (kN)	Mean Maximum Pressure (kPa)
Amphibious Carrier M29C Weasel	Link track	26.5	27
Armoured Personnel Carrier M113	Link track	108	119
Caterpillar D4 Tractor	Link track	59	82
Caterpillar D7 Tractor	Link track	131	80
Main Battle Tank AMX 30	Link track	370	249
Main Battle Tank Leopard I	Link track	393	198
Main Battle Tank Leopard II	Link track	514	201
Main Battle Tank M60	Link track	510–545	221–236
Main Battle Tank T62	Link track	370	242
Swedish S-Tank	Link track	370	267
Volvo BV202 All-Terrain Carrier	Belt track, pneumatic tire	42	33

Source: Reference 2.27.

To evaluate whether a particular vehicle with a specific value of MMP will have adequate mobility over a specific terrain, a set of desired values of the mean maximum pressure for different conditions is proposed as shown in Table 2.2 [2.27].

It should be pointed out that in the empirical equations 2.44 and 2.45, terrain characteristics are not explicitly taken into account in the calculation of MMP. Thus, the values of MMP calculated are independent of terrain conditions. In reality, the pressure distribution under a track is strongly influenced by terrain characteristics [2.4]. Furthermore, Eqs. 2.44 and 2.45, together with Table 2.2, can only be employed to evaluate the soft ground performance of tracked vehicles on a "go/no go" basis, and cannot be used to quantitatively predict the performance of a vehicle, such as the motion resistance, thrust, drawbar pull, and tractive efficiency under a given operating condition.

Empirical methods are simple to use, and would be useful in estimating the performance of vehicles with design features similar to those that have been tested under similar operating conditions. It should be pointed out, however, that empirical relations cannot normally be extrapolated beyond the conditions upon which they were derived. Consequently, empirical methods have inherent limitations. For instance, it is uncertain that they could play a useful role in the evaluation of new vehicle design concepts or in the prediction of vehicle performance in new operating environments. Furthermore, an entirely empirical approach is only feasible where the number of variables involved in the problem is relatively small. If a large number of parameters are required to define the problem, then an empirical approach may not necessarily be cost-effective.

TABLE 2.2   Desired Values of the Mean Maximum Pressure

	Mean Maximum Pressure (kPa)		
Terrain	Ideal (Multipass operation or good gradability)	Satisfactory	Maximum acceptable (mostly trafficable at single-pass level)
Wet, fine-grained			
—Temperate	150	200	300
—Tropical	90	140	240
Muskeg	30	50	60
Muskeg floating mat and European bogs	5	10	15
Snow	10	25–30	40

Source: Reference 2.27.

2.4   MEASUREMENT AND CHARACTERIZATION OF TERRAIN RESPONSE

Owing to the limitations of the theories of elasticity and plastic equilibrium, as well as the empirical methods described above, methods for parametric analysis

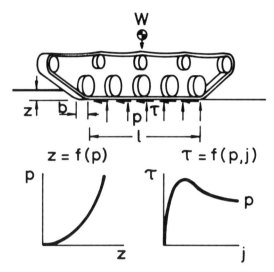

Fig. 2.32 A simplified model for predicting tracked vehicle performance.

of off-road vehicle performance based on the measurement of terrain response under loading conditions similar to those exerted by an off-road vehicle and on a detailed analysis of the mechanics of vehicle–terrain interaction have been developed [2.3, 2.4]. The measurement and characterization of terrain response are discussed in this section, while the mechanics of vehicle–terrain interaction and methods for the parametric analysis of off-road vehicle performance will be described in subsequent sections.

A ground vehicle, through its running gear, applies normal load to the terrain surface, which results in sinkage giving rise to motion resistance, as shown in Fig. 2.32. Also, the torque applied to the sprocket of a track or to the tire initiates shearing action between the running gear and the terrain, which results in the development of thrust and associated slip. The measurement of both the normal pressure–sinkage and shear stress–shear displacement relationships, therefore, is of prime importance in the prediction and evaluation of off-road vehicle performance. Furthermore, when an off-road vehicle is in a straight line motion, an element of the terrain under the vehicle is subject to the repetitive loading of the consecutive wheels in a multiaxle wheeled vehicle (or the roadwheels in a tracked vehicle). To realistically predict the performance of an off-road vehicle, the response of the terrain to repetitive loading should also be measured [2.4, 2.28, 2.29].

One of the well-known techniques for measuring the response of terrain to loading pertinent to vehicle mobility studies is that proposed by Bekker [2.2, 2.3, 2.30]. This technique has now become known as the bevameter technique. It comprises two basic sets of tests: one is a set of plate penetration tests, and the other is a set of shear tests. In the penetration tests, a plate of suitable size is used to simulate the contact area of the vehicle running gear, and the pressure–sinkage relationship of the terrain is measured. It is used to predict the normal pressure distribution on the vehicle–terrain interface, as well as vehicle sinkage. To minimize the uncertainty in applying the measured data to the prediction of the performance of full-size vehicles, it is preferable that the size of the plate used in the tests should be comparable to that of the contact area of a track link or a tire [2.4, 2.29]. In the shear tests, a shear ring or a shear plate, shown in Fig. 2.12, is used to simulate the shearing action of the vehicle running gear. The shear stress–shear displacement relationship and the shear strength of the terrain are measured. This provides the necessary data for predicting the shear stress distribution on the vehicle–terrain interface and the tractive effort developed by the vehicle.

The basic features of a bevameter designed to carry out the tests described above are illustrated in Fig. 2.33. A hydraulic ram is usually used to apply normal load to the sinkage plate in the pressure–sinkage test. Plates of circular shape are commonly used. The applied pressure and the resulting sinkage of the plate are recorded as shown in Fig. 2.33. In shear tests, a shear ring is usually employed to apply shear loading to the terrain surface under various normal pressures. The torque applied and the resulting angular displacement of the shear ring are recorded, as shown in Fig. 2.33, from which the shear stress–shear displacement relationship and the shear strength parameters of the terrain can be derived. To predict the traction developed by a rubber tire or by a rubber track, the characteristics of rubber–terrain shearing should be measured. These can be obtained using a shear ring covered with a layer of rubber of the same composition as that for the tire tread or the track.

Figure 2.34 shows a bevameter mounted in front of a vehicle for measuring terrain properties in the field.

2.4.1 Characterization of Pressure–Sinkage Relationship

After the pressure–sinkage data have been collected, they should be properly characterized so that they may be integrated into a select framework for predicting the performance of off-road vehicles. Dependent upon the type, structure, and con-

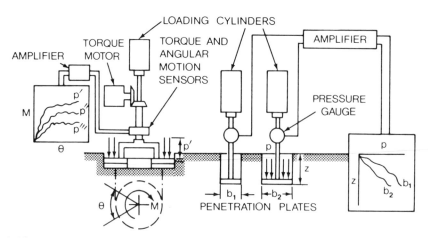

Fig. 2.33 Schematic view of a bevameter for measuring terrain properties. (From *Introduction to Terrain-Vehicle Systems* by M.G. Bekker, copyright © by the University of Michigan, 1969, reproduced with permission of the University of Michigan Press.)

ditions of the terrain, different mathematical functions are used to characterize the pressure–sinkage relationship.

Homogeneous Terrain   If a terrain is considered to be homogeneous within the depth of interest, its pressure–sinkage relationship may take one of the forms shown in Fig. 2.35, and it may be characterized by the following equation proposed by Bekker [2.3]:

$$p = \left(\frac{k_c}{b} + k_\phi\right) z^n \tag{2.46}$$

Fig. 2.34   A vehicle-mounted bevameter in field operation.

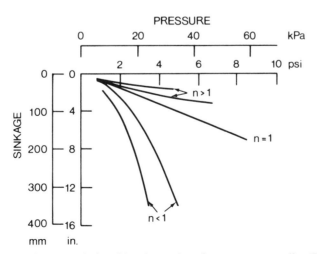

Fig. 2.35   Pressure–sinkage relationships for various homogeneous soils. (From *Introduction to Terrain-Vehicle Systems* by M.G. Bekker, copyright © by the University of Michigan, 1969, reproduced with permission of the University of Michigan Press.)

where p is pressure, b is the smaller dimension of the contact patch, that is, the width of a rectangular contact area, or the radius of a circular contact area, z is sinkage, and n, k_c, and k_ϕ are pressure–sinkage parameters. It has been shown by Bekker that k_c and k_ϕ are insensitive to the width of rectangular plates for plates with large aspect ratios (larger than 5–7) in homogeneous terrain. In view of the possible localized nonhomogeneity in the field, however, the width of the plate designed for field use should not be less than 5 cm (2 in.), and preferably not less than 10 cm (4 in.). A number of tests have been performed to determine the degree of dependence of the values of k_c, k_ϕ, and n on the shape of the test plate. Experimental results obtained so far indicate that there is little difference between the values of k_c, k_ϕ, and n obtained with a set of rectangular plates of high aspect ratios (larger than 5–7) and those obtained with a set of circular plates having radii equal to the widths of the rectangular plates. Because of this, circular plates are commonly used since they require less total load than the corresponding rectangular plates to produce the same ground pressure.

The values of k_c, k_ϕ, and n can be derived from the results of a minimum of two tests with two sizes of plates having different widths (or radii). The tests produce two curves:

$$p_1 = \left(\frac{k_c}{b_1} + k_\phi\right) z^n$$

$$p_2 = \left(\frac{k_c}{b_2} + k_\phi\right) z^n$$
(2.47)

On the logarithmic scale, the above equations can be rewritten as follows:

$$\log p_1 = \log \left(\frac{k_c}{b_1} + k_\phi\right) + n \log z$$

$$\log p_2 = \log \left(\frac{k_c}{b_2} + k_\phi\right) + n \log z$$
(2.48)

They represent two parallel straight lines of the same slope on the log–log scale, as shown in Fig. 2.36. It is evident that $\tan \alpha_s = n$ (Fig. 2.36). Thus, the exponent of deformation n can be determined from the slope of the straight lines. At sinkage $z = 1$, the values of the normal pressure for the two sizes of plates are

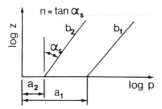

Fig. 2.36 Method for determining sinkage moduli and exponent.

$$(p_1)_{z=1} = \frac{k_c}{b_1} + k_\phi = a_1$$

$$(p_2)_{z=1} = \frac{k_c}{b_2} + k_\phi = a_2 \tag{2.49}$$

In the above equations, $(p_1)_{z=1}$ and $(p_2)_{z=1}$ are measured values, and the only unknowns are k_c and k_ϕ. Thus, k_c and k_ϕ can be determined by the following equations:

$$k_\phi = \frac{a_2 b_2 - a_1 b_1}{b_2 - b_1}$$

$$k_c = \frac{(a_1 - a_2) b_1 b_2}{(b_2 - b_1)} \tag{2.50}$$

Owing to the nonhomogeneity of the terrain in the field and possible experimental errors, the pressure–sinkage lines may not be quite parallel on the log–log scale in some cases. Thus, two values of the exponent of deformation may be produced. Under these circumstances, the value of n is usually taken as the mean of the two values obtained. It should be mentioned that the above-noted procedure relies on the skill of the investigator to plot the appropriate straight lines to represent the pressure–sinkage data on the log–log scale. Consequently, it is liable to error for inexperienced personnel. Furthermore, the values of k_c and k_ϕ are determined using only the pressures measured at sinkage $z = 1$. To provide a more rational approach for deriving the values of n, k_c, and k_ϕ from measured pressure–sinkage data, a computerized procedure based on the weighted least squares method has been developed and successfully used to process field data [2.4, 2.31].

The values of k_c, k_ϕ, and n for a sample of terrains are given in Table 2.3 [2.3, 2.4, 2.32].

It should be emphasized that Eq. 2.46 is essentially an empirical equation. Furthermore, the parameters k_c and k_ϕ have variable dimensions, depending on the value of the exponent n. Influenced by the work of a more fundamental nature in soil mechanics and by experimental evidence, Reece proposed a new equation for the pressure–sinkage relationship [2.33]:

$$p = (ck_c' + \gamma_s b k_\phi') \left(\frac{z}{b}\right)^n \tag{2.51}$$

where n, k_c', and k_ϕ' are pressure–sinkage parameters, γ_s is the weight density of the terrain, and c is cohesion. A series of penetration tests were carried out to verify the validity of the principal features of the above equation. Plates with various widths and with an aspect ratio of at least 4.5 were used. The test results are shown in Fig. 2.37. For a frictionless clay, the term k_ϕ' should be negligible. The results shown in Fig. 2.37 indicate that this is true, the curves for clay collapsing

TABLE 2.3 Terrain Values

Terrain	Moisture Content (%)	n	k_c (lb/in.$^{n+1}$)	k_c (kN/m^{n+1})	k_ϕ (lb/in.$^{n+2}$)	k_ϕ (kN/m^{n+2})	c (lb/in.^{2})	c (kPa)	ϕ (deg)
Dry sand (Land Locomotion Lab., LLL)	0	1.1	0.1	0.99	3.9	1528.43	0.15	1.04	28°
Sandy loam (LLL)	15	0.7	2.3	5.27	16.8	1515.04	0.25	1.72	29°
	22	0.2	7	2.56	3	43.12	0.2	1.38	38°
Sandy loam Michigan (Strong, Buchele)	11	0.9	11	52.53	6	1127.97	0.7	4.83	20°
	23	0.4	15	11.42	27	808.96	1.4	9.65	35°
Sandy loam (Hanamoto)	26	0.3	5.3	2.79	6.8	141.11	2.0	13.79	22°
	32	0.5	0.7	0.77	1.2	51.91	0.75	5.17	11°
Clayey soil (Thailand)	38	0.5	12	13.19	16	692.15	0.6	4.14	13°
	55	0.7	7	16.03	14	1262.53	0.3	2.07	10°
Heavy clay (Waterways Experiment Stn., WES)	25	0.13	45	12.70	140	1555.95	10	68.95	34°
	40	0.11	7	1.84	10	103.27	3	20.69	6°
Lean clay (WES)	22	0.2	45	16.43	120	1724.69	10	68.95	20°
	32	0.15	5	1.52	10	119.61	2	13.79	11°
LETE sand (Wong)		0.79	32	102	42.2	5301	0.19	1.3	31.1°
Upland sandy loam (Wong)	51	1.10	7.5	74.6	5.3	2080	0.48	3.3	33.7°
Rubicon Sandy loam (Wong)	43	0.66	3.5	6.9	9.7	752	0.54	3.7	29.8°
North Gower Clayey loam (Wong)	46	0.73	16.3	41.6	24.5	2471	0.88	6.1	26.6°
Grenville loam (Wong)	24	1.01	0.008	0.06	20.9	5880	0.45	3.1	29.8°
Snow (U.S.) (Harrison)		1.6	0.07	4.37	0.08	196.72	0.15	1.03	19.7°
		1.6	0.04	2.49	0.10	245.90	0.09	0.62	23.2°
Snow (Sweden)		1.44	0.3	10.55	0.05	66.08	0.87	6	20.7°

Source: References 2.3, 2.4, and 2.32.

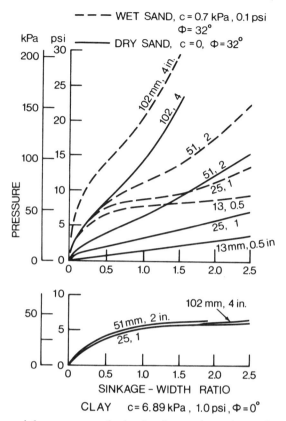

Fig. 2.37 Pressure–sinkage curves obtained using various sizes of rectangular plates in different soils. (Reproduced with permission of the Council of the Institution of Mechanical Engineers from reference 2.33.)

to almost a single line for all plates regardless of their width when plotted against z/b. For dry, cohesionless sand, the term k_c' should be negligible. The equation thus suggests that pressure increases linearly with the width of the plate for a given value of z/b. Wetting the sand would not alter its value of ϕ, but would add a cohesive component. This would add a pressure term independent of width represented by the first term in Eq. 2.51. This again seems to be well borne out by test results.

Reece pointed out that although Eq. 2.51 only differs from Eq. 2.46 in the effect of the width, this is sufficient to mark a radical improvement. The soil values k_c' and k_ϕ' in Eq. 2.51 are dimensionless, whereas k_c and k_ϕ in Eq. 2.46 have dimensions dependent upon n. Furthermore, Eq. 2.51 seems to allow itself to fit in with the conceivable theoretical approach. For instance, Eq. 2.51 and Terzaghi's bearing capacity equation (Eq. 2.29) have a similar form. In dry, cohesionless sand, both equations show that increasing width can cause a linear increase in pressure for the same value of z/b. On the other hand, in frictionless clay, both equations show that the increase of width has no effect on pressure for the same ratio of z/b.

Organic Terrain (Muskeg)   For a commonly encountered organic terrain (muskeg) in North America, there is a mat of living vegetation on the surface with a layer of saturated peat beneath it. A representative pressure–sinkage curve for the organic terrain obtained in the field is shown in Fig. 2.38 [2.4, 2.28, 2.34]. It can be seen that, initially, the pressure increases with an increase in sinkage. However, when the applied pressure (or load) reaches a certain level, the surface mat is broken. Since the saturated peat beneath the mat is often weaker than the mat and offers lower resistance, the pressure decreases with an increase of sinkage after the surface mat is broken, as shown in Fig. 2.38. Based on experimental observations, a mathematical model for the failure of the surface mat has been developed [2.4, 2.34]. In formulating the model, it is assumed that the organic terrain consists of two layers: one is the surface mat, and the other is the peat. The surface mat is idealized as a membrane-like structure, which means that it can only sustain a force of tension directed along the tangent to the surface and cannot offer any resistance to bending. The underlying peat is assumed to be a medium that offers a resistance proportional to its deformation in the vertical direction.

Based on this model, the pressure–sinkage relationship for an organic terrain up to the critical sinkage z_{cr}, where the breaking of the surface mat is initiated, is given by [2.4, 2.28, 2.34]

$$p = k_p z + 4 m_m z^2 / D_h \tag{2.52}$$

where p is the pressure, z is the sinkage, k_p is a stiffness parameter for the peat, m_m is a strength parameter for the surface mat, and D_h is the hydraulic diameter of the contact area (or sinkage plate), which is equal to $4A/L$, where A and L are the area and the perimeter of the contact patch, respectively.

A computerized procedure based on the least squares method has been developed to derive the values of k_p and m_m from measured data [2.4, 2.28, 2.34].

Table 2.4 shows the values of k_p, m_m, and z_{cr} for two types of organic terrain found in the Petawawa area in Ontario, Canada. It should be noted that the value

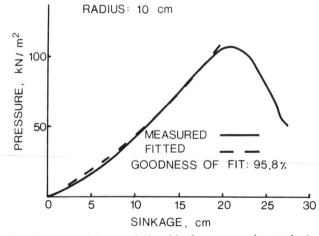

Fig. 2.38 Pressure–sinkage relationship for an organic terrain (muskeg).

TABLE 2.4 Values of k_p, m_m, and z_{cr} for Organic Terrains (Muskeg)

Terrain Type	Penetration Rate		k_p		m_m		z_{cr}	
	cm/s	in./s	kN/m³	lb/in.³	kN/m³	lb/in.³	cm	in.
Petawawa	2.5	1	407	1.5	97	0.36	20	7.9
Muskeg A	10	4	471	1.7	112	0.41	17	6.7
Petawawa	2.5	1	954	3.5	99	0.36	21	8.3
Muskeg B	10	4	1243	4.6	99	0.36	22	8.7

Source: References 2.4 and 2.28.
Note: Data obtained using a circular plate of 10 cm (4 in.) in diameter.

of k_p varies with the penetration rate. For Petawawa Muskeg A and B shown in Table 2.4, increasing the penetration rate from 2.5 to 10 cm/s (1–4 in./s), the value of k_p increases from 407 to 471 kN/m³ (1.5–1.7 lb/in.³) and from 954 to 1243 kN/m³ (3.5–4.6 lb/in.³), respectively. The increase in the apparent stiffness is probably due to the movement of water within the saturated peat, which creates an additional hydrodynamic resistance related to the penetration rate.

Snow Covers with Ice Layers   In the northern temperate zone, the snow on the ground is often subject to the "melt–freeze" cycle during the winter season. Consequently, crusts (ice layers) of significant strength form at the surface of snow covers in open areas. With subsequent snow fall on top of the crusts, snow covers containing ice layers are formed. Figure 2.39 shows the pressure–sinkage data obtained in a snow cover in the Petawawa area, Ontario, Canada. It contains a significant ice layer at a depth of approximately 10 cm (4 in.) from the surface and with a frozen ground at the base [2.4, 2.35].

It can be seen from Fig. 2.39 that the pressure first increases gradually with sinkage as the snow within a certain boundary under the plate is deformed. When the lower boundary of the deformation zone of the snow under the plate reaches the ice layer, the pressure increases rapidly with an increase of sinkage. When the applied pressure exceeds a certain level, the ice layer is broken, resulting in a sudden drop in pressure. After the ice layer is fractured, further penetration of the plate produces increasing deformation of the snow beneath the ice layer. As the plate approaches the frozen ground at the base of the snow cover, the pressure again increases rapidly, and the pressure–sinkage curve approaches an asymptote.

Based on the results shown in Fig. 2.39, the pressure–sinkage relationship, before as well as after the failure of the ice layer, may be described by an exponential function of the following form [2.4, 2.35]:

$$z = z_\omega [1 - \exp(-p/p_\omega)]$$

or

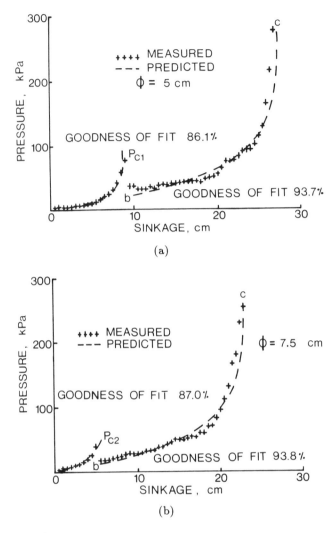

Fig. 2.39 Pressure–sinkage relationships for a snow measured using different sizes of circular plates.

$$p = p_\omega \left[-\ln \left(1 - z/z_\omega \right) \right] \tag{2.53}$$

where p is the pressure, z is the sinkage, z_w defines the asymptote of the pressure–sinkage curve, and in a first approximation may be taken as the depth of the ice layer or that of the frozen ground, and p_ω is an empirical parameter which may be taken as $1/3$ of the pressure where the sinkage z is 95% of the value of z_ω. For instance, the value of z_ω for defining the pressure–sinkage relationship in the range between 0 and 10 cm (0–4 in.) shown in Fig. 2.39(a) is approximately 9 cm (3.5 in.). The pressure p at 95% of z_ω (8.6 cm or 3.4 in.) is approximately 58.8 kPa (8.5 psi). Therefore, p_ω is equal to 19.6 kPa (2.8 psi).

A computerized procedure based on the least squares principle has been developed for deriving the values of z_ω and p_ω from measured data [2.4, 2.35].

The pressures p_{c1} and p_{c2} that cause the failure of the ice layer shown in Fig. 2.39 (a) and (b) may be predicted using a method based on the theory of plasticity [2.4, 2.35].

2.4.2 Characterization of the Response to Repetitive Loading

When an off-road vehicle is in a straight line motion, an element of the terrain under the running gear is first subject to the load applied by the leading wheel (or roadwheel in a track system). When the leading wheel has passed, the load on the terrain element is reduced. Load is reapplied as the succeeding wheel rolls over it. A terrain element is thus subject to the repetitive loading of the consecutive wheels of a multiaxle wheeled vehicle or the roadwheels of a tracked vehicle. The loading–unloading–reloading cycle continues until the rear wheel of the vehicle has passed over it. To predict the normal pressure distribution under a moving off-road vehicle and hence its sinkage and motion resistance, the response of the terrain to repetitive normal load must be measured, in addition to the pressure–sinkage relationship described above.

Figures 2.40, 2.41, and 2.42 show the response to repetitive normal load of a

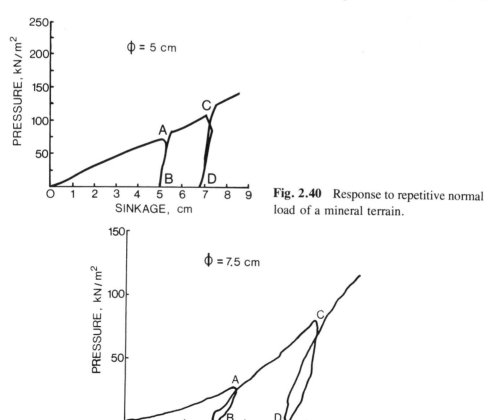

Fig. 2.40 Response to repetitive normal load of a mineral terrain.

Fig. 2.41 Response to repetitive normal load of an organic terrain (muskeg).

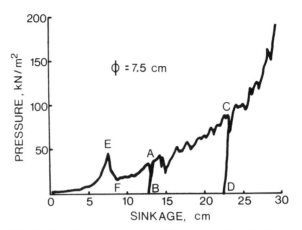

Fig. 2.42   Response to repetitive normal load of a snow.

sandy terrain, an organic terrain, and a snow-covered terrain, repsectively [2.4, 2.29]. It can be seen that the pressure initially increases with sinkage along curve *OA*. However, when the load applied to the terrain is reduced at *A*, the pressure–sinkage relationship during unloading follows line *AB*. When the load is reapplied at *B*, the pressure–sinkage relationship follows, more or less, the same path as that during unloading for the sandy terrain and the snow-covered terrain, as shown in Figs. 2.40 and 2.42, respectively. For the organic terrain, however, when the load is reapplied at *B*, the pressure–sinkage relationship follows a different path from that during unloading, as shown in Fig. 2.41. This indicates that a significant amount of hysteresis exists during the unloading–reloading cycle. When the reapplied load exceeds that at which the preceding unloading begins (point *A* in the figures), additional sinkage results. With the further increase of pressure, the pressure–sinkage relation appears to follow the continuous loading path as *AC* shown in the figures. The characteristics of the second unloading–reloading cycle which begins at point *C* are similar to those of the first one.

Based on experimental observations, for the three types of terrain described above, the pressure–sinkage relationship during both unloading and reloading, such as *AB* and *BA* shown in the figures, may be approximated by a linear function which represents the average response of the terrain [2.4]:

$$p = p_u - k_u(z_u - z) \tag{2.54}$$

where p and z are the pressure and sinkage, respectively, during unloading or reloading; p_u and z_u are the pressure and sinkage, respectively, when unloading begins; and k_u is the pressure–sinkage parameter representing the average slope of the unloading–reloading line *AB*.

It should be noted that the slope of the unloading–reloading line *AB* (i.e., k_u) represents the degree of elastic rebound during unloading. If line *AB* is vertical, then during unloading, there is no elastic rebound, and the terrain deformation is entirely plastic.

From measured data, it is found that the parameter k_u is a function of the sinkage z_u where unloading begins. As a first approximation, their relationship may be expressed by [2.4]

$$k_u = k_0 + A_u z_u \qquad (2.55)$$

where k_0 and A_u are parameters characterizing the response of the terrain to repetitive loading, and z_u is the sinkage where unloading begins.

The values of k_0 and A_u for different types of terrain are given in Table 2.5.

TABLE 2.5   Values of k_0 and A_u for Various Types of Terrain

Terrain Type	k_0		A_u	
	kN/m^3	lb/in.^{3}	kN/m^4	lb/in.^{4}
LETE Sand	0	0	503,000	47.07
Petawawa Muskeg A	123	0.46	23,540	2.20
Petawawa Muskeg B	147	0.54	29,700	2.78
Petawawa Snow A	0	0	109,600	10.26
Snow (Sweden)	0	0	87,985	8.23

Source: References 2.4 and 2.29.

2.4.3   Characterization of the Shear Stress–Shear Displacement Relationship

When a torque is applied to the tire or the sprocket of a track, shearing action is initiated on the vehicle running gear–terrain interface, as shown in Fig. 2.43. To predict vehicle thrust and associated slip, the shear stress–shear displacement relationship of the terrain is required, and this can be measured using the bevameter technique described previously. Figure 2.44 shows the shear stress–shear displacement relationships for a sand under various normal pressures obtained using different shear devices [2.37]. If the maximum shear stress of the terrain is plotted against the corresponding normal pressure, a straight line may be obtained, as shown in Fig. 2.45. The slope of the straight line determines the angle of internal shearing resistance ϕ, and the intercept of the straight line with the shear stress axis determines the apparent cohesion c of the terrain, as discussed previously.

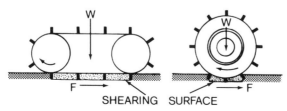

Fig. 2.43   Shearing action of a track and a wheel.

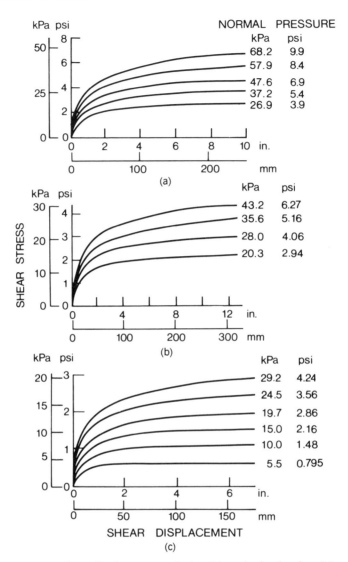

Fig. 2.44 Shear stress–shear displacement relationships obtained using (a) a shear ring with outside diameter of 22.2 cm (8.75 in.), (b) a shear ring with outside diameter of 29.8 cm (11.75 in.), and (c) a rigid track of 13.2 × 71.1 cm (5.18 × 28 in.) in sand. (Reproduced with permission of the *Journal of Agricultural Engineering Research* from reference 2.37.)

The results shown in Fig. 2.45 indicate that the shear strength determined by various shearing devices, including translational shear box, shear ring, rectangular shear plate, and rigid track, is comparable.

Based on a considerable amount of field data, it is found that there are three types of shear stress-shear displacement relationship commonly observed.

A. For loose sand, saturated clay, dry fresh snow, and most of the disturbed soils, the shear stress–shear displacement relationship exhibits characteristics shown in Fig. 2.46. The shear stress initially increases rapidly with an increase in shear displacement, and then approaches a constant value with a further increase in shear displacement. This type of shear stress–shear displacement relationship may be described by an exponential function of the following form proposed by Janosi and Hanamoto [2.3, 2.4]:

$$\tau = \tau_{max} \, (1 - e^{-j/K})$$

$$= (c + \sigma \tan \phi)(1 - e^{-j/K}) \qquad (2.56)$$

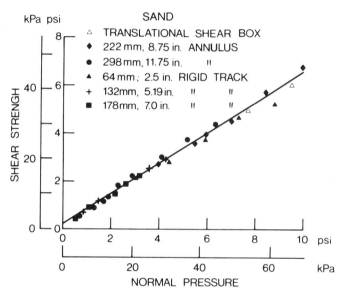

Fig. 2.45 Shear strength of sand determined by various methods. (Reproduced with permission of the *Journal of Agricultural Engineering Research* from reference 2.37.)

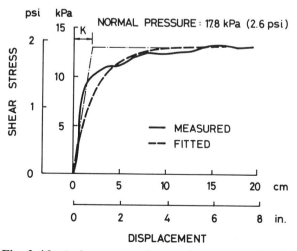

Fig. 2.46 A shear curve of a simple exponential form.

where τ is the shear stress, j is the shear displacement, c and ϕ are the cohesion and the angle of internal shearing resistance of the terrain, respectively, and K is referred to as the shear deformation modulus.

K may be considered as a measure of the magnitude of the shear displacement required to develop the maximum shear stress. The value of K determines the shape of the shear curve. Its value may be represented by the distance between the vertical axis and the point of intersection of the straight line tangent to the shear curve at the origin and the horizontal line representing the maximum shear stress τ_{max}. The slope of the shear curve at the origin can be obtained by differentiating τ with respect to j in Eq. 2.56:

$$\frac{d\tau}{dj}\bigg|_{j=0} = \frac{\tau_{max}}{K} e^{-j/K}\bigg|_{j=0} = \frac{\tau_{max}}{K} \tag{2.57}$$

Thus, the value of K can be determined from the slope of the shear curve at the origin and τ_{max}.

The value of K may also be taken as $1/3$ of the shear displacement where the shear stress τ is 95% of the maximum shear stress τ_{max}.

In practice, shear curves, particularly those for natural terrains obtained in the field, are not smooth, as shown in Fig. 2.46. The optimum value of K that minimizes the overall error in fitting Eq. 2.56 to the measured curve may be obtained from the following equation, based on the weighted least squares principle [2.4, 2.31, 2.36]:

$$K = -\frac{\sum(1 - \tau/\tau_{max})^2 j^2}{\sum(1 - \tau/\tau_{max})^2 j \left[\ln\left(1 - \tau/\tau_{max}\right)\right]} \tag{2.58}$$

where τ_{max} is the measured maximum shear stress, and τ and j are the measured shear stress and the corresponding shear displacement, respectively.

Based on the experimental data collected, the value of K varies from 1 cm (0.4 in.) for firm sandy terrain to 2.5 cm (1 in.) for loose sand, and is approximately 0.6 cm (1/4 in.) for clay at maximum compaction [2.4, 2.33]. For undisturbed, fresh snow, the value of K varies in the range from 2.5 to 5 cm (1–2 in.) [2.32]. Available experimental results also suggest that the value of K may be a function of normal pressure. However, their precise relationship is yet to be determined.

B. For organic terrain (muskeg) with a mat of living vegetation on the surface and saturated peat beneath it, the shear stress–shear displacement relationship exhibits characteristics shown in Fig. 2.47. It can be seen that the shear stress initially increases rapidly with the increase of shear displacement, and reaches a "hump" of maximum shear stress where the "shear-off" of the surface mat is initiated. With a further increase of shear displacement, the shear stress continually decreases, as the peat beneath the mat offers a lower shearing resistance than the surface mat. This type of shearing behavior may be characterized by the following equation [2.4, 2.28, 2.34, 2.36]:

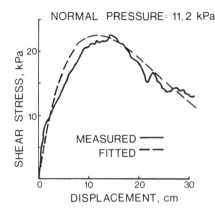

Fig. 2.47 A shear curve exhibiting a peak and decreasing residual shear stress.

$$\tau = \tau_{\max} \, (j/K_\omega) \exp (1 - j/K_\omega) \qquad (2.59)$$

where K_ω is the shear displacement where the maximum shear stress $\tau_{\max}$ occurs.

It should be mentioned that in many cases, the values of $\tau_{\max}$ and K_ω may be directly identified from the measured shear curve. However, in some cases, the value of K_ω may not be distinct or easy to identify. Under these circumstances, the optimum value of K_ω that minimizes the overall error in fitting Eq. 2.59 to the measured curve may be obtained by solving the following equation which is derived from the weighted least squares principle [2.4, 2.28, 2.34]:

$$\Sigma (\tau/\tau_{\max})^2 \, [\ln (\tau/\tau_{\max}) - (1 + \ln (j/K_\omega) - j/K_\omega)] \, (K_\omega - j) = 0 \quad (2.60)$$

A computerized procedure has been developed to derive the optimum value of K_ω from measured data [2.4, 2.28, 2.34].

Based on the experimental data collected, the value of K_ω varies from 14.4 to 16.4 cm (5.7–6.5 in.) for various types of organic terrain tested in the Petawawa area, Ontario, Canada [2.4, 2.28, 2.34].

C. For compact sand, silt and loam, and frozen snow, they may exhibit shearing characteristics shown in Fig. 2.48. It can be seen that the shear stress initially increases rapidly and reaches a "hump" of maximum shear stress at a particular shear displacement. However, with a further increase in shear displacement, the shear stress decreases and approaches a more or less constant residual value. This type of shearing behavior may be characterized by the following function proposed by Wong [2.4, 2.36]:

$$\tau = \tau_{\max} \, K_r \, \{1 + [1/(K_r(1 - 1/e)) - 1] \exp (1 - j/K_\omega)\}$$
$$\cdot \, [1 - \exp (-j/K_\omega)] \qquad (2.61)$$

where K_r is the ratio of the residual shear stress τ_r to the maximum shear stress $\tau_{\max}$, and K_ω is the shear displacement where the maximum shear stress $\tau_{\max}$ occurs.

It should be noted that in many cases, the values of K_r, K_ω, and $\tau_{\max}$ may

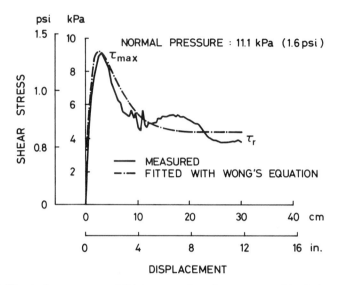

Fig. 2.48   A shear curve exhibiting a peak and constant residual shear stress.

be directly identified from the measured shear curve. However, in some cases, their values are not distinct or easy to identify. A computerized procedure for determining the optimum values of K_r, K_ω, and τ_{max} for a given measured shear curve has been developed, which is based on the least squares principle [2.4, 2.36].

Based on the field data collected, for various types of firm, mineral terrain, the values of K_ω and K_r vary from 2.7 to 7.1 cm (1.1–2.8 in.) and from 0.38 to 0.72, respectively. For a firm snow, the values of K_ω and K_r are approximately 2.2 cm (0.9 in.) and 0.66, respectively.

It is interesting to note that the tractive (braking) effort–longitudinal slip (skid) relationships for pneumatic tires on road surfaces described in Chapter 1 exhibit characteristics similar to those of the shear stress–shear displacement relationship shown in Fig. 2.48. The peak value of tractive effort $\mu_p W$ and the sliding value $\mu_s W$ shown in Fig. 1.16 are analogous to τ_{max} and τ_r shown in Fig. 2.48, respectively.

It should be mentioned that during shear tests, as a shear ring is being rotated or a rectangular shear plate is being moved horizontally, additional sinkage results. This additional sinkage due to shear loading (or shear displacement) is usually referred to as slip sinkage. This means that in operation, the total sinkage of a vehicle consists of two parts: one is due to the static normal load, and the other is due to the slip of the running gear. Figure 2.49 shows the relationships between sinkage and shear displacement under various normal pressures on different types of terrain [2.33]. It can be seen that under a given normal pressure, the sinkage of the shear plate increases continually with the increase of shear displacement. To accurately predict the total sinkage of a vehicle in operation, the phenomenon of slip sinkage should be taken into account.

It should also be noted that when an all-wheel-drive vehicle is in a straight line motion, an element of the terrain under the vehicle is subject to the repetitive

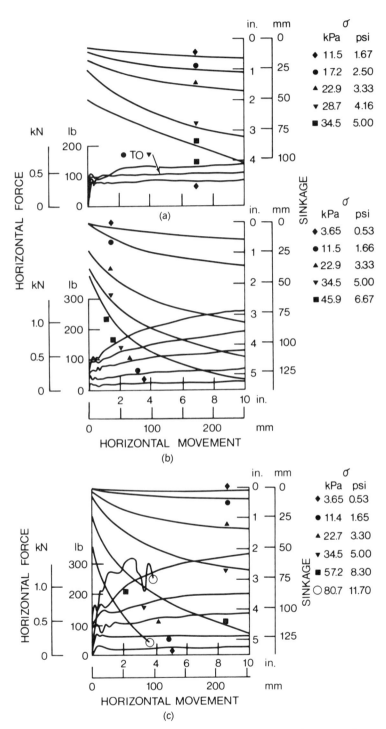

Fig. 2.49 Slip–sinkage phenomenon in three types of soil. (a) Clay, $\phi = 0$, $c = 6.9$ kPa (1.0 psi); (b) dry sand, $\phi = 32$, $c = 0$; (c) wet sand, $\phi = 32°$, $c = 0.69$ kPa (0.1 psi). (Reproduced with permission of the Council of the Institution of Mechanical Engineers from reference 2.33.)

shearing of consecutive tires. To realistically predict the shear stress distribution on the vehicle running gear–terrain interface and the thrust developed by the vehicle, the response of the terrain to repetitive shear loading should be measured. Figure 2.50 shows the response of a frictional terrain (a dry sand) to repetitive shearing under a constant normal load [2.4, 2.29]. It is shown that when the shear load is reduced from B to zero and is then reapplied at C, the shear stress–shear displacement relationship during reshearing, such as CDE, is similar to that when the terrain is being sheared in its virgin state, such as OAB. This means that when reshearing takes place after the completion of a loading–unloading cycle, the shear stress does not instantaneously reach its maximum value for a given normal pressure. Rather, a certain amount of additional shear displacement must take place before the maximum shear stress can be developed, similar to that when the terrain is being sheared in its virgin state.

Results of an investigation by Keira [2.38] on the shearing force developed beneath a rectangular shear plate under a cyclic normal load lead to a similar conclusion. Figure 2.51 shows the variation of the shearing force beneath a rectangular shear plate on a dry sand subject to a vertical harmonic load at a frequency of 10.3 Hz. It indicates that during the loading portion of each cycle, the shear force does not reach its maximum value instantaneously ($S_{max} = P \tan \phi$, where P is the instantaneous value of the normal load and ϕ is the angle of shearing resistance). This is demonstrated by the fact that the slope of the normal load curve

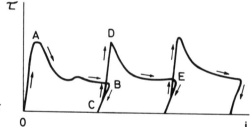

Fig. 2.50 Response to repetitive shear loading of a dry sand.

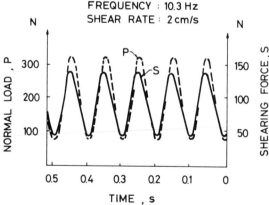

Fig. 2.51 Development of shear force under a rectangular shear plate subject to cyclic normal load on a dry sand. (Reproduced from reference 2.38.)

is steeper than that of the shearing force curve. During the unloading portion of the cycle, however, the shearing force decreases in proportion to the instantaneous value of the normal load.

The response of the terrain under repetitive shear loading and its shearing behavior under cyclic normal loads described above have a significant effect on the development of the shear stress on the vehicle running gear–terrain interface. Figure 2.52 (b) illustrates the development of the shear stress under a track when the response of the terrain to repetitive shear loading is taken into account for an idealized case, as compared with that when it is not taken into account, shown in Fig. 2.52 (a). Since the tractive effort developed by a track is the summation of the shear stress over the entire contact area, it can be seen that when the repetitive shearing characteristics of the terrain are taken into consideration, the predicted total tractive effort of the vehicle at a given slip may be considerably lower than that when they are not taken into account, particularly at low slips.

The response of the terrain to repetitive normal and shear loading has been taken into consideration in the development of the computer-aided methods for predicting and evaluating off-road vehicle performance, which will be discussed later in this chapter. It will be shown that predictions based on the computer-aided methods are in closer agreement with vehicle test data obtained in the field than other methods previously developed.

2.5 METHODS FOR PARAMETRIC ANALYSIS OF TRACKED VEHICLE PERFORMANCE

The track and the wheel constitute two basic forms of running gear for off-road vehicles. The study of the mechanics of the track and of the wheel over unprepared terrain is, therefore, of fundamental importance. The objective is to establish reliable methods for predicting their performance in relation to their design parameters and terrain characteristics.

One of the earlier methods for parametric analysis of track system performance was developed by Bekker [2.1–2.3]. In this method, it is assumed that the track in contact with the terrain is similar to a rigid footing. Making use of the pressure–

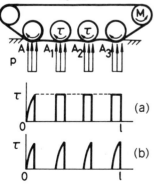

Fig. 2.52 Development of shear stress under a track on a frictional terrain predicted by (a) the conventional method and (b) the improved method, taking into account the response of terrain to repetitive shear loading.

sinkage relationship of the terrain measured by the bevameter technique described in the previous section, track sinkage and motion resistance due to compacting the terrain are predicted. Based on the shear stress–shear displacement relationship and the shear strength of the terrain, the thrust–slip relationship and the maximum traction of a track are determined.

2.5.1 Motion Resistance of a Track

As mentioned above, in the method developed by Bekker, the track is assumed to be similar to a rigid footing. The normal reaction exerted on the track by the terrain can then be equated to that beneath a sinkage plate at the same depth in a pressure-sinkage test. If the center of gravity of the vehicle is located at the midpoint of the track contact area, the normal pressure distribution may be assumed to be uniform, as shown in Fig. 2.32. On the other hand, if the center of gravity of the vehicle is located ahead of or behind the midpoint of the track contact area, a sinkage distribution of trapezoidal form may be assumed.

Using the pressure–sinkage equation proposed by Bekker (Eq. 2.46), for a track with uniform contact pressure, the sinkage z_0 is given by

$$z_0 = \left(\frac{p}{k_c/b + k_\phi} \right)^{1/n} = \left(\frac{W/bl}{k_c/b + k_\phi} \right)^{1/n} \tag{2.62}$$

where p is the normal pressure, W is the normal load on the track, and b and l are the width and length of the track in contact with the terrain, respectively.

The work done in compacting the terrain and making a rut of width b, length l, and depth z_0 is given by

$$\text{Work} = bl \int_0^{z_0} p\,dz$$

$$= bl \int_0^{z_0} (k_c/b + k_\phi)\, z^n dz$$

$$= bl\, (k_c/b + k_\phi) \left(\frac{z_0^{n+1}}{n+1} \right) \tag{2.63}$$

Substituting for z_0 from Eq. 2.62 yields

$$\text{Work} = \frac{bl}{(n+1)(k_c/b + k_\phi)^{1/n}} \left(\frac{W}{bl} \right)^{(n+1)/n} \tag{2.64}$$

If the track is pulled a distance l in the horizontal direction, the work done by the towing force, which is equal to the magnitude of the motion resistance due to terrain compaction R_c, can be equated to the vertical work done in making a rut of length l, as expressed by Eq. 2.64:

$$R_c l = \frac{bl}{(n+1)\,(k_c/b + k_\phi)^{1/n}} \left(\frac{W}{bl}\right)^{(n+1)/n}$$

and

$$R_c = \frac{b}{(n+1)\,(k_c/b + k_\phi)^{(1/n)}} \left(\frac{W}{bl}\right)^{(n+1)/n}$$

$$= \frac{1}{(n+1)b^{1/n}\,(k_c/b + k_\phi)^{(1/n)}} \left(\frac{W}{l}\right)^{(n+1)/n} \tag{2.65}$$

This is the equation for calculating the motion resistance due to terrain compaction of a track with uniform pressure distribution, based on Bekker's pressure–sinkage relationship. Expressions for motion resistance based on other pressure–sinkage relationships described in Section 2.4 may be derived in a similar way.

On soft terrain where vehicle sinkage is significant, Bekker suggested that a bulldozing resistance acting in the front of the track should be taken into account, in addition to the compaction resistance R_c. The bulldozing resistance may be calculated using the earth pressure theory described in Section 2.2 [2.2, 2.3].

The idealization of a track as a rigid footing may not be unreasonable for tracked vehicles with a relatively long track pitch and a large number of small diameter roadwheels, commonly used in agriculture and construction industry at low speeds. For this type of vehicle, the normal pressure usually does not exhibit pronounced peaks under the roadwheels. However, this idealization is not realistic for tracked vehicles designed for high-speed operations, such as military tracked vehicles. To achieve high operating speeds, it is necessary to have relatively short track pitch to minimize speed fluctuation and the associated vibrations. Furthermore, to have adequate ability to ride over large obstacles, large roadwheels with sufficient suspension travel are required. As a result of using a relatively small number (typically 5–7) of large diameter roadwheels and a short track pitch, the normal pressure distribution under the track is nonuniform, and significant pressure peaks are observed under the roadwheels. Figure 2.53 shows the normal pressure distributions measured at a depth of 0.23 m (9 in.) below the terrain surface under tracked vehicles with different design features [2.26]. It can be seen that for military tracked vehicles with a relatively small number of large diameter roadwheels and having a short track pitch, the peak pressure is much higher than the average ground pressure. For this type of tracked vehicle, Eqs. 2.62 and 2.65 will not yield realistic predictions of vehicle sinkage and motion resistance. A new method has recently been developed for predicting the performance of tracked vehicles with large diameter roadwheels and short track pitch [2.4, 2.29, 2.39–2.42]. This will be discussed later in this chapter.

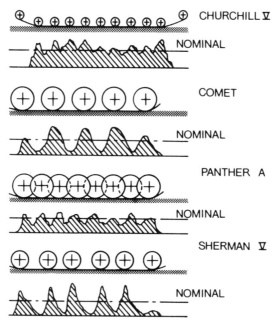

Fig. 2.53 Measured normal pressure distributions at a depth of 23 cm (9 in.) below the soil surface under various tracked vehicles. (Reproduced with permission from reference 2.26.)

2.5.2   Tractive Effort and Slip of a Track

The tractive effort of a track is produced by the shearing of the terrain, as shown in Fig. 2.43. The maximum tractive effort F_{max} that can be developed by a track is determined by the shear strength of the terrain τ_{max} and the contact area A:

$$F_{max} = A\tau_{max}$$

$$= A(c + p \tan \phi)$$

$$= Ac + W \tan \phi \qquad (2.66)$$

where A is the contact area of the track, W is the normal load, and c and ϕ are the apparent cohesion and the angle of internal shearing resistance of the terrain, respectively. It can be seen that in frictional soil, such as dry sand, the cohesion c is negligible; the maximum tractive effort, therefore, depends on the vehicle weight. The heavier the vehicle, the higher the tractive effort it can develop. The dimensions of the track do not affect the maximum tractive effort. For dry sand, the angle of internal shearing resistance could be as high as 35°. The maximum tractive effort of a vehicle on dry sand can therefore be expected to be approximately 70% of the vehicle weight. In cohesive soil, such as saturated clay, the value of ϕ is low, the maximum tractive effort primarily depends on the contact area of the track, and the weight has little effect. Thus, the dimensions of the track are crucial in this case; the larger the contact area, the higher the thrust the track can develop.

It should be noted that Eq. 2.66 can only be used for predicting the maximum tractive effort of a tracked vehicle. In vehicle performance evaluation, it is, however, desirable to determine the variation of thrust with track slip over the full operating range. To predict the relationship between thrust and slip, it is necessary to examine the development of shear displacement beneath a track since shear stress is a function of shear displacement. The shear displacement at various points beneath a track is shown schematically in Fig. 2.54 [2.1]. At point 1, the grouser is just coming into contact with the terrain; it cannot develop the same shear displacement as the other grousers 2, 3, 4, and 5 since they have been shearing the terrain for a certain period of time. The amount of horizontal shear displacement j increases along the contact length, and reaches its maximum value at the rear of the contact area. To examine the development of shear displacement beneath a track quantitatively, the slip of a track i has to be defined first:

$$i = 1 - \frac{V}{r\omega} = 1 - \frac{V}{V_t} = \frac{V_t - V}{V_t} = \frac{V_j}{V_t} \tag{2.67}$$

where V is the actual forward speed of the track, V_t is the theoretical speed which can be determined from the angular speed ω and the radius r of the pitch circle of the sprocket, and V_j is the speed of slip of the track with reference to the ground. When the vehicle is slipping, V_j will be in the direction opposite that of vehicle motion. On the other hand, when the vehicle is skidding, V_j will be in the same direction as that of vehicle motion. It should be noted that the definition for the slip of a track given by Eq. 2.67 is the same as that of a tire given by Eq. 1.5. Since the track cannot stretch, the speed of slip V_j is the same for every point of the track in contact with the terrain. The shear displacement j at a point located at a distance x from the front of the contact area (Fig. 2.55) can be determined by

$$j = V_j t \tag{2.68}$$

where t is the contact time of the point in question with the terrain and is equal to x/V_t. Rearranging Eq. 2.68, the expression for shear displacement j becomes

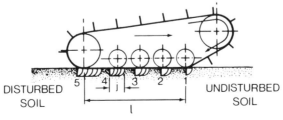

Fig. 2.54 Development of shear displacement under a track. (From *Theory of Land Locomotion* by M.G. Bekker, copyright © by the University of Michigan, 1956, reproduced with permission of the University of Michigan Press.)

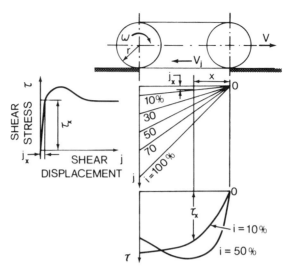

Fig. 2.55 Distribution of shear stress under a track.

$$j = \frac{V_j x}{V_t} = ix \tag{2.69}$$

This indicates that the shear displacement beneath a flat track increases linearly from the front to the rear of the contact area, as shown in Fig. 2.55. Since the development of shear stress is related to shear displacement as discussed previously, the shear stress distribution along the contact area can be found. For instance, to determine the shear stress developed at a point located at a distance x from the front of the contact area, the shear displacement at that point should first be calculated using Eq. 2.69. Making use of the shear stress–shear displacement relationships obtained from shear tests, such as those shown in Figs. 2.46, 2.47, and 2.48, or from the semi-empirical equations, such as Eqs. 2.56, 2.59, and 2.61, the shear stress at that point can then be determined. As an example, the shear stress distribution beneath a track on a particular type of terrain at a given slip is shown in Fig. 2.55. The total tractive effort developed by a track at a particular slip is represented by the area beneath the shear stress curve in Fig. 2.55. Alternatively, if Eq. 2.56 is used to describe the shear stress–shear displacement relationship, the total tractive effort of a track can be calculated as follows:

$$F = b \int_0^l \tau dx$$

$$= b \int_0^l (c + p \tan \phi)(1 - e^{-j/K})\, dx \tag{2.70}$$

The above equation indicates that the tractive effort of a track depends on the normal pressure distribution over the contact area, among other factors. For a uniform normal pressure distribution, p is independent of x and equal to W/bl. In this case, the total tractive effort of a track is determined by

$$F = b \int_0^l \left(c + \frac{W}{bl} \tan \phi \right) (1 - e^{-ix/K}) \, dx$$

$$= (Ac + W \tan \phi) \left[1 - \frac{K}{il} (1 - e^{-il/K}) \right] \qquad (2.71)$$

Equation 2.71 expresses the functional relationship among tractive effort, vehicle design parameters, terrain values, and track slip. If the slip is 100%, then Eqs. 2.71 and 2.66 are partically identical. Among the vehicle design parameters, the contact length of the track deserves special attention. Consider two tracked vehicles with identical ground contact area and normal load (i.e., $A_1 = A_2$ and $W_1 = W_2$) operating over the same terrain. However, the track length of one vehicle is twice that of the other (i.e., $l_1 = 2l_2$). To keep the total contact area the same, the width b_1 of the track with length l_1 is half that of the other (i.e., $b_1 = 0.5b_2$). If these two tracked vehicles are to develop the same tractive effort, then from Eq. 2.71, the slip of the vehicle with contact length l_1 will be half that of the other with contact length l_2. It may be concluded, therefore, that in general, a shorter track will slip more than a longer one, if they are to develop the same tractive effort.

The above analysis is applicable to predicting the tractive effort of a track with uniform normal pressure distribution. In practice, the normal pressure distribution is seldom uniform, as mentioned previously. It is, therefore, of interest to assess the effect of normal pressure distribution on the tractive effort developed by a track. This problem has been investigated by Wills, among others [2.37]. Consider the case of the multipeak sinusoidal pressure distribution described by

$$p = \frac{W}{bl} \left(1 + \cos \frac{2n\pi x}{l} \right) \qquad (2.72)$$

where n is the number of periods, as shown in Fig. 2.56. In a frictional soil, the shear stress developed along the contact length can be expressed by

$$\tau = \frac{W}{bl} \tan \phi \left(1 + \cos \frac{2n\pi x}{l} \right) (1 - e^{-ix/K}) \qquad (2.73)$$

and hence the tractive effort is given by

$$F = b \int_0^l \frac{W}{bl} \tan \phi \left(1 + \cos \frac{2n\pi x}{l} \right) (1 - e^{ix/K}) \, dx$$

$$= W \tan \phi \left[1 + \frac{K}{il} (e^{-il/K} - 1) + \frac{K (e^{-il/K} - 1)}{il (1 + 4n^2 K^2 \pi^2 / i^2 l^2)} \right] \qquad (2.74)$$

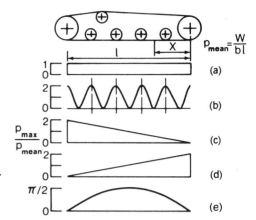

Fig. 2.56 Various types of idealized normal pressure distribution under a track. (Reproduced with permission of the *Journal of Agricultural Engineering Research* from reference 2.37.)

The tractive effort of a track with other types of normal pressure distribution can be evaluated in a similar way. In the case of normal pressure increasing linearly from front to rear [i.e., $p = 2(W/bl)(x/l)$] as shown in Fig. 2.56, the tractive effort of a track in a frictional soil is given by

$$F = W \tan \phi \left[1 - 2 \left(\frac{K}{il} \right)^2 \left(1 - e^{-il/K} - \frac{il}{K} e^{-il/K} \right) \right] \qquad (2.75)$$

In the case of normal pressure increasing linearly from rear to front [i.e., $p = 2(W/bl)(l - x)/l$], as shown in Fig. 2.56, the tractive effort in a frictional soil is calculated by

$$F = 2W \tan \phi \left[1 - \frac{K}{il} (1 - e^{-il/K}) \right]$$

$$- W \tan \phi \left[1 - 2 \left(\frac{K}{il} \right)^2 \left(1 - e^{-il/K} - \frac{il}{K} e^{-il/K} \right) \right] \qquad (2.76)$$

In the case of sinusoidal distribution with maximum pressure at the center and zero pressure at the front and rear end [i.e., $p = (W/bl)(\pi/2) \sin(\pi x/l)$], as shown in Fig. 2.56, the tractive effort in a frictional soil is determined by

$$F = W \tan \phi \left[1 - \frac{e^{-il/K} + 1}{2(1 + i^2 l^2 / \pi^2 K^2)} \right] \qquad (2.77)$$

Figure 2.57 shows the variation of the tractive effort with slip of a track with various types of normal pressure distribution discussed above. It can be seen that the normal pressure distribution has a noticeable effect on the development of tractive effort, particularly at low slips.

Example 2.3. Two tracked vehicles with the same gross weight of 135 kN (30,350 lb) travel over a terrain, which is characterized by $n = 1.6$, $k_c = 4.37$ kN/m$^{2.6}$ (0.07 lb/in.$^{2.6}$), $k_\phi = 196.72$ kN/m$^{3.6}$ (0.08 lb/in.$^{3.6}$), $K = 5$ cm (2 in.), $c =$

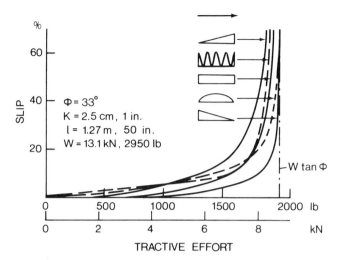

Fig. 2.57 Effect of normal pressure distribution on the tractive effort–slip relationship of a track on sand. (Reproduced with permission of the *Journal of Agricultural Engineering Research* from reference 2.37.)

1.0 kPa (0.15 psi), and $\phi = 19.7°$. Both vehicles have the same ground contact area of 7.2 m² (77.46 ft²). However, the width b and contact length l of the tracks of the two vehicles are not the same. For vehicle A, $b = 1$ m (3.28 ft) and $l = 3.6$ m (11.8 ft), and for vehicle B, $b = 0.8$ m (2.62 ft) and $l = 4.5$ m (14.76 ft). Estimate the motion resistance due to terrain compaction and the thrust–slip characteristics of these two vehicles. In the calculations, uniform ground contact pressure may be assumed.

Solution.

A. Motion resistance of vehicle A

Sinkage:

$$z_0 = \left(\frac{p}{k_c/b + k_\phi} \right)^{1/n} = \left(\frac{135.0/7.2}{4.37/1 + 196.72} \right)^{0.625}$$

$$= 0.227 \text{ m (9 in.)}$$

Compaction resistance:

$$R_c = 2b\,(k_c/b + k_\phi)\,\frac{z_0^{n+1}}{n+1}$$

$$= \frac{2 \times 1 \times 201.09 \times 0.227^{2.6}}{2.6}$$

$$= 3.28 \text{ kN (738 lb)}$$

B. Motion resistance of vehicle B

Sinkage:

TABLE 2.6 Thrust–Slip Relationships for Vehicles A and B

Vehicle Type	Slip $i\%$	5	10	20	40	60	80
A	Thrust kN	40.54	47.82	51.68	53.62	54.25	54.57
	lb	9114	10,750	11,618	12,054	12,196	12,268
B	Thrust kN	43.32	49.37	52.46	54.0	54.51	54.77
	lb	9739	11,099	11,794	12,140	12,254	12,313

$$z_0 = 0.226 \text{ m (9 in.)}$$

Compaction resistance:

$$R_c = 2.60 \text{ kN (585 lb)}$$

C. Thrust–slip characteristics of vehicle A

$$F = (2blc + W \tan \phi) \left[1 - \frac{K}{il} (1 - e^{-il/K}) \right]$$

$$= F_{\max} \left[1 - \frac{K}{il} (1 - e^{-il/K}) \right]$$

$$F_{\max} = 2 \times 1 \times 3.6 \times 1 + 135 \times 0.358$$

$$= 7.2 + 48.34 = 55.54 \text{ kN (12,486 lb)}$$

The thrust of vehicle A at various slips is given in Table 2.6.

D. Thrust–slip characteristics of vehicle B

The maximum thrust of vehicle B will be the same as vehicle A since the contact area and the weight of the two vehicles are identical. The thrust–slip relationship will, however, be different, as the contact lengths of the two vehicles are not the same. The thrust of vehicle B at various slips is given in Table 2.6.

It can be seen that the performance of vehicle B is somewhat better than that of vehicle A in the terrain specified. For instance, the compaction resistance of vehicle B is approximately 20.7% lower than that of vehicle A. At 10% slip, the thrust of vehicle B is approximately 3.2% higher than that of vehicle A.

2.6 COMPUTER-AIDED METHODS FOR EVALUATING TRACKED VEHICLE PERFORMANCE

The method for parametric analysis of tracked vehicle performance described in the previous section is based on the simplifying assumption that a track in contact with the terrain is equivalent to a rigid footing. Consequently, it will not yield realistic predictions of the performance of tracked vehicles with a relatively small number of large diameter roadwheels and having a short track pitch, designed for high-speed operations. A comprehensive method has recently been developed for parametric analysis of the performance of this type of tracked vehicle [2.4, 2.29, 2.39–2.42]. It takes into account all major design parameters of the vehicle, including the track system configuration, number of roadwheels, dimensions of roadwheels, roadwheel spacing, track dimensions and geometry, initial track tension, track longitudinal elasticity, suspension characteristics, location of the center of gravity, arrangements for the sprockets, idlers, and supporting rollers, and vehicle hull (belly) shape (for the analysis of vehicle hull–terrain interaction when the hull is in contact with the terrain surface). All pertinent terrain characteristics, such as the pressure–sinkage and shearing characteristics and the response to repetitive loading, are taken into consideration. The prediction procedures have been computerized, and a user-friendly computer-aided method (computer simulation model) for the performance and design evaluation of tracked vehicles has been developed [2.4, 2.29, 2.39–2.42].

The computer-aided method can be used to predict the normal and shear stress distributions on the track–terrain interface, and the external motion resistance, tractive effort (thrust), drawbar pull, and tractive efficiency of the vehicle as functions of track slip. The basic features of the method have been validated by means of full-scale vehicle tests on various types of terrain, including mineral terrain, organic terrain, and snow.

The method is particularly suited for the evaluation of competing designs, for the optimization of design parameters, and for the selection of vehicle candidates for a given mission and environment. It has been gaining increasingly wide acceptance in industry and governmental agencies in North America, Europe, and Asia.

The basic approach to the development of the computer-aided method is outlined in this section, and the details are given in references [2.4, 2.29, 2.39–2.42].

2.6.1 Approach to the Prediction of Normal Pressure Distribution Under a Track

When a tracked vehicle rests on a hard surface, the track lies flat on the ground. In contrast, when the vehicle travels over a deformable terrain, the normal load applied through the track system causes the terrain to deform. The track segments between the roadwheels take up load, and as a result, they deflect and have the form of a curve. The actual length of the track in contact with the terrain between the front and rear roadwheels increases in comparison with that when the track rests on a firm ground. This causes a reduction in the sag of the top run of the track and a change in track tension. Furthermore, the passage of each consecutive roadwheel will usually cause additional sinkage, and the vehicle may assume a nose-up attitude. It should also be noted that when a tracked vehicle travels in a straight line, an element of terrain is subject to the repetitive loading of consecutive roadwheels. To predict the normal pressure distribution under a moving tracked vehicle, the pressure–sinkage relationship and the response to repetitive loading of the terrain should be taken into consideration.

When the terrain characteristics are known or specified, the prediction of the normal pressure distribution is reduced to the determination of the shape of the deflected track in contact with the terrain. To achieve this, the mechanics of track–terrain interaction is analyzed.

In the analysis, the track is assumed to be equivalent to a flexible belt. This assumption is considered to be reasonable for rubber-belt tracks and for link tracks with a relatively short track pitch designed for high-speed operations, such as those commonly used in military tracked vehicles. The longitudinal elasticity of the track and the elongation of the track under tension are taken into account in the analysis. Over highly compressible terrain, such as deep snow, track sinkage may be greater than the ground clearance of the vehicle. If this occurs, the hull (belly) of the vehicle will be in contact with the terrain surface and will support part of the vehicle weight. This will reduce the load carried by the tracks and will adversely affect the traction of the vehicle. Furthermore, the contact of the hull with the terrain will give rise to an additional drag component. The characteristics of vehicle hull–terrain interaction have been taken into consideration. In the latest version of the computer-aided method, the characteristics of the independent suspension of the roadwheels are fully taken into account as well. Torsion bar, hydropneumatic, and other types of independent suspension can be realistically simulated.

A schematic of a track–roadwheel system traveling on a deformable terrain under steady-state conditions is shown in Fig. 2.58. The deflected track in contact with the terrain may be divided into two sections [Fig. 2.58 (b)]: one in contact with both the roadwheel and the terrain (such as segments AC and FH), and the other in contact with the terrain only (such as segment CF). The shape of the track

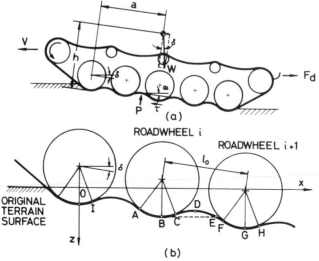

Fig. 2.58 Geometry of a flexible track system in contact with a deformable terrain.

segment in contact with the roadwheel, such as AC, is defined by the shape of the roadwheel, whereas the shape of the track segment in contact with the terrain only, such as CF, is determined by the track tension, roadwheel spacing, and the pressure–sinkage relationship of the terrain.

Along segment AB, the pressure exerted on the terrain increases from A to B. From B to D, the pressure decreases, corresponding to the unloading portion of the repetitive loading cycle shown in Figs. 2.40–2.42. Along segment DE, the pressure increases again, corresponding to the reloading portion of the repetitive loading cycle shown in Figs. 2.40–2.42. Beyond point E, which is at the same level as point B, the sinkage is higher than that at B. As a result, the pressure increases, and the sinkage of the succeeding roadwheel will be greater than that of the preceding roadwheel. Beyond point G, the pressure exerted on the terrain decreases again, and another unloading–reloading cycle begins.

Based on the understanding of the physical nature of track–terrain interaction described above, a set of equations for the equilibrium of forces and moments acting on the track system, including the independently suspended roadwheels, and for the evaluation of the overall track length are derived. They establish the relationship between the shape of the deflected track in contact with the terrain and vehicle design parameters and terrain characteristics. The solution to this set of equations defines the sinkage of the roadwheels, the inclination of the vehicle body, the track tension, and the track shape in contact with the terrain. From these, the normal pressure distribution under a moving tracked vehicle can be predicted.

2.6.2 Approach to the Prediction of Shear Stress Distribution Under a Track

The tractive performance of a tracked vehicle is closely related to both its normal pressure and shear stress distributions on the track–terrain interface. To predict the shear stress distribution under a track, the shear stress–shear displacement relationship, the shear strength and the response to repetitive shear loading of the terrain, as discussed in Section 2.4, are used as input. Over a given terrain, the shear stress at a given point on the track–terrain interface is a function of the shear displacement, measured from the point where shearing (or reshearing) begins, and the normal pressure at that point. The shear displacement developed under a flexible track, shown in Fig. 2.59, may be determined from the analysis of the slip velocity V_j similar to that described in Section 2.5. The slip velocity V_j of a point P on a flexible track relative to the terrain surface is the tangential component of the absolute velocity V_a shown in Fig. 2.59. The magnitude of the slip velocity V_j is expressed by

$$V_j = V_t - V \cos \alpha$$

$$= r\omega - r\omega (1 - i) \cos \alpha$$

$$= r\omega [1 - (1 - i) \cos \alpha] \qquad (2.78)$$

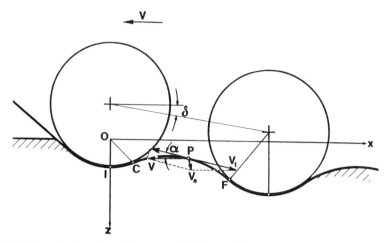

Fig. 2.59 Slip velocity of a point on a flexible track in contact with a deformable terrain.

where r and ω are the pitch radius and angular speed of the sprocket, respectively, i is the slip of the track, α is the angle between the tangent to the track at point P and the horizontal, V_t is the theoretical speed of the vehicle (i.e., $V_t = r\omega$), and V is the actual forward speed of the vehicle.

The shear displacement j along the track–terrain interface is given by

$$j = \int_0^t r\omega \, [1 - (1 - i) \cos \alpha] \, dt$$

$$= \int_0^l r\omega \, [1 - (1 - i) \cos \alpha] \, \frac{dl}{r\omega}$$

$$= l - (1 - i) \, x \tag{2.79}$$

where l is the distance along the track between point P and the point where shearing (or reshearing) begins, and x is the corresponding horizontal distance between point P and the initial shearing (or reshearing) point.

If the shear stress–shear displacement relationship of the terrain is described by Eq. 2.56, then the shear stress distribution may be expressed by

$$\tau(x) = [c + p(x) \tan \phi] \left\{ 1 - \exp \left[- \left(\frac{l - (1 - i) \, x}{K} \right) \right] \right\} \tag{2.80}$$

where $p(x)$ is the normal pressure on the track, which is a function of x.

In using Eq. 2.80 to predict the shear stress distribution under a flexible track, the response to repetitive shear loading of the terrain discussed in Section 2.4 and the shearing characteristics of the terrain under varying normal pressure should be taken into consideration [2.4, 2.29].

2.6.3 Prediction of Motion Resistance and Drawbar Pull as Functions of Track Slip

When the normal pressure and shear stress distributions under a tracked vehicle at a given slip have been determined, the tractive performance of the vehicle can be predicted. The tractive performance of an off-road vehicle is usually characterized by its motion resistance, tractive effort, and drawbar pull (the difference between the tractive effort and motion resistance) as functions of slip.

The external motion resistance R_t of the track can be determined from the horizontal component of the normal pressure acting on the track in contact with the terrain. For a vehicle with two tracks, R_t is given by

$$R_t = 2b \int_0^{l_t} p \sin \alpha dl \tag{2.81}$$

where b is the contact width of the track, l_t is the contact length of the track, p is the normal pressure, and α is the angle between a track element and the horizontal.

If the track sinkage is greater than the ground clearance of the vehicle, the hull (belly) will be in contact with the terrain, giving rise to an additional drag, known as the belly drag R_{be}. It can be determined from the horizontal components of the normal and shear stresses acting on the hull–terrain interface, and is expressed by

$$R_{be} = b_b \left[\int_0^{l_b} p_b \sin \alpha_b dl + \int_0^{l_b} \tau_b \cos \alpha_b dl \right] \tag{2.82}$$

where b_b is the contact width of the hull, l_b is the contact length of the hull, α_b is the angle between the hull and the horizontal, and p_b and τ_b are the normal pressure and shear stress on the hull–terrain interface, respectively.

The tractive effort of the vehicle can be calculated from the horizontal component of the shear stress acting on the track in contact with the terrain. For a vehicle with two tracks, F is given by

$$F = 2b \int_0^{l_t} \tau \cos \alpha dl \tag{2.83}$$

where τ is shear stress on the track–terrain interface.

Since both the normal pressure p and shear stress τ are functions of track slip, the track motion resistance R_t, belly drag R_{be} (if any), and tractive effort F vary with slip.

For a track with rubber pads, part of the tractive effort is generated by rubber–terrain shearing. To predict the tractive effort developed by the rubber pads, the portion of the vehicle weight supported by the rubber pads, the area of the rubber pads in contact with the terrain, and the characteristics of rubber–terrain shearing are taken into consideration.

It should be noted that the tractive effort F calculated by Eq. 2.83 is due to the shearing action of the track across the grouser tips. For a track with high grousers, additional thrust will be developed due to the shearing action on the vertical surfaces on either side of the track. This additional thrust may be estimated using a method proposed by Reece [2.33]

The drawbar pull F_d is the difference between the total tractive effort (including the thrust developed by vertical shearing surfaces on both sides of the tracks) and the total external motion resistance of the vehicle (including the belly drag, if any), and is expressed by

$$F_d = F - R_t - R_{be} \qquad (2.84)$$

From Eq. 2.84, the relationship between drawbar pull F_d and track slip i can be determined.

2.6.4 Experimental Validation of the Computer-Aided Method

To validate the basic features of the computer-aided method, the tractive performance of a single-unit tracked vehicle and that of a two-unit articulated vehicle were measured over various types of terrain and compared with the predicted ones [2.4, 2.29, 2.41–2.43]. Figures 2.60 and 2.61 show a comparison between the predicted and measured normal pressure distribution under the track pad of a test vehicle on a sandy terrain and an organic terrain, respectively [2.4, 2.41]. Figures 2.62 and 2.63 show a comparison between the predicted and measured drawbar performance of the test vehicle over the sandy terrain and the organic terrain, respectively. It can be seen that there is a close agreement between the predicted and measured normal pressure distribution and drawbar performance. Thus, the basic features of the computer-aided method have been substantiated.

Since the method takes into account all major design parameters of the vehicle as well as terrain characteristics, it is particularly suited to the detailed parametric analysis of tracked vehicle design, and to the evaluation of the effects on performance of the operational environment. The method has been employed to assist vehicle manufacturers in the development of new tracked vehicles, and governmental agencies in the selection of vehicle candidates to suit specific operational requirements.

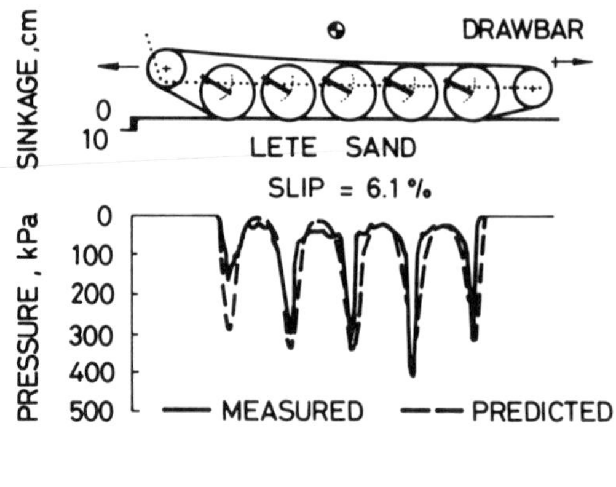

Fig. 2.60 Comparison of the measured normal pressure distribution under the track pad of an M113 and the predicted one using a computer-aided method on sand.

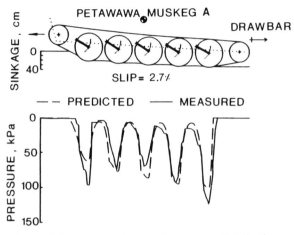

Fig. 2.61 Comparison of the measured normal pressure distribution under the track pad of an M113 and the predicted one using a computer-aided method on organic terrain (muskeg).

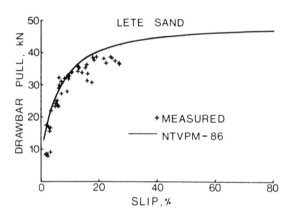

Fig. 2.62 Comparison of the measured drawbar performance of an M113 and the predicted one using a computer-aided method on sand.

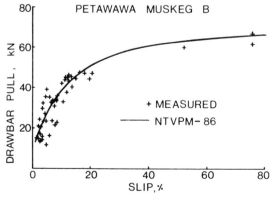

Fig. 2.63 Comparison of the measured drawbar performance of an M113 and the predicted one using a computer-aided method on organic terrain (muskeg).

2.7 METHODS FOR PARAMETRIC ANALYSIS OF WHEELED VEHICLE PERFORMANCE

2.7.1 Motion Resistance of a Rigid Wheel

Although pneumatic tires have long replaced rigid wheels in off-road wheeled vehicles, the mechanics of a rigid wheel over unprepared terrain is still of interest, as a pneumatic tire may behave like a rigid rim in soft terrain. One of the earlier methods for predicting the motion resistance of a rigid wheel is that proposed by Bekker [2.1–2.3]. In developing the method, it is assumed that the terrain reaction at all points on the contact patch is purely radial, and is equal to the normal pressure beneath a horizontal plate at the same depth in a pressure–sinkage test. The equilibrium equations of a towed rigid wheel can be written as (Fig. 2.64)

$$R_c = b \int_0^{\theta_0} \sigma r \sin \theta d\theta \tag{2.85}$$

$$W = b \int_0^{\theta_0} \sigma r \cos \theta d\theta \tag{2.86}$$

where R_c is the motion resistance, W is the vertical load, σ is the normal pressure, and b and r are the width and radius of the wheel, respectively. Since it is assumed that the normal pressure σ acting on the wheel rim is equal to the normal pressure p beneath a plate at the same depth z, $\sigma r \sin \theta d\theta = p dz$ and $\sigma r \cos \theta d\theta = p dx$. Using the pressure–sinkage relationship defined by Eq. 2.46, Eq. 2.85 becomes

$$
\begin{aligned}
R_c &= b \int_0^{z_0} \left(\frac{k_c}{b} + k_\phi \right) z^n dz \\
&= b \left[\left(\frac{k_c}{b} + k_\phi \right) \frac{z_0^{n+1}}{n+1} \right]
\end{aligned}
\tag{2.87}
$$

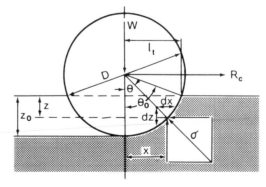

Fig. 2.64 Simplified wheel–soil interaction model. (From *Theory of Land Locomotion* by M.G. Bekker, copyright © by the University of Michigan, 1956, reproduced with permission of the University of Michigan Press.)

The value of R_c calculated by Eq. 2.87 is equivalent to the vertical work done per unit length in pressing a plate of width b into the ground to a depth of z_0. The assumption for the stress distribution made by Bekker implies that the motion resistance of a rigid wheel is due to the vertical work done in making a rut of depth z_0. The motion resistance R_c is referred to as the compaction resistance.

Using Eq. 2.87 to calculate the compaction resistance, the sinkage z_0 expressed in terms of wheel parameters and terrain properties has to be determined first. From Eq. 2.86,

$$W = -b \int_0^{z_0} p\,dx = -b \int_0^{z_0} \left(\frac{k_c}{b} + k_\phi \right) z^n dx \tag{2.88}$$

From the geometry shown in Fig. 2.64,

$$x^2 = [D - (z_0 - z)](z_0 - z) \tag{2.89}$$

where D is the wheel diameter.

For small sinkages,

$$x^2 = D(z_0 - z) \tag{2.90}$$

and

$$2x\,dx = -D\,dz \tag{2.91}$$

Substituting Eq. 2.91 into Eq. 2.88, one obtains

$$W = b\,(k_c/b + k_\phi) \int_0^{z_0} \frac{z^n \sqrt{D}}{2\sqrt{z_0 - z}}\,dz \tag{2.92}$$

Let $z_0 - z = t^2$, then $dz = -2t\,dt$ and

$$W = b \left(\frac{k_c}{b} + k_\phi \right) \sqrt{D} \int_0^{\sqrt{z_0}} (z_0 - t^2)^n\,dt \tag{2.93}$$

Expanding $(z_0 - t^2)^n$ and only taking the first two terms of the series $(z_0^n - nz_0^{n-1}t^2 + n(n-1)z_0^{n-2}t^4/2 - n(n-1)(n-2)z_0^{n-3}t^6/6 + n(n-1)(n-2)(n-3)z_0^{n-4}t^8/24 + \cdots)$, one obtains

$$W = \frac{b(k_c/b + k_\phi)\sqrt{z_0 D}}{3} z_0^n\,(3 - n) \tag{2.94}$$

Rearranging Eq. 2.94, it becomes

$$z_0^{(2n+1)/2} = \frac{3W}{b(k_c/b + k_\phi)\sqrt{D}\,(3-n)}$$

or

$$z_0 = \left[\frac{3W}{b(3-n)\,(k_c/b + k_\phi)\sqrt{D}}\right]^{(2/(2n+1))} \tag{2.95}$$

Substituting Eq. 2.95 into Eq. 2.87, the compaction resistance R_c becomes

$$R_c = \frac{1}{(3-n)^{(2n+2)/(2n+1)}\,(n+1)\,b^{1/(2n+1)}\,(k_c/b + k_\phi)^{1/(2n+1)}}$$
$$\cdot \left[\frac{3W}{\sqrt{D}}\right]^{(2n+2)/(2n+1)} \tag{2.96}$$

It can be seen from Eq. 2.96 that to reduce the compaction resistance, it seems more effective to increase the wheel diameter D than the wheel width b, as D enters the equation in higher power than b. It should be noted that Eq. 2.96 is derived from Eq. 2.94, which is obtained using only the first two terms of a series to represent $(z_0 - t^2)^n$ in Eq. 2.93. As a result, Eq. 2.96 works well only for values of n up to about 1.3. Beyond that, the error in predicting the compaction resistance R_c increases, and when the value of n approaches 3, R_c approaches infinity—an obvious anomaly. For values of n greater than 1.3, the first five terms in the series should be taken to represent the function $(z_0 - t)^n$ in Eq. 2.93 in the integration. This will greatly improve the accuracy in the prediction of the compaction resistance R_c.

Bekker pointed out that acceptable predictions may be obtained using Eq. 2.96 for moderate sinkages (i.e., $z_0 \leq D/6$), and that the larger the wheel diameter and the smaller the sinkage, the more accurate the predictions are [2.3]. He also mentioned that predictions based on Eq. 2.96 for wheels smaller than 50 cm (20 in.) in diameter becomes less accurate, and that predictions of sinkage based on Eq. 2.95 in dry, sandy soil are not accurate if there is significant slip sinkage [2.3]. Experimental evidence shows that the actual normal pressure distribution beneath a rigid wheel is different from that assumed in the theory described above (Fig. 2.65) [2.13, 2.45, 2.46]. According to the theory, the maximum normal pressure should occur at the lowest point of contact (bottom–dead-center) where the sinkage is a maximum. Experimental results, however, show that the maximum normal pressure occurs in front of the bottom–dead-center, and that its location varies with slip, as shown in Fig. 2.65. It has been found that the maximum normal pressure occurs at the junction of the two flow zones, as shown in Figs. 2.19 and 2.20 [2.13, 2.46]. The variation of normal pressure distribution with slip implies that the motion resistance should be expected as a function of slip. This indicates that the actual interaction between the wheel and the terrain is much more complicated than that assumed in the simplified method described above.

In soft terrain where wheel sinkage is significant, Bekker suggested that a bull-dozing resistance acting in front of the wheel should be taken into consideration, in addition to the compaction resistance R_c given by Eq. 2.96. The bulldozing resistance may be calculated using the earth pressure theory described in Section 2.2.

2.7.2 Motion Resistance of a Pneumatic Tire

The motion resistance of a pneumatic tire depends on the mode of operation. If the ground is sufficiently soft and the sum of the inflation pressure p_i and the pressure produced by the stiffness of the carcass p_c is greater than the maximum pressure that the terrain can support at the lowest point of the tire circumference, the tire will remain round like a rigid rim, as shown in Fig. 2.66. This is usually referred to as the rigid mode of operation. On the other hand, if the terrain is firm enough, a portion of the circumference of the tire will be flattened. This is referred to as the elastic mode of operation. When predicting the motion resistance of a tire, it is necessary, first of all, to determine whether the pneumatic tire behaves like a rigid rim or an elastic wheel under a given operating condition. If the tire behaves like a rigid rim, using Bekker's pressure–sinkage relationship, the normal pressure at the lowest point of contact (bottom–dead–center) p_g is

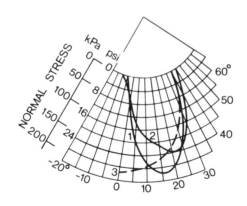

Fig. 2.65 Comparison of the measured normal pressure distribution on a rigid wheel with the predicted one using the simplified soil–wheel interaction model. Curve 1, measured at 3.1% slip; curve 2, measured at 35.1%; and curve 3, predicted.

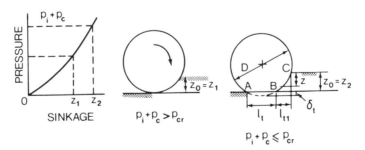

Fig. 2.66 Behavior of a pneumatic tire in different operating modes.

$$p_g = [k_c/b + k_\phi]\, z_0^n \tag{2.97}$$

Substituting Eq. 2.95 into the above equation, the expression for p_g becomes [2.45]

$$p_g = [k_c/b + k_\phi]^{1/(2n+1)} \left[\frac{3W}{(3-n)b\sqrt{D}}\right]^{2n/(2n+1)} \tag{2.98}$$

If the sum of the inflation pressure p_i and the pressure due to carcass stiffness p_c is greater than the pressure defined by Eq. 2.98, which may be called the critical pressure p_{gcr}, the tire will remain round like a rigid wheel [2.47]. Under this condition, the motion resistance due to compacting the terrain can be predicted using Eq. 2.96. On the other hand, if the sum of p_i and p_c is less than p_{gcr} calculated from Eq. 2.98, a portion of the circumference of the tire will be flattened, and the contact pressure on the flat portion will be equal to $p_i + p_c$. In this case, the sinkage of the tire z_0 can be determined by the following equation if Bekker's pressure–sinkage equation is used:

$$z_0 = \left(\frac{p_i + p_c}{k_c/b + k_\phi}\right)^{1/n} \tag{2.99}$$

Substituting Eq. 2.99 into Eq. 2.87, the expression for the motion resistance of an elastic wheel due to compacting the terrain becomes

$$R_c = b(k_c/b + k_\phi)\left(\frac{z_0^{n+1}}{n+1}\right)$$

$$= \frac{b(p_i + p_c)^{(n+1)/n}}{(n+1)\,(k_c/b + k_\phi)^{1/n}} \tag{2.100}$$

It should be mentioned that, in practice, the pressure p_c exerted on the terrain due to carcass stiffness is difficult to determine, as it varies with the inflation pressure and normal load of the tire. As an alternative, Bekker proposed to use the average ground pressure p_{gr} of a tire on a hard ground to represent the sum of p_i and p_c. The average ground pressure p_{gr} for a specific tire at a given normal load and inflation pressure can be derived from the so-called ''generalized deflection chart,'' normally available from tire manufacturers, as shown in Fig. 2.67. The average ground pressure of the tire p_{gr} is equal to the load carried by the tire divided by the corresponding ground contact area A shown in the figure. As an example, Fig. 2.68 shows the relationship between the average ground pressure p_{gr} and the inflation pressure p_i for a 11.00 R16XL tire at various normal loads. It appears that for the particular tire shown, the pressure p_c exerted on the ground due to carcass stiffness is not a constant, and that its value varies with inflation pressure and load. It is interesting to note from Fig. 2.68 that when the tire load and inflation pressure are within certain ranges, the average ground pressure p_{gr} is

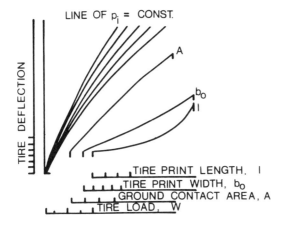

Fig. 2.67 Generalized deflection chart for a tire.

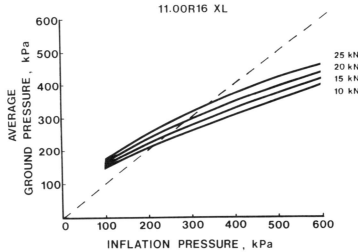

Fig. 2.68 Variation of average ground pressure with inflation pressure and normal load for an off-road tire.

lower than the inflation pressure p_i. Using the average ground pressure p_{gr} to represent the sum of p_i and p_c, Eqs. 2.99 and 2.100 can be rewritten as

$$z_0 = \left(\frac{p_{gr}}{k_c/b + k_\phi}\right)^{1/n} \tag{2.101}$$

$$R_c = \frac{bp_{gr}^{(n+1)/n}}{(n+1)(k_c/b + k_\phi)^{1/n}} \tag{2.102}$$

For tires that are wide in comparison with the diameter, such as terra tires and rolligons, care must be taken in using Eqs. 2.101 and 2.102 to predict the sinkage and compaction resistance. For this type of tire, the smaller dimension of the loading area (i.e., the denominator of k_c in the pressure sinkage equation, Eq. 2.46) is not necessarily the width of the tire, and the contact length l_t shown in Fig. 2.66

may well be the smaller dimension of the contact patch. This indicates that to predict the performance of this type of tire, the contact length l_t has to be determined by considering the vertical equilibrium of the tire. An approximate method for analyzing the performance of this type of tire is given below.

In a first approximation, it may be assumed that the contact length l_t is a function of tire deflection δ_t shown in Fig. 2.66:

$$l_t = 2\sqrt{D\delta_t - \delta_t^2} \qquad (2.103)$$

When l_t is less than the width of the tire, its value should be used as the denominator of k_c in calculating the sinkage z_0:

$$z_0 = \left(\frac{p_{gr}}{k_c/l_t + k_\phi}\right)^{1/n} \qquad (2.104)$$

The normal load W on the tire is supported by the ground pressure p_{gr} on the flat portion AB, as well as by the reaction on the curved portion BC shown in Fig. 2.66. In a first approximation, BC may be assumed to be a circular arc with radius $r = D/2$. The vertical reaction W_{cu} along BC may be determined following an approach similar to that for analyzing a rigid wheel described in the previous section:

$$W_{cu} = -b \int_0^{z0} p\,dx = -b\,(k_c/l_t + k_\phi) \int_0^{z0} \frac{z^n\sqrt{D}\,dz}{2\sqrt{z_0 + \delta_t - z}} \qquad (2.105)$$

Denote $z_0 + \delta_t - z = t^2$; then $dz = -2t\,dt$ and

$$W_{cu} = b(k_c/l_t + k_\phi)\sqrt{D} \int_{\sqrt{\delta_t}}^{\sqrt{z_0 + \delta_t}} (z_0 + \delta_t - t^2)^n\,dt \qquad (2.106)$$

By expanding $(z_0 + \delta_t - t^2)^n$ into a series and taking only the first two terms of the series, one obtains

$$
\begin{aligned}
W_{cu} &= b(k_c/l_t + k_\phi)\sqrt{D} \int_{\sqrt{\delta_t}}^{\sqrt{z_0 + \delta_t}} [(z_0 + \delta_t)^n - n(z_0 + \delta_t)^{n-1}t^2]\,dt \\
&= [b(k_c/l_t + k_\phi)\sqrt{D}\,(z_0 + \delta_t)^{n-1}] \times \\
&\quad \frac{[(3-n)(z_0 + \delta_t)^{3/2} - (3-n)\delta_t^{3/2} - 3z_0\sqrt{\delta_t}]}{3}
\end{aligned}
\qquad (2.107)
$$

The equilibrium equation for the vertical forces acting on the tire is

$$W = bp_{gr}l_t + W_{cu} \qquad (2.108)$$

It can be seen that the normal reaction of a given tire is a function of δ_t, l_t, and z_0, and that the relationships among l_t, z_0, and δ_t are governed by Eqs. 2.103 and 2.104. This indicates that for a given tire with known normal load, there is a particular value of tire deflection δ_t that satisfies Eq. 2.108 over a specific terrain. In principle, the tire deflection δ_t, therefore, can be determined by solving Eqs. 2.103, 2.104, 2.107, and 2.108 simultaneously. In practice, however, it is more convenient to follow an iterative procedure to determine the value of tire deflection. In the iteration process, a value of δ_t is first assumed and is substituted into Eq. 2.103 to calculate the contact length l_t. Then use is made of Eq. 2.104 to calculate the sinkage z_0. With the values of δ_t, l_t, and z_0 known, the normal reaction of the tire for the assumed value of δ_t can be determined. If the assumed value of δ_t is a correct one, the calculated normal reaction should be equal to the given normal load. If not, a new value of δ_t should be assumed, and the whole process should be repeated until convergence is achieved. After the correct value of δ_t is obtained, the appropriate contact length l_t and sinkage z_0 can be calculated using Eqs. 2.103 and 2.104. The compaction resistance can then be determined by

$$R_c = b(k_c/l_t + k_\phi) \left(\frac{z_0^{n+1}}{n+1} \right) \qquad (2.109)$$

For a pneumatic tire in the elastic mode of operation, it deforms. As a result, in addition to the compaction resistance, energy is dissipated in the hysteresis of tire material and in other internal losses, which appears as a resisting force acting on the tire. The resistance due to tire deformation depends on tire design, construction, and material, and on operating conditions. The value of this resistance is usually determined experimentally. Bekker and Semonin proposed the following equation for predicting the motion resistance due to tire deformation [2.48]:

$$R_h = [3.581 b D^2 p_{gr} \epsilon \, (0.0349\alpha - \sin 2\alpha)]/\alpha(D - 2\delta_t) \qquad (2.110)$$

where p_{gr} is the average ground pressure, and b, D, and δ_t are the tire width, diameter, and deflection, respectively. The parameters α and ϵ are calculated as follows:

$$\alpha = \cos^{-1} [(D - 2\delta_t)/D] \qquad (2.111)$$

and

$$\epsilon = 1 - \exp (-k_e\delta_t/h) \qquad (2.112)$$

where α is the contact angle in degrees, h is the tire section height and k_e is a parameter related to tire construction. The value of k_e is 15 for bias-ply tires and 7 for radial-ply tires.

When the tire sinkage is significant, Bekker suggested that a bulldozing resist-

ance also be taken into account in the calculation of the total motion resistance of
a tire.

It should be mentioned that the methods described above are for the prediction
of a single tire (wheel). In practice, quite often the rear tires of a vehicle travel in
the ruts formed by the front tires. To predict the overall tractive performance of a
multiaxle wheeled vehicle, the response of the terrain to repetitive normal and
shear loading should be taken into account.

Example 2.4. A pneumatic tire 11.00 R16XL is to be installed on an off-road
wheeled vehicle. The tire has a diameter of 97.5 cm (38.4 in.), a section height
of 28.4 cm (11.2 in.), and a width of 28 cm (11 in.). It is to carry a load of 20
kN (4496 lb). The vehicle is to operate on a soil with pressure–sinkage parameters
$n = 1$ and $k_\phi = 680$ kN/m³ (2.5 lb/in.³). Two inflation pressures, 100 and 200
kPa (14.5 and 29 psi), are proposed. The relationships between the inflation pressure p_i and the average ground pressure p_{gr} for the tire under various normal loads
are shown in Fig. 2.68. Compare the sinkage and compaction resistance of the tire
at the two inflation pressures proposed.

Solution. On the soil specified, the critical pressure p_{gcr} for the tire can be determined using Eq. 2.98:

$$p_{gcr} = [k_\phi]^{1/(2n+1)} \left[\frac{3W}{(3-n)\, b\sqrt{D}} \right]^{2n/(2n+1)}$$

$$= 200 \text{ kPa (29 psi)}.$$

   A. From Fig. 2.68, for a normal load of 20 kN (4496 lb) at an inflation pressure
$p_i = 100$ kPa (14.5 kPa), the average ground pressure p_{gr} is 170 kPa (24.7 psi).
Since $p_{gcr} > p_{gr}$, the tire is operating in the elastic mode, and the lower part of
the tire in contact with the terrain is flattened. Using Eq. 2.101, the sinkage z_0 is
given by

$$z_0 = \left(\frac{p_{gr}}{k_\phi} \right)^{1/n} = 0.25 \text{ m (10 in.)}$$

and using Eq. 2.87, the compaction resistance R_c is given by

$$R_c = b(k_\phi) \left(\frac{z_0^{n+1}}{n+1} \right)$$

$$= 5.95 \text{ kN (1338 lb)}$$

   B. From Fig. 2.68, for a normal load of 20 kN (4496 lb) at an inflation pressure
$p_i = 200$ kPa (29 psi), the average ground pressure p_{gr} is 230 kPa (33.4 psi). Since
$p_{gcr} < p_{gr}$, the tire behaves like a rigid wheel.

Using Eq. 2.95, the sinkage z_0 is given by

$$z_0 = \left[\frac{3W}{b(3 - n)k_\phi \sqrt{D}} \right]^{2/(2n + 1)}$$

$$= 0.294 \text{ m } (11.6 \text{ in.})$$

and using Eq. 2.87, the compaction resistance R_c is given by

$$R_c = b(k_\phi) \left(\frac{z_0^{n + 1}}{n + 1} \right)$$

$$= 8.23 \text{ kN } (1850 \text{ lb})$$

It can be seen that the compaction resistance of the tire at an inflation pressure of 200 kPa (29 psi) is approximately 38.3% higher than that at an inflation pressure of 100 kPa (14.5 psi).

2.7.3 Tractive Effort and Slip of a Wheel

To evaluate the relationship between the tractive effort and slip of a rigid wheel, the development of shear displacement along the wheel–soil interface has to be determined first. The shear displacement developed along the contact area of a rigid wheel may be determined based on the analysis of the slip velocity V_j. For a rigid wheel, the slip velocity V_j of a point on the rim relative to the terrain is the tangential component of the absolute velocity at the same point, as illustrated in Fig. 2.69 [2.46]. The magnitude of the slip velocity V_j of a point on the rim defined by angle θ (Fig. 2.69) can be expressed by [2.46]

$$V_j = r\omega \left[1 - (1 - i) \cos \theta \right] \tag{2.113}$$

It can be seen that the slip velocity for a rigid wheel varies with angle θ and slip.

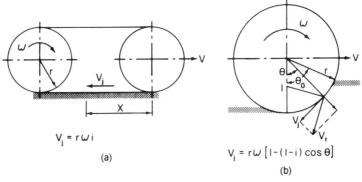

Fig. 2.69 Development of shear displacement under a wheel as compared with that under a track.

The shear displacement j along the wheel–soil interface is given by

$$j = \int_0^t V_j \, dt = \int_\theta^{\theta_0} r\omega \, [1 - (1 - i) \cos] \frac{d\theta}{\omega}$$

$$= r[(\theta_0 - \theta) - (1 - i)(\sin \theta_0 - \sin \theta)] \qquad (2.114)$$

where θ_0 is the entry angle that defines the angle where a point on the rim comes into contact with the terrain (Fig. 2.69).

Based on the relationship between the shear stress and shear displacement discussed previously, the shear stress distribution along the contact area of a rigid wheel can be determined. For instance, using Eq. 2.56, the shear stress distribution may be described by

$$\tau(\theta) = [c + p(\theta) \tan \phi] (1 - e^{j/K})$$

$$= [c + p(\theta) \tan \phi] [1 - \exp^{-(r/K)[\theta_0 - \theta - (1-i)(\sin\theta_0 - \sin\theta)]}] \qquad (2.115)$$

The normal pressure distribution along a rigid wheel $p(\theta)$ may be estimated by a variety of methods, including the simplified method proposed by Bekker described previously [2.3, 2.46].

Figure 2.70 shows a comparison of the measured shear stress distribution on the contact area of a rigid wheel at 22.1% slip on a compact sand and the predicted one using the method described above. The details of the prediction procedures followed are given in reference [2.46].

By integrating the horizontal component of tangential stress over the entire contact area, the total tractive effort F can be determined:

$$F = \int_0^{\theta_0} \tau(\theta) \cos \theta \, d\theta \qquad (2.116)$$

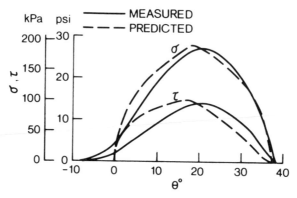

Fig. 2.70 Comparison of the measured and predicted normal and shear stress distribution on the contact area of a rigid wheel at 22.1% slip on compact sand.

It should be mentioned that the vertical component of shear stress at the contact area supports part of the vertical load on the wheel. This fact has been neglected in the simplified wheel–soil interaction model shown in Fig. 2.64. In a more complete analysis of wheel–soil interaction, the effect of shear stress should be taken into consideration, and the equations for predicting the tractive performance of a rigid wheel are given by the following [2.4, 2.46].

For vertical load,

$$W = rb \left[\int_0^{\theta_0} p(\theta) \cos \theta d\theta + \int_0^{\theta_0} \tau(\theta) \sin \theta d\theta \right] \qquad (2.117)$$

for drawbar pull,

$$F_d = rb \left[\int_0^{\theta_0} \tau(\theta) \cos \theta d\theta - \int_0^{\theta_0} p(\theta) \sin \theta d\theta \right] \qquad (2.118)$$

and for wheel torque,

$$M_\omega = r^2 b \int_0^{\theta_0} \tau(\theta) \, d\theta \qquad (2.119)$$

It should be pointed out that Eq. 2.115 is for the prediction of shear stress distribution along the contact area of a driven rigid wheel. For a free-rolling, towed rigid wheel, the shear stress distribution has different characteristics, and is shown in Fig. 2.71. It is noted that the shear stress changes its direction at a particular point on the wheel–soil interface, which may be called the transition point. It has been determined that this transition point corresponds to that where the two flow zones in the soil beneath a towed wheel meet each other, as shown in Fig. 2.20. Under the action of section AD of the rim, the soil in the region ABD moves upward and forward, while the rim rotates around the instantaneous center I. The soil, therefore, slides along AD in such a way as to produce shear stress in the direction opposite that of wheel rotation, which is denoted as positive. Between A and E, the soil moves forward slowly, while the wheel rim moves forward relatively fast. In this region, the shear stress acts in the direction of wheel rotation, which is denoted as negative. As a result, the resultant moment about the wheel center due to the shear force acting on the rim of a free-rolling, towed wheel is zero.

The method for predicting the tractive effort of a pneumatic tire depends on its mode of operation. If the average ground pressure p_{gr} is greater than the critical pressure p_{gcr} defined by Eq. 2.98, the tire will behave like a rigid wheel, and the shear displacement, shear stress, and tractive effort can be predicted using Eqs. 2.114, 2.115, and 2.116, respectively. On the other hand, if p_{gr} is less than p_{gcr}, then a portion of the tire circumference will be flattened, as shown in Fig. 2.72.

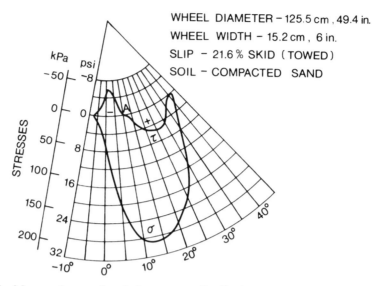

Fig. 2.71 Measured normal and shear stress distribution on the contact area of a towed rigid wheel on compact sand.

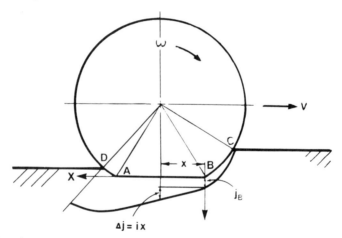

Fig. 2.72 Development of shear displacement beneath a tire in the elastic operating mode.

Under these circumstances, the shear displacement developed along BC in Fig. 2.72 can be determined in the same way as that described earlier for a rigid wheel. For the flat portion AB, the slip velocity is considered to be a constant, similar to that beneath a rigid track described in Section 2.5.2. The increase in shear displacement Δj along section AB is proportional to the slip of the tire i and the distance x between the point in question and point B, and is expressed by

$$\Delta j = ix \qquad (2.120)$$

The cumulative shear displacement j_x at a distance x from point B is then given by

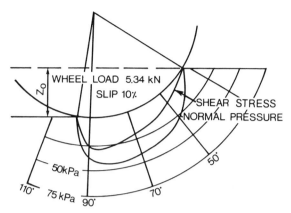

Fig. 2.73 Measured normal and shear stress distribution on the contact patch of a tractor tire on sandy loam. (Reproduced with permission from reference 2.49.)

$$j_x = j_B + \Delta j = j_B + ix \qquad (2.121)$$

where j_B is shear displacement at point B, which can be determined using Eq. 2.114.

The shear displacement along section AD, which is due to the elastic rebound of the terrain upon unloading, can again be determined in the same way as that for a rigid wheel. The development of shear displacement beneath a tire is illustrated in Fig. 2.72.

After the shear displacement along the tire-terrain interface has been determined, the corresponding shear stress distribution can be defined using the appropriate shear stress-shear displacement relationship for the terrain under consideration. The tractive effort can then be determined by integrating the horizontal component of the shear stress over the entire contact area.

Figure 2.73 shows the measured normal and shear stress distributions on the contact patch of a tractor tire (11.5–15) at 10% slip on a sand loam [2.49]. For a pneumatic tire operating in the elastic mode, the stress distribution is more uniform than that for a rigid wheel.

A user-friendly computer-aided method incorporating the procedures described above has been developed for predicting the overall tractive performance of tires. Taking into account the longitudinal interaxle load transfer due to drawbar pull, the suspension stiffness of the axles, and the response of the terrain to repetitive loading, a computer-aided method for predicting the overall tractive performance of multiaxle wheeled vehicles has also been developed [2.4].

REFERENCES

2.1 M.G. Bekker, *Theory of Land Locomotion.*   Ann Arbor, MI: University of Michigan Press, 1956.

2.2 M.G. Bekker, *Off-the-Road Locomotion.*   Ann Arbor, MI: University of Michigan Press, 1960.

2.3   M.G. Bekker, *Introduction to Terrain-Vehicle Systems.* Ann Arbor, MI: University of Michigan Press, 1969.

2.4   J.Y. Wong, *Terramechanics and Off-Road Vehicles.* Amsterdam, The Netherlands: Elsevier Science Publishers B.V., 1989.

2.5   W. Söhne, "Fundamentals of Pressure Distribution and Soil Compaction Under Tractor Tires," *Agricultural Engineering*, May 1958.

2.6   W. Söhne, "Agricultural Engineering and Terramechanics," *Journal of Terramechanics*, vol. 6, no. 4, 1969.

2.7   M.S. Osman, "The Mechanics of Soil Cutting Blades," *Journal of Agricultural Engineering Research*, vol. 9, no. 4, 1964.

2.8   K. Terzaghi, *Theoretical Soil Mechanics.* New York: Wiley, 1966.

2.9   D.R.P. Hettiaratchi and A.R. Reece, "The Calculation of Passive Soil Resistance," *Geotechnique*, vol. 24, no. 3, 1974.

2.10 L.L. Karafiath and E.A. Nowatzki, *Soil Mechanics for Off-Road Vehicle Engineering.* Aedermannsdorf, Switzerland: Trans Tech Publications, 1978.

2.11 E. McKyes, *Soil Cutting and Tillage, Developments in Agricultural Engineering 7.* Amsterdam, The Netherlands: Elsevier Science Publishers B.V., 1985.

2.12 J.Y. Wong and A.R. Reece, "Soil Failure Beneath Rigid Wheels," in *Proc. 2nd Int. Conf. of the International Society for Terrain Vehicle Systems.* Toronto, Canada: University of Toronto Press, 1966.

2.13 J.Y. Wong, "Behaviour of Soil Beneath Rigid Wheels," *Journal of Agricultural Engineering Research*, vol. 12, no. 4, 1967.

2.14 L.L. Karafiath, "Plasticity Theory and Stress Distribution Beneath Wheels," *Journal of Terramechanics*, vol. 8, no. 2, 1971.

2.15 J.Y. Wong, "Review of 'Soil Mechanics for Off-Road Vehicle Engineering,'" *Canadian Geotechnical Journal*, vol. 16, no. 3 and *Journal of Terramechanics*, vol. 16, no. 4, 1979.

2.16 R.N. Yong and E.A. Fattah, "Prediction of Wheel-Soil Interaction and Performance Using the Finite Element Method," *Journal of Terramechanics*, vol. 13, no. 4, 1976.

2.17 R.N. Yong, E.A. Fattah, and N. Skiadas, *Vehicle Traction Mechanics, Developments in Agricultural Engineering 3.* Amsterdam, The Netherlands: Elsevier Science Publishers B.V., 1984.

2.18 P. Boonsinsuk and R.N. Yong, "Soil Compliance Influence on Tyre Performance," in *Proc. 8th Int. Conf. of the International Society for Terrain-Vehicle Systems*, vol. I. 1984.

2.19 J.Y. Wong, "Discussion on 'Prediction of wheel-soil interaction and performance using the finite element method,'" *Journal of Terramechanics*, vol. 14, no. 4, 1977.

2.20 "Off-Road Vehicle Mobility Evaluation," SAE J939, Society of Automotive Engineers, 1967.

2.21 A.A. Rula and C.J. Nuttall, "An Analysis of Ground Mobility Models (ANA-MOB)," Technical Report M-71-4, U.S. Army Engineer Waterways Experiment Station, Vicksburg, MS, 1971.

2.22 D.R. Freitag, "A Dimensional Analysis of the Performance of Pneumatic Tires on Soft Soils," Technical Report 3-688, U.S. Army Engineer Waterways Experiment Station, Vicksburg, MS, 1965.

2.23 G.W. Turnage, "A Synopsis of Tire Design and Operational Considerations Aimed at Increasing In-Soil Tire Drawbar Performance," in *Proc. 6th Int.Conf. of the International Society for Terrain-Vehicle Systems*, vol. II, 1978.

2.24 R.D. Wismer and H.J. Luth, "Off-Road Traction Prediction for Wheeled Vehicles," American Society of Agricultural Engineers, Paper no. 72-619, 1972.

2.25 G.W. Turnage, "Prediction of In-Sand Tire and Wheeled Vehicle Drawbar Performance," in *Proc. 8th Int. Conf. of the International Society for Terrain-Vehicle Systems*, vol. I, 1984.

2.26 D. Rowland, "Tracked Vehicle Ground Pressure and Its Effect on Soft Ground Performance," in *Proc. 4th Int. Conf. of the International Society for Terrain Vehicle Systems*, vol. 1, Stockholm, Sweden, 1972.

2.27 D. Rowland, "A Review of Vehicle Design for Soft-Ground Operation," in *Proc. 5th Int. Conf. of the International Society for Terrain Vehicle Systems*, vol. 1, Detroit, MI, 1975.

2.28 J.Y. Wong, J.R. Radforth, and J. Preston-Thomas, "Some Further Studies of the Mechanical Properties of Muskeg," *Journal of Terramechanics*, vol. 19, no. 2, 1982.

2.29 J.Y. Wong, M. Garber, and J. Preston-Thomas, "Theoretical Prediction and Experimental Substantiation of the Ground Pressure Distribution and Tractive Performance of Tracked Vehicles," *Proc. Institution of Mechanical Engineers*, vol. 198, no. D15, 1984.

2.30 J.Y. Wong and M.G. Bekker, "Terrain Vehicle Systems Analysis," Monograph, Department of Mechanical and Aerospace Engineering, Carleton Univeristy, Ottawa, Ont., Canada, 1976, 1977, 1978, 1980, 1985.

2.31 J.Y. Wong, "Data Processing Methodology in the Characterization of the Mechanical Properties of Terrain," *Journal of Terramechanics*, vol. 17, no. 1, 1980.

2.32 W.L. Harrison, "Vehicle Performance Over Snow," U.S. Army Cold Regions Research and Engineering Laboratory, Technical Report 268, Dec. 1975.

2.33 A.R. Reece, "Principles of Soil-Vehicle Mechanics," *Proc. Institution of Mechanical Engineers*, vol. 180, part 2A, 1965–1966.

2.34 J.Y. Wong, M. Garber, J.R. Radforth, and J.T. Dowell, "Characterization of the Mechanical Properties of Muskeg with Special Reference to Vehicle Mobility," *Journal of Terramechanics*, vol. 16, no. 4, 1979.

2.35 J.Y. Wong and J. Preston-Thomas, "On the Characterization of the Pressure-Sinkage Relationship of Snow Covers Containing an Ice Layer," *Journal of Terramechanics*, vol. 20, no. 1, 1983.

2.36 J.Y. Wong and J. Preston-Thomas, "On the Characterization of the Shear Stress-Displacement Relationship of Terrain," *Journal of Terramechanics*, vol. 19, no. 4, 1983.

2.37 B.M.D. Wills, "The Measurement of Soil Shear Strength and Deformation Moduli and a Comparison of the Actual and Theoretical Performance of a Family of Rigid Tracks," *Journal of Agricultural Engineering Research*, vol. 8, no. 2, 1963.

2.38 H.M.S. Keira, "Effects of Vibration on the Shearing Characteristics of Soil Engaging Machinery," unpublished Ph.D. dissertation, Carleton University, Ottawa, Ont., Canada, 1979.

2.39 J.Y. Wong, "Computer-Aided Analysis of the Effects of Design Parameters on the Performance of Tracked Vehicles," *Journal of Terramechanics*, vol. 23, no. 2, 1986.

2.40   J.Y. Wong and J. Preston-Thomas, "Parametric Analysis of Tracked Vehicle Performance Using an Advanced Computer Simulation Model," *Proc. Institution of Mechanical Engineers*, vol. 200, no. D2, 1986.

2.41   J.Y. Wong and J. Preston-Thomas, "Investigation into the Effects of Suspension Characteristics and Design Parameters on the Performance of Tracked Vehicles Using an Advanced Computer Simulation Model," *Proc. Institution of Mechanical Engineers*, vol. 202, no. D3, 1988.

2.42   J.Y. Wong, "Optimization of the Tractive Performance of Articulated Tracked Vehicles Using an Advanced Computer Simulation Model," *Proc. Institution of Mechanical Engineers*, vol. 206, no. D1, 1992.

2.43   J.Y. Wong, "Expansion of the Terrain Input Base for the Nepean Tracked Vehicle Performance Model NTVPM to Accept Swiss Rammsonde Data from Deep Snow," *Journal of Terramechanics*, vol. 29, no. 3, 1992.

2.44   J.Y. Wong, "Computer-Aided Methods for the Optimization of the Mobility of Single-Unit and Two-Unit Articulated Tracked Vehicles," *Journal of Terramechanics*, vol. 29, no. 4/5, 1992.

2.45   O. Onafeko and A.R. Reece, "Soil Stresses and Deformations Beneath Rigid Wheels," *Journal of Terramechanics*, vol. 4, no. 1, 1967.

2.46   J.Y. Wong and A.R. Reece, "Prediction of Rigid Wheel Performance Based on the Analysis of Soil-Wheel Stresses, Part I and Part II," *Journal of Terramechanics*, vol. 4, nos. 1 and 2, 1967.

2.47   J.Y. Wong, "Performance of the Air Cushion-Surface Contacting Hybrid Vehicle for Overland Operation," *Proc. Institution of Mechanical Engineers*, vol. 186, no. 50/72, 1972.

2.48   M.G. Bekker and E.V. Semonin, "Motion Resistance of Pneumatic Tires," *Journal of Automotive Engineering*, vol. 6, no. 2, 1975.

2.49   G. Krick, "Radial and Shear Stress Distribution Under Rigid Wheels and Pneumatic Tires Operating on Yielding Soils with Consideration of Tire Deformation," *Journal of Terramechanics*, vol. 6, no. 3, 1969.

PROBLEMS

2.1   The contact area of a tire on a fairly hard and dry soil may be approximated by a circle having a radius of 20 cm (7.9 in.). The contact pressure is assumed to be a uniform 68.95 kPa (10 psi). For this type of soil, the concentration factor ν is assumed to be 3. Calculate the resultant vertical stress σ_z in the soil at depths of 20 and 40 cm (7.9 and 15.8 in.) below the center of the contact area. At what depth below the center is the vertical stress one-tenth of the contact pressure?

2.2   A steel cage wheel with 18 lugs on a narrow rim is to be attached to an off-road wheeled vehicle to increase its traction over a wet soil. The outside diameter of the steel wheel across the tips of the lugs is 1.5 m (4.92 ft). The lugs are 25 cm (10 in.) wide and penetrate 12.5 cm (5 in) into the soil at the vertical position. Estimate the tractive effort that a lug in the vertical position can develop in a soil with c = 13.79 kPa (2 psi), ϕ = 5°, and γ_s = 16 kN/m³ (102 lb/ft³). Also calculate the corresponding driving torque required. The rim of the wheel is narrow, and its effect may be neglected. The surface of the lugs is assumed to be smooth.

2.3 A tracked vehicle with uniform contact pressure weighs 155.68 kN (35,000 lb). Each of its two tracks is 102 cm (40 in.) wide and 305 cm (120 in.) long. Estimate the motion resistance and thrust–slip relationship of the vehicle on a terrain with n = 0.5, k_c = 0.77 kN/m^{n+1} (0.7 lb/in.$^{n+1}$), k_ϕ = 51.91 kN/m^{n+2} (1.2 lb/in.$^{n+2}$), c = 5.17 kPa (0.75 psi), ϕ = 11°, and K = 5 cm (2 in.). What will be the changes in its performance if the width of the track is reduced by 20% and its length is increased by 25%?

2.4 A four-wheel-drive tractor weighs 60 kN (13,489 lb), with equal weight distribution between the axles. All four tires are of 11.00 R16XL radial tires with dimensions as given in Example 2.4, and the relationship between the average ground pressure and the inflation pressure for the tires is given in Fig. 2.68. The tire inflation pressure is 150 kPa (21.75 psi). Estimate the motion resistance and the thrust of the front axle at 20% slip on a terrain with n = 0.8, k_c = 29.76 kN/m^{n+1}(9 lb/in.$^{n+1}$), k_ϕ = 2083 kN/m^{n+2} (16 lb/in.$^{n+2}$), c = 8.62 kPa (1.25 psi), ϕ = 22.5°, and K = 2.5 cm (1 in.).

CHAPTER 3

PERFORMANCE CHARACTERISTICS OF ROAD VEHICLES

Performance characteristics of a road vehicle are primarily concerned with its capability to accelerate, decelerate, and negotiate grades in a straight-line motion. The tractive (or braking) effort developed by the tires and the resisting forces acting on the vehicle determine the performance potential of the vehicle, and will be discussed in detail in this chapter. Procedures for predicting and evaluating the performance characteristics of road vehicles will also be presented.

3.1 EQUATION OF MOTION AND MAXIMUM TRACTIVE EFFORT

The major external forces acting on a two-axle vehicle are shown in Fig. 3.1. In the longitudinal direction, they include the aerodynamic resistance R_a, rolling resistance of the front and rear tires R_{rf} and R_{rr}, drawbar load R_d, grade resistance R_g ($W \sin \theta_s$), and tractive effort of the front and rear tires F_f and F_r. For a rear-wheel-drive vehicle, $F_f = 0$, whereas for a front-wheel-drive vehicle, $F_r = 0$.

The equation of motion along the longitudinal axis x of the vehicle is expressed by

$$m \frac{d^2x}{dt^2} = \frac{W}{g} a = F_f + F_r - R_a - R_{rf} - R_{rr} - R_d - R_g \qquad (3.1)$$

where d^2x/dt^2 or a is the linear acceleration of the vehicle along the longitudinal axis, g is acceleration due to gravity, and m and W are vehicle mass and weight, respectively.

By introducing the concept of inertia force, the above equation may be rewritten

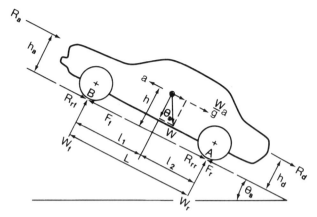

Fig. 3.1 Forces acting on a two-axle vehicle.

as

$$F_f + F_r - \left(R_a + R_{rf} + R_{rr} + R_d + R_g + \frac{aW}{g} \right) = 0$$

or

$$F = R_a + R_r + R_d + R_g + \frac{aW}{g} \tag{3.2}$$

where F is the total tractive effort and R_r is the total rolling resistance of the vehicle.

To evaluate the performance potential, the maximum tractive effort that the vehicle can develop has to be determined. There are two limiting factors to the maximum tractive effort of a road vehicle: one is determined by the coefficient of road adhesion and the normal load on the drive axle or axles; the other is determined by the characteristics of the power plant and the transmission. The smaller of these two determines the performance potential of the vehicle.

To predict the maximum tractive effort that the tire–ground contact can support, the normal loads on the axles have to be determined. They can be computed readily by summation of the moments about points A and B shown in Fig. 3.1. By summing moments about A, the normal load on the front axle W_f can be determined:

$$W_f = \frac{Wl_2 \cos \theta_s - R_a h_a - haW/g - R_d h_d \mp Wh \sin \theta_s}{L} \tag{3.3}$$

where l_2 is the distance between the rear axle and the center of gravity of the vehicle, h_a is the height of the point of application of the aerodynamic resistance, h is the height of the center of gravity, h_d is the height of the drawbar hitch, L is the wheelbase, and θ_s is the slope angle. When the vehicle is climbing up a hill, the negative sign is used for the term $Wh \sin \theta_s$.

Similarly, the normal load on the rear axle can be determined by summing moments about B:

$$W_r = \frac{Wl_1 \cos \theta_s + R_a h_a + haW/g + R_d h_d \pm Wh \sin \theta_s}{L} \tag{3.4}$$

where l_1 is the distance between the front axle and the center of gravity of the vehicle. In the above expression, the positive sign is used for the term $Wh \sin \theta_s$ when the vehicle is climbing up a hill.

For small angles of slope, $\cos \theta_s$ is approximately equal to 1. For passenger cars, the height of the point of application of the aerodynamic resistance h_a and the height of the drawbar hitch h_d may be assumed to be near the height of the center of gravity h. With these simplifications and assumptions, Eqs. 3.3 and 3.4 may be rewritten as

$$W_f = \frac{l_2}{L} W - \frac{h}{L} \left(R_a + \frac{aW}{g} + R_d \pm W \sin \theta_s \right) \tag{3.5}$$

and

$$W_r = \frac{l_1}{L} W + \frac{h}{L} \left(R_a + \frac{aW}{g} + R_d \pm W \sin \theta_s \right) \tag{3.6}$$

Substituting Eq. 3.2 into the above equations, one obtains

$$W_f = \frac{l_2}{L} W - \frac{h}{L} (F - R_r) \tag{3.7}$$

and

$$W_r = \frac{l_1}{L} W + \frac{h}{L} (F - R_r) \tag{3.8}$$

It should be noted that the first term on the right-hand side of each equation represents the static load on the axle when the vehicle is at rest on level ground. The second term on the right-hand side of each equation represents the dynamic component of the normal load or dynamic load transfer.

The maximum tractive effort that the tire–ground contact can support can be determined in terms of the coefficient of road adhesion μ and vehicle parameters. For a rear-wheel-drive vehicle,

$$F_{\max} = \mu W_r = \mu \left[\frac{l_1}{L} W + \frac{h}{L} (F_{\max} - R_r) \right]$$

and

$$F_{\max} = \frac{\mu W (l_1 - f_r h)/L}{1 - \mu h/L} \qquad (3.9)$$

where the total rolling resistance R_r is expressed as the product of the coefficient of rolling resistance f_r and the weight of the vehicle W. For a front-wheel-drive vehicle,

$$F_{\max} = \mu W_f = \mu \left[\frac{l_2}{L} W - \frac{h}{L} (F_{\max} - R_r) \right]$$

and

$$F_{\max} = \frac{\mu W (l_2 + f_r h)/L}{1 + \mu h/L} \qquad (3.10)$$

It should be noted that in deriving the above equations, the transverse load transfer due to engine torque for a longitudinally mounted engine or the longitudinal load transfer due to engine torque for a transversely mounted engine has been neglected, and that both the right- and left-hand side tires are assumed to have identical performance.

For a tractor–semitrailer, the calculation of the maximum tractive effort that the tire–ground contact can support is more involved than a two-axle vehicle. The major forces acting on a tractor–semitrailer are shown in Fig. 3.2. For most of the tractor–semitrailers, the tractor rear axle is driven. To compute the maximum tractive effort as determined by the nature of tire–road adhesion, it is necessary to calculate the normal load on the tractor rear axle under operating conditions. This

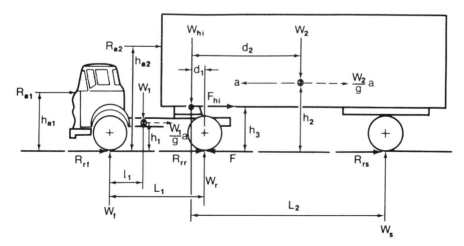

Fig. 3.2 Forces acting on a tractor–semitrailer.

can be calculated by considering the tractor and the semitrailer as free bodies separately. By taking the semitrailer as a free body, the normal load on the semitrailer axle W_s and the vertical and horizontal loads at the hitch point W_{hi} and F_{hi} can be determined.

The normal load on the semitrailer axle, for small angles of slope, is given by

$$W_s = \frac{W_2 d_2 + R_{a2} h_{a2} + h_2 a W_2/g \pm W_2 h_2 \sin \theta_s - F_{hi} h_3}{L_2} \tag{3.11}$$

where R_{a2} is the aerodynamic resistance acting on the semitrailer, h_{a2} is the height of the point of application of R_{a2}, and W_2 is the weight of the semitrailer. Other parameters and dimensions are shown in Fig. 3.2. When the vehicle is climbing up a hill, the positive sign for the term $W_2 h_2 \sin \theta_s$ in Eq. 3.11 should be used.

If $h_{a2} \simeq h_3 \simeq h_2$, the expression for W_s may be simplified as

$$W_s = \frac{d_2}{L_2} W_2 + \frac{h_2}{L_2} \left(R_{a2} + \frac{a W_2}{g} \pm W_2 \sin \theta_s - F_{hi} \right) \tag{3.12}$$

The longitudinal force at the hitch point is given by

$$F_{hi} = R_{a2} + \frac{a W_2}{g} \pm W_2 \sin \theta_s + f_r W_s \tag{3.13}$$

Substituting Eq. 3.13 into Eq. 3.12, the expression for W_s becomes

$$W_s = \frac{W_2 d_2}{L_2 + f_r h_2}$$

and the load at the hitch point is given by

$$W_{hi} = W_2 - W_s = \left(1 - \frac{d_2}{L_2 + f_r h_2} \right) W_2$$

$$= C_{hi} W_2 \tag{3.14}$$

By taking the tractor as a free body and summing moments about the front tire–ground contact point, the normal load on the tractor rear axle W_r can be determined:

$$W_r = \frac{W_1 l_1 + R_{a1} h_{a1} + h_1 a W_1/g \pm W_1 h_1 \sin \theta_s + F_{hi} h_3 + (L_1 - d_1) W_{hi}}{L_1}$$

$$\tag{3.15}$$

where R_{a1} is the aerodynamic resistance acting on the tractor, h_{a1} is the height of the point of application of R_{a1}, and W_1 is the weight of the tractor. Other parameters and dimensions are shown in Fig. 3.2. When the vehicle is climbing up a hill, the positive sign for the term $W_1 h_1 \sin \theta_s$ in Eq. 3.15 should be used.

If $h_{a_1} \cong h_3 \cong h_1$, the expression for W_r may be simplified as

$$W_r = \frac{W_1 l_1 + (R_{a_1} + aW_1/g \pm W_1 \sin \theta_s + F_{hi}) h_1 + (L_1 - d_1) W_{hi}}{L_1} \quad (3.16)$$

By equating the forces acting on the tractor in the longitudinal direction, the following expression for the required tractive effort F can be obtained:

$$F = R_{a_1} + \frac{aW_1}{g} \pm W_1 \sin \theta_s + f_r (W_1 + W_{hi}) + F_{hi} \quad (3.17)$$

From Eqs. 3.16 and 3.17, the maximum tractive effort that the tire–ground contact can support with the tractor rear axle driven can be expressed by

$$F_{\max} = \mu W_r = \frac{\mu [l_1 W_1 - h_1 f_r (W_1 + W_{hi}) + (L_1 - d_1) W_{hi}]/L_1}{1 - \mu h_1/L_1}$$

Substitution of Eq. 3.14 into the above equation yields

$$F_{\max} = \frac{\mu [l_1 W_1 - h_1 f_r (W_1 + C_{hi} W_2) + (L_1 - d_1) C_{hi} W_2]/L_1}{1 - \mu h_1/L_1} \quad (3.18)$$

The maximum tractive effort as determined by the nature of the tire–road interaction imposes a fundamental limit on the vehicle performance characteristics, including maximum speed, acceleration, gradability, and drawbar pull.

3.2 AERODYNAMIC FORCES AND MOMENTS

With growing emphasis on fuel economy and on the reduction of undesirable exhaust emissions, it has become increasingly important to optimize vehicle power requirements. To achieve this, it is necessary to reduce the aerodynamic resistance, rolling resistance, and inertia resistance, which is proportional to vehicle weight. For a typical passenger car cruising at a speed higher than approximately 80 km/h (50 mph), the power required to overcome the aerodynamic resistance is greater than that required to overcome the rolling resistance of the tires and the resistance in the transmission, as shown in Fig. 3.3 [3.1]. Because of the significant effects of aerodynamic resistance on vehicle power requirements at moderate and higher speeds, continual effort has been expended in improving the aerodynamic performance of road vehicles.

The aerodynamic resistance is generated by two sources: one is the air flow over the exterior of the vehicle body, and the other is the flow through the engine

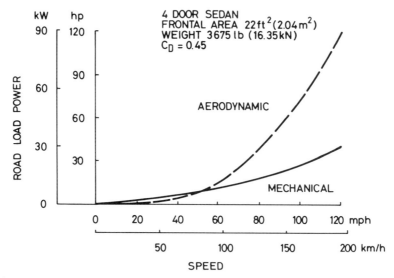

Fig. 3.3 Power requirements of a full-size passenger car as a function of speed. (Reproduced with permission of the Society of Automotive Engineers from reference 3.1.)

radiator system and the interior of the vehicle for purposes of cooling, heating, and ventilating. Of the two, the former is the dominant one, which accounts for more than 90% of the total aerodynamic resistance of a passenger car.

The external air flow generates normal pressure and shear stress on the vehicle body. According to the aerodynamic nature, the external aerodynamic resistance comprises two components, commonly known as the pressure drag and skin friction. The pressure drag arises from the component of the normal pressure on the vehicle body acting against the motion of the vehicle, while the skin friction is due to the shear stress in the boundary layer adjacent to the external surface of the vehicle body. Of the two components, the pressure drag is by far the larger, and constitutes more than 90% of the total external aerodynamic resistance of a passenger car with normal surface finish. The skin friction may become more significant, however, for a long vehicle, such as a bus or a tractor–trailer train. It should be noted that the momentum losses of the air in the wake of the vehicle and the energy imparted to the air by the vortices generated by the vehicle are not additional, but are an alternative measure of the pressure drag and skin friction [3.2].

In practice, the aerodynamic resistance is usually expressed in the following form:

$$R_a = \frac{\rho}{2} C_D A_f V_r^2 \tag{3.19}$$

where ρ is the mass density of the air, C_D is the coefficient of aerodynamic resistance that represents the combined effects of all of the factors described above, A_f is a characteristic area of the vehicle, usually taken as the frontal area, which is the projected area of the vehicle in the direction of travel, and V_r is the speed of the vehicle relative to the wind. It is interesting to note that aerodynamic resistance is proportional to the square of speed. Thus, the horsepower required to overcome aerodynamic resistance increases with the cube of speed. When the speed of a vehicle is doubled, the power required for overcoming aerodynamic resistance increases eightfold.

It should be mentioned that atmospheric conditions affect air density ρ, and hence aerodynamic resistance. For instance, an increase in ambient temperature from $0°$ to $38°C$ ($32°-100°F$) will cause a 14% reduction in aerodynamic resistance, and an increase in altitude of 1219 m (4000 ft) will lead to a decrease in aerodynamic resistance by 17%. In view of the significant effects of ambient conditions on the aerodynamic resistance, it is necessary to establish a standard set of conditions to which all aerodynamic test data may be referred. The commonly used standard conditions are: temperature $520°$ Rankine ($15.5°C$ or $60°F$) and barometric pressure 101.32 kPa (76 cm or 29.92 in. Hg). In performance calculations, the mass density of the air ρ may be taken as 1.23 kg/m^3 (0.00236 slug/ft^3, and its equivalent weight density 0.076 lb/ft^3).

The frontal area A_f of the vehicle may be determined from a photograph taken from the front if accurate drawings of the vehicle are not available. For passenger cars, the frontal area varies in the range of 79–84% of the area calculated from the overall vehicle width and height. Based on data collected, for passenger cars with mass in the range of 800–2000 kg (or 1760–4400 lb in weight), the relationship between the frontal area and the vehicle mass may be approximately expressed by

$$A_f = 1.6 + 0.00056 \, (m_v - 765) \tag{3.20}$$

where A_f is the frontal area in m^2 and m_v is the mass of the vehicle in kg.

The coefficient of aerodynamic resistance C_D may be obtained by wind-tunnel testing of scale models or full-scale vehicles. The deceleration method of road testing, commonly referred to as the coast-down test, may also be used to determine the aerodynamic resistance [3.3–3.5]. Using this method, the vehicle is first run up to a certain speed, then the driveline is disconnected from the engine, and the vehicle decelerates. The deceleration of the vehicle due to the combined effects of the rolling resistance of the tires, the driveline resistance, and the aerodynamic resistance can be derived from the coast-down test data, such as the speed–time or speed–distance data. By separating the effects of the motion resistance of the tires and the driveline resistance from the test data, the aerodynamic resistance can be derived. It has been shown that this method can yield sufficiently accurate results if care is taken to determine the motion resistance of the tires and the driveline resistance. In comparison with wind-tunnel testing, this method does not require expensive facilities. However, it requires a straight and level road, and it is subject to the influence of ambient conditions.

The coefficient of aerodynamic resistance C_D is a function of a number of vehicle design and operational factors. The shape of the vehicle body, including the forebody, afterbody, underbody, wheel-wells, drip-rails, window recesses, external mirrors, and mud-flaps, has a significant effect on the coefficient of aerodynamic resistance. The values of the coefficient of aerodynamic resistance for passenger cars with various shapes are shown in Fig. 3.4 [3.6], and those for a select group of automobiles are listed in Table 3.1 [3.7]. The influence of shape variations on the aerodynamic resistance coefficient of a passenger car is shown in Fig. 3.5 [3.8]. The effects of the shape of the forebody and afterbody of a passenger car on the aerodynamic resistance coefficient are shown in Figs. 3.6 and 3.7, respectively [3.7, 3.8]. To improve the aerodynamic performance of vehicles, add-on devices are often used. Figures 3.8 and 3.9 show the effects of front and rear spoilers on the aerodynamic resistance coefficient, respectively [3.8].

In addition to the shape of the vehicle body, the attitude of the vehicle defined by the angle of attack (i.e., the angle between the longitudinal axis of the vehicle and the horizontal), ground clearance, loading conditions, and other operational factors, such as radiator open or blanked, and window open or closed, also affect the aerodynamic resistance coefficient. Figure 3.10 shows the effect of the angle of attack on the value of C_D for three types of passenger car, while Fig. 3.11 shows the effect of ground clearance on the value of C_D for different types of vehicle [3.8]. The loading conditions and the distribution of load among axles may change the attitude (angle of attack) and ground clearance of the vehicle, and hence the aerodynamic resistance coefficient. The influence of loading conditions on the value of C_D for a passenger car is shown in Fig. 3.12 [3.8]. The influence of operational factors on the aerodynamic resistance coefficient of a car is shown in Fig. 3.13 [3.8].

The various components of aerodynamic resistance of a representative passenger car and their potential for reduction are summarized in Table 3.2 [3.2]. It can be seen that the greatest potential for reduction lies in the optimization of the body

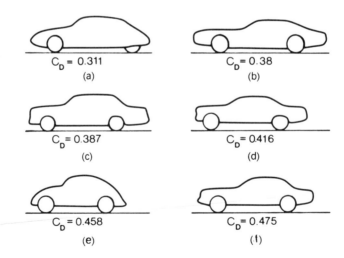

Fig. 3.4 Aerodynamic resistance coefficient for passenger cars. (a) Citroen DS 19. (b) Oldsmobile Toronado. (c) Mercedes-Benz 300 SE. (d) Ford Falcon Futura. (e) VW 1200. (f) Ford Mustang. (Reproduced with permission of the Society of Automotive Engineers from reference 3.6.)

TABLE 3.1 Values of Aerodynamic Resistance Coefficient and Frontal Area for Passenger Cars

Vehicle Type	Aerodynamic Resistance Coefficient C_D	Frontal Area A_f	
		m^2	ft^2
Mini Cars			
Fiat Uno ES	0.33–0.34	1.83	19.70
Peugeot 205GL	0.35–0.37	1.74	18.73
Honda Civic 1.2	0.37–0.39	1.72	18.51
VW Polo Coupe	0.39–0.40	1.72	18.51
Nissan Micra GL	0.40–0.41	1.78	19.16
Low Medium Size			
VW Golf GTI	0.35–0.36	1.91	20.56
VW Jetta GT	0.36–0.37	1.91	20.56
Ford Escort 1.3 GL	0.39–0.41	1.83	19.70
Mazda 323 1.5	0.41–0.43	1.78	19.16
Toyota Corolla 1300 DX	0.45–0.46	1.76	18.95
Medium Size			
VW Passat CL	0.36–0.37	1.89	20.34
Audi 80CC	0.38–0.39	1.86	20.02
BMW 318i (320i)	0.39–0.40	1.86	20.02
Honda Accord 1.8 EX	0.40–0.42	1.88	20.24
Nissan Stanza Notchback	0.41–0.43	1.88	20.24
Upper Medium Size			
Audi 100 1.8	0.30–0.31	2.05	22.07
Mercedes 190E (190D)	0.33–0.35	1.90	20.45
BMW 518i (520i, 525e)	0.36–0.38	2.02	21.74
Saab 900 GLi	0.40–0.42	1.95	20.99
Volvo 740 GLE	0.40–0.42	2.16	23.25
Luxury Cars			
Saab 9000 Turbo 16	0.34–0.36	2.05	22.07
Jaguar XJ-S	0.4–0.41	1.92	20.67
Mercedes 500 SEL	0.36–0.37	2.16	23.25
Peugeot 604 STI	0.41–0.43	2.05	22.07
BMW 728i (732i/735i)	0.42–0.44	2.13	22.93
Sports Cars			
Porsche 924	0.31–0.33	1.80	19.38
Renault Fuego GTX	0.34–0.37	1.82	19.59
VW Scirocco GTX	0.38–0.39	1.74	18.73
Toyota Celica Supra 2.8i	0.37–0.39	1.83	19.70
Honda Prelude	0.38–0.40	1.84	19.81

Source: Reference 3.7.

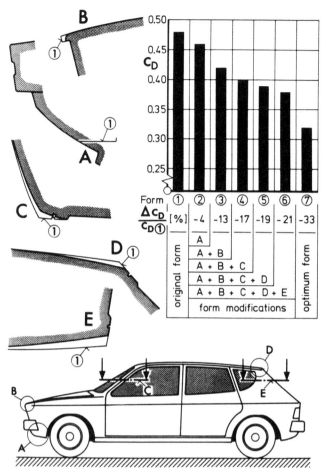

Fig. 3.5 Influence of body shape details on aerodynamic resistance coefficient of a passenger car. (Reproduced with permission from reference 3.8.)

shape. It is estimated that the component of aerodynamic resistance coefficient due to body shape can be reduced from a typical value of 0.28 to a practical minimum of 0.1. The total scope for reduction in aerodynamic resistance of a typical modern car is approximately 55%, as indicated in Table 3.2 [3.2].

The effects of the aerodynamic resistance coefficient on the fuel economy under steady-state conditions of a passenger car, with mass 1060 kg (2332 lb), frontal area 1.77 m^2 (19 ft^2), and radial tires, are shown in Fig. 3.14 [3.9]. It can be seen that at a steady speed of 96 km/h (60 mph), a reduction of the aerodynamic resistance coefficient from 0.5 to 0.3 will improve the fuel economy by approximately 23%. Figure 3.15 shows the effects of the reduction in aerodynamic resistance coefficient on fuel saving of a tractor–semitrailer under different operating conditions [3.10]. It can be seen from Fig. 3.15 that operating on a level road, the reduction in aerodynamic resistance coefficient has the most significant effect on fuel saving of a tractor–semitrailer.

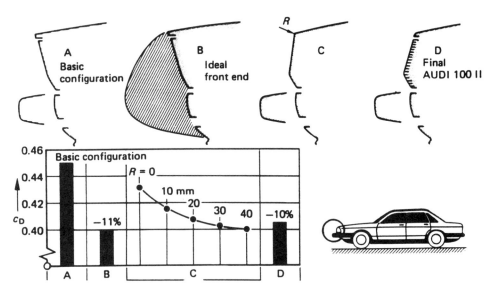

Fig. 3.6 Influence of the shape of the front end on aerodynamic resistance coefficient of a passenger car. (Reproduced with permission from reference 3.7.)

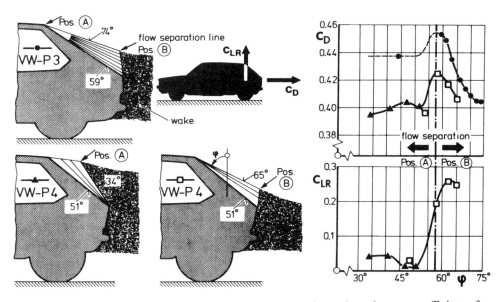

Fig. 3.7 Influence of the shape of the rear end on aerodynamic resistance coefficient of a passenger car. (Reproduced with permission from reference 3.8.)

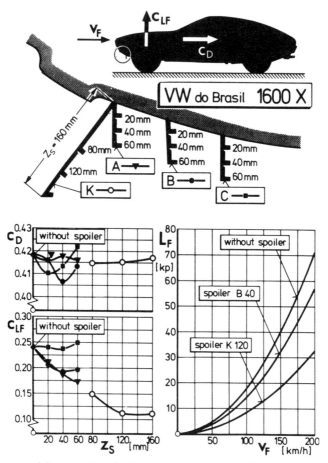

Fig. 3.8 Influence of front spoiler design on aerodynamic resistance coefficient and aerodynamic lift coefficient of a passenger car. (Reproduced with permission from reference 3.8.)

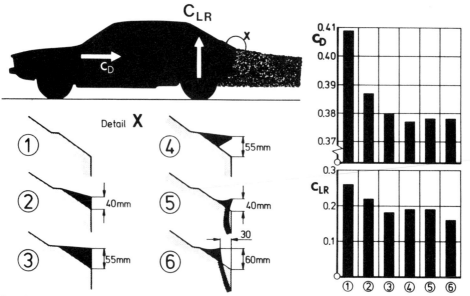

Fig. 3.9 Influence of rear spoiler design on aerodynamic resistance coefficient and aerodynamic lift coefficient of a passenger car. (Reproduced with permission from reference 3.8.)

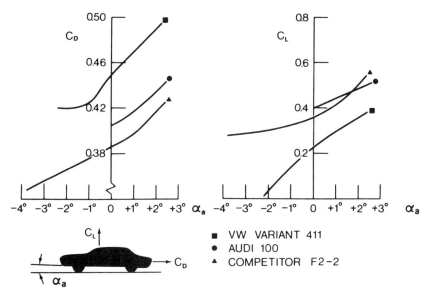

Fig. 3.10 Influence of the angle of attack on aerodynamic resistance coefficient and aerodynamic lift coefficient of passenger cars. (Reproduced with permission from reference 3.8.)

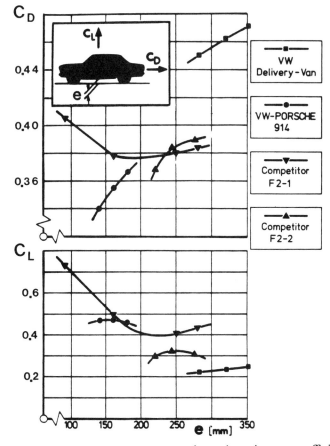

Fig. 3.11 Influence of ground clearance on aerodynamic resistance coefficient and aerodynamic lift coefficient of a passenger car. (Reproduced with permission from reference 3.8.)

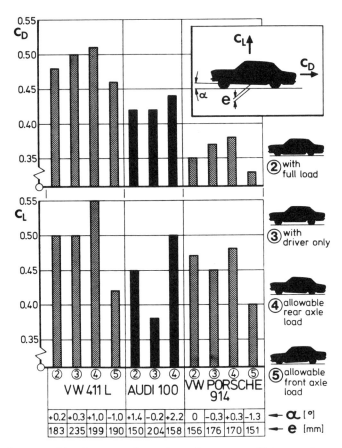

Fig. 3.12 Influence of load on aerodynamic resistance coefficient and aerodynamic lift coefficient of a passenger car. (Reproduced with permission from reference 3.8.)

In comparison with passenger cars, heavy commercial vehicles, such as trucks, tractor–semitrailers, and truck–trailers, usually have much higher values of aerodynamic resistance coefficient. This is primarily due to their essentially box-shaped body. Figure 3.16 shows the variations of the aerodynamic resistance coefficient of a tractor–semitrailer and a truck–trailer with the yaw angle, which is the angle between the direction of travel of the vehicle and that of the wind [3.10]. It also shows the contributions of the tractor (or truck) and semitrailer (or trailer) to the total aerodynamic resistance coefficient of the combination. It can be seen that for a tractor–semitrailer, the aerodynamic resistance of the tractor is not sensitive to yaw angle, and that the tractor contributes approximately 60% of the total aerodynamic resistance of the tractor–semitrailer combination at 0° yaw angle. For the truck–trailer combination, the truck contributes approximately 62% of the total aerodynamic resistance of the combination at 0° yaw angle.

Table 3.3 shows representative values of the aerodynamic resistance coefficient of passenger cars, vans, buses, tractor–semitrailers, and truck–trailers [3.10].

To improve the aerodynamic performance of heavy commercial vehicles, add-on devices, such as the air deflector mounted on the roof of the tractor or truck, have

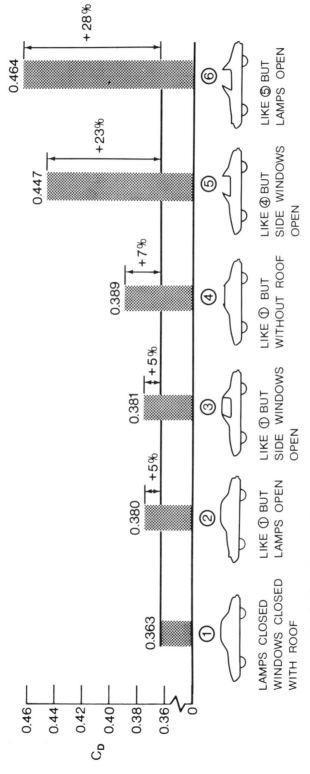

Fig. 3.13 Influence of operational factors on aerodynamic resistance coefficient of a passenger car. (Reproduced with permission from reference 3.8.)

TABLE 3.2 Components of Aerodynamic Resistance Coefficient and Potential for Reduction

Components of Aerodynamic Resistance Coefficient	Typical Value*	Minimum Feasible Value
Forebody	0.055	−0.015
Afterbody	0.14	0.07
Underbody	0.06	0.02
Skin friction	0.025	0.025
Total body drag	0.28	0.10
Wheel and wheel wells	0.09	0.07
Drip-rails	0.01	0
Window recesses	0.01	0.005
External mirror (one)	0.01	0.005
Total protuberance drag	0.12	0.08
Cooling system	0.035	0.015
Total internal drag	0.035	0.015
Overall total drag	0.435	0.195

Source: Reference 3.2.

*Based on cars of 1970's and early 1980's.

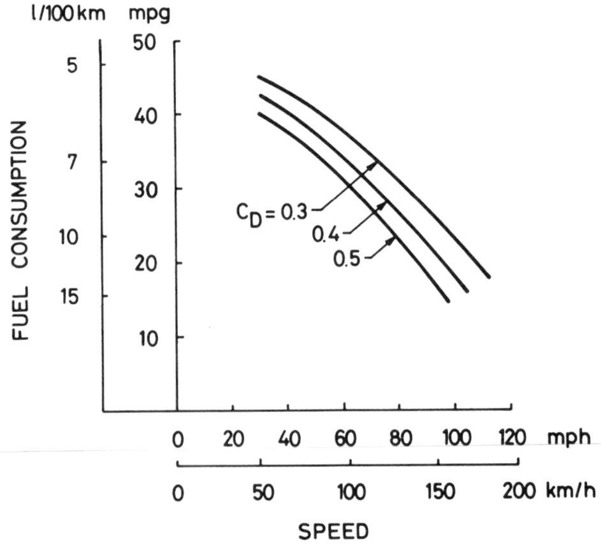

Fig. 3.14 Effect of reduction in aerodynamic resistance coefficient on fuel economy at different speeds for a midsize passenger car. (Reproduced with permission of the Society of Automotive Engineers from reference 3.9.)

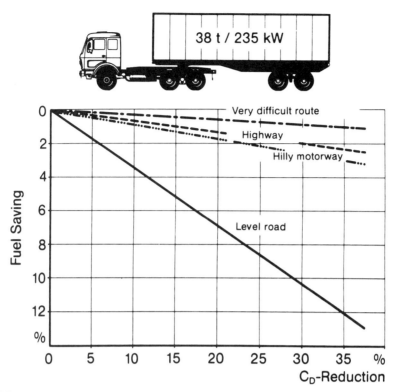

Fig. 3.15 Effect of reduction in aerodynamic resistance coefficient on fuel saving for a tractor–semitrailer. (Reproduced with permission from reference 3.10.)

been introduced. Figure 3.17 shows the effects of various types of air deflector on the aerodynamic resistance coefficient of a tractor–semitrailer [3.11]. It can be seen that with the best air deflector among those investigated (type 6 shown in the figure), the aerodynamic resistance coefficient can be reduced by 24%, in comparison with that of the baseline vehicle (type 1). The installation of a gap seal between the tractor and semitrailer (type 8) does not cause a noticeable decrease in the aerodynamic resistance coefficient. With rounded vertical edges in the front of the semitrailer and with smooth, flat panels on the semitrailer body (type 9), the aerodynamic resistance coefficient is reduced by 22%. If this is coupled with the installation of the best air deflector (type 10), a total reduction of 34% in aerodynamic resistance coefficient can be achieved. Figure 3.18 shows the variations of the aerodynamic resistance coefficient of tractor–semitrailers with various add-on devices and tractor shapes with the yaw angle [3.10].

Aerodynamic lift acting on a vehicle is caused by the pressure differential across the vehicle body from the bottom to the top. It may become significant at moderate speeds. The aerodynamic lift usually causes the reduction of the normal load on the tire–ground contact. Thus, the performance characteristics and directional control and stability of the vehicle may be adversely affected. For racing cars, to improve their cornering and tractive capabilities, externally mounted aerodynamic

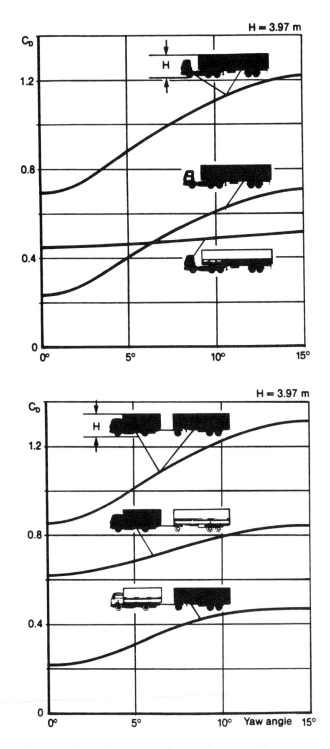

Fig. 3.16 Distribution of aerodynamic resistance between (a) tractor and semitrailer and (b) truck and trailer at different yaw angles. (Reproduced with permission from reference 3.10.)

**TABLE 3.3 Values of Aerodynamic Resistance
Coefficient for Various Types of Vehicle**

Vehicle Type	Aerodynamic Resistance Coefficient C_D
Passenger cars	0.3–0.52
Vans	0.4–0.58
Buses	0.5–0.8
Tractor–semitrailers	0.64–1.1
Truck–trailers	0.74–1.0

Source: Reference 3.10.

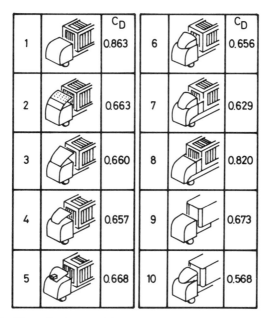

Fig. 3.17 Effect of add-on devices and body details on aerodynamic resistance coefficient of tractor–semitrailers. (Reproduced with permission of the Society of Automotive Engineers from reference 3.11.)

surfaces that generate a downward aerodynamic force are widely used. This increases the normal load on the tire–ground contact.

The aerodynamic lift R_L acting on a vehicle is usually expressed by

$$R_L = \frac{\rho}{2} C_L A_f V_r^2 \tag{3.21}$$

where C_L is the coefficient of aerodynamic lift usually obtained from wind-tunnel testing. Typical values of C_L for passenger cars vary in the range 0.2–0.5 using the frontal area of the vehicle as the characteristic area. As for the coefficient of aerodynamic resistance, it depends not only on the shape of the vehicle, but also

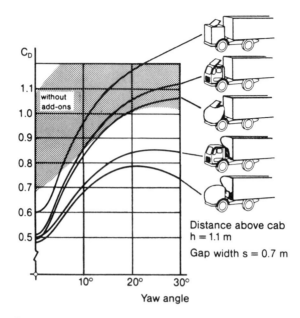

Fig. 3.18 Effect of add-on devices on aerodynamic resistance coefficient of tractor–semi-trailers at different yaw angles. (Reproduced with permission from reference 3.10.)

on a number of operational factors. The effects of the shape of the afterbody on the rear axle aerodynamic lift coefficient C_{LR} are shown in Fig. 3.7. Figures 3.8 and 3.9 show the influence of the front and rear spoilers on the front and rear axle aerodynamic lift coefficients, C_{LF} and C_{LR}, respectively. The effects of the angle of attack, ground clearance, and loading conditions on the aerodynamic lift coefficient C_L are illustrated in Figs. 3.10, 3.11, and 3.12, respectively.

The aerodynamic pitching moment may also affect the behavior of a vehicle. This moment is the resultant of the moments of the aerodynamic resistance and aerodynamic lift about the center of gravity of the vehicle. It may cause significant load transfer from one axle to the other at moderate and higher speeds. Thus, it would affect the performance, as well as the directional control and stability of the vehicle.

The aerodynamic pitching moment M_a is usually expressed by

$$M_a = \frac{\rho}{2} C_M A_f L_c V_r^2 \qquad (3.22)$$

where C_M is the coefficient of aerodynamic pitching moment usually obtained from wind-tunnel testing and L_c is the characteristic length of the vehicle. The wheelbase or the overall length of the vehicle may be used as the characteristic length in Eq. 3.22. Most passenger cars have a value of C_M between 0.05 and 0.20, using the wheelbase as the characteristic length and the frontal area as the characteristic area.

3.3 VEHICLE POWER PLANT AND TRANSMISSION CHARACTERISTICS

As mentioned previously, there are two limiting factors to the performance of a road vehicle: one is the maximum tractive effort that the tire–ground contact can support, and the other is the tractive effort that the engine torque with a given transmission can provide. The smaller of these two will determine the performance potential of the vehicle. In low gears with the engine throttle fully open, the tractive effort may be limited by the nature of tire–road adhesion. In higher gears, the tractive effort is usually determined by the engine and transmission characteristics. To predict the overall performance of a road vehicle, the engine and transmission characteristics must be taken into consideration. In this section, the general characteristics of vehicle power plants and transmissions will be presented.

3.3.1 Power Plant Characteristics

For vehicular applications, the ideal performance characteristics of a power plant are constant power output over the full speed range. Consequently, the engine output torque varies with speed hyperbolically, as shown in Fig. 3.19. This will provide the vehicle with high tractive effort at low speeds where demands for acceleration, drawbar pull, or grade climbing capability are high. There are power plants that have power–torque–speed characteristics close to the ideal for vehicular applications, such as series-wound electric motors and steam engines. Figure 3.20 shows the torque–speed characteristics of a series-wound dc motor. The internal

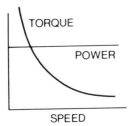

Fig. 3.19 Ideal performance characteristics for vehicular power plants.

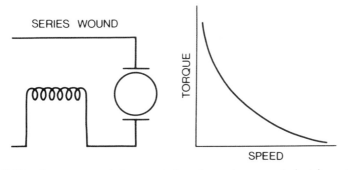

Fig. 3.20 Torque–speed characteristics of a series-wound electric motor.

190 PERFORMANCE CHARACTERISTICS OF ROAD VEHICLES

combustion engine has less favorable performance characteristics, and can be used only with a suitable transmission. Despite this shortcoming, it has found the widest application in automotive vehicles to date because of its relatively high power to weight ratio, good fuel economy, low cost, and easiness to start.

In addition to the continuous search for improving the efficiency, power-to-weight ratio, size, and fuel economy of vehicle power plants, considerable emphasis has been placed on the control and reduction of undesirable exhaust emissions in recent years. Various technological options, including further modification of the internal combustion engine, are being investigated. In general, the two basic approaches to reducing undesirable emissions are to prevent them from forming, and to remove them from the exhaust once formed. Improved combustion using fuel injection, stratified charge techniques, and others can reduce undesirable emissions. Pollutants can also be removed after they have left the combustion chamber by injecting air into an exhaust manifold reactor for more complete oxidation, or by a catalytic converter in the direct-flame afterburner [3.12].

Alternatives to the internal combustion engine are also being studied [3.12]. They include gas turbine engines, Rankine-cycle external combustion engines, noncondensing external combustion (Stirling-cycle) engines, electric propulsion systems, and hybrid power systems, such as a combination of the internal combustion engine and electric propulsion. The gas turbine has several advantages as a vehicular power plant. It has a favorable power-to-weight ratio, and can be used with a wide range of fuels. The carbon monoxide and hydrocarbon in the exhausts of a gas turbine are lower than those of an equivalent gasoline engine. There is evidence to suggest that nitrogen oxide emissions could also be reduced. The gas turbine is, however, not without drawbacks as an automotive power plant. The greatest disadvantage is its low efficiency and poor fuel economy under no load or partial load conditions that constitute a significant portion of the operation of automotive vehicles. The Rankine vapor-cycle external combustion engine has torque–speed characteristics close to the ideal. Coupled with its high overload capacity, the Rankine-cycle engine would eliminate the need for a transmission. It can use a wide range of hydrocarbon fuels, and yet undesirable emissions including nitrogen oxides are very low. Among the disadvantages of this kind of power plant are the time required to put the engine into operation and a relatively poor power-to-weight ratio. The Stirling-cycle engine utilizes alternate heating and cooling of the working medium, such as compressed helium and hydrogen gas, at constant volume to develop useful mechanical work. To date, it has a rather poor power-to-weight ratio and is mechanically complex. The emission characteristics of the Stirling engine are, however, extremely good. It also has excellent performance characteristics at higher speeds, which suggests its potential value in a hybrid power system for automotive vehicles, where it could run continuously under optimum operating conditions [3.12].

Since the internal combustion engine is still the most commonly used power plant in automotive vehicles to date, it is appropriate to review the basic features of its characteristics that are essential to the prediction of vehicle performance. Representative characteristics of a gasoline engine and a diesel engine are shown in Figs. 3.21 and 3.22, respectively. The internal combustion engine starts operating smoothly at a certain speed (the idle speed). Good combustion quality and maximum engine torque are reached at an intermediate engine speed. As speed increases further, the mean effective pressure decreases because of growing losses in the air-induction manifolds, and the engine torque also declines. Power output, however, increases with an increase of speed up to the point of maximum power. Beyond this point, the engine torque decreases more rapidly with an increase of speed. This results in a decline of power output. In vehicular applications, the

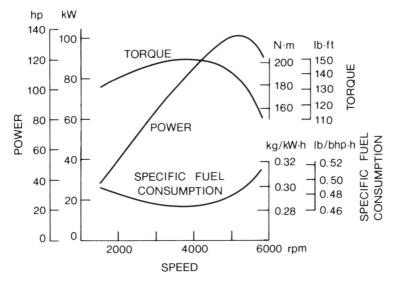

Fig. 3.21 Performance characteristics of a gasoline engine.

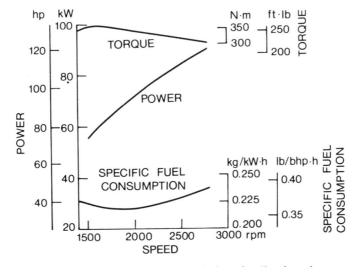

Fig. 3.22 Performance characteristics of a diesel engine.

maximum permissible speed of the engine is usually set just above the speed of the maximum power output. Vehicles designed for traction, such as agricultural and industrial tractors, usually operate at much lower engine speeds since the maximum torque, and not power, determines the limits to their tractive performance. To limit the maximum operating speed, engines for heavy-duty vehicles are often equipped with a governor.

It should be mentioned that engine performance diagrams supplied by manufacturers usually represent the gross engine performance, which is the performance measured when all installations and accessories not essential to the operation are stripped off. The effective engine power available at the transmission input shaft is therefore reduced by the power consumed by the accessories, such as the fan and water pump for the cooling system, and by losses arising from the exhaust system, air cleaner, etc. There are also auxiliaries, such as the alternator, air conditioning unit, and power-assisted steering and braking, that make a demand on engine power. Figure 3.23 shows the variations of the power consumed by the air conditioning unit, the water pump and fan, power steering, and alternator with engine speed for a representative full-size passenger car [3.13]. In vehicle performance prediction, the power consumption of all accessories over the full engine speed range should be evaluated and subtracted from the gross engine power to obtain the effective power available to the transmission input shaft.

Atmospheric conditions affect engine performance. To allow comparison of the performance of different engines on a common basis, standard atmospheric con-

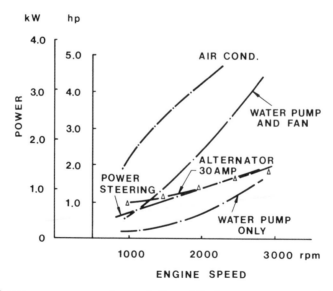

Fig. 3.23   Accessory power requirements for a full-size passenger car. (Reproduced with permission of the Society of Automotive Engineers from reference 3.13.)

ditions are used. The commonly used standard conditions are temperature $T_0 =$ 520° Rankine (15.5°C or 60°F), and barometric pressure $B_0 = 101.32$ kPa (76 cm or 29.92 in. Hg). For a gasoline engine, the relationship between the engine power under standard atmospheric conditions P_0 and that under given atmospheric conditions P is given by [3.14]

$$P = \frac{P_0 (B_a - B_v)}{B_0} \sqrt{\frac{T_0}{T}} \qquad (3.23)$$

where B_a and T are the barometric pressure at the engine air intake and ambient temperature (°R) respectively. B_v is the vapor pressure, which represents the effect of air humidity. Usually, it may be neglected, except under extreme conditions. For a diesel engine, the effects of atmospheric conditions on its performance characteristics are more complicated than those for a gasoline engine. As an approximation, the following relation may be used [3.14]:

$$P = \frac{P_0 (B_a - B_v)}{B_0} \frac{T_0}{T} \qquad (3.24)$$

Atmospheric conditions can change engine performance considerably. The effects of engine inlet temperature and ambient pressure on engine performance are shown in Fig. 3.24 [3.14]. It can be seen that if the engine air inlet temperature is higher and the ambient pressure is lower than the standard conditions, the power output of the engine will be lower.

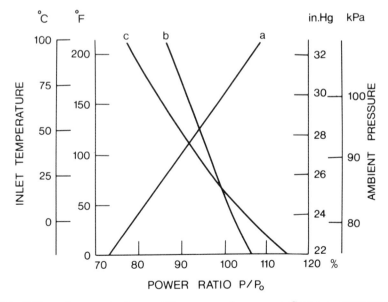

Fig. 3.24 Effect of atmospheric conditions on engine power. Curve *a*—power ratio versus ambient pressure. Curve *b*— power ratio versus intake temperature for gasoline engines. Curve *c*—power ratio versus intake temperature for diesel engines.

3.3.2 Transmission Characteristics

As mentioned previously, the power–torque–speed characteristics of the internal combustion engine are not suited for direct vehicle propulsion. A transmission, therefore, is required to provide the vehicle with the tractive effort–speed characteristics that will satisfy the load demands under various operating conditions. The term "transmission" includes all of those systems or subsystems employed for transmitting the engine power to the driven wheels or sprockets. There are two common types of transmission for road vehicles: the manual gear transmission, and the automatic transmission with a torque converter. Other types of transmission, such as the continuous variable transmission (CVT) and the hydrostatic transmission, are also in use.

Manual Gear Transmissions   The principal requirements for the transmission are:

1. to achieve the desired maximum vehicle speed with an appropriate engine
2. to be able to start, fully loaded, in both forward and reverse directions on a steep gradient, typically 33% (1 in 3), and to be able to maintain a speed of 88–96 km/h (55–60 mph) on a gentle slope, such as 3%, in high gear for passenger cars
3. to properly match the characteristics of the engine to achieve the desired operating fuel economy and acceleration characteristics.

The manual gear transmission usually consists of a clutch, a gearbox, a propeller shaft, and a drive axle with a differential (to allow relative rotation of the driven tires during turning maneuvers). In front-engined and front-wheel-drive vehicles or in rear-engined and rear-drive-vehicles, the gearbox and differential are usually integrated into a unit, commonly referred to as a transaxle. As a general rule, the drive axle has a constant gear reduction ratio, which is determined by the usual practice requiring direct drive (nonreducing drive) in the gearbox in the highest gear. For vehicles requiring extremely high torque at low speeds, an additional reduction gear (final drive) may be placed at the driven wheels. The gearbox provides a number of gear reduction ratios ranging from 3 to 5 for passenger cars, and 5 to 16 or more for heavy commercial vehicles. The number of gear ratios is selected to provide the vehicle with the tractive effort–speed characteristics as close to the ideal as possible in a cost-effective manner, as indicated in Fig. 3.25.

The gear ratio of the highest gear (i.e., the smallest gear reduction ratio) is chosen so that the desired maximum vehicle speed can be achieved with an appropriate engine. The engine should have sufficient power to overcome the internal resistance in the transmission, rolling resistance of the tires, and aerodynamic resistance at the maximum vehicle speed on a level road. The common practice is to select a gear ratio such that at the maximum vehicle speed, the engine speed is slightly higher than that at the maximum engine power, as indicated in Fig. 3.26. This ensures sufficient power reserve to maintain a given vehicle speed against a

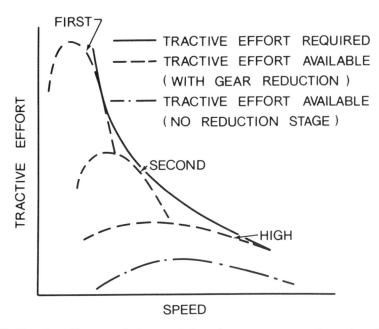

Fig. 3.25 Tractive effort–speed characteristics of a passenger car. (Reproduced with permission from reference 3.14.)

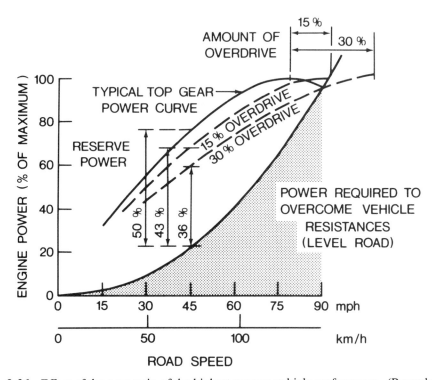

Fig. 3.26 Effect of the gear ratio of the highest gear on vehicle performance. (Reproduced with permission from reference 3.16.)

temporary increase in headwind or gradient during operation or against the possible deterioration in engine performance after extended use. Based on this principle, the gear ratio of the highest gear in the gearbox may be determined as follows:

$$\xi_n = \frac{n_{e1} r (1 - i)}{V_{\max} \xi_{ax}} \tag{3.25}$$

where ξ_n is the gear ratio of the highest gear in a gearbox with n-speed; n_{e1} is the engine speed corresponding to the maximum vehicle speed, which for passenger cars is usually about 10% higher than the speed at the maximum engine power; r is the rolling radius of the tire; i is the tire slip; $V_{\max}$ is the desired maximum vehicle speed; and ξ_{ax} is the gear ratio in the drive axle.

If, in the highest gear, the gearbox is in direct drive (i.e., $\xi_n = 1$), then Eq. 3.25 can be used to determine the gear ratio ξ_{ax} in the drive axle.

The gear ratio of the lowest gear (i.e., the largest gear reduction ratio) is selected on the basis that the vehicle should be able to climb a steep gradient, usually 33% for passenger cars. There is also a suggestion that the gear ratio of the lowest gear in the gearbox should be such that the vehicle can climb the maximum gradient possible without tire spin on a typical road surface. If this approach is followed, then the gear ratio of the lowest gear in the gear box can be determined as follows.

For a rear-wheel-drive vehicle, from Eq. 3.9, the maximum slope $\theta_{s\max}$ that the vehicle can climb, as determined by the maximum tractive effort that the tire–ground contact can support, is expressed by

$$W \sin \theta_{s\max} = \frac{\mu W (l_1 - f_r h)/L}{1 - \mu h/L} - f_r W \tag{3.26}$$

In the above equation, the aerodynamic resistance is neglected because on a steep slope, the vehicle speed is usually low.

From Eq. 3.26, the gear ratio of the lowest gear ξ_1 in the gearbox is given by

$$\xi_1 = \frac{W (\sin \theta_{s\max} + f_r) r}{M_{e\max} \xi_{ax} \eta_t} \tag{3.27}$$

where $M_{e\max}$ is the maximum engine torque and η_t is the efficiency of the transmission.

For a front-wheel-drive vehicle, a similar expression for the gear ratio of the lowest gear can be derived from Eqs. 3.10 and 3.27.

The method for selecting the gear ratios for the intermediate gears between the highest and the lowest is, to a great extent, dependent upon the type of vehicle (heavy commercial vehicles or passenger cars). For heavy commercial vehicles, the gear ratios are usually arranged in a geometric progression. The basis for this is to have the engine operating within the same speed range in each gear, as shown in Fig. 3.27. This would ensure that in each gear, the operating fuel economy is similar.

For instance, for a four-speed gearbox, the following relationship can be established (see Fig. 3.27):

$$\frac{\xi_2}{\xi_1} = \frac{\xi_3}{\xi_2} = \frac{\xi_4}{\xi_3} = \frac{n_{e2}}{n_{e1}} = K_g$$

and

$$K_g = \sqrt[3]{\frac{\xi_4}{\xi_1}} \tag{3.28}$$

where ξ_1, ξ_2, ξ_3, and ξ_4 are the gear ratios of the first, second, third, and fourth gears, respectively. In a more general case, if the ratio of the highest gear ξ_n and that of the lowest gear ξ_1 have been determined, and the number of speeds in the gearbox n_g is known, the factor K_g can be determined by

$$K_g = \sqrt[n_g-1]{\frac{\xi_n}{\xi_1}} \tag{3.29}$$

and

$$\xi_n = K_g \xi_{n-1}$$

Table 3.4 gives the gear ratios of gearboxes designed for heavy commercial

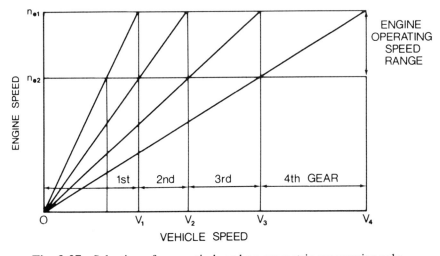

Fig. 3.27 Selection of gear ratio based on geometric progression rule.

TABLE 3.4   Gear Ratios of Transmissions for Heavy Commercial Vehicles

Gear	Allison HT70	Eaton Fuller RT-11608	Eaton Fuller RT/RTO-15615	Eaton Fuller RT-6613	ZF Ecomid 16S 109
1	3.0	10.23	7.83	17.93	11.86
2	2.28	7.23	6.00	14.04	10.07
3	1.73	5.24	4.63	10.96	8.40
4	1.31	3.82	3.57	8.61	7.13
5	1.00	2.67	2.80	6.74	5.71
6	0.76	1.89	2.19	5.26	4.85
7		1.37	1.68	4.11	3.97
8		1.00	1.30	3.29	3.37
9			1.00	2.61	2.99
10			0.78	2.05	2.54
11				1.60	2.12
12				1.25	1.80
13				1.00	1.44
14					1.22
15					1.00
16					0.85
Value of K_g Calculated from Eq. 3.29	0.76	0.717	0.774	0.786	0.839

vehicles. It can be seen that the ratios for these gearboxes are basically arranged in a geometric progression. It should be noted that because the number of teeth of a gear is an integer, it is not possible, in some cases, to arrange gear ratios in an exact geometric progression.

For passenger cars, the gear ratios are not usually arranged in a geometric progression. The ratios of intermediate gears may be chosen to minimize the time required to reach a specific speed, such as 100 km/h (or 60 mph) or the maximum speed of the vehicle. Consideration is also given to the fact that shifting between upper gears happens more frequently than between lower gears, particularly in city driving. As a result, the gear ratios of the upper gears are usually closer than those of the lower gears. For instance, for the gearbox in the Cadillac (Seville) shown in Table 3.5, the ratio of the gear ratio of the fourth gear to that of the third gear is 0.7 (0.7/1.00), whereas the ratio of the gear ratio of the third gear to that of the second gear is 0.637 (1.00/1.57) and the ratio of the gear ratio of the second gear to that of the first gear is 0.538 (1.57/2.92). Similar situations can be observed in the gear ratios of the transmissions for other passenger cars shown in Table 3.5.

It is interesting to note that while the gear ratios for passenger cars are not arranged in a geometric progression, the average value of the ratios of two consecutive gear ratios is quite close to the value of K_g obtained using Eq. 3.29. For instance, the average value of the ratios of two consecutive gear ratios for the Cadillac (Seville) is 0.625 ((0.7 + 0.637 + 0.538)/3), whereas the value of K_g obtained using Eq. 3.29 is 0.621 ($\sqrt[3]{0.7/2.92}$).

TABLE 3.5 Gear Ratios of Transmissions for Passenger Cars

Vehicle	Transmission Type	Transmission Ratios					Final Drive Ratio
		1st	2nd	3rd	4th	5th	
Audi 80 1.8S	Manual	3.545	1.857	1.156	0.838	0.683	4.111
100	Manual	3.545	2.105	1.429	1.029	0.838	4.111
100 Quattro 2.8E	Manual	3.500	1.842	1.300	0.943	0.789	4.111
BMW 325i	Manual	4.202	2.49	1.67	1.24	1.00	3.15
535i	Manual	3.83	2.20	1.40	1.00	0.81	3.64
750i	Automatic	2.48	1.48	1.00	0.73		3.15
Buick Park Avenue	Automatic	2.92	1.57	1.00	0.70		2.84
Cadillac Seville	Automatic	2.92	1.57	1.00	0.70		2.97
Chrysler Voyager SE	Automatic	2.84	1.57	1.00	0.69		3.47
Ford Mustang GT	Manual	3.97	2.34	1.46	1.00	0.79	3.45
Crown Victoria	Automatic	2.40	1.47	1.00	0.67		3.08
Honda Accord GT2.2i	Manual	3.307	1.809	1.230	0.933	0.757	4.266
Mazda 323 1.6i GLX	Manual	3.42	1.84	1.29	0.92	0.73	4.11
929 3.0i GLX	Manual	3.48	2.02	1.39	1.00	0.76	3.73
Mercedes-Benz 230CE	Manual	3.91	2.17	1.37	1.00	0.81	3.46
300E	Automatic	3.87	2.25	1.44	1.00		3.27
600SEL	Automatic	3.87	2.25	1.44	1.00		2.65
Mercury Cougar LS	Manual	2.40	1.47	1.00	0.67		3.27
Nissan Micra LX	Manual	3.41	1.96	1.26	0.92	0.72	3.81
Toyota Camry 2.0G i	Manual	3.285	2.041	1.322	1.028	0.820	3.944
Volkswagen Passat GT	Manual	3.78	2.12	1.43	1.03	0.84	3.68
Volvo 960	Automatic	2.80	1.53	1.00	0.75		3.73

In the transmission, there are losses due to friction between gear teeth and in the bearings and seals, and due to oil churning. The mechanical efficiency of the transmission is a function of load (torque) and speed. Figure 3.28 shows the variations of the mechanical efficiency with the input speed for a three-speed automatic gearbox. The transmission is connected to an engine operating at wide open throttle and developing a maximum torque of 407 N · m (300 lb · ft) [3.15]. In vehicle performance predictions, as a first approximation, the following average values for the mechanical efficiency of the major subsystems in the transmission may be used:

gearbox—direct drive   98%

gearbox—indirect drive   95%

drive axle   95%.

For a vehicle with a manual gear transmission, the tractive effort of the vehicle is given by

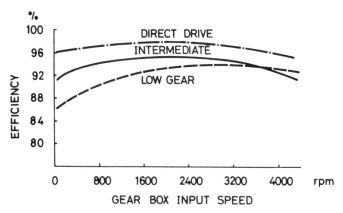

Fig. 3.28 Mechanical efficiency of a three-speed automatic gearbox at wide open throttle. (Reproduced with permission of the Society of Automotive Engineers from reference 3.15.)

$$F = \frac{M_e \xi_0 \eta_t}{r} \tag{3.30}$$

where M_e is the engine output torque, ξ_0 is the overall reduction ratio of the transmission (including both the gearbox and drive axle gear ratios), η_t is the overall transmission efficiency, and r is the radius of the tire (or sprocket). It is important to note that the maximum tractive effort that the tire–ground contact can support usually determines the traction capability of the vehicle in low gears.

The relationship between vehicle speed and engine speed is given by

$$V = \frac{n_e r}{\xi_0} (1 - i) \tag{3.31}$$

where n_e is the engine speed and i is the slip of the vehicle running gear. For a road vehicle, the slip is usually assumed to be 2–5% under normal operating conditions.

Figure 3.29 shows the variation of the tractive effort with speed for a passenger car equipped with a three-speed manual gear transmission [3.14].

Automatic Transmissions   The automatic transmission with a torque converter is used widely in passenger cars in North America. It usually comprises a torque converter and an automatic gear box. The torque converter consists of at least three rotary elements known as the pump (impeller), the turbine, and the reactor, as shown in Fig. 3.30. The pump is connected to the engine shaft, and the turbine is connected to the output shaft of the converter, which in turn is coupled with the input shaft of a multispeed gearbox. The reactor is coupled to an external casing to provide a reaction on the fluid circulating in the converter. The

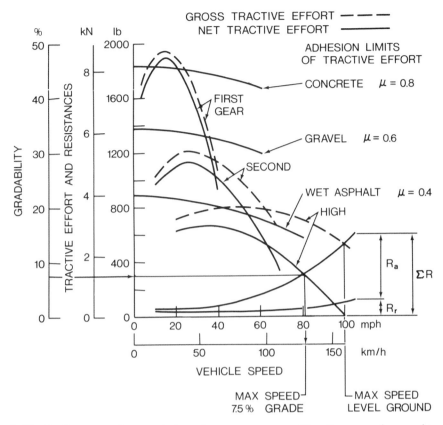

Fig. 3.29 Performance characteristics of a passenger car with a three-speed manual transmission (Reproduced with permission from reference 3.14.)

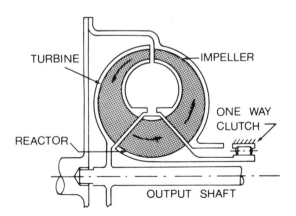

Fig. 3.30 Schematic view of a torque converter.

function of the reactor is to enable the turbine to develop an output torque higher than the input torque of the converter, thus to obtain a torque multiplication. The reactor is usually mounted on a free wheel (one-way clutch) so that when the starting period has been completed and the turbine speed is approaching that of the pump, the reactor is in free rotation. At this point, the converter operates as a fluid coupling, with a ratio of output torque to input torque equal to 1.0 [3.16].

The major advantages of incorporating a torque converter into the transmission may be summarized as follows:

1. When properly matched, it will not stall the engine.
2. It provides a flexible coupling between the engine and the driven wheels (or sprockets).
3. Together with a suitably selected multispeed gearbox, it provides torque-speed characteristics that approach the ideal.

The performance characteristics of a torque converter are usually described in terms of the following four parameters:

Speed ratio C_{sr} = output speed/input speed

Torque ratio C_{tr} = output torque/input torque

Efficiency η_c = output speed $\times$ output torque/input speed $\times$ input torque = $C_{sr}C_{tr}$

Capacity factor (size factor) K_{tc} = speed/$\sqrt{\text{torque}}$

The capacity factor is an indication of the ability of the converter to absorb or to transmit torque, which is proportional to the square of the rotating speed.

Representative performance characteristics of the torque converter are shown in Fig. 3.31, in which the torque ratio, efficiency, and input capacity factor, which is the ratio of the input speed to the square root of the input torque, are plotted against the speed ratio [3.15]. The torque ratio of the converter reaches a maximum at stall condition where the speed ratio is zero. The torque ratio decreases as the speed ratio increases, and the converter eventually acts as a hydraulic coupling with a torque ratio of 1.0. At this point, a small difference between the input and output speed remains because of the slip between the pump (impeller) and the turbine. The efficiency of the converter is zero at stall condition, and increases with an increase of the speed ratio. It reaches a maximum when the converter acts as a fluid coupling. The input capacity factor is an important parameter defining the operating conditions of the torque converter and governing the matching be-tween the converter and the engine. The input capacity factor of the converter has a minimum value at stall condition, and increases with an increase of the speed ratio.

Since the converter is driven by the engine, to determine the actual operating conditions of the converter, the engine operating point has to be specified. To characterize the engine operating conditions for purposes of determining the com-

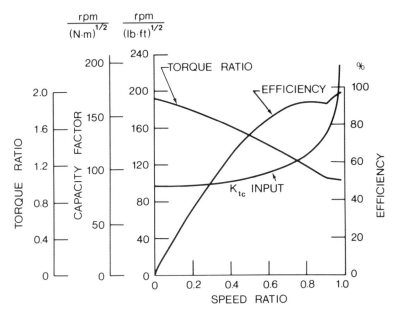

Fig. 3.31 Performance characteristics of a torque converter. (Reproduced with permission of the Society of Automotive Engineers from reference 3.15.)

bined performance of the engine and the converter, an engine capacity factor K_e is introduced and is defined as

$$K_e = \frac{n_e}{\sqrt{M_e}}$$

where n_e and M_e are the engine speed and torque, respectively. The variation of the capacity factor with speed for a particular engine is shown in Fig. 3.32 [3.15]. To achieve proper matching, the engine and the converter should have a similar range of capacity factor.

As mentioned above, the engine shaft is usually connected to the input shaft of the converter; therefore,

$$K_e = K_{tc}$$

The matching procedure begins with specifying the engine speed and engine torque. Knowing the engine operating point, one can determine the engine capacity factor K_e (Fig. 3.32). Since $K_e = K_{tc}$, the input capacity factor of the converter corresponding to the specific engine operating point is then known. For a particular value of the input capacity factor of the converter K_{tc}, the converter speed ratio and torque ratio can be determined from the converter performance curves, as shown in Fig. 3.31. The output torque and output speed of the converter are then given by

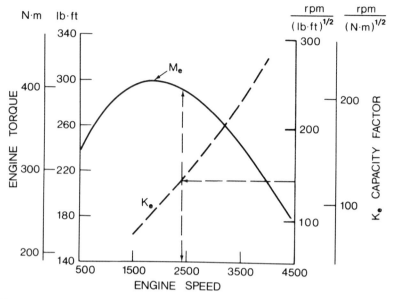

Fig. 3.32   Capacity factor of an internal combustion engine. (Reproduced with permission of the Society of Automotive Engineers from reference 3.15.)

$$M_{tc} = M_e C_{tr} \qquad \cdot \tag{3.32}$$

and

$$n_{tc} = n_e C_{sr} \tag{3.33}$$

where M_{tc} and n_{tc} are the output torque and output speed of the converter, respectively.

With the reduction ratios of the gearbox and the drive axle known, the tractive effort and speed of the vehicle can be calculated:

$$F = \frac{M_{tc}\xi_0\eta_t}{r} = \frac{M_e C_{tr}\xi_0\eta_t}{r} \tag{3.34}$$

and

$$V = \frac{n_{tc}r}{\xi_0}(1 - i) = \frac{n_e C_{sr}r}{\xi_0}(1 - i) \tag{3.35}$$

Figure 3.33 shows the variation of the tractive effort with speed for a passenger car equipped with a torque converter and a three-speed gearbox [3.15].

It should be mentioned that the efficiency of a torque converter is low over a considerable range of speed ratio, as shown in Fig. 3.31. To improve the overall

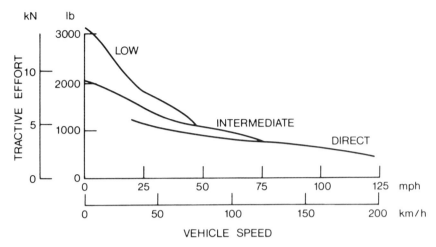

Fig. 3.33 Tractive effort–speed characteristics of a passenger car with a three-speed automatic transmission. (Reproduced with permission of the Society of Automotive Engineers from reference 3.15.)

efficiency of the automatic transmission and hence fuel economy, a "lock-up" clutch is incorporated in the torque converter. It is programmed to engage in a predetermined vehicle speed range. When the "lock-up" clutch is engaged, the engine power is directly transmitted to the output shaft of the torque converter.

Example 3.1. An engine with torque–speed characteristics as shown in Fig. 3.32 is coupled with a torque converter with characteristics as shown in Fig. 3.31. Determine the output speed and output torque of the torque converter when the engine is operating at 2450 rpm with an engine output torque of 393 N · m (290 lb · ft).

Solution. The engine capacity factor K_e

$$K_e = \frac{n_e}{\sqrt{M_e}} = \frac{2450}{\sqrt{393}} = 123 \text{ rpm}/(\text{N} \cdot \text{m})^{1/2}$$

Since the capacity factor K_e is equal to that of the torque converter K_{tc},

$$K_{tc} = 123 \text{ rpm}/(\text{N} \cdot \text{m})^{1/2}$$

From Fig. 3.31, when $K_{tc} = 123$, the speed ratio $C_{sr} = 0.9$ and the torque ratio $C_{tr} = 1.02$. The output speed of the torque converter n_{tc} is

$$n_{tc} = 0.9 \times 2450 = 2205 \text{ rpm}$$

The output torque of the torque converter M_{tc} is

$$M_{tc} = 393 \times 1.02 = 400 \text{ N} \cdot \text{m} \ (295 \text{ lb} \cdot \text{ft})$$

The efficiency of the torque converter under this operating condition is

$$\eta_c = 0.9 \times 1.02 = 91.8\%$$

Continuously Variable Transmissions With growing interest in improving the fuel economy of automotive vehicles, continuously variable transmissions have attracted a geat deal of interest. This type of transmission provides a continuously variable reduction ratio that enables the engine to operate under the most economical conditions over a wide range of vehicle speed. The operating fuel economy of automotive vehicles will be discussed later in this chapter.

Two representative types of continuously variable transmission are the Van Doorne belt system and the Perbury system. The Van Doorne system has a pair of conically faced pulleys, as shown in Fig. 3.34. The effective radius of the pulleys, and hence the reduction ratio, can be varied by adjusting the distance between the two sides of the pulleys. On the original system, the reduction ratio was controlled by mechanical means through centrifugal weights on the driving pulley and an engine vacuum actuator. More recently, a microprocessor-based control system has been developed [3.17, 3.18]. This type of continuously variable transmission can achieve a reduction ratio ranging from 4 to 6. The mechanical efficiency of this transmission varies with the load and speed. The variations of the efficiency with input torque and speed at a reduction ratio of 1 for a system designed for a lightweight passenger car are shown in Fig. 3.35 [3.17]. To improve the efficiency of the system and to reduce noise and wear, a "segmented steel belt" or a "push belt system" has been developed [3.19]. It comprises a set of belt elements about 2 mm (0.078 in.) thick, with slots on each side to fit two high-tensile steel bands which hold them together. Unlike the conventional V-belt, it transmits power by the compressive force between the belt elements, instead of tension. The Van Doorne system is most suited to low power applications, and has been used in small size passenger cars and snowmobiles.

The Perbury system is schematically shown in Fig. 3.36 [3.20]. The key component of this system is the variator, which consists of three disks, with the outer pair connected to the input shaft and the inner one connected to the output shaft. The inner surfaces of the disks are of a toroidal shape, upon which the spherical

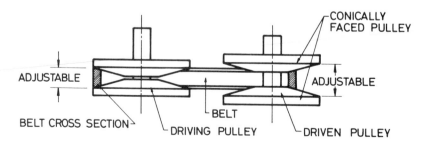

Fig. 3.34 A Van Doorne type continuously variable transmission.

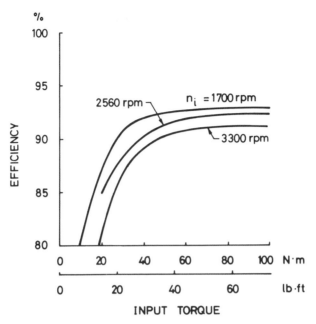

Fig. 3.35 Variation of mechanical efficiency with input torque at a constant reduction ratio for a Van Doorne type continuously variable transmission. (Reproduced with permission of the Society of Automotive Engineers from reference 3.17.)

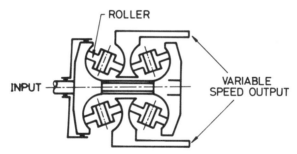

Fig. 3.36 A Perbury type continuously variable transmission. (Reproduced with permission of the Council of the Institution of Mechanical Engineers from reference 3.20.)

rollers roll. The rollers can rotate about their own axes. By varying the inclination of the roller axes, a continuously variable reduction ratio can be achieved. It should be noted that the carriers for the rollers are fixed. To minimize wear, lubrication is provided between the rollers and the disks. To transmit adequate torque, high normal forces across the contact points are required, as the coefficient of traction between the roller and the disk surfaces is low, typically less than 0.1. The relative slip between the two is 1–2% under normal operating conditions. This system can provide a reduction ratio of about 5. Common with the Van Doorne belt system, it cannot provide zero output and a reverse ratio. Consequently, separate devices are required for starting and for reverse. The Perbury system is suited to higher power applications than the Van Doorne belt system, and has been designed for buses and delivery trucks with a rated power of 375 kW (502 hp). The average value of the mechanical efficiency of this system is approximately 90%.

Hydrostatic Transmissions   Hydrostatic transmissions are used in some road vehicles, as well as off-road vehicles, particularly those of a specialized nature, and have enjoyed a certain degree of success [3.21]. Hydrostatic drives may be divided into three categories.

Constant Displacement Pump with Fixed Displacement Motor   This type of hydrostatic drive usually consists of a gear or vane pump driving a gear, vane, or piston motor through control valves. The maximum working pressure of the fluid in this type of system is usually about 20,685 kPa (3000 psi). This simple hydrostatic transmission has been quite widely used in construction machinery such as excavators to drive the tracks. Each gear pump drives its own hydraulic motor, which allows the two tracks to be operated individually, thus providing a mechanism for steering. The tractive effort–speed characteristics of this system with a multispeed gearbox are illustrated in Fig. 3.37(a).

Variable Displacement Pump with Fixed Displacement Motor   This type of hydrostatic drive has certain advantages over the fixed displacement pump and motor system. Variable displacement pumps are piston pumps that permit higher pressure to be used. They also permit stepless speed control from zero to maximum. Closed-loop fluid circuits can be employed to provide both forward and reverse motions and braking functions. To extend the tractive effort and vehicle speed range, a gearbox is frequently employed. The performance characteristics of this type of system coupled with a two-speed gearbox are shown in Fig. 3.37(b).

Variable Displacement Pump and Motor   In this system, the displacement of both the pump and the motor can be varied continuously. The performance characteristics of the vehicle are approaching the ideal ones, as shown in Fig. 3.37(c). Although the performance and control of this type of transmission are

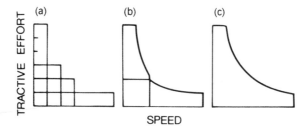

Fig. 3.37   Tractive effort–speed characteristics of a vehicle equipped with various types of hydrostatic transmission. (Reproduced with permission of the Council of the Institution of Mechanical Engineers, from "Why has the British Manufacturer been Hesitant to Adopt Hydrostatic Drives?" by Wardill, I. Mech. E. Conference on Making Technology Profitable—Hydrostatic Drives, 1974.)

beyond question, the problems of cost, reliability, maintenance, and service remain to be solved.

In comparison with the automatic transmission with a torque converter, the hydrostatic drive can provide a more positive speed control and flexibility in vehicle layout. Figure 3.38 shows the efficiencies of a hydrostatic drive and a comparable automatic transmission (a torque converter with a two-speed gearbox) [3.21]. It appears that there is relatively little difference between the two types of transmission from the point of view of efficiency over the operating range. However, for vehicles designed for traction operating with a high tractive effort at low

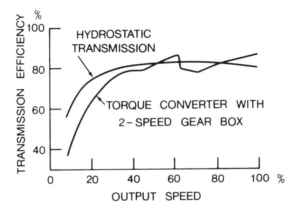

Fig. 3.38 Variation of transmission efficiency with output speed of an automatic transmission with a torque converter and of a hydrostatic transmission. (Reproduced with permission of the Council of the Institution of Mechanical Engineers from reference 3.21.)

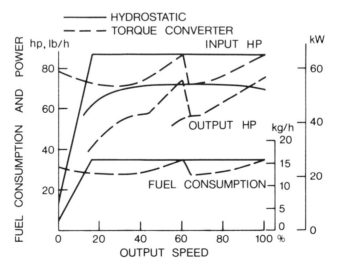

Fig. 3.39 Variation of fuel consumption and output power with output speed of an automatic transmission with a torque converter and of a hydrostatic transmission. (Reproduced with permission of the Council of the Institution of Mechanical Engineers from reference 3.21.)

speeds, the hydrostatic transmission seems to be more suitable. Figure 3.39 shows the fuel consumption and power output of a particular vehicle equipped with the two types of transmission [3.21]. It is apparent that the hydrostatic transmission permits full power to be developed by the engine once the output speed of the transmission is high enough. Thus, a faster rate of work can be achieved with the hydrostatic drive. Tests of off-road vehicles equipped with hydrostatic transmissions have shown improved productivity as compared with those equipped with manual gear transmissions, even though manual gear transmissions have higher efficiency [3.21].

3.4 PREDICTION OF VEHICLE PERFORMANCE

The relationship between tractive effort and vehicle speed discussed in the previous section provides the basis for predicting the performance characteristics of a road vehicle. The passenger car with characteristics shown in Fig. 3.29 will be used as an example to illustrate the procedure for predicting acceleration characteristics and gradability.

To fully describe the performance of a vehicle, in addition to the relationship between the tractive effort and vehicle speed, the resistance of the vehicle as a function of speed must also be determined. On level ground without a drawbar load, the major resisting forces are the rolling resistance R_r and the aerodynamic resistance R_a, and they can be predicted using methods discussed previously. The variation of R_r and R_a with speed for the passenger car is shown in Fig. 3.29. The difference between the tractive effort and the resultant resisting force is the net thrust F_{net} available for accelerating the vehicle or for overcoming grade resistance. The intersection of the vehicle thrust and the resultant resistance curves determines the maximum speed that the vehicle can achieve, as shown in Fig. 3.29. It should be noted that the nature of tire–road adhesion imposes a fundamental limit on the maximum tractive effort. The maximum tractive efforts of the passenger car that the tire–ground contact can support on various surfaces including concrete, gravel, and wet asphalt are shown in the figure. They are determined using the method discussed in Section 3.1. It can be seen, for instance, that with the second gear engaged, the maximum tractive effort as determined by the engine torque and transmission characteristics is about 5.5 kN (1240 lb), whereas the maximum tractive effort on wet asphalt that the tire–road contact can support is only 4 kN (900 lb). This indicates that, in fact, the maximum tractive effort that the car can develop with the second gear engaged is 4 kN. Figure 3.29 also shows that with the second gear engaged, when the vehicle speed is below 112 km/h (70 mph), the tractive effort of the vehicle on wet asphalt is limited by the tire–road adhesion, and not by the engine torque.

3.4.1 Acceleration Time and Distance

Having determined the net thrust of the vehicle as a function of speed, one can then compute the acceleration of the vehicle using Newton's second law. It should be noted, however, that the translational motion of the vehicle is coupled to the rotational motion of the components connected with the wheels, including the engine and the driveline. Any change of translational speed of the vehicle will therefore be accompanied by a corresponding change of the rotational speed of the components coupled with the wheels. To take into account the effect of the inertia of the rotating parts on vehicle acceleration characteristics, a mass factor γ_m is introduced into the following equation for calculating vehicle acceleration a:

$$F - \Sigma R = F_{net} = \gamma_m ma \qquad (3.36)$$

where m is the vehicle mass.

γ_m can be determined from the moments of inertia of the rotating parts by

$$\gamma_m = 1 + \frac{\Sigma I_w}{mr^2} + \frac{\Sigma I_1 \xi_1^2}{mr^2} + \frac{\Sigma I_2 \xi_2^2}{mr^2} + \cdots + \frac{\Sigma I_n \xi_n^2}{mr^2} \qquad (3.37)$$

where I_w is the mass moment of inertia of the wheel, $I_1, I_2 \cdots I_n$ are the mass moments of inertia of the rotating components connected with the driveline having gear ratios $\xi_1, \xi_2 \cdots \xi_n$, respectively, with reference to the driven wheel, and r is the rolling radius of the wheel. For passenger cars, the mass factor γ_m may be calculated using the following empirical relation [3.14]:

$$\gamma_m = 1.04 + 0.0025\xi_0^2 \qquad (3.38)$$

The first term on the right-hand side of the above equation represents the contribution of the rotating inertia of the wheels, while the second term represents the contribution of the inertia of the components rotating at the equivalent engine speed with the overall gear reduction ratio ξ_0 with respect to the driven wheel.

In the evaluation of vehicle acceleration characteristics, time–speed and time–distance relationships are of prime interest. These relationships can be derived using the equation of motion of the vehicle in a differential form:

$$\gamma_m m \frac{dV}{dt} = F - \Sigma R = F_{net}$$

and

$$dt = \frac{\gamma_m m dV}{F_{net}} \qquad (3.39)$$

As can be seen from Fig. 3.29, the net tractive effort F_{net} available for accelerating the vehicle is a function of vehicle speed:

$$F_{net} = f(V) \qquad (3.40)$$

This makes the expression relating the time and speed of the following form not integrable by analytic methods:

$$t = \gamma_m m \int_{V_1}^{V_2} \frac{dV}{f(V)} \tag{3.41}$$

To predict the time required to accelerate the vehicle from speed V_1 to V_2, the integration is best handled by numerical methods using a computer, although graphic methods of integration can also offer solutions of sufficient accuracy [3.14].

The distance S that the vehicle travels during an acceleration period from speed V_1 to V_2 can be calculated by integrating the following equation:

$$S = \int_{V_1}^{V_2} \frac{VdV}{F_{net}/\gamma_m m} = \gamma_m m \int_{V_1}^{V_2} \frac{VdV}{f(V)} \tag{3.42}$$

When a vehicle having a manual gear transmission starts from rest, in the initial period, slip occurs between the driving and driven parts of the clutch, and the vehicle speed is not directly related to the engine speed. There are mathematical models available for analyzing the dynamics of the clutch engagement process. In a first approximation, however, it can be assumed that during the clutch engagement period, the maximum engine torque is transmitted to the input shaft of the gearbox. The acceleration time and distance from zero vehicle speed to the next speed increment can then be calculated using the procedures outlined above.

In the evaluation of acceleration time and distance, the engine is usually assumed to be operating at wide open throttle. It should be noted that a certain amount of time is required for gear changing during acceleration. For manual transmissions, gear changing causes a time delay of 1–2 s; for automatic transmissions, the delay is typically 0.5–1 s. To obtain a more accurate estimate of acceleration time and distance, this delay should be taken into consideration.

Figure 3.40 shows the acceleration time–distance curve and the acceleration time–speed curve for a passenger car with a gross weight of 17.79 kN (4000 lb) and with thrust–speed characteristics as shown in Fig. 3.29 [3.14]. The kinks in the time–speed curve represent the delays caused by gear changing.

Example 3.2. A vehicle weighs 21.24 kN (4775 lb), including the four road wheels. Each of the wheels has a rolling radius of 33 cm (13 in.) and a radius of gyration of 25.4 cm (10 in.), and weighs 244.6 N (55 lb). The engine develops a torque of 325 N · m (240 lb · ft) at 3500 rpm. The equivalent mass of moment of inertia of the parts rotating at engine speed is 0.733 kg · m^2 (0.54 slug · ft^2). The transmission efficiency is 85%, and the total reduction ratio of the driveline in the third gear is 4.28 to 1. The vehicle has a frontal area of 1.86 m^2 (20 ft^2), and the aerodynamic drag coefficient is 0.38. The coefficient of rolling resistance is 0.02. Determine the acceleration of the vehicle on a level road under these conditions.

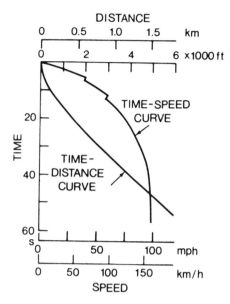

Fig. 3.40 Acceleration characteristics of a passenger car with a three-speed manual transmission. (Reproduced with permission from reference 3.14.)

Solution.

a) The mass factor γ_m for the vehicle in the third gear can be calculated using Eq. 3.37:

$$\gamma_m = 1 + \frac{\sum I_w + \sum I \xi^2}{mr^2}$$

$$= 1 + \frac{4 \times 1.61 + 0.733 \times 4.28^2}{2165 \times 0.33^2} = 1.084$$

b) The thrust of the vehicle F is determined using Eq. 3.30:

$$F = \frac{M_e \xi_0 \eta_t}{r} = 3585 \text{ N } (806 \text{ lb})$$

c) The vehicle speed V can be calculated using Eq. 3.31:

$$V = \frac{n_e r}{\xi_0} (1 - i)$$

Assume that $i = 3\%$; the vehicle speed V is

$$V = 98.7 \text{ km/h } (61.3 \text{ mph})$$

d) The total resistance of the vehicle is the sum of the aerodynamic resistance R_a and the rolling resistance R_r:

$$\Sigma R = R_a + R_r = 752 \text{ N } (169 \text{ lb})$$

e) The acceleration a of the vehicle can be determined using Eq. 3.36:

$$a = \frac{F - \Sigma R}{\gamma_m m} = 1.2 \text{ m/s}^2 \ (3.94 \text{ ft/s}^2)$$

3.4.2 Gradability

Gradability is usually defined as the maximum grade a vehicle can negotiate at a given steady speed. This parameter is primarily intended for the evaluation of the performance of heavy commercial vehicles and off-road vehicles. On a slope at a constant speed, the tractive effort has to overcome grade resistance, rolling resistance, and aerodynamic resistance:

$$F = W \sin \theta_s + R_r + R_a$$

For a relatively small angle of θ_s, $\tan \theta_s \simeq \sin \theta_s$. Therefore, the grade resistance may be approximated by $W \tan \theta_s$ or WG, where G is the grade in percent.

The maximum grade a vehicle can negotiate at a constant speed therefore is determined by the net tractive effort available at that speed:

$$G = \frac{1}{W} (F - R_r - R_a) = \frac{F_{net}}{W} \tag{3.43}$$

Use can be made of the performance curves of a vehicle, such as those shown in Fig. 3.29, to determine the speed obtainable on each particular grade. For instance, the grade resistance of the passenger car with a weight of 17.79 kN (4000 lb) on a grade of 7.5% is 1.34 kN (300 lb). A horizontal line representing this grade resistance can be drawn on the diagram, which intersects the net tractive effort curve at a speed of 133 km/h (82 mph). This indicates that for the passenger car under consideration, the maximum speed obtainable at a grade of 7.5% is 133 km/h (82 mph). It should be noted that the limits of tractive effort set by the nature of tire–road adhesion usually determine the maximum gradability of the vehicle. For instance, it can be seen from Fig. 3.29 that the maximum grade the vehicle can negotiate at low speeds on a gravel surface with $\mu = 0.6$ will be approximately 35%.

3.5 OPERATING FUEL ECONOMY

The operating fuel economy of an automotive vehicle depends on a number of factors, including the fuel consumption characteristics of the engine, transmission characteristics, weight of the vehicle, aerodynamic resistance, rolling resistance of the tires, driving cycle (conditions), and driver behavior.

Typical fuel economy characteristics of a gasoline and a diesel engine are shown in Figs. 3.41 and 3.42, respectively [3.16]. They usually have reduced fuel economy at low throttle and low torque settings. Operations at low engine speed and high torque are always more economical than at higher speed and lower torque settings with the same power output. For instance, it can be seen from Fig. 3.41 that for the engine to develop 22 kW (30 hp) of power, it can run at a speed of 2500 rpm or 4000 rpm. At 2500 rpm, the specific fuel consumption is approximately 0.29 kg/kW · h (0.48 lb/hp · h), whereas at 4000 rpm, it is 0.37 kg/kW · h (0.60 lb/hp · h). By connecting the engine operating points with the lowest specific fuel consumption for each power setting, an optimum fuel economy line (maximum efficiency line) of the engine can be drawn, as shown in Fig. 3.41 [3.16].

For a given power requirement at a specific vehicle speed, the engine operating point is determined by the gear ratio of the transmission. Ideally, the gear ratio of the transmission can be continuously varied to any desired value so that the engine operating point will follow the optimum fuel economy line for all power settings.

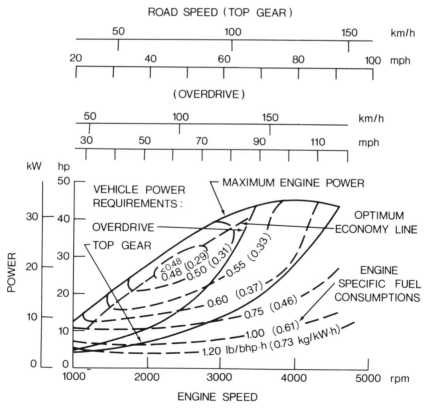

Fig. 3.41 Fuel economy characteristics of a gasoline engine. (Reproduced with permission from reference 3.16.)

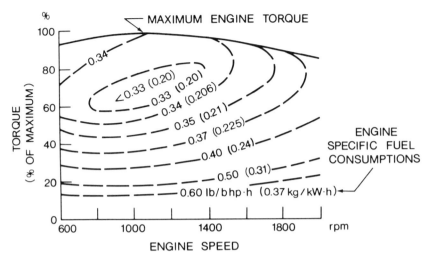

Fig. 3.42 Fuel economy characteristics of a diesel engine. (Reproduced with permission from reference 3.16.)

This has stimulated the development of a variety of continuously variable transmissions, as described in Section 3.3.2. The potential gain in fuel economy using the continuously variable transmission may be illustrated using the example given above. As shown in Fig. 3.41, when the vehicle is operating in the top gear at 128 km/h (80 mph), the horsepower required is 22 kW (30 hp), and the engine is running at 4000 rpm with a specific fuel consumption of 0.37 kg/kW · h (0.60 lb/hp · h). However, if a continuously variable transmission is used, the transmission gear ratio can be varied so that at the same vehicle speed with the same power output, the engine is running at 2500 rpm with a specific fuel consumption of approximately 0.29 kg/kW · h (0.48 lb/hp · h). This represents a potential fuel saving of 21.6%. It should be noted, however, that the mechanical efficiency of the current generation of continuously variable transmissions is generally lower than that of the manual gear transmission. The actual saving in fuel using the continuously variable transmission may not be as high as that given in the above example. Figure 3.43 shows a comparison of fuel consumption of a small passenger car with a 1.6 L engine equipped with a Van Doorne type of continuously variable transmission and that with a manual five-speed transmission [3.18]. It can be seen that under steady operating conditions in the speed range 60–150 km/h (37–93 mph), the vehicle with the Van Doorne transmission achieves better fuel economy than the manual five-speed transmission, in spite of its lower mechanical efficiency (approximately 86–90%).

To further illustrate the effect of the gear ratios of the transmission on the operating fuel economy of road vehicles, let us consider the overdrive gear of a passenger car as an example. As shown in Fig. 3.26, the gear ratio of the top gear in the transmission is usually selected in such a way that the curve representing the power available at the driven wheels meets the resultant resistance curve at a speed slightly higher than that of maximum power [3.16]. This typical choice of

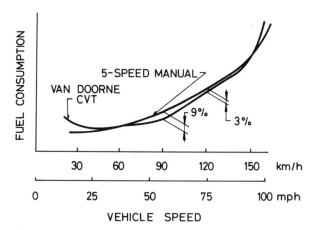

Fig. 3.43 Comparison of fuel consumption of a small car equipped with a continuously variable transmission to that with a manual transmission. (Reproduced with permission of the Council of the Institution of Mechanical Engineers from reference 3.18.)

gear ratio provides the vehicle with sufficient power reserve to maintain a given vehicle speed against a temporary increase in resistance due to headwind or gradient. The vehicle power requirements at various vehicle speeds in top gear can be plotted in the engine performance diagram as shown in Fig. 3.41. It will be noted that a maximum vehicle speed of 145 km/h (90 mph) is equivalent to an engine speed of 4500 rpm in top gear in the example shown, and that the power required to overcome the resultant resistance at that speed is about 32.8 kW (44 hp). When the engine is running at 4500 rpm and developing 32.8 kW (44 hp), the specific fuel consumption will be 0.40 kg/kW · h (0.65 lb/hp · h), as shown in Fig. 3.41. Thus, in 1 h at 145 km/h (90 mph), the vehicle will consume 13.1 kg (28.8 lb) of fuel in top gear.

If, however, an overdrive gear with a gear ratio of approximately 30% less than that of the top gear is introduced into the transmission, the vehicle can still achieve a maximum speed of 145 km/h (90 mph), as shown in Fig. 3.26, but with reduced power reserve over the entire speed range. Owing to the lower gear ratio that an overdrive gear introduces, for the same vehicle speed the engine speed will be lower than that when using the top gear, as shown in Fig. 3.41. For instance, at a speed of 145 km/h (90 mph), with the overdrive gear, the engine is running at 3400 rpm as compared with 4500 rpm when using the top gear. Accordingly, using the overdrive gear, the engine specific fuel consumption is reduced to 0.32 kg/kW · h (0.53 lb/hp · h) as compared with 0.40 kg/kW · h (0.65 lb/hp · h) when using the top gear. Thus, with the overdrive gear, the vehicle will consume only 10.5 kg (23.1 lb) of fuel per hour at a speed of 145 km/h (90 mph). This represents a saving of fuel of approximately 20%. Although this example is for a particular engine and vehicle, most cars will show similar gains with an overdrive. The improvement in fuel economy obtained by an overdrive gear under steady-state cruising conditions is an exploitation of the fact that for the same power output, the internal combustion engine is always more economical to operate at low speed and high torque than at higher speed and lower torque settings.

The reduction of vehicle weight is also one of the important methods for achieving improved fuel economy. This is because the propelling force, and hence power, required to accelerate a vehicle is proportional to its weight. In "stop and go" driving conditions in the city or an urban environment, the frequent acceleration leads to higher fuel consumption for a heavier vehicle than a lighter vehicle. To reduce vehicle weight, unibody construction has largely replaced the separate body-frame construction, computer-aided techniques have been introduced to optimize the design of vehicle structure, and lightweight materials, such as composites, high-strength low-alloy steel, plastics, aluminum, and metal–plastic laminates, have found increasing use in vehicle components. The reconfiguration of the vehicle from front engine–rear wheel drive to front engine–front wheel drive would also lead to a considerable reduction in vehicle weight. It is estimated that a reduction of 1 kg in vehicle mass is equivalent to a reduction in fuel consumption of 7.24×10^{-5} L/km (or each pound of weight saved will result in a reduction in fuel consumption of 1.4×10^{-5} gal/mi) [3.22]. It is observed that a 10% change in tire rolling resistance will result in an approximately 2% change in fuel economy for passenger cars. The effect of aerodynamic resistance on vehicle fuel consumption is also noticeable, which has been discussed in Section 3.2.

Driving cycle (conditions) is another factor that significantly affects fuel consumption. It is obvious that the fuel consumption for driving in the city with slow speeds and frequent "stop and go" is substantially higher than that for driving on the highway with steadier and higher speeds. To provide a common basis for comparing the fuel economy of different vehicles, the Environmental Protection Agency (EPA) of the United States has devised a city (urban) driving cycle and a highway (suburban) driving cycle. Vehicle manufacturers are required to conduct fuel economy tests according to these EPA cycles. The EPA city driving cycle consists of 10 "stop and go" driving segments within 766 s and with a maximum speed of 60 mph (96 km/h). The EPA highway driving cycle consists of four segments to simulate the driving conditions on a local road, a collector lane, a principal arterial, and a minor arterial within 765 s and with a maximum speed of 60 mph (96 km/h) [3.22]. Based on the test results for the EPA city and highway driving cycle, a composite fuel economy indicator [also known as the Corporate Average Fuel Economy (CAFE)] expressed in miles per gallon (mpg) is established according to the following formula [3.22]:

$$\text{mpg}_{\text{composite}} = \frac{1}{(0.55/\text{city mpg}) + (0.45/\text{highway mpg})} \qquad (3.44)$$

A number of other operating factors, including engine start-up and warm-up behavior, ambient conditions, road surface conditions, vehicle maintenance, and driver behavior (habits), also affect the operating fuel economy.

The fuel consumption data for some passenger cars are given in Table 3.6. It can be seen that for the same vehicle with the same engine, the fuel consumption is dependent upon the type of transmission installed. From the data shown, in most

TABLE 3.6 Fuel Consumption Ratings of Passenger Cars

Vehicle	Engine Displacement (L.iter)	No. of Cylinders	Transmission	Fuel Consumption City L/100 km	City mpg	Highway L/100 km	Highway mpg
Acura Integra	1.8	4	M5+	9.6	29	7.0	40
Integra	1.8	4	A4+	10.2	28	7.0	40
Audi 90	2.8	6	M5+	12.1	23	8.2	34
90	2.8	6	A4+	12.9	22	8.2	34
BMW 525i	2.5	6	M5	12.2	23	7.7	37
525i	2.5	6	A4+	12.7	22	8.5	33
Cadillac Seville	4.6	8	E4+	14.3	20	8.7	32
Chevrolet Cavalier	2.2	4	M5+	10.1	28	6.1	46
Cavalier	2.2	4	A3	9.9	29	7.0	40
Chrysler Concorde	3.3	6	E4+	12.4	23	7.9	36
Ford Contour	2.0	4	M5	9.6	29	6.2	46
Contour	2.0	4	E4+	9.9	29	6.8	42
Honda Accord	2.2	4	M5+	9.5	30	6.9	41
Accord	2.2	4	A4+	10.3	27	7.3	39
Lincoln Town Car	4.6	8	E4+	13.5	21	8.4	34
Mercedes-Benz							
C280	2.8	6	A4	12.0	24	8.5	33
E320	3.2	6	A4	11.9	24	8.4	34
SL600	6.0	12	A4	17.7	16	12.0	24
Nissan Maxima	3.0	6	M5+	10.8	26	8.0	35
Maxima	3.0	6	E4+	11.4	25	7.8	36
Toyota Camry	2.2	4	M5+	10.4	27	6.9	41
Camry	2.2	4	E4+	11.3	25	7.9	36
Volkswagen							
Passat GLX	2.8	6	M5+	12.9	22	8.6	33
Passat GLX	2.8	6	A4+	13.1	22	8.7	32
Volvo 940	2.3	4	A4+	12.4	23	8.3	34

Source: 1995 Fuel Consumption Guide, Ministry of Transport, Canada (The city ratings are based on a 12 km drive of 22 minutes which includes 16 complete stops, with an average speed of 32 km/h. The highway ratings are based on a 16 km trip of 12 minutes with no stops, at an average speed of 77 km/h.)

Note: A—automatic, E—electronic automatic, M—manual, 1, 2, 3, 4, 5—number of gears, +—with overdrive, L/100 km—liters per 100 km, mpg—miles per imperial gallon.

cases, fuel consumption with an automatic transmission is higher than that with a manual transmission by 1–11% for both city and highway driving.

3.6 ENGINE AND TRANSMISSION MATCHING

From the discussions presented previously, it can be seen that the engine and transmission characteristics are two of the most significant design factors that affect the performance and fuel economy of a vehicle. For a given vehicle to achieve a desired level of performance and fuel economy, proper matching of the engine to the transmission is of importance. The performance of a road vehicle may be characterized by its acceleration time from standstill to a given speed, usually 100 km/h or 60 mph or the time required to travel a given distance, such as 1/4 mi or 0.4 km. This can be predicted using the method described in Section 3.4. The fuel economy may be characterized by the fuel consumed for a given distance traveled under a specific driving cycle. This may be evaluated using the general procedure outlined in Section 3.5. In the United States, the fuel consumption data obtained under EPA city and highway driving cycle and/or the EPA Corporate Average Fuel Economy (CAFE) described by the mpg$_{composite}$ calculated from Eq. 3.44 are generally used as indicators for fuel economy.

For a given vehicle with a particular engine and gearbox having a specific gear ratio span (i.e., the ratio of the gear ratio of the lowest gear to that of the highest gear), the acceleration time and fuel economy are a function of the drive axle gear ratio. Figure 3.44 shows the effects of the gear ratio of the drive axle on the performance and fuel economy of a vehicle with different engine sizes (small, midsize, and large) [3.23]. The enveloping curve shown in Fig. 3.44 represents the optimum performance versus fuel economy tradeoff curve. For instance, points A, B, and C represent the gear ratios of the drive axle with a specific gearbox that

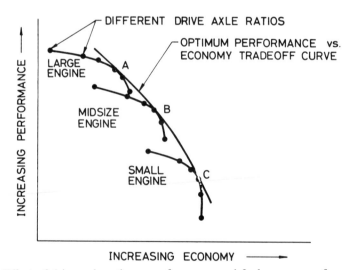

Fig. 3.44 Effect of drive axle ratio on performance and fuel economy of a passenger car. (Reproduced with permission of the Society of Automotive Engineers from reference 3.23.)

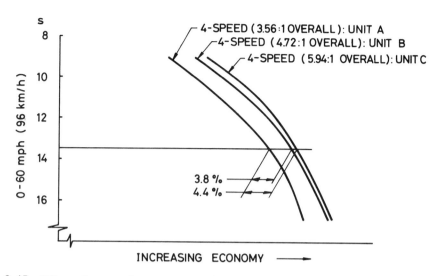

Fig. 3.45 Effect of gear ratio span of a four-speed manual transmission on performance and fuel economy of a passenger car. (Reproduced with permission of the Society of Automotive Engineers from reference 3.23.)

achieve the optimum tradeoff between performance and fuel economy for the large, midsize, and small engine, respectively. Figure 3.45 shows the optimum performance versus economy tradeoff curves for various four-speed gearboxes having different gear ratio spans from 3.56 to 5.94. If the vehicle is to achieve an acceleration time of 13.5 s from standstill to 60 mph (96 km/h) with a given engine, then using gearbox unit C with a gear ratio span of 5.94 and with an optimum drive axle ratio will improve the fuel economy by 4.4%, in comparison with that using gearbox unit A with a gear ratio span of 3.56. The fuel economy of the vehicle is measured by the EPA Corporate Average Fuel Economy (CAFE) in $mpg_{composite}$ defined by Eq. 3.44.

Figure 3.46 shows the effects of the gear ratio span of a three-speed automatic transmission with an optimum drive axle gear ratio and of the engine displacement (in liters) on the performance and fuel economy of a General Motors front-wheel-drive car [3.24]. It shows the gain in fuel economy that can be obtained by changing the transmission gear ratio span or engine size for a given performance level, expressed in terms of the time taken to travel 1/4 mi (0.4 km). This provides the vehicle engineer with quantitative information to select the proper combination of engine and transmission to achieve a desired level of performance and fuel economy.

3.7 BRAKING PERFORMANCE

Braking performance of motor vehicles is undoubtedly one of the most important characteristics that affect vehicle safety. With increasing emphasis on traffic safety in recent years, intensive efforts have been directed towards improving the braking

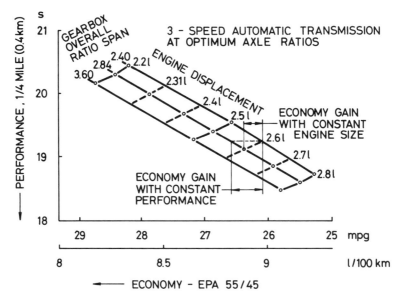

Fig. 3.46 Effect of engine size and transmission gear ratio span on performance and fuel economy of a passenger car. (Reproduced with permission of the Society of Automotive Engineers from reference 3.24.)

performance. Safety standards that specify performance requirements of various types of brake system have been introduced in many countries.

In this section, the method of approach to the analysis of the braking performance of motor vehicles will be presented. Criteria for the evaluation of braking capability and approaches to improving braking performance will be discussed.

3.7.1 Braking Characteristics of a Two-Axle Vehicle

The major external forces acting on a decelerating two-axle vehicle are shown in Fig. 3.47.

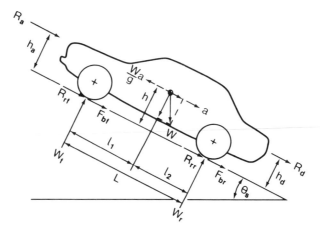

Fig. 3.47 Forces acting on a two-axle vehicle during braking.

The braking force F_b originating from the brake system and developed on the tire–road interface is the primary retarding force. When the braking force is below the limit of tire–road adhesion, the braking force F_b is given by

$$F_b = \frac{T_b - \Sigma I\alpha_{an}}{r} \qquad (3.45)$$

where T_b is the applied brake torque, I is the rotating inertia connected with the wheel being decelerated, α_{an} is the corresponding angular deceleration, and r is the rolling radius of the tire.

In addition to the braking force, the rolling resistance of tires, aerodynamic resistance, transmission resistance, and grade resistance (when traveling on a slope) also affect vehicle motion during braking. Thus, the resultant retarding force F_{res} can be expressed by

$$F_{\mathrm{res}} = F_b + f_r W \cos\theta_s + R_a \pm W \sin\theta_s + R_t \qquad (3.46)$$

where f_r is the rolling resistance coefficient, W is the vehicle weight, θ_s is the angle of the slope with the horizontal, R_a is the aerodynamic resistance, and R_t is the transmission resistance. When the vehicle is moving uphill, the positive sign for the term $W \sin\theta_s$ should be used. On a downhill grade, the negative sign should, however, be used. Normally, the magnitude of the transmission resistance is small and can be neglected in braking performance calculations.

During braking, there is a load transfer from the rear axle to the front axle. By considering the equilibrium of moments about the front and rear tire–ground contact points, the normal loads on the front and rear axles, W_f and W_r, can be expressed as

$$W_f = \frac{1}{L}\left[Wl_2 + h\left(\frac{W}{g}a - R_a \pm W\sin\theta_s\right)\right] \qquad (3.47)$$

and

$$W_r = \frac{1}{L}\left[Wl_1 - h\left(\frac{W}{g}a - R_a \pm W\sin\theta_s\right)\right] \qquad (3.48)$$

where a is the deceleration. When the vehicle is moving uphill, the negative sign for the term $W \sin\theta_s$ should be used. In the above expression, it is assumed that the aerodynamic resistance is applied at the center of gravity of the vehicle, and that there is no drawbar load.

By considering the force equilibrium in the horizontal direction, the following relationship can be established:

$$F_b + f_r W = F_{bf} + F_{br} + f_r W = \frac{W}{g}a - R_a \pm W\sin\theta_s \qquad (3.49)$$

where F_{bf} and F_{br} are the braking forces of the front and rear axles, respectively.

Substituting Eq. 3.49 into Eqs. 3.47 and 3.48, the normal loads on the axles become

$$W_f = \frac{1}{L} [Wl_2 + h(F_b + f_r W)] \tag{3.50}$$

and

$$W_r = \frac{1}{L} [Wl_1 - h(F_b + f_r W)] \tag{3.51}$$

The maximum braking force that the tire–ground contact can support is determined by the normal load and the coefficient of road adhesion. With four-wheel brakes, the maximum braking forces on the front and rear axles are given by (assuming the maximum braking force of the vehicle $F_{b\,\text{max}} = \mu W$)

$$F_{bf\text{max}} = \mu W_f = \frac{\mu W [l_2 + h(\mu + f_r)]}{L} \tag{3.52}$$

$$F_{br\text{max}} = \mu W_r = \frac{\mu W [l_1 - h(\mu + f_r)]}{L} \tag{3.53}$$

where μ is the coefficient of road adhesion. It should be noted that when the braking forces reach the values determined by Eqs. 3.52 and 3.53, tires are at the point of sliding. Any further increase in the braking force would cause the tires to lock up.

It should be pointed out that the distribution of the braking forces between the front and rear axles is a function of the design of the brake system when no wheels are locked. For conventional brake systems, the distribution of the braking forces is primarily dependent on the hydraulic (or air) pressures and brake cylinder (or chamber) areas in the front and rear brakes. From Eqs. 3.52 and 3.53, it can be seen that only when the distribution of the braking forces between the front and rear axles is in exactly the same proportion as that of normal loads on the front and rear axles will the maximum braking forces of the front and rear tires be developed at the same time.

$$\frac{K_{bf}}{K_{br}} = \frac{F_{bf\text{max}}}{F_{br\text{max}}} = \frac{l_2 + h(\mu + f_r)}{l_1 - h(\mu + f_r)} \tag{3.54}$$

where K_{bf} and K_{br} are the proportions of the total braking force on the front and rear axles, respectively, and are determined by the brake system design.

For instance, for a light truck with 68% of the static load on the rear axle ($l_2/L = 0.32$, $l_1/L = 0.68$), $h/L = 0.18$, $\mu = 0.85$, and $f_r = 0.01$, the maximum braking forces of the front and rear tires that the tire–ground contact can support will be developed at the same time only if the braking force distribution between the front and rear brakes satisfies the following condition:

$$\frac{K_{bf}}{K_{br}} = \frac{0.32 + 0.18(0.85 + 0.01)}{0.68 - 0.18(0.85 + 0.01)} = \frac{47}{53}$$

In other words, 47% of the total braking force must be placed on the front axle and 53% on the rear axle to achieve optimum utilization of the potential braking capability of the vehicle. The braking force distribution that can ensure the maximum braking forces of the front and rear tires developed at the same time is referred to as the ideal braking force distribution. If the braking force distribution is not ideal, then either the front or the rear tires will lock up first.

When the rear tires lock up first, the vehicle will lose directional stability. This can be visualized with the aid of Fig. 3.48. The figure shows the top view of a two-axle vehicle acted upon by the braking force and the inertia force. When the rear tires lock, the capability of the rear tires to resist lateral force is reduced to zero. If some slight lateral movement of the rear tires is initiated by side wind, road camber, or centrifugal force, a yawing moment due to the inertia force about the yaw center of the front axle will be developed. As the yaw motion progresses, the moment arm of the inertia force increases, resulting in an increase in yaw acceleration. As the rear end of the vehicle swings around 90°, the moment arm gradually decreases, and eventually the vehicle rotates 180°, with the rear end leading the front end. Figure 3.49 shows the measured angular deviation of a vehicle when the front and rear tires do not lock at the same instant [3.25].

The lock-up of front tires will cause a loss of directional control, and the driver will no longer be able to exercise effective steering. It should be pointed out, however, that front tire lock-up does not cause directional instability. This is because whenever lateral movement of the front tires occurs, a self-correcting moment due to the inertia force of the vehicle about the yaw center of the rear axle

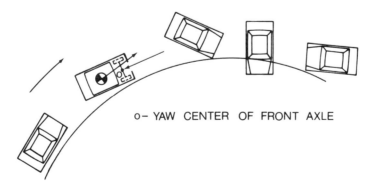

o— YAW CENTER OF FRONT AXLE

Fig. 3.48 Loss of directional stability due to lock-up of rear tires.

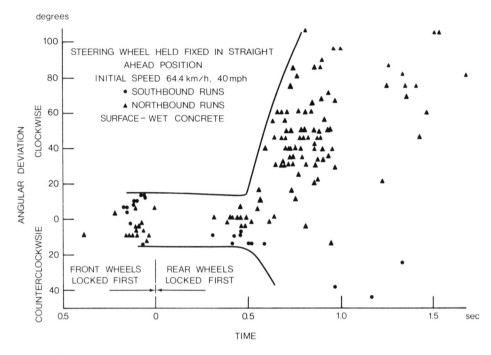

Fig. 3.49 Angular deviation of a car when the front and rear tires do not lock at the same instant. (Reproduced with permission of the Society of Automotive Engineers from reference 3.25.)

will be developed. Consequently, it tends to bring the vehicle back to a straight line path.

Loss of steering control may be detected more readily by the driver, and control may be regained by release or partial release of the brakes. Contrary to the case of front tire lock-up, when rear tires lock and the angular deviation of the vehicle exceeds a certain level, control cannot be regained, even by complete release of the brakes and by the most skillful driver. This suggests that rear tire lock-up is a more critical situation, particularly on a road surface with a low coefficient of adhesion. Since on slippery surfaces, the value of the available braking force is low, the kinetic energy of the vehicle will dissipate at a slow rate, and the vehicle will experience a serious loss of directional stability over a considerable distance. Because of the importance of the sequence of locking of the tires to vehicle behavior during braking, the braking standards in some countries, such as those in Western Europe, require that the braking effort distribution be such that the front tires lock before the rear tires on roads with a coefficient of adhesion lower than a certain value.

The conditions under which the front or the rear tires will lock first can be quantitatively determined. To facilitate the understanding of the problem, only the braking force and rolling resistance will be considered in the following analysis. Thus,

$$F_b + f_r W = F_{bf} + F_{br} + f_r W = \frac{W}{g} a \qquad (3.55)$$

Substituting Eq. 3.55 into Eqs. 3.50 and 3.51 yields

$$W_f = \frac{W}{L}\left(l_2 + \frac{a}{g} h\right) \qquad (3.56)$$

$$W_r = \frac{W}{L}\left(l_1 - \frac{a}{g} h\right) \qquad (3.57)$$

The braking forces of the front and rear axles as determined by the brake sytem design are expressed by

$$F_{bf} = K_{bf} F_b = K_{bf} W \left(\frac{a}{g} - f_r\right) \qquad (3.58)$$

and

$$F_{br} = K_{br} F_b = (1 - K_{bf}) F_b = (1 - K_{bf}) W \left(\frac{a}{g} - f_r\right) \qquad (3.59)$$

The front tires approach lock-up when

$$F_{bf} = \mu W_f \qquad (3.60)$$

Substituting Eqs. 3.56 and 3.58 into Eq. 3.60 yields

$$K_{bf} W \left(\frac{a}{g} - f_r\right) = \mu W \left(\frac{l_2}{L} + \frac{a}{g}\frac{h}{L}\right) \qquad (3.61)$$

From Eq. 3.61, the vehicle deceleration rate (in g-units) associated with the impending lock-up of the front tires can be defined by

$$\left(\frac{a}{g}\right)_f = \frac{\mu l_2 / L + K_{bf} f_r}{K_{bf} - \mu h / L} \qquad (3.62)$$

Similarly, it can be shown that the rear tires approach lock-up when the deceleration rate is

$$\left(\frac{a}{g}\right)_r = \frac{\mu l_1 / L + (1 - K_{bf}) f_r}{1 - K_{bf} + \mu h / L} \qquad (3.63)$$

For a given vehicle with a particular braking force distribution on a given road surface, the front tires will lock first if

$$\left(\frac{a}{g}\right)_f < \left(\frac{a}{g}\right)_r \tag{3.64}$$

On the other hand, the rear tires will lock first if

$$\left(\frac{a}{g}\right)_r < \left(\frac{a}{g}\right)_f \tag{3.65}$$

From the above analysis, it can readily be seen that for a given vehicle with a fixed braking force distribution, both the front and rear tires will lock at the same deceleration rate only on a particular road surface. Under this condition, the maximum braking forces of the front and rear axles that the tire–ground contact can support are developed at the same time, which indicates an optimum utilization of the potential braking capability of the vehicle. Under all other conditions, either the front or rear tires will lock first, resulting in a loss of either steering control or directional stability. This suggests that, ideally, the braking force distribution should be adjustable to ensure optimum braking performance under various operating conditions.

Based on the analysis described above, the interrelationships among the sequence of locking of tires, the deceleration achievable prior to any tire lock-up, the design parameters of the vehicle, and operating conditions can be quantitatively defined. As an illustrative example, Fig. 3.50 shows the braking characteristics of a light truck as a function of the braking effort distribution on the front axle under loaded and unloaded conditions [3.26]. For the loaded condition, the gross vehicle weight is 44.48 kN (10,000 lb), and for the unloaded case, it is 26.69 kN (6000 lb). The ratio of the height of the center of gravity to the wheelbase is 0.18 for both loaded and unloaded conditions. The coefficient of road adhesion is 0.85.

In Fig. 3.50, the solid line and the dotted line represent the boundaries of the deceleration rate that the vehicle can achieve prior to the locking of any tires under loaded and unloaded conditions, respectively. Lines OA and $O'A'$ represent the limiting values of the deceleration rate the vehicle can achieve without locking the rear tires, whereas lines AB and $A'B'$ represent the limiting values of the deceleration rate the vehicle can achieve without locking the front tires. Use can be made of Fig. 3.50 to determine the braking characteristics of the light truck under various operating conditions. For instance, if the brake system is designed to have 40% of the total braking force placed on the front axle, then for the loaded vehicle, the lock-up of the rear tires will take place prior to the lock-up of the front tires and the highest deceleration rate the vehicle can achieve just prior to rear tire lock-up will be 0.75 g. Conversely, if 60% of the total braking force is placed on the front, then for the loaded case, the lock-up of the front tires will take place prior to that of the rear tires, and the highest deceleration rate the vehicle can achieve without the locking of any tires will be 0.6 g. It is interesting to note that

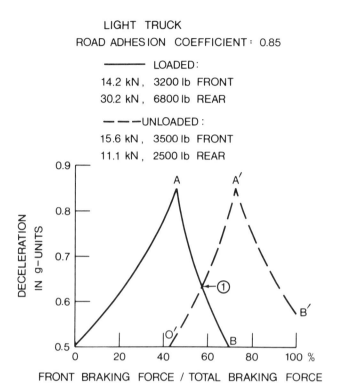

LIGHT TRUCK
ROAD ADHESION COEFFICIENT : 0.85

———— LOADED :
14.2 kN , 3200 lb FRONT
30.2 kN , 6800 lb REAR

— — —UNLOADED :
15.6 kN , 3500 lb FRONT
11.1 kN , 2500 lb REAR

Fig. 3.50 Effect of braking effort distribution on the braking performance of a light truck. (Reproduced with permission of the Society of Automotive Engineers from reference 3.26.)

to achieve the maximum deceleration rate of 0.85 g, which indicates the optimum utilization of the potential braking capability on a surface with a coefficient of road adhesion of 0.85, 47% of the total braking force on the front is required for the loaded case as compared to 72% for the unloaded case. Therefore, there is a difference of 25% in the optimum braking force distribution between the loaded and unloaded cases. A compromise in the selection of the braking force distribution has to be made. Usually, the value of the braking force distribution on the front axle corresponding to the intersection of lines AB and $O'A'$, point 1, in Fig. 3.50 is selected as a compromise. Under these circumstances, the maximum deceleration that the truck can achieve without locking any tires under both loaded and unloaded conditions is 0.64 g on a surface with a coefficient of road adhesion of 0.85.

Figure 3.51 illustrates the braking characteristics of a passenger car [3.26]. Because the difference in vehicle weight between the loaded and unloaded cases for a passenger car is much smaller than that for a truck, the braking characteristics under these two conditions are very close, which can readily be seen from Fig. 3.51. To achieve the maximum deceleration rate of 0.85 g, 62% of the total braking force on the front is required for the loaded case as compared to 67% for the unloaded case, a difference of 5%. A braking force distribution with 64.5% of the total braking force on the front, corresponding to point 1 in Fig. 3.51, may be selected as a compromise under these circumstances. The maximum deceleration

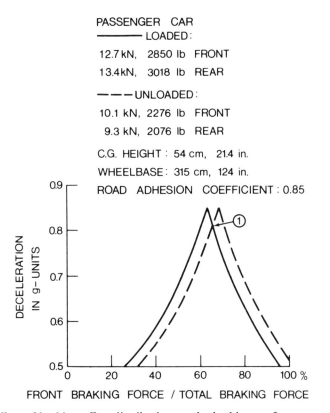

Fig. 3.51 Effect of braking effort distribution on the braking performance of a passenger car. (Reproduced with permission of the Society of Automotive Engineers from reference 3.26.)

that the vehicle can achieve prior to any tire lock-up under both loaded and unloaded conditions is therefore 0.82 *g*.

The analysis and examples given above indicate the complex nature of the braking process. It is shown that the optimum braking force distribution, which ensures the maximum deceleration rate, varies with the loading conditions of the vehicle, vehicle design parameters, and road surface conditions. In practice, the operating conditions vary in a wide range; thus, for a given vehicle with a fixed braking force distribution, only under a specific set of loading and road conditions will the maximum braking forces on the front and rear axles be developed at the same time and will the maximum deceleration rate be achieved. Under all other conditions, the achievable deceleration rate without causing a loss of steering control or directional stability will be reduced. To improve braking performance, pressure proportioning valves or load-sensing proportioning valves have been used. Pressure proportioning valves commonly in use provide equal pressure to both front and rear brakes up to a certain pressure level, and then reduce the rate of pressure rise to the rear brakes. Load-sensing proportioning valves are used on trucks, particularly in Europe. These valves adjust the braking effort distribution as a function of load distribution between the axles. To ensure steering control and directional stability under all possible operating conditions, antilock devices have been introduced. The prime function of these devices is to prevent tires from locking; thus, the capability of the tires to sustain a side force can be maintained. The operating principles of the antilock braking system will be briefly described in Section 3.7.4.

Example 3.3. A passenger car weighs 21.24 kN (4775 lb) and has a wheelbase of 2.87 m (113 in.). The center of gravity is 1.27 m (50 in.) behind the front axle and 0.508 m (20 in.) above ground level. The braking effort distribution on the front axle is 60%. The coefficient of rolling resistance is 0.02. Determine which set of the tires will lock first on two road surfaces: one with a coefficient of adhesion $\mu = 0.8$, and the other with $\mu = 0.2$.

Solution.
a) On the road surface with $\mu = 0.8$, the vehicle deceleration associated with the impending lock-up of the front tires is determined by Eq. 3.62:

$$\left(\frac{a}{g}\right)_f = \frac{\mu l_2/L + K_{bf}f_r}{K_{bf} - \mu h/L} = \frac{0.8 \times 0.558 + 0.6 \times 0.02}{0.6 - 0.8 \times 0.177} = 1.0$$

The vehicle deceleration associated with the impending lock-up of the rear tires is determined by Eq. 3.63:

$$\left(\frac{a}{g}\right)_r = \frac{\mu l_1/L + (1 - K_{bf})f_r}{1 - K_{bf} + \mu h/L} = \frac{0.8 \times 0.442 + 0.4 \times 0.02}{0.4 + 0.8 \times 0.177} = 0.67$$

Since $(a/g)_f > (a/g)_r$, the rear tires will lock first on the road surface with $\mu = 0.8$.
b) On the road surface with $\mu = 0.2$,

$$\left(\frac{a}{g}\right)_f = \frac{0.2 \times 0.558 + 0.6 \times 0.02}{0.6 - 0.2 \times 0.177} = 0.219$$

$$\left(\frac{a}{g}\right)_r = \frac{0.2 \times 0.442 + 0.4 \times 0.02}{0.4 + 0.2 \times 0.177} = 0.221$$

Since $(a/g)_f < (a/g)_r$, the front tires will lock first on the road surface with $\mu = 0.2$.

3.7.2 Braking Efficiency and Stopping Distance

To characterize the braking performance of a road vehicle, braking efficiency may be used. Braking efficiency η_b is defined as the ratio of the maximum deceleration rate in g units (a/g) achievable prior to any tire lock-up to the coefficient of road adhesion μ, and is given by

$$\eta_b = \frac{a/g}{\mu} \qquad (3.66)$$

The braking efficiency indicates the extent to which the vehicle utilizes the coefficient of road adhesion available during braking. Thus, when $a/g < \mu$, hence $\eta_b < 1.0$, the deceleration is less than the maximum achievable, resulting in an unnecessarily long stopping distance. Referring to Fig. 3.50, if 57% of the total braking force is placed on the front axle, corresponding to point 1, the maximum deceleration achievable prior to any tire lock-up is 0.64 g. This indicates that on a surface with a coefficient of road adhesion of 0.85, the braking efficiency is 75.3%.

Stopping distance is another parameter widely used for evaluating the overall braking performance of a road vehicle. To predict the stopping distance, the basic principles in dynamics are employed. The interrelationships among stopping distance, braking force, vehicle mass, and vehicle speed, in differential form, may be expressed as

$$ads = \left(\frac{F_b + \Sigma R}{\gamma_b W/g}\right) ds = VdV \qquad (3.67)$$

where γ_b is an equivalent mass factor taking into account the mass moments of inertia of the rotating components involved during braking. Since during braking the clutch is usually disengaged, the value of γ_b is not necessarily the same as that of γ_m used in the calculation of acceleration. For passenger cars, γ_b may be taken as approximately 1.05.

Equation 3.67 may be integrated to determine the stopping distance S from an initial speed V_1 to a final speed V_2:

$$S = \int_{V_2}^{V_1} \frac{\gamma_b W}{g} \frac{VdV}{F_b + \Sigma R} \qquad (3.68)$$

Substituting Eq. 3.46 into the above equation and neglecting the transmission resistance R_t, Eq. 3.68 becomes

$$S = \frac{\gamma_b W}{g} \int_{V_2}^{V_1} \frac{VdV}{F_b + f_r W \cos \theta_s \pm W \sin \theta_s + R_a} \qquad (3.69)$$

The aerodynamic resistance is proportional to the square of speed, and it may be expressed as

$$R_a = \frac{\rho}{2} C_D A_f V^2 = C_{ae} V^2 \qquad (3.70)$$

With substitution of $C_{ae}V^2$ for R_a and integration, the stopping distance can be expressed by [3.14]

$$S = \frac{\gamma_b W}{2gC_{ae}} \ln \left(\frac{F_b + f_r W \cos \theta_s \pm W \sin \theta_s + C_{ae}V_1^2}{F_b + f_r W \cos \theta_s \pm W \sin \theta_s + C_{ae}V_2^2} \right) \qquad (3.71)$$

For final speed $V_2 = 0$, Eq. 3.71 reduces to the form

$$S = \frac{\gamma_b W}{2gC_{ae}} \ln \left(1 + \frac{C_{ae}V_1^2}{F_b + f_r W \cos \theta_s \pm W \sin \theta_s} \right) \qquad (3.72)$$

For a given vehicle, if the braking force distribution and road conditions are such that the maximum braking forces of the front and rear tires that the tire–ground contact can support are developed at the same time, that is, the braking efficiency $\eta_b = 100\%$, the minimum stopping distance will be achieved. In this case, the braking torque generated by the brakes has already overcome the inertia of the rotating parts connected with the wheels; the maximum braking forces developed at the tire–ground contact are retarding only the translational inertia. The mass factor γ_b is therefore one. The minimum stopping distance $S_{\min}$ can be expressed as

$$S_{\min} = \frac{W}{2gC_{ae}} \ln \left(1 + \frac{C_{ae}V_1^2}{\mu W + f_r W \cos \theta_s \pm W \sin \theta_s} \right) \qquad (3.73)$$

If the braking efficiency η_b is less than 100% (i.e., the maximum deceleration rate in g units achievable prior to tire lock-up is less than the coefficient of road adhesion available), then the stopping distance will be longer than that determined using Eq. 3.73. In this case, the stopping distance may be calculated from

$$S = \frac{W}{2gC_{ae}} \ln \left(1 + \frac{C_{ae}V_1^2}{\eta_b \mu W + f_r W \cos \theta_s \pm W \sin \theta_s} \right) \qquad (3.74)$$

It should be pointed out that, in practice, there is a time lag between the application of brakes and the full development of the braking force. This time lag depends on the response of the brake system. The actual stopping distance therefore will be longer than that calculated using the equations given above. In general, the distance the vehicle travels during the transient period between the application of brakes and the attainment of steady-state braking has to be taken into consideration in determining the total stopping distance. In a first approximation, this additional stopping distance S_a may be calculated from

$$S_a = t_d V_1$$

where t_d is the response time of the brake system and V_1 is the initial speed of the vehicle. For preliminary braking performance calculations, an average value of 0.3 s for t_d may be assumed [3.26]. The delay in applying brakes due to the driver's reaction time further increases the actual stopping distance in practice. This reaction time usually varies from 0.5 to 2 s [3.14].

3.7.3   Braking Characteristics of a Tractor–Semitrailer

In comparison with a two-axle vehicle, the braking characteristics of a tractor–semitrailer are more complex. For a given two-axle vehicle, the load transfer is only a function of the deceleration rate, whereas for a tractor–semitrailer, the load transfer during braking is dependent not only on the deceleration rate, but also on the braking force of the semitrailer. Consequently, the optimum braking for a tractor–semitrailer is even more difficult to achieve than for a two-axle vehicle. A tractor–semitrailer during emergency braking could exhibit behavior of a more complex nature than that of a two-axle vehicle. In addition to the possibility of loss of directional control due to the lock-up of tractor front tires, directional instability of a tractor–semitrailer may be caused by the locking of either the tractor rear tires or the semitrailer tires. The locking of the tractor rear tires first usually causes jackknifing, which puts the vehicle completely out of control and often causes considerable damage both to the vehicle itself and to other road users. On the other hand, the lock-up of the semitrailer tires causes trailer swing. Although trailer swing has little effect on the stability of the tractor, it could be very dangerous to other road users, particularly to the oncoming traffic [3.27].

To reach a better understanding of the braking characteristics of a tractor–semitrailer, it is necessary to review its mechanics of braking. Figure 3.52 shows the major forces acting on a tractor–semitrailer during braking. To simplify the analysis, the aerodynamic drag and rolling resistance will be neglected.

The equilibrium equations are as follows.

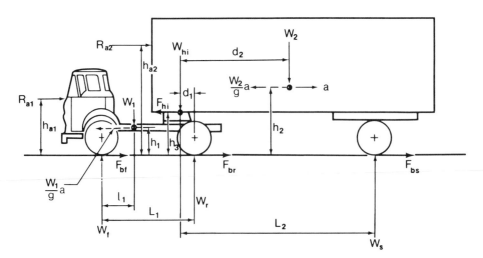

Fig. 3.52   Forces acting on a tractor–semitrailer during braking.

1. For the tractor,

$$W_f + W_r = W_1 + W_{hi} \tag{3.75}$$

$$C_f W_f + C_r W_r = a/g W_1 + F_{hi} \tag{3.76}$$

$$(a/g) W_1 h_1 + F_{hi} h_3 + W_1 (L_1 - l_1 - d_1)$$
$$+ W_r d_1 = W_f (L_1 - d_1) \tag{3.77}$$

2. For the semitrailer,

$$W_{hi} + W_s = W_2 \tag{3.78}$$

$$F_{hi} + C_{se} W_s = (a/g) W_2 \tag{3.79}$$

$$W_2 d_2 + F_{hi} h_3 = (a/g) W_2 h_2 + W_s L_2 \tag{3.80}$$

3. For the tractor–semitrailer combination,

$$W_f + W_r + W_s = W_1 + W_2 \tag{3.81}$$

$$C_f W_f + C_r W_r + C_{se} W_s = (a/g)(W_1 + W_2) \tag{3.82}$$

$$(a/g) W_1 h_1 + (a/g) W_2 h_2 + W_r L_1 + W_s [L_1 - d_1 + L_2]$$
$$= W_1 l_1 + W_2 [L_1 - d_1 + d_2] \tag{3.83}$$

where W_{hi} is the vertical load on the fifth wheel, F_{hi} is the horizontal load on the fifth wheel, a is the deceleration of the vehicle, and C_f, C_r, and C_{se} are the ratios of the braking force to the normal load of the tractor front axle, rear axle, and semitrailer axle, respectively. Other parameters are shown in Fig. 3.52.

It should be mentioned that the equations described above are applicable to tractors with a single rear axle and semitrailers with a single axle. For tractors and semitrailers having tandem axles without equalization, the equations have to be modified, because of interaxle load transfer.

From the above equations, the normal loads on various axles can be expressed by the following.

1. Tractor front axle:

$$W_f = \frac{W_1 [L_1 - l_1 + (a/g) h_1 + (C_r - a/g) h_3]}{L_1 + (C_r - C_f) h_3}$$
$$+ \frac{W_2 [L_2 - d_2 + (C_{se} - a/g) h_3 + (a/g) h_2](d_1 + C_r h_3)}{(L_2 + C_{se} h_3)[L_1 + (C_r - C_f) h_3]}$$

$$\tag{3.84}$$

2. Tractor rear axle:

$$W_r = \frac{W_1 \left[l_1 - (a/g)\, h_1 + (a/g - C_f)\, h_3 \right]}{L_1 + (C_r - C_f)\, h_3}$$

$$+ \frac{W_2 \left[(L_2 - d_2) + (C_{se} - a/g)\, h_3 + (a/g)\, h_2 \right] \left[(L_1 - d_1) - C_f h_3 \right]}{(L_2 + C_{se}h_3)\, [L_1 + (C_r - C_f)\, h_3]}$$

$$(3.85)$$

3. Semitrailer axle:

$$W_s = W_2 \frac{[d_2 + (h_3 - h_2)\, a/g]}{C_{se} h_3 + L_2} \tag{3.86}$$

It can be seen that to determine the normal loads on various axles of a given tractor-semitrailer, the deceleration rate and the braking force coefficient of the semitrailer axle C_{se} have to be specified. When the deceleration and the braking force of the semitrailer axle are known, the normal load on the semitrailer axle can be determined from Eq. 3.86, and the vertical and horizontal loads on the fifth wheel, W_{hi} and F_{hi}, can be calculated from Eqs. 3.78 and 3.79. With the values of W_{hi} and F_{hi} known, from Eqs. 3.75 and 3.77, the normal loads on the front and rear axles of the tractor can be calculated.

For the optimum braking condition where the maximum braking forces of all axles that the tire–ground contact can support are developed at the same time, the braking force coefficients for all axles and the deceleration rate in g units are equal to the coefficient of road adhesion, $C_f = C_r = C_{se} = a/g = \mu$. The expressions for the axle loads given above can be simplified as follows.

1. Tractor front axle:

$$W_f = \frac{W_1 \left[L_1 - l_1 + \mu h_1 \right]}{L_1}$$

$$+ \frac{W_2 \left[L_2 - d_2 + \mu h_2 \right] (d_1 + \mu h_3)}{L_1 (L_2 + \mu h_3)} \tag{3.87}$$

2. Tractor rear axle:

$$W_r = \frac{W_1 \left[l_1 - \mu h_1 \right]}{L_1}$$

$$+ \frac{W_2 \left[L_2 - d_2 + \mu h_2 \right] \left[L_1 - d_1 - \mu h_3 \right]}{L_1 (L_2 + \mu h_3)} \tag{3.88}$$

3. Semitrailer axle:

$$W_s = \frac{W_2\,[d_2 + \mu(h_3 - h_2)]}{\mu h_3 + L_2} \tag{3.89}$$

Under the optimum braking condition, the braking forces on the axles are proportional to the corresponding normal loads. The required braking force distribution among the axles, therefore, can be determined from Eqs. 3.87–3.89. Figure 3.53 shows the variation of the optimum braking force distribution with the coefficient of road adhesion for a particular tractor–semitrailer under various loading conditions [3.27]. The parameters of the vehicle used in the analysis are as follows: $W_1 = 75.62$ kN (17,000 lb), $W_2 = 75.62$ kN (17,000 lb) (semitrailer empty), $W_2 = 170.14$ kN (38,250 lb) (semitrailer partially loaded), $W_2 = 245.75$ kN (55,250 lb) (semitrailer fully loaded), $L_1 = 5.0$ m (16.5 ft), $L_2 = 9.75$ m (32 ft), $l_1 = 2.75$ m (9 ft), $d_1 = 0.3$ m (1 ft), $d_2 = 4.88$ m (16 ft), $h_1 = 0.84$ m (2.75 ft), $h_2 = 2.44$ m (8 ft), and $h_3 = 0.98$ m (3.20 ft). It can be seen that the optimum value of the braking force distribution on the tractor rear axle K_{br} varies very little over a wide range of road and loading conditions. On the other hand, the optimum value of the braking force distribution on the tractor front axle K_{bf} and that on the semitrailer axle K_{bs} vary considerably with the coefficient of road adhesion and with the loading conditions of the semitrailer. This indicates that for a tractor–semitrailer combination with a fixed braking force distribution, the optimum braking condition can be achieved only with a particular load configuration over a

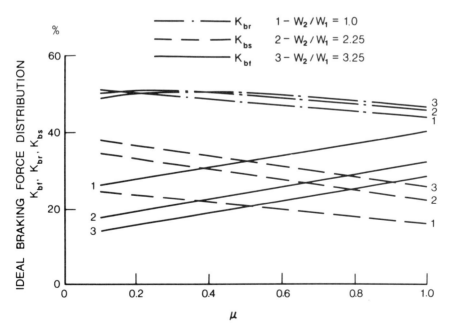

Fig. 3.53 Variation of ideal braking force distribution with road adhesion coefficient and loading conditions for a tractor–semitrailer.

specific road surface. Under all other conditions, one of the axles will lock first. As mentioned previously, the locking of tractor front tires results in a loss of steering control, the locking of tractor rear tires first results in jackknifing, and the locking of semitrailer tires causes trailer swing. This indicates that the locking sequence of the tires is of particular importance to the behavior of the tractor-semitrailer during braking. As jackknifing is the most critical situation, the preferred locking sequence, therefore, appears to be tractor front tires locking up first, then semitrailer tires, and then tractor rear tires. A procedure for predicting the locking sequence of tires of tractor-semitrailers has been developed [3.27]. It has been shown that by careful selection of the braking force distribution among the axles coupled with the proper control of loading conditions, the preferred locking sequence may be achieved over a certain range of road conditions, thus minimizing the undesirable directional response. However, a loss of braking efficiency will result under certain operating conditions [3.27].

The dynamic behavior and directional response of tractor-semitrailers during braking is of practical importance to traffic safety. Extensive study has been made, and the results have been reported in the literature, including references [3.27–3.34].

3.7.4 Antilock Brake Systems

As mentioned previously, when a tire is locked (i.e., 100% skid), the coefficient of road adhesion falls to its sliding value, and its ability to sustain side force is reduced to almost null. As a result, the vehicle will lose directional control and/or stability, and the stopping distance will be longer than the minimum achievable. Figure 3.54 shows the general characteristics of the braking effort coefficient (i.e.,

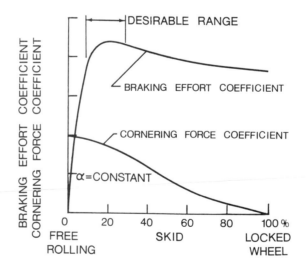

Fig. 3.54 Effect of skid on cornering force coefficient of a tire.

the ratio of the braking effort to the normal load of the tire) and the coefficient of cornering force (i.e., the ratio of the cornering force to the normal load of the tire) at a given slip angle as a function of skid for a pneumatic tire.

The prime function of an antilock brake system is to prevent the tire from locking, and ideally to keep the skid of the tire within a desired range, such as that shown in Fig. 3.54. This will ensure that the tire can develop a sufficiently high braking force for stopping the vehicle, and at the same time it can retain an adequate cornering force for directional control and stability. Data collected in Germany and other countries in the mid-1980's have shown that the introduction of antilock brake systems has reduced a noticeable number of traffic accidents involving passenger cars, and has also mitigated the consequences of a number of accidents [3.35]. In some countries, the insurance premium is reduced for passenger cars equipped with antilock devices.

To appreciate the operation of an antilock brake system, it would be useful to briefly review the dynamics of the tire during braking. When a braking torque T_b is applied to the tire, a corresponding braking effort F_b is developed on the tire–ground contact patch, as shown in Fig. 3.55. This braking effort F_b has a moment T_t about the tire center, which acts in the opposite direction of the applied braking torque T_b. The difference between T_t and T_b causes an angular acceleration $\dot{\omega}$ of the tire:

$$\dot{\omega} = (T_t - T_b)/I_w = (F_b r - T_b)/I_w \qquad (3.90)$$

where I_w is the mass of moment of inertia of the tire assembly about its center and r is the radius of the tire.

When the difference between $F_b r$ and T_b is positive, the tire accelerates, and when it is negative, the tire decelerates.

The braking effort F_b also causes a linear deceleration a_c of the tire center:

$$a_c = F_b/(W/g) \qquad (3.91)$$

where W is the load carried by the tire and g is the acceleration due to gravity.

It should be noted that because of the skid of the tire during braking, the linear deceleration of the tire center a_c is not equal to $r\dot{\omega}$. As noted previously, the skid

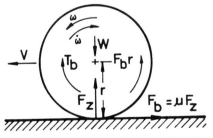

Fig. 3.55 Forces and moments acting on a tire during braking.

i_s of the tire is defined by Eq. 1.30 as follows:

$$i_s = \left(1 - \frac{r\omega}{V}\right) \times 100\%$$

where ω and V are the angular speed and linear speed of the center of the tire, respectively.

If the applied braking torque T_b is large and the angular deceleration $\dot{\omega}$ is high, the tire will become locked (i.e., its angular speed ω becomes zero, while the linear speed of the tire center V is not zero) within a short period of time. The basic function of an antilock device is to monitor the operating conditions of the tire and to control the applied braking torque by modulating the brake pressure so as to prevent the tire from becoming locked, and ideally to keep it operating within a desired range of skid.

A modern antilock brake system is an electronic feedback control system. It consists of a sensor (or sensors), an electronic control unit, and a brake pressure modulator, as schematically shown in Fig. 3.56. In practice, the skid of the tire is difficult to determine accurately, primarily due to the lack of a practical and cost-effective means to directly measure the linear speed V of the tire center during braking. The control logic of an antilock device, therefore, is usually formulated based on some easily measurable parameters, such as the angular speed and angular deceleration (or acceleration) of the tire and linear deceleration of the vehicle.

Sensors with electromagnetic pulse pickups and toothed wheels are usually used to monitor the rotation of the tires or the rotating components of the driveline. To monitor the average angular speed of the tires on a drive axle, the sensor may be mounted at the speedometer cable take-out of the transmission case or on the propeller shaft. To monitor the rotation of individual tires, sensors are mounted directly to the wheel hubs. They usually generate 90–100 pulses per wheel revolution. The angular speed and angular deceleration (or acceleration) of the tire are derived from these digital pulse signals by differentiation with respect to time. A linear accelerometer is used in some antilock devices to monitor the longitudinal deceleration of the vehicle. The signals generated by the sensors are transmitted to the electronic control unit for processing.

The control unit usually consists of four modules: a signal processing module, a module for predicting whether the tire is at the point of locking, a module for

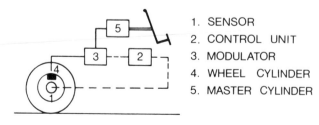

1. SENSOR
2. CONTROL UNIT
3. MODULATOR
4. WHEEL CYLINDER
5. MASTER CYLINDER

Fig. 3.56   Elements of an antilock braking system.

determining whether the danger of locking the tire is averted, and a module for generating a command signal for activating the pressure modulator.

In the control unit, after the signals generated by the sensors have been processed, the measured parameters and/or those derived from them are compared with the corresponding predetermined threshold values. When certain conditions that indicate the impending lock-up of the tire are met by the measured parameters and/or their derivatives, a command signal is sent to the modulator to release the brake. The methods for predicting the locking of the tire used in some antilock systems are described below [3.36–3.40].

1. In some of the existing antilock devices, the locking of the tire is predicted, and a command signal is transmitted to the modulator to release the brake, whenever the product of the angular deceleration $\dot{\omega}$ of the tire and its rolling radius r exceeds a predetermined value. In some systems, the threshold value used is in the range 1–1.6 g.

2. In an antilock system designed for passenger cars, the angular speed signal of the tire is tracked by a track-and-hold circuit in the control unit, and when the value of $r\dot{\omega}$ is greater than 1.6 g, the tracked signal is held in a memory circuit for about 140 ms. During this period of time, if the measured angular speed of the tire decreases by 5% of the already held value, and at the same time if the deceleration of the vehicle measured by a linear accelerometer is not higher than 0.5 g, it is predicted that the tire is at the point of locking, and a command signal for releasing the brake is sent to the modulator. On the other hand, if the deceleration of the vehicle is higher than 0.5 g, locking of the tire is predicted, and the brake is released whenever the decrease in angular speed of the tire is 15% of the already stored value.

3. In many current antilock brake systems, the brake pressure will be reduced if the following two conditions are met [3.39, 3.40]: the estimated tire skid $i_s > i_{s0}$ and $r\dot{\omega} = r\dot{\omega}_0$, where i_{s0} is the threshold value for tire skid, typically 10%, and $r\dot{\omega}_0$ is the threshold value for the circumferential deceleration of the tire, typically 1–1.6 g.

As mentioned previously, the actual skid of the tire during braking is difficult to determine accurately, due to a lack of practical means for directly measuring the linear speed of the tire center. Therefore, in many cases, the tire skid i_s is calculated from the estimated linear speed of the tire center based on the radius r and the measured angular speed ω of the tire, using various estimation methods. To avoid excessive operation of the antilock device at low vehicle speeds due to errors in estimating the tire skid, the threshold value for skid i_{s0} is increased with a decrease in the vehicle speed.

During the braking process, the operating conditions of the tire and the vehicle are continuously monitored by the sensors and the control unit. After the danger of locking the tire is predicted and the brake is released, another module in the control unit will determine at what point the brake should be reapplied. There is a variety of criteria employed in existing antilock systems; some of them are described below [3.36-3.40].

1. In some systems, a command signal will be sent to the modulator to reapply the brake, whenever the criteria for releasing the brake discussed previously are no longer satisfied.
2. In certain devices, a fixed time delay is introduced to ensure that the brake is reapplied only when a fixed time has elapsed after the release of the brake.
3. When the brake is released, the forward momentum of the vehicle causes the tire to have an angular acceleration. In some systems, the brake is reapplied as soon as the product of the angular acceleration $\dot{\omega}$ of the tire and the rolling radius r exceeds a predetermined value. Threshold values for $r\dot{\omega}$ in the range 2.2–3 g have been used. In some devices, the brake pressure build-up rate is made dependent upon the angular acceleration of the tire.

As an example, Fig. 3.57 shows the characteristics of an antilock system designed for heavy commercial vehicles [3.41]. The variations of the brake pressure, tire skid, vehicle speed, circumferential speed $r\omega$, and circumferential acceleration $r\dot{\omega}$ of the tire with time during a simulated braking maneuver over a wet pavement are shown. As can be seen, the brake pressure fluctuates during the operation of an antilock device. The cycle of reducing, holding, and restoring the brake pressure is repeated several times, typically from 5 to 16, per second until the vehicle has slowed to a speed of approximately 3–5 km/h (2–3 mph), at which the antilock device is usually deactivated.

Various layouts for antilock devices on road vehicles have been used. The primary consideration is to ensure directional control and stability of the vehicle, not only when braking in a straight line, but also when braking in a turn and on an

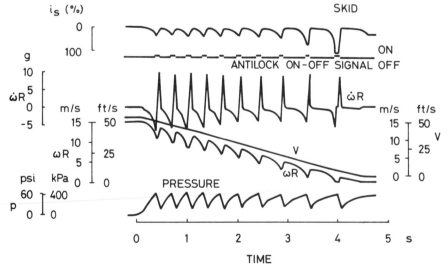

Fig. 3.57 Operating characteristics of an antilock system for heavy commercial vehicles with pneumatic braking systems.

asymmetrical road surface having different values of coefficient of road adhesion for the left- and right-hand side tires.

The common layouts for passenger cars are the four-channel and four-sensor, three-channel and three-sensor, and three-channel and four-sensor configurations, as schematically shown in Fig. 3.58 [3.42]. A channel refers to the portion of the brake system which the control unit/modulator controls independently of the rest of the brake system. For instance, the four-channel and four-sensor configuration shown in the figure has four hydraulic brake circuits with sensors for monitoring the operating conditions of the four tires separately. The two front tires are controlled individually, based on the information obtained by the respective sensors. However, the two tires on the rear axle are jointly controlled in the "select-low" operating mode. "Select-low" means that the control unit will use the information from the slower of the two tires to jointly control both tires with the same brake pressure, whereas "select-high" means that the control unit will use the information from the faster of the two tires to control the brake pressure applied to both tires. It has been shown that using the "select-low" operating mode for controlling the two tires on the rear axle will ensure vehicle directional stability when braking on an asymmetrical road or on a turn, in contrast to using the "select-high" op-

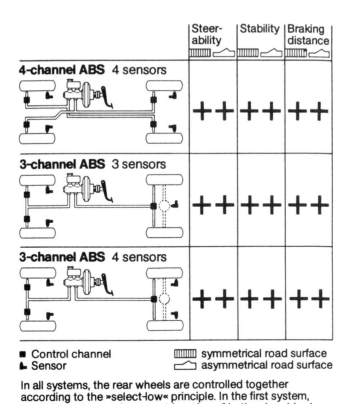

Fig. 3.58 Various layouts of antilock systems for passenger cars. (Reproduced with permission of the Society of Automotive Engineers from reference 3.42.)

erating mode. This is because, with the "select-high" mode, the tire on the low friction side of an asymmetrical road or on the inside of a turn will be locked up, while the other tire on the high friction side of the road or on the outside of a turn develops a higher braking force. This results in a reduction of the cornering force available for the axle, and a large yawing moment which will have an adverse effect on the directional stability of the vehicle. It should be pointed out, however, that using the "select-low" operating mode will have a lower braking efficiency and a longer stopping distance than using the "select-high" mode. It is also interesting to note that with the four tires individually controlled, different braking forces are acting on the left- and right-hand side tires on the front axle, as well as on the rear axle on an asymmetrical road. This results in a large yawing moment which will adversely affect the directional stability of the vehicle. The three-channel and three-sensor configuration has three hydraulic circuits for the control of the two front tires individually and the two rear tires jointly, based on the information obtained by the two sensors mounted on the two front tires and by the one sensor for monitoring the average operating conditions of the two rear tires. The operation of the three-channel and four-sensor configuration with the "select-low" operating mode for the rear tires is similar to that of the four-channel and four-sensor configuration described above.

A two-channel and four-sensor configuration in which the two front tires are jointly controlled by the "select-high" operating mode and the two rear tires by the "select-low" operating mode has also been developed [3.43]. It is claimed that this system can substantially curb the excessive operation of the antilock brake system on rough roads, and that the combination of the "select-high" for the front axle and the "select-low" for the rear axle offers a reasonable compromise between achieving a sufficiently short stopping distance and retaining adequate directional stability.

3.7.5 Traction Control Systems

Similar to the functions of antilock devices for improving vehicle braking performance, traction control systems have been developed for improving vehicle tractive performance and for maintaining directional control and stability during acceleration [3.44, 3.45]. The prime functions of a traction control system are as follows:

1. to improve traction on an asymmetrical road surface with different values of coefficient of road adhesion for the left- and right-hand side tires
2. to prevent the tire from spinning during acceleration or on slippery surfaces, and ideally to keep the slip of the tire within a desired range so as to retain an adequate cornering force for direction control and stability.

Similar to an antilock brake system, a typical traction control system consists of a sensor (or sensors), an electronic control unit, a brake pressure modulator, and an engine control device, which controls the throttle, fuel injection system, or ignition. Because of the similarity between the two systems, the traction control system is usually integrated with the antilock brake system, sharing a large number of common components, such as the sensor, electronic control unit, and brake pressure modulator.

For a drive axle with a simple differential, the driving torque is evenly distributed between the left- and right-hand side half-shafts. As a result, when operating on an asymmetrical road, the tire on the side of the road having a low value of coefficient of road adhesion will slip excessively, and will impose a limit on the tractive effort that the other tire with a high value of coefficient of road adhesion can develop. While a differential lock, limited-slip differential or viscous coupling would provide a solution to this problem, a traction control system is a viable alternative. When the slip of a tire on one side of a drive axle is determined to be excessive, a braking torque is applied to that tire through brake pressure modulation so as to increase the driving torque available to the other tire for improving traction. For a vehicle with only one drive axle, the slip of the driven tires can be determined directly using the angular speed of the free-rolling tires on the non-driven axle as a reference.

When the vehicle operates on a slippery surface with a low coefficient of road adhesion or during start-up, both tires on the drive axle may slip excessively. Under these circumstances, the traction control system will apply braking torques to both driven tires and/or decrease the engine output torque to reduce the tractive effort and slip. This ensures adequate directional control for a front-wheel-drive vehicle or directional stability for a rear-wheel-drive vehicle. When operating on a long stretch of slippery road, to avoid brake overheating, a combined brake pressure modulation and engine control is necessary. It should be pointed out that the response of traction control to brake pressure modulation is usually faster than that to engine control because of the actuation time of the engine control device, engine rotating inertia, and the elasticity of the driveline.

REFERENCES

3.1 K.B. Kelly and H.J. Holcombe, "Aerodynamics for Body Engineers," *Automotive Aerodynamics*, Progress in Technology Series, vol. 16, Society of Automotive Engineers, 1978.

3.2 C.W. Carr, "Potential for Aerodynamic Drag Reduction in Car Design," in M.A. Dorgham, Ed., *Impact of Aerodynamics on Vehicle Design*, Technological Advances in Vehicle Design Series, SP3. Jersey, Channel Islands, U.K.: Inderscience Enterprises Limited, 1983.

3.3 G. Rousillon, J. Marzin, and J. Bourhis, "Contribution to the Accurate Measurement of Aerodynamic Drag by the Deceleration Method," in *Advances in Road Vehicle Aerodynamics*, BHRA Fluid Engineering, Cranfield, England, 1973.

3.4 R.A. White and H.H. Korst, "A Generalized Method for Determining Drag Coefficient or Rolling Resistances from Coast Down Tests," in *Advances in Road Vehicle Aerodynamics*, BHRA Fluid Engineering, Cranfield, England, 1973.

3.5   G.W. Eaker, "Wind Tunnel-to-Road Aerodynamic Drag Correlation," in *Research in Automotive Aerodynamics*, Society of Automotive Engineers, Special Publication SP-747, 1988.

3.6   R.G.S. White, "A Method of Estimating Automobile Drag Coefficient," *SAE Transactions*, vol. 78, paper 690189, 1969.

3.7   W.H. Hucho, "Aerodynamic Drag of Passenger Cars," in W.H. Hucho, Ed., *Aerodynamics of Road Vehicles*. London: Butterworths, 1987.

3.8   L.J. Janssen and W.H. Hucho, "The Effect of Various Parameters on the Aerodynamic Drag of Passenger Cars," in *Advances in Road Vehicle Aerodynamics*, BHRA Fluid Engineering, Cranfield, England, 1973.

3.9   W.H. Hucho, L.J. Janssen, and H.J. Emmelmann, "The Optimization of Body Details—A Method for Reducing the Aerodynamic Drag of Road Vehicles," Society of Automotive Engineers, paper 760185, 1976.

3.10 H. Gotz, "Commercial Vehicles," in W.H. Hucho, Ed., *Aerodynamics of Road Vehicles*. London: Butterworths, 1987.

3.11 C. Berta and B. Bonis, "Experimental Shape Research of Ideal Aerodynamic Characteristics for Industrial Vehicles," Society of Automotive Engineers, paper 801402, 1980.

3.12 R.V. Agres and R.P. McKenna, *Alternatives to the Internal Combustion Engine*. Baltimore, MD: The Johns Hopkins University Press, 1972.

3.13 C.W. Coon and C.D. Wood, "Improvement of Automobile Fuel Economy," Society of Automotive Engineers, paper 740969, 1974.

3.14 J.J. Taborek, "Mechanics of Vehicles," *Machine Design*, 1957.

3.15 H.I. Setz, "Computer Predicts Car Acceleration," *SAE Transactions*, vol. 69, 1961.

3.16 J.G. Giles, *Gears and Transmissions*, Automotive Technology Series, vol. 4. London: Butterworths, 1969.

3.17 A. Bonthron, "CVT—Efficiency Measured Under Dynamic Running Conditions," Society of Automotive Engineers, paper 850569, 1985.

3.18 D. Hahne, "A Continuously Variable Automatic Transmission for Small Front Wheel Drive Cars," in *Driveline '84*, Institution of Mechanical Engineers, 1984.

3.19 K. Newton, W. Steeds, and T.K. Garrett, *The Motor Vehicle*, 10th ed. London: Butterworths, 1983.

3.20 C.J. Greenwood, "The Design, Construction and Operation of a Commercial Vehicle Continuously Variable Transmission," in *Driveline '84*, Institution of Mechanical Engineers, 1984.

3.21 C.K.J. Price and S.A. Beasley, "Aspects of Hydraulic Transmissions for Vehicles of Specialized Nature," *Proc. Institution of Mechanical Engineers*, vol. 178, part 3C, 1963–1964.

3.22 D. Cole, "Automotive Fuel Economy," in J.C. Hilliard and G.S. Springer, Ed., *Fuel Economy in Road Vehicles Powered by Spark Ignition Engines*. New York: Plenum Press, 1984.

3.23 H.E. Chana, W.L. Fedewa, and J.E. Mahoney, "An Analytical Study of Transmission Modifications as Related to Vehicle Performance and Economy," Society of Automotive Engineers, paper 770418, 1977.

3.24 F.C. Porter, "Design for Fuel Economy—The New GM Front Drive Cars," Society of Automotive Engineers, paper 790721, 1979.

3.25 R.D. Lister, "Retention of Directional Control When Braking," *SAE Transactions*, vol. 74, paper 650092, 1965.

3.26 D.J. Bickerstaff and G. Hartley, "Light Truck Tire Traction Properties and Their Effect on Braking Performance," *SAE Transactions*, vol. 83, paper 741137, 1974.

3.27 J.Y. Wong and R.R. Guntur, "Effects of Operational and Design Parameters on the Sequence of Locking of the Wheels of Tractor-Semitrailers," *Vehicle Systems Dynamics*, vol. 7, no. 1, 1978.

3.28 J.R. Ellis, *Vehicle Dynamics*. London, England: Business Books, 1969.

3.29 E.C. Mikulcik, "The Dynamics of Tractor-Semitrailer Vehicles: The Jackknifing Problem," *SAE Transactions*, vol. 80, paper 710045, 1971.

3.30 R.W. Murphy, J.E. Bernard, and C.B. Winkler, "A Computer Based Mathematical Method for Predicting the Braking Performance of Trucks and Tractor-Trailers," Report of the Highway Safety Research Institute, University of Michigan, Ann Arbor, September 1972.

3.31 C.B. Winkler, J.E. Bernard, P.S. Fancher, C.C. MacAdam, and T.M. Post, "Predicting the Braking Performance of Trucks and Tractor-Trailers," Report of the Highway Safety Research Institute, University of Michigan, Ann Arbor, June 1976.

3.32 R.R. Guntur and J.Y. Wong, "Application of the Parameter Plane Method to the Analysis of Directional Stability of Tractor-Semitrailers," *Transactions of the ASME, Journal of Dynamic Systems, Measurement and Control*, vol. 100, no. 1, Mar. 1978.

3.33 C.P. Lam, R.R. Guntur, and J.Y. Wong, "Evaluation of the Braking Performance of a Tractor-Semitrailer Equipped with Two Different Types of Antilock System," *SAE Transactions*, vol. 88, paper 791046, 1979.

3.34 V.S. Verma, R.R. Guntur, and J.Y. Wong, "Directional Behavior During Braking of a Tractor-Semitrailer Fitted with Antilock Devices," *International Journal of Vehicle Design*, vol. 1, no. 3, 1980.

3.35 H.-C. Klein, "Anti-Lock Brake Systems for Passenger Cars, State of the Art 1985," in *Proc. XXI FISITA Congress*, paper 865139, Belgrade, Yugoslavia, 1986.

3.36 R.R. Gunter and H. Ouwerkerk, "Adaptive Brake Control Systems," in *Proc. Institution of Mechanical Engineers*, vol. 186, 68/72, 1972.

3.37 J.Y. Wong, J.R. Ellis, and R.R. Guntur, *Braking and Handling of Heavy Commercial Vehicles*, Monograph, Department of Mechanical and Aeronautical Engineering, Carleton University, Ottawa, Ont., Canada, 1977.

3.38 R.R. Guntur and J.Y. Wong, "Some Design Aspects of Anti-Lock Brake Systems for Commercial Vehicles," *Vehicle System Dynamics*, vol. 9, no. 3, 1980.

3.39 M. Satoh and S. Shiraishi, "Excess Operation of Antilock Brake System on a Rough Road," in *Braking of Road Vehicles 1983*, Institution of Mechanical Engineers, 1983.

3.40 H. Leiber and A. Czinczel, "Antiskid System for Passenger Cars with a Digital Electronic Control Unit," Society of Automotive Engineers, paper 790458, 1979.

3.41 R. Srinivasa, R.R. Gunter, and J.Y. Wong, "Evaluation of the Performance of Anti-Lock Brake Systems Using Laboratory Simulation Techniques," *International Journal of Vehicle Design*, vol. 1, no. 5, 1980.

3.42 H. Leiber and A. Czinczel, "Four Years of Experience with 4-Wheel Antiskid Brake Systems (ABS)," Society of Automotive Engineers, paper 830481, 1983.

3.43 M. Satoh and S. Shiraishi, "Performance of Antilock Brakes with Simplified Control Technique," Society of Automotive Engineers, paper 830484, 1983.

3.44 H.W. Bleckmann, H. Fennel, J. Graber, and W.W. Selbert, "Traction Control System with Teves ABS Mark II," Society of Automotive Engineers, paper 860506, 1986.

3.45 H. Demel and H. Hemming, "ABS and ASR for Passenger Cars—Goals and Limits," Society of Automotive Engineers, paper 890834, 1989.

PROBLEMS

3.1 A vehicle weighs 20.02 kN (4500 lb) and has a wheelbase of 279.4 cm (110 in.). The center of gravity is 127 cm (50 in.) behind the front axle and 50.8 cm (20 in.) above ground level. The frontal area of the vehicle is 2.32 m² (25 ft²) and the aerodynamic drag coefficient is 0.45. The coefficient of rolling resistance is given by $f_r = 0.0136 + 0.4 \times 10^{-7} V^2$, where V is the speed of the vehicle in kilometers per hour. The rolling radius of the tires is 33 cm (13 in.). The coefficient of road adhesion is 0.8. Estimate the possible maximum speed of the vehicle on level ground and on a grade of 25% as determined by the maximum tractive effort that the tire–road contact can support if the vehicle is (a) rear-wheel-drive, and (b) front-wheel-drive. Plot the resultant resistance versus vehicle speed, and show the maximum thrust of the vehicle with the two types of drive.

3.2 The vehicle described in Problem 3.1 is equipped with an engine having torque–speed characteristics as shown in the following table. The gear ratios of the gearbox are: first, 4.03; second, 2.16; third, 1.37; and fourth, 1.0. The gear ratio of the drive axle is 3.54. The transmission efficiency is 88%. Estimate the maximum speed of the vehicle on level ground and on a grade of 25% as determined by the tractive effort that the engine torque with the given transmission can provide if the vehicle is rear-wheel-drive. Plot the vehicle thrust in various gears versus vehicle speed.

Engine Characteristics

Engine speed, rpm	500	1000	1750	2500	3000	3500	4000	4500	5000
Engine torque, N · m	339	379.7	406.8	393.2	363.4	325.4	284.8	233.2	189.8

3.3 A vehicle is equipped with an automatic transmission consisting of a torque converter and a three-speed gearbox. The torque converter and the engine characteristics are shown in Figs. 3.31 and 3.32, respectively. The total gear reduction ratio of the gearbox and the drive axle is 2.91 when the third gear is engaged. The combined efficiency of the gearbox, propeller shaft, and the drive axle is 0.90. The rolling radius of the tire is 33.5 cm (1.1 ft). Calculate the tractive effort and speed of the vehicle when the third gear is engaged and the engine is running at 2000 rpm with an engine torque of 407 N · m (300 lb · ft). Also determine the overall efficiency of the transmission, including the torque converter.

3.4 A passenger car weighs 12.45 kN (2800 lb), including the four tires. Each of the tires has an effective diameter of 67 cm (2.2 ft) and a radius of gyration of 27.9 cm (11 in.), and weighs 222.4 N (50 lb). The engine develops 44.8 kW (60 hp) at 4000 rpm, and the equivalent weight of the rotating parts of the driveline at engine speed is 444.8 N (100 lb) with a radius of gyration of 10 cm (4 in.). The transmission efficiency is 88% and the total reduction ratio of the driveline in the second gear is 7.56 to 1. The vehicle has a frontal area of 1.67 m² (18 ft²) and the aerodynamic drag coefficient is 0.45. The average coefficient of rolling resistance is 0.015. Calculate the acceleration of the vehicle on a level road under these conditions.

3.5 A passenger car weighs 20.02 kN (4500 lb) and has a wheelbase of 279.4 cm (110 in.). The center of gravity is 127 cm (50 in.) behind the front axle and 50.8 cm (20 in.) above ground level. In practice, the vehicle encounters a variety of surfaces, with the coefficient of road adhesion ranging from 0.2 to 0.8 and the coefficient of rolling resistance of 0.015. With a view to avoiding the loss of directional stability on surfaces with a low coefficient of adhesion under emergency braking conditions, what would you recommend regarding the braking effort distribution between the front and rear axles?

3.6 For a tractor–semitrailer combination, the tractor weighs 66.72 kN (15,000 lb) and the semitrailer weighs 266.88 kN (60,000 lb). The wheelbase of the tractor is 381 cm (150 in.), and the trailer axle is 1016 cm (400 in.) behind the rear axle of the tractor. The hitch point is 25 cm (10 in.) in front of the tractor rear axle and 122 cm (48 in.) above the ground level. The center of gravity of the tractor is 203.2 cm (80 in.) behind the tractor front axle and 96.5 cm (38 in.) above the ground. The center of gravity of the semitrailer is 508 cm (200 in.) in front of the trailer axle and 177.8 cm (70 in.) above the ground. What is the ideal braking effort distribution between the axles that ensures all the tires being locked up at the same time on a surface with a coefficient of road adhesion $\mu = 0.6$? Also calculate the normal loads on the axles and the forces acting at the hitch point.

3.7 A "coast-down" test was performed to estimate the aerodynamic resistance coefficient C_D and the rolling coefficient f_r of a road vehicle. The test was conducted on a level road with a tail wind of 8 km/h (5 mph). The vehicle was first run up to a speed of 96 km/h (60 mph) and then the gear was shifted to neutral. The vehicle decelerated under the action of the aerodynamic resistance, the rolling resistance of the tires, and the internal resistance of the driveline. The vehicle slowed down from 96 km/h (60 mph) to 88.5 km/h (55 mph) in a distance of 160 m (525.5 ft), and from 80 km/h (50 mph) to 72.4 km/h (45 mph) in a distance of 162.6 m (533.5 ft). The vehicle weighs 15.568 kN (3500 lb) and has a frontal area of 2.32 m² (25 ft²). Assuming that the rolling resistance of the tires is independent of speed and that the internal resistance of the driveline may be neglected, estimate the values of the aerodynamic resistance coefficient C_D and the rolling resistance coefficient of the tires f_r.

CHAPTER 4

PERFORMANCE CHARACTERISTICS OF OFF-ROAD VEHICLES

Depending on the functional requirements, different criteria are employed to evaluate the performance characteristics of various types of off-road vehicle. For tractors, their main function is to provide adequate draft to pull various types of implement and machinery; the drawbar performance is, therefore, of prime interest. It may be characterized by the ratio of drawbar pull to vehicle weight, drawbar horsepower, and drawbar efficiency. For cross-country transport vehicles, the transport productivity and efficiency are often used as basic criteria for evaluating their performance. For military vehicles, on the other hand, the maximum feasible operating speed between two specific points in a given area may be employed as a criterion for the evaluation of their mobility.

Although differing criteria are used to assess the performance of different kinds of off-road vehicle, there is a basic requirement common to all cross-country vehicles, that is, mobility over unprepared terrain. Mobility in the broad sense is concerned with the performance of the vehicle in relation to soft terrain, obstacle negotiation and avoidance, ride quality over rough terrain, and water crossing. The performance on soft terrain constitutes a basic problem in vehicle mobility, and a detailed analysis of the relationship among vehicle performance, vehicle design parameters, and the terrain is, therefore, of prime importance.

In this chapter, methods for evaluating and predicting the tractive performance of cross-country vehicles will be discussed. Performance criteria for various types of off-road vehicle will also be examined in detail.

4.1 DRAWBAR PERFORMANCE

4.1.1 Drawbar Pull and Drawbar Power

For off-road vehicles designed for traction (i.e., tractors), the drawbar performance is of prime importance, as it represents the ability of the vehicle to pull or push

250

various types of working machinery, including agricultural implements and construction and earth-moving equipment. Drawbar pull F_d is the force available at the drawbar, and is equal to the difference between the tractive effort F developed by the running gear and the resultant resisting force ΣR acting on the vehicle:

$$F_d = F - \Sigma R \tag{4.1}$$

For a vehicle with known power plant and transmission characteristics, the tractive effort and vehicle speed can be determined using methods similar to those described in Chapter 3. It should be pointed out, however, that in cross-country operations, the maximum tractive effort is often limited by the characteristics of vehicle–terrain interaction, as described in Chapter 2. Furthermore, the development of thrust often results in considerable slip over unprepared terrain. Thus, the drawbar pull and vehicle speed are functions of slip.

The resisting forces acting on an off-road vehicle include the internal resistance of the running gear, resistance due to vehicle–terrain interaction, obstacle resistance, grade resistance, as well as aerodynamic drag.

Internal Resistance of the Running Gear   For wheeled vehicles, the internal resistance of the running gear is mainly due to hysteresis losses in the tire, which has been discussed in Chapter 1. For tracked vehicles, the internal resistance of the track and the associated suspension system may be substantial. Frictional losses in track pins, between the driving sprocket teeth and the track, and in sprocket hub and roadwheel bearings, and the rolling resistance of the roadwheels on the track constitute the major portion of the internal resistance of the track-suspension system. Experimental results show that of the total power consumed in the track-suspension system, 63–75% is due to losses in the track itself. Among the oper-

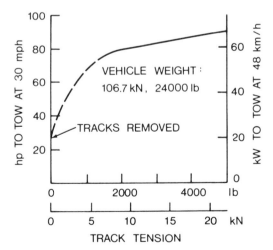

Fig. 4.1 Effect of track tension on power consumption. (Reproduced with permission of the Council of the Institution of Mechanical Engineers from reference 4.1.)

ational parameters, track tension and vehicle speed have noticeable effects on the internal resistance, as shown in Figs. 4.1 and 4.2, respectively [4.1, 4.2].

Because of the complex nature of the internal resistance in the track-suspension system, it is difficult, if not impossible, to establish an analytic procedure to predict the internal resistance with sufficient accuracy. As a first approximation, the following formula proposed by Bekker may be used for calculating the average value of the internal resistance R_{in} of a conventional tracked vehicle [4.2]:

$$R_{in} = W (222 + 3V) \tag{4.2}$$

where R_{in} is in newtons, W is the vehicle weight in tonnes, and V is the vehicle speed in kilometers per hour.

For modern lightweight tracked vehicles, the internal resistance may be less, and the empirical formula is [4.2]

$$R_{in} = W (133 + 2.5V) \tag{4.3}$$

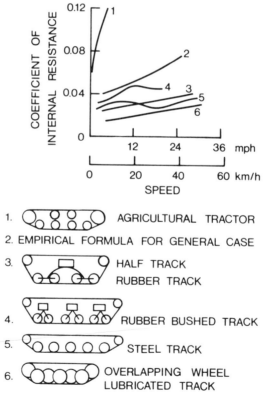

Fig. 4.2 Effect of speed on the coefficient of internal resistance of various types of track. (From *Introduction to Terrain-Vehicle Systems* by M.G. Bekker, copyright © by the University of Michigan, 1969, reproduced with permission of the University of Michigan Press.)

For military tracked vehicles operating on hard, smooth road surfaces, the coefficient of motion resistance f_r, which is the ratio of the motion resistance to vehicle weight, may be estimated by the following empirical equation [4.3]:

$$f_r = f_0 + f_s V \tag{4.4}$$

where f_0 and f_s are empirical coefficients, and V is in kilometers per hour. For tracks having double, rubber-bushed pins and rubber pads, the value of f_0 is typically 0.03; for all-steel, single-pin tracks, it is 0.025; and for tracks having sealed, lubricated pin joints with needle bearings, it can be as low as 0.015. The value of f_s varies with the type of track, and as a first approximation, may be taken as 0.00015.

Resistance Due to Vehicle–Terrain Interaction   This type of resistance is the most significant one for off-road vehicles, and determines, to a great extent, the mobility of the vehicle over unprepared terrain. It includes the resistance due to compacting the terrain and the bulldozing effect, and it may be predicted using the methods described in Chapter 2 or determined experimentally.

Ground Obstacle Resistance   In off-road operations, obstacles such as stumps and stones may be encountered. The obstacle resistance may be considered as a resisting force, usually variable in magnitude, acting parallel to the ground at a certain effective height. When the line of action of this resisting force is high above ground level, it produces a moment that would cause significant load transfer, and it should be taken into consideration in formulating the equations of motion for the vehicle. In general, the value of the obstacle resistance is obtained from experiments.

Aerodynamic Resistance   Aerodynamic resistance is usually not a significant factor for off-road vehicles operating at speeds below 48 km/h (30 mph). For vehicles designed for higher speeds, such as military vehicles, aerodynamic resistance may have to be taken into consideration in performance calculations. The aerodynamic resistance can be predicted using the methods described in Chapter 3.

The aerodynamic resistance coefficient mainly depends on the shape of the vehicle, as mentioned previously. For heavy fighting vehicles, such as battle tanks, the aerodynamic resistance coefficient C_D is approximately 1.0, and the frontal area is of the order of 6–8 m² (65–86 ft²) [4.3]. For a tank weighing 50 tonnes and having an aerodynamic resistance coefficient of 1.17 and a frontal area of 6.5 m² (70 ft²), the power required to overcome aerodynamic resistance at 48 km/h (30 mph) amounts to about 11.2 kW (15 hp). A light tracked vehicle weighing 10 tonnes and having a frontal area of 3.7 m² (40 ft²) may require 10.5 kW (14 hp) to overcome the aerodynamic resistance at a speed of 56 km/h (35 mph).

In addition to the resisting forces described above, the grade resistance must be taken into consideration when the vehicle is climbing up a slope. For heavy fighting vehicles, the usual requirement is that they should be able to climb up a gradient of 30° (58%).

To characterize the drawbar performance, the slip of the running gear and the vehicle speed in each gear are usually plotted against tractive effort and drawbar pull, as shown in Fig. 4.3. The product of drawbar pull and vehicle speed is usually referred to as the drawbar power that represents the potential productivity of the vehicle, that is, the rate at which productive work may be done. The drawbar power P_d is given by

$$P_d = F_d V = \left(F - \Sigma R\right) V_t \,(1 - i) \qquad (4.5)$$

where V and V_t are the actual forward speed and the theoretical speed of the vehicle, respectively. The theoretical speed is the speed of the vehicle if there is no slip (or skid), and is determined by the engine speed, reduction ratio of the transmission, and the radius of the tire (or sprocket). Usually, the variation of drawbar power with drawbar pull in each gear is also shown in the drawbar performance diagram. As an example, Fig. 4.4 shows the measured drawbar performance of an MF-165 tractor on tarmacadam [4.4]. The drawbar performance diagram provides a basis for comparing and evaluating the tractive performance of tractors. It also provides the operator with the required information to achieve proper matching of the tractor with the working machinery.

4.1.2 Tractive Efficiency

To characterize the efficiency of an off-road vehicle in transforming the engine power to the power available at the drawbar, the tractive (drawbar) efficiency is often used. It is defined as the ratio of drawbar power P_d to the corresponding power delivered by the engine P:

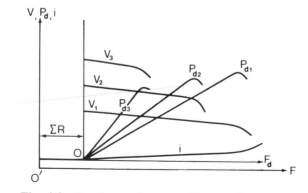

Fig. 4.3 Tractive performance diagram for tractors.

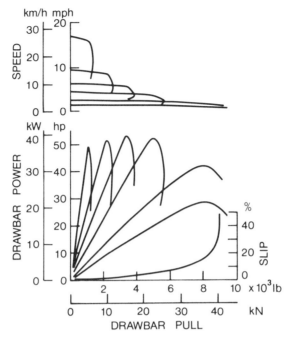

Fig. 4.4 Drawbar performance of an MF-165 tractor on tarmacadam. (Reproduced with permission of the *Journal of Agricultural Engineering Research* from reference 4.4.)

$$\eta_d = \frac{P_d}{P} = \frac{F_d V}{P} = \frac{\left(F - \Sigma R\right) V_t \left(1 - i\right)}{P} \tag{4.6}$$

The power delivered by the engine may be expressed in terms of the power available at the driven wheel (or sprocket) and the transmission efficiency η_t:

$$P = \frac{F V_t}{\eta_t} \tag{4.7}$$

Substituting Eq. 4.7 into Eq. 4.6, the expression for tractive efficiency becomes

$$\eta_d = \frac{\left(F - \Sigma R\right)}{F} \left(1 - i\right) \eta_t = \frac{F_d}{F} \left(1 - i\right) \eta_t$$

$$= \eta_m \eta_s \eta_t \tag{4.8}$$

where η_m is the efficiency of motion equal to F_d/F, and η_s is the efficiency of slip equal to $1 - i$.

The efficiency of motion indicates the losses in transforming the tractive effort at the driven wheels to the pull at the drawbar. For motion resistance having a constant value, the efficiency of motion η_m increases with an increase of drawbar pull, as shown in Fig. 4.5.

The efficiency of slip characterizes the power losses, and also the reduction in speed of the vehicle due to the slip of the running gear. Since slip increases with an increase of tractive effort and drawbar pull, the efficiency of slip decreases as the drawbar pull increases, as shown in Fig. 4.5. Usually, slip is a major source of power losses in the operation of off-road vehicles over unprepared terrain. Reducing the slip is, therefore, of practical significance in increasing the operational efficiency of off-road vehicles.

As can be seen from Eq. 4.8, the tractive efficiency is the product of the efficiency of transmission, efficiency of motion, and efficiency of slip. In general, it exhibits a peak at an intermediate value of drawbar pull, as shown in Fig. 4.5. To increase the tractive efficiency, optimization of the form and size of the vehicle running gear is of importance. In this respect, the terramechanics described in Chapter 2 plays an important role.

Example 4.1. An off-road wheeled vehicle is equipped with an engine having the torque–speed characteristics given in Table 4.1. The vehicle is to operate on a soil

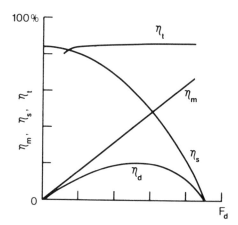

Fig. 4.5 Variation of tractive efficiency with drawbar pull.

TABLE 4.1   Engine Characteristics

Engine Speed n_e (rpm)	Engine Torque M_e	
	N · m	lb · ft
800	393	290
1200	650	479
1600	732	540
2000	746	550
2400	705	520
2800	610	450

with the thrust–slip characteristics given in Table 4.2. The total motion resistance is 2.23 kN (500 lb). The transmission efficiency is 0.85, and the rolling radius of the tire is 0.76 m (2.5 ft). Determine the drawbar power and tractive efficiency of the vehicle when the fourth gear with a total reduction ratio of $\xi_0 = 20.5$ is engaged.

Solution. The thrust can be calculated using Eq. 3.30 in Chapter 3:

$$F = \frac{M_e \xi_0 \eta_t}{r}$$

From Table 4.2, the slip at a particular thrust can be determined. The vehicle speed can be determined using Eq. 3.31 in Chapter 3:

$$V = \frac{n_e r}{\xi_0} (1 - i)$$

For a given engine operating point, the vehicle speed and thrust are related. Therefore, the slip at a particular theoretical speed can be determined, and the actual speed of the vehicle can be calculated. The results of the calculations for F and V are tabulated in Table 4.3. The drawbar pull is given by

$$F_d = F - \Sigma R$$

Since the total motion resistance is given, the drawbar pull can be calculated, and the results are given in Table 4.3. The drawbar power can be determined using Eq. 4.5:

$$P_d = F_d V$$

and the tractive efficiency can be calculated using either Eq. 4.6 or Eq. 4.8:

TABLE 4.2 Thrust–Slip Characteristics

Slip (%)	Thrust F	
	kN	lb
5	10.24	2303
10	16.0	3597
15	20.46	4600
20	24.0	5396
25	26.68	5998
30	28.46	6398
40	32.02	7199

TABLE 4.3 Drawbar Performance

Engine Speed n_e (rpm)	Thrust F		Slip (%)	Vehicle speed V		Drawbar Pull F_d		Drawbar Power P_d		Transmission Efficiency η_t (%)	Efficiency of Slip η_s (%)	Tractive Efficiency η_d (%)
	kN	lb		km/h	mph	kN	lb	kW	hp			
800	9.01	2025	4.4	10.7	6.7	6.78	1525	20.1	27	85	95.6	61.1
1200	14.90	3350	9.0	15.3	9.5	12.67	2850	53.8	72.2	85	91.0	65.7
1600	16.78	3772	10.9	19.9	12.4	14.55	3272	80.4	107.8	85	89.1	65.6
2000	17.10	3844	11.23	24.9	15.5	14.87	3344	102.8	137.9	85	88.7	65.6
2400	16.16	3633	10.2	30.2	18.8	13.93	3133	116.8	156.7	85	89.8	65.8
2800	13.98	3143	8.3	36.0	22.4	11.75	2643	117.5	157.5	85	91.7	65.5

$$\eta_d = \frac{F_d V}{P}$$

The results of the calculations for P_d and η_d are tabulated in Table 4.3. It can be seen that the maximum drawbar efficiency of the vehicle under the operating conditions specified is approximately 66%, which indicates that 34% of the engine power is lost in the transmission, in overcoming the motion resistance, and in vehicle slip.

It should be mentioned that engines for off-road vehicles are often equipped with a governor to limit its maximum operating speed. When the engine characteristics over the operating range of the governor (i.e., between the full load and no load settings of the governor) are known, the drawbar performance of the vehicle in that range can be predicted in the same way as that described above.

In agriculture, earth-moving, logging, and cross-country transport, there is a growing demand for higher productivity. Consequently, there has been a steady increase in the installed power of new vehicles. For wheeled tractors to fully utilize the high engine power available and to maintain high tractive efficiency, four-wheel-drive has gained increasingly wide acceptance since the total weight of a four-wheel-drive tractor is utilized for the development of thrust, whereas only about 60–70% of the total weight is applied on the driven wheels of a two-wheel-drive vehicle. Consequently, over soft terrain, a four-wheel-drive tractor has the potential of developing higher thrust than an equivalent two-wheel-drive vehicle at the same slip. Furthermore, a four-wheel-drive vehicle with the same size tires for the front and rear axles usually has a lower overall coefficient of rolling resistance than an equivalent two-wheel-drive vehicle. This is because its rear tires run in the ruts formed by the front tires, thus reducing their motion resistance. Figure 4.6(a) and (b) show a comparison of the drawbar performance of a two-wheel-drive and a four-wheel-drive tractor on a dry loam, stubble field and on a wet, clayey loam, respectively [4.6]. It can be seen that on the dry loam, stubble field, the drawbar pull of the four-wheel-drive tractor at 20% slip is 27% higher and at 50% slip is 20% higher than the corresponding values of the two-wheel-drive tractor. The peak tractive efficiency of the four-wheel-drive tractor and that of the two-wheel-drive tractor are 77 and 70%, respectively [4.5]. On the wet clayey loam, the drawbar pull of the four-wheel-drive tractor at 30% slip is as much as 57% higher and at 50% slip is 44% higher than the corresponding values of the two-wheel-drive tractor. The values of the peak tractive efficiency of the four-wheel-drive and two-wheel-drive tractor are 51 and 40%, respectively.

For a four-wheel-drive tractor to achieve the optimum tractive efficiency, certain requirements have to be met. To define these requirements quantitatively, it is necessary to examine the tractive efficiency, particularly the efficiency of slip, of a four-wheel-drive off-road vehicle. For a four-wheel-drive vehicle, the power losses due to slip occur at both the front and rear driven wheels. The slip efficiency η_{s4} of a four-wheel-drive vehicle is determined by [4.7]

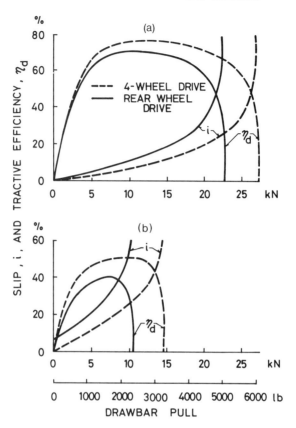

Fig. 4.6 Comparison of drawbar performance between a four-wheel-drive and a rear-wheel-drive tractor on (a) dry loam, stubble field and (b) wet clayey loam. (Reproduced with permission from reference 4.6.)

$$\eta_{s4} = 1 - \frac{i_f V_{tf} F_f + i_r V_{tr} F_r}{V_{tf} F_f + V_{tr} F_r} \tag{4.9}$$

where V_{tf} and V_{tr} are the theoretical speed of the front and rear wheels, F_f and F_r are the tractive effort of the front and rear wheels, and i_f and i_r are the slip of the front and rear wheels, respectively.

There is a relationship between the translatory speed of the front wheel and that of the rear wheel of a four-wheel-drive vehicle in a straight line motion. The relationship can be expressed by

$$V_{tf}(1 - i_f) = V_{tr}(1 - i_r) = V \tag{4.10}$$

This is due to the fact that the front and rear wheels are connected with the same frame, and the actual translatory speeds of the front and rear wheels must be the same in a straight line motion.

Therefore,

$$\eta_{s4} = 1 - \frac{[(1 - i_r)/(1 - i_f)] \, i_f V_{tr} F_f + i_r V_{tr} F_r}{[(1 - i_r)/(1 - i_f)] \, V_{tr} F_f + V_{tr} F_r}$$

$$= 1 - \frac{i_f (1 - i_r) - (i_f - i_r) K_d}{(1 - i_r) - (i_f - i_r) K_d} \tag{4.11}$$

where K_d is the coefficient of thrust distribution and is equal to $F_r/(F_f + F_r)$.

Equation 4.11 shows that, in general, the efficiency of slip of a four-wheel-drive vehicle depends not only on the slips of the front and rear wheels, but also on the distribution of thrust between them. From Eq. 4.11, it is clear that under a particular condition, there is an optimum thrust distribution that can make the efficiency of slip reach its peak. To find this optimum thrust distribution, the first partial derivative of η_{s4} with respect to K_d is taken and set equal to zero:

$$\frac{\partial \eta_{s4}}{\partial K_d} = \frac{(1 - i_f)(1 - i_r)(i_f - i_r)}{[(1 - i_r) - (i_f - i_r) K_d]^2} = 0 \tag{4.12}$$

This condition can only be satisfied if the slip of the front wheels or that of the rear wheels is 100%, or the slip of the front wheels is equal to that of the rear wheels. When the slip of either the front or the rear wheels is 100%, the vehicle cannot move forward at all, and the tractive efficiency is equal to zero. Therefore, under normal operating conditions, only when the slip of the front wheels equals that of the rear wheels will the first partial derivative be zero. This is the necessary condition for achieving the maximum efficiency of slip.

The above analysis leads to an interesting result, which shows that for the most efficient operation of a four-wheel-drive vehicle, the slip of the front wheels must be the same as that of the rear wheels. In other words, the optimum thrust distribution will make the slips of the front and rear wheels equal. Only in this case can the efficiency of slip reach its peak. It is interesting to point out that when the slips of the front and rear wheels are equal, $i_f = i_r$, the efficiency of slip, η_{s4}, is simply equal to $1 - i_f$ or $1 - i_r$, and the coefficient of thrust distribution no longer has an effect on the efficiency of slip (see Eq. 4.11). As an example, Fig. 4.7 shows the variation of the efficiency of slip with the coefficient of thrust distribution of a four-wheel-drive vehicle on a farm soil [4.7].

Since the thrust distribution affects the tractive efficiency of a four-wheel-drive vehicle considerably, it is of importance to analyze the factors that in practice affect the thrust distribution. Generally speaking, there are two basic factors: first, the type of coupling between the front and rear axles, which may be rigid coupling, interaxle differential, overrunning clutch, viscous coupling, etc.; and second, the difference in theoretical speed (wheel speed when no slip or skid occurs) between the front and rear wheels.

A difference in theoretical speed often exists under operating conditions, and is usually caused by the variation of the radii of the front or rear tires, owing to unequal tire inflation pressure, uneven wear of tires, or load transfer. It has been shown that the difference in theoretical speed between the drive axles of an all-wheel-drive military vehicle could be as much as 7% in practice. When the sizes of the front and rear tires are not the same, sometimes it is difficult to provide the right gear ratio that exactly matches the sizes of the tires, and this also causes the difference in theoretical speed between them.

The most common configuration of four-wheel-drive off-road vehicles has rigid coupling between the front and rear drive axles. For this type of vehicle, the ratio of the angular speed of the front wheel to that of the rear wheel is fixed. The relationship between the slip of the front wheel and that of the rear wheel in a straight line motion is therefore a function of the ratio of the theoretical speed of the front wheel to that of the rear wheel, K_v:

$$i_r = 1 - \frac{V_{tf}}{V_{tr}}(1 - i_f) = 1 - K_v(1 - i_f) \tag{4.13}$$

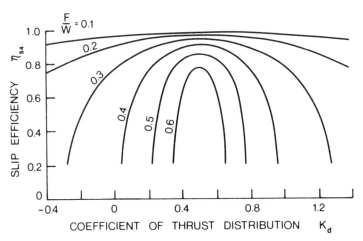

Fig. 4.7 Effect of thrust distribution between driven axles on the slip efficiency of a four-wheel-drive tractor.

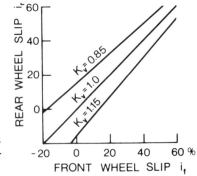

Fig. 4.8 Effect of theoretical speed ratio on the slips of the front and rear tires of a four-wheel-drive tractor with rigid interaxial coupling.

The variation of i_r with i_f and K_v is shown in Fig. 4.8. When the theoretical speed ratio K_v is equal to 0.85 (i.e., the theoretical speed of the front wheel is 85% of that of the rear wheel) and i_r is less than 15%, the front wheel skids and develops negative thrust (braking force). On the other hand when K_v is equal to 1.15 (i.e., the theoretical speed of the front wheel is 15% higher than that of the rear wheel) and i_f is less than 13%, the rear wheel skids and also develops negative thrust. In both cases, the maximum forward thrust of the vehicle is reduced, and torsional wind-up in the transmission inevitably occurs. This results in an increase of stress in the components of the driveline and a reduction of transmission efficiency. Figure 4.9 shows the torques on the front and rear axles of a four-wheel-drive vehicle on a dry concrete surface in forward motion as well as in reverse [4.8]. It shows that when the radius of the front wheel is smaller than that of the rear wheel, then in forward motion, after the initial start-up period, the torque on the front axle is negative, while that on the rear axle is positive. This indicates that the front wheel skids and develops a braking force, while the rear wheel slips and develops a forward thrust. Under these circumstances, torsional wind-up occurs. When the vehicle is in reverse, a similar situation can be observed.

In a turning maneuver, the wheels on the front and rear axles usually follow different paths with different turning radii, which requires the front and rear wheels to have different translatory speeds. If the front and rear axles are rigidly coupled, the front wheel will skid and develop a braking force. Figure 4.10 shows the torques on the front and rear axles of a four-wheel-drive vehicle during a turning maneuver on dry concrete [4.8]. It can be seen that when the vehicle is in forward motion, after the initial start-up period, the torque on the front axle is negative, while that on the rear axle is positive. This indicates that the front wheel skids and develops a braking force, while the rear wheel slips and develops a forward thrust. Under these circumstances, torsional wind-up again occurs.

Since wheel slip is related to thrust as described in Chapter 2, the thrust distribution between the front and rear drive axles depends on the theoretical speed ratio. Figure 4.11 shows the relationship between the coefficient of thrust distribution K_d and the theoretical speed ratio K_v of a four-wheel-drive vehicle having

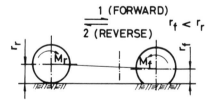

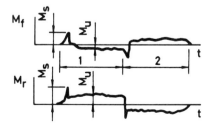

Fig. 4.9 Torque distribution between the front and rear axles of a four-wheel-drive tractor with rigid interaxial coupling when the dynamic radius of the front tire is smaller than that of the rear tire. (Reproduced with permission from reference 4.8.)

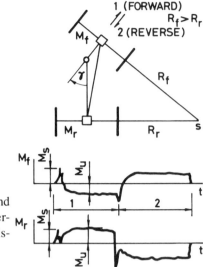

Fig. 4.10 Torque distribution between the front and rear axles of a four-wheel-drive tractor with rigid inter-axial coupling during a turn. (Reproduced with permission from reference 4.8.)

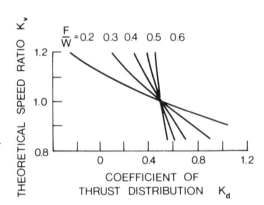

Fig. 4.11 Variation of coefficient of thrust distribution with theoretical speed ratio of a four-wheel-drive tractor with rigid interaxial coupling.

equal weight distribution between the axles at various values of thrust/weight ratio, F/W, in a straight line motion on a farm soil [4.7]. It is shown that when the value of the thrust/weight ratio is high (i.e., the vehicle is pulling a heavy load), the difference in the theoretical speed has less effect on the thrust distribution. It is interesting to note that when the thrust/weight ratio is 0.2 and the theoretical speed ratio K_v is 0.9, the coefficient of thrust distribution K_d is equal to 1.0. This indicates that the vehicle is essentially a rear-wheel-drive vehicle, and that the potential advantage of four-wheel-drive has not been realized.

Since the theoretical speed ratio K_v affects the relationship between the slip of the front wheel and that of the rear wheel, and hence the thrust distribution between the drive axles, the slip efficiency η_{s4} is a function of the theoretical speed ratio. Figure 4.12 shows the variation of the slip efficiency with the thrust/weight ratio for a four-wheel-drive vehicle at various theoretical speed ratios in a straight line motion. It can be seen that when the theoretical speed ratio K_v is equal to 1.0, the slip of the front wheel equals that of the rear wheel, and the slip efficiency is an optimum.

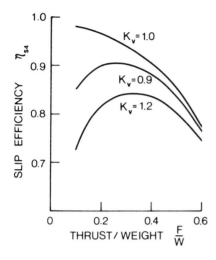

Fig. 4.12 Variation of slip efficiency with thrust/weight ratio at various theoretical speed ratios of a four-wheel-drive tractor with rigid interaxial coupling.

The results of the above analysis indicate that care must be taken in the design and operation of four-wheel-drive off-road vehicles to achieve optimum efficiency. For a four-wheel-drive vehicle with rigid coupling between the drive axles to achieve a high efficiency of operation, the theoretical speed of the front wheel and that of the rear wheel must be equal in a straight line motion, so that the slip of the front wheel and that of the rear wheel are the same under operating conditions. This requires that the rolling radii of the tires be equal (when the front and rear tires are of the same size) under working conditions, an important matter that the vehicle operator must control.

4.1.3 Coefficient of Traction

In the evaluation of the drawbar performance of off-road vehicles, the ratio of the drawbar pull to the normal load on the driven wheels W_d, which is usually referred to as the coefficient of traction μ_{tr}, is a widely used parameter. It is expressed by

$$\mu_{tr} = \frac{F_d}{W_d} = \frac{F - \Sigma R}{W_d} \tag{4.14}$$

It should be pointed out that since drawbar pull is a function of slip, the coefficient of traction of different vehicles should be compared at the same slip. Figure 4.13 shows a comparison of the coefficient of traction of a two-wheel-drive and a comparable four-wheel-drive tractor on a farm soil [4.5].

4.1.4 Weight-to-Power Ratio for Off-Road Vehicles

For off-road vehicles designed for traction, the desirable weight-to-engine-power ratio is determined by the necessity for the optimum utilization of the engine power to produce the required drawbar pull. It is, therefore, a function of the operating

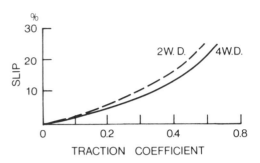

Fig. 4.13 Variation of coefficient of traction with slip for a two-wheel-drive and a four-wheel-drive tractor. (Reproduced with permission of the Council of the Institution of Mechanical Engineers from reference 4.5.)

speed. From Eq. 4.7, the relationship between the vehicle-weight-to-engine-power ratio and the operating speed can be expressed by [4.9]

$$P = \frac{FV_t}{\eta_t} = \frac{(F_d + \Sigma R)V_t}{\eta_t}$$

$$= \frac{(W_d\mu_{tr} + Wf_r)V}{(1 - i)\eta_t} \qquad (4.15)$$

and

$$\frac{W}{P} = \frac{(1 - i)\eta_t}{(\mu_{tr}W_d/W + f_r)V} = \frac{(1 - i)\eta_t}{(\mu_{tr}K_{we} + f_r)V} \qquad (4.16)$$

where W is the total vehicle weight, f_r is the coefficient of motion resistance, and K_{we} is called the weight utilization factor and is the ratio of W_d to W. The weight utilization factor K_{we} is less than unity for a two-wheel-drive tractor, and is equal to unity for a four-wheel-drive or a tracked vehicle. If there is load transfer from the implement to the vehicle, the value of K_{we} may be greater than unity.

Equation 4.16 indicates that for a vehicle designed to operate in a given speed range, the weight-to-engine-power ratio should be within a particular limit, so that a specific level of tractive efficiency can be maintained. Figure 4.14 shows the variations of the desirable weight-to-engine-power ratio with operating speed for a two-wheel-drive and a four-wheel-drive tractor under a particular operating environment.

In agriculture, attempts are being made to achieve higher productivity in the field by increasing the operating speed of the tractor–implement system. This would require the development of appropriate implements as well as tractors, so that full advantage of high-speed operation can be realized. Equation 4.16 provides guiding principles for the selection of the design and performance parameters of tractors designed for operation at increased speeds. It shows that to achieve optimum utilization of engine power and to maintain a high level of tractive efficiency, an

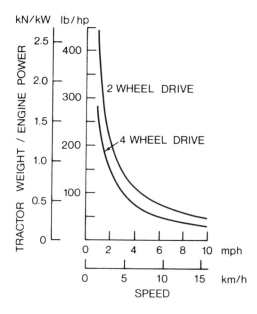

Fig. 4.14 Variation of the optimum weight-to-power ratio with operating speed for a two-wheel-drive and a four-wheel-drive tractor. (Reproduced with permission of the Council of the Institution of Mechanical Engineers from reference 4.9.)

increase of the operating speed must be accompanied by a corresponding reduction of the tractor weight-to-engine-power ratio.

4.2 FUEL ECONOMY OF CROSS-COUNTRY OPERATIONS

The fuel economy of off-road vehicles depends not only on the fuel consumption characteristics of the engine, but also on the transmission characteristics, internal resistance of the running gear, external resisting forces, drawbar pull, and operating speed. When the resultant resisting force, drawbar pull, and operating speed are known, the required engine output power P is determined by

$$P = \frac{\left(\sum R + F_d\right) V}{(1 - i)\eta_t} \tag{4.17}$$

The fuel consumed per hour of operation u_h can then be calculated by

$$u_h = Pu_s \tag{4.18}$$

where u_s is the specific fuel consumption of the engine in kg/kW · h (or lb/hp · h). For changing operating conditions, the basic equations given above can still be used to compute step by step the changing power requirements and fuel consumption.

The motion resistance and slip of an off-road vehicle over a given terrain affect the power requirements, and are dependent, to a great extent, on the design of the running gear and vehicle configuration, as discussed in Chapter 2. Consequently, the tractive performance of the vehicle has a considerable impact on the fuel economy of cross-country operations. This may be illustrated by the following example.

Example 4.2. Referring to Example 2.3 in Chapter 2, if vehicles A and B are to pull a load that requires a drawbar pull of 45 kN (10,117 lb), estimate the difference in fuel consumption of the two vehicles when traveling at a speed of 10 km/h (6.2 mph). In the calculations, an average specific fuel consumption of 0.25 kg/kW · h (0.41 lb/hp · h) for a diesel engine may be assumed.

Solution. Referring to Example 2.3, the compaction resistance of vehicle A is 3.28 kN (738 lb) and that of vehicle B is 2.6 kN (585 lb). Both vehicles have a weight of 135 kN (30,350 lb). The internal resistance of the two vehicles traveling at 10 km/h may be estimated using Eq. 4.2:

$$R_{in} = W(222 + 3V) = 3.47 \text{ kN (780 lb)}$$

a) To pull the load specified, vehicle A should develop a thrust, F, equal to the sum of the resultant motion resistance and drawbar pull:

$$F = \Sigma R + F_d = 3.28 + 3.47 + 45 = 51.75 \text{ kN (11,634 lb)}$$

From Table 2.6, to develop this thrust, the slip of vehicle A is 20.7%. Assume that the transmission efficiency η_t is 0.85. The engine power required for vehicle A traveling at 10 km/h (6.2 mph) can be calculated using Eq. 4.17:

$$P = \frac{(\Sigma R + F_d)V}{(1 - i)\eta_t} = 213.3 \text{ kW (286 hp)}$$

The fuel consumption per hour of operation is

$$u_h = Pu_s = 53.3 \text{ kg/h (117.3 lb/h)}$$

b) To pull the load specified, the thrust that vehicle B should develop is

$$F = 2.6 + 3.47 + 45 = 51.07 \text{ kN (11,482 lb)}$$

From Table 2.6, to develop this thrust, the slip of vehicle B is 15.5%. The required engine power for vehicle B traveling at 10 km/h (6.2 mph) is

$$P = 197.5 \text{ kW (264.8 hp)}$$

The fuel consumption per hour of operation

$$u_h = 49.4 \text{ kg/h (108.6 lb/h)}$$

The results indicate that vehicle A consumes about 7.9% more fuel than vehicle B because vehicle A has higher motion resistance and slip than vehicle B under the circumstances. The difference in tractive performance between the two vehicles is due to the difference in the dimensions of the tracks.

The operational fuel economy of various types of cross-country vehicle may also be evaluated using parameters reflecting the productive work performed by the vehicle. For instance, for an agricultural tractor, the operating fuel economy may be expressed in terms of fuel consumed for work performed in unit area, u_a:

$$u_a = \frac{Pu_s}{B_m V_m} \tag{4.19}$$

where B_m is the working width of the implement or machinery which the tractor pulls and V_m is the average operating speed.

To evaluate the fuel economy of a tractor in developing drawbar power, the fuel consumption per unit drawbar power per hour u_d may be used as a criterion:

$$u_d = \frac{u_h}{P_d} = \frac{Pu_s}{P\eta_m \eta_s \eta_t} = \frac{u_s}{\eta_m \eta_s \eta_t} \tag{4.20}$$

where u_h is the fuel consumed per hour of operation, P is the engine power, P_d is the drawbar power, u_s is the specific fuel consumption of the engine, η_m is the efficiency of motion, η_s is the efficiency of slip, and η_t is the transmission efficiency.

In the University of Nebraska's test programs, the energy obtained at the drawbar E_d per unit volume of fuel consumed, u_e, is used as an index for evaluating fuel economy:

$$u_e = \frac{E_d}{u_t} = \frac{F_d Vt}{u_t} = \frac{P_d t}{u_t} \tag{4.21}$$

where u_t is the fuel consumed during time t.

For cross-country transporters, the fuel consumption per unit payload transported over a unit distance, u_{tr}, may be used as a criterion for evaluating fuel economy:

$$u_{tr} = \frac{Pu_s}{W_p V_m} \tag{4.22}$$

where W_p is the payload. u_{tr} may be expressed in liters per tonne $\cdot$ kilometer or gallons per ton $\cdot$ mile.

When operating in areas where fuel is not readily available, special fuel carriers have to be used to supply the payload carriers with the required fuel. Thus, the total fuel consumption per unit payload transported should include the consumption of the fuel carriers [4.2].

4.3   TRANSPORT PRODUCTIVITY AND TRANSPORT EFFICIENCY

The absolute criterion for comparing one commercial off-road transporter with another is the relative cost of transporting a unit payload on a particular route. This involves not only the performance and fuel consumption characteristics of the vehicle, but also factors not known before a vehicle has been operated, such as load factor and customer's preference. However, certain basic performance criteria exist that enable some assessment and comparison to be made in the preliminary stage of development. Some of these are discussed below.

Transport productivity, which is defined as the product of payload and the average cross-country speed through a specific region, may be used as a criterion for evaluating the performance of off-road transporters. For an existing vehicle, the average speed may be measured experimentally. However, for a vehicle under development, the prediction of its average operating speed through a particular region may be quite complex, as the terrain conditions may vary considerably from one patch to another.

In addition to vehicle tractive performance, a number of other factors, such as ability in obstacle negotiation, mobility in a riverine environment, and vehicle vibrations excited by ground roughness, also affect the cross-country speed of the vehicle.

To characterize the efficiency of a transport system, the transport efficiency η_{tr}, which is defined as the ratio of the transport productivity to the corresponding power input to the system, may also be used [4.10, 4.11]:

$$\eta_{tr} = \frac{W_p V}{P} \tag{4.23}$$

where W_p is the payload and P is the power input to the system. The transport efficiency as defined has three basic components, namely, the lift/drag ratio C_{ld} (the ratio of the vehicle total weight to the resultant motion resistance), structural efficiency η_{st} (the ratio of the payload to the vehicle total weight), and propulsive efficiency η_p:

$$\eta_{tr} = \frac{W_p V}{P} = \frac{W_p V}{(\Sigma R) \, V / \eta_p} = \frac{W}{\Sigma R} \frac{W_p}{W} \eta_p$$

$$= C_{ld} \eta_{st} \eta_p \tag{4.24}$$

The propulsive efficiency includes the transmission efficiency and slip efficiency of the vehicle.

The reciprocal of transport efficiency expressed in terms of power consumption per unit transport productivity may also be used to characterize the performance of a transport system.

4.4 MOBILITY MAP AND MOBILITY PROFILE

To characterize the mobility of military vehicles, such as logistics vehicles and armored personnel carriers, the maximum feasible speed between two points in a given region may be used as a basic criterion [4.12]. The maximum feasible speed is a highly aggregated parameter representing the net results of numerous interactions between the vehicle and the operational environment. This criterion has found increasingly wide acceptance, particularly among military strategic planners and military vehicle operators.

To predict the maximum feasible speed, various computer simulation models, such as the AMC-71, AMM-75, and NATO Reference Mobility Model (NRMM), have been developed [4.12–4.14]. In view of the variation of environmental conditions in the field, in these computer models, the area of interest is first divided into patches, within each of which the terrain is considered sufficiently uniform to permit the use of the maximum speed of the vehicle in a straight line motion to define its mobility.

For these computer models, the characteristics of the terrain, the vehicle, and the driver are required as inputs. Terrain surface composition, surface geometry, vegetation, and linear geometry, such as stream cross section and water speed and depth, have to be specified. Vehicle geometric characteristics, inertia characteristics, and mechanical characteristics together with the driver's reaction time, recognition distance, and ride comfort limits also have to be defined.

For the computer models, the terrain is classified into three categories: areal patch, linear feature segment, such as a stream, ditch, or embankment, and road or trail segment.

When a vehicle is crossing an areal terrain unit, the maximum speed may be limited by one or a combination of the following factors:

1. the tractive effort available for overcoming the resisting forces due to sinkage, slope, obstacles, vegetation, etc.
2. the driver's tolerance to ride discomfort when traversing rough terrain and to obstacle impacts
3. the driver's reluctance to proceed faster than the speed at which the vehicle would be able to decelerate to a stop, within the limited visibility distance prevailing in that patch
4. vehicle maneuverability to avoid obstacles

5. the acceleration and deceleration between obstacles, and speed reduction due to maneuvering to avoid obstacles.

The speed limited by each of the above factors is calculated and compared, and the maximum attainable speed within a particular terrain patch is determined.

When the vehicle is traversing a linear feature segment, such as a stream, man-made ditch, canal, escarpment, railroad, and highway embankment, appropriate models are used to determine the maximum attainable speed. In the models, the time required to enter and cross the segment and that required to egress from it are taken into consideration. Both include allowance for engineering effort, such as winching and excavating, whenever required.

To predict the maximum attainable speed of a vehicle on roads or trails, in addition to the speed limited by the motion resistance, the speed limited by ride discomfort, visibility, tire characteristics, or road curvature has to be taken into consideration. The least of them is taken as the maximum feasible speed for the road or trail segment.

The results obtained from the analysis may be conveniently shown in a mobility map, as illustrated in Fig. 4.15 [4.12]. The numbers in the map indicate the speed (in miles per hour) of which a particular vehicle is capable in each patch throughout the region under consideration. This provides the basis for selecting the optimum route for the vehicle to maximize the average speed through a given area. The information contained in the mobility map may be generalized in a mobility profile shown in Fig. 4.16 [4.12], which conveys a complete statistical description of vehicle mobility in a particular area. It indicates the speed which the vehicle can sustain as a function of the percentage of the total area under consideration. For instance, the intercept of 90% point (point A) in Fig. 4.16 indicates that the vehicle can achieve an average speed of 13.7 km/h (8.5 mph) over 90% of the area. The mobility map and mobility profile are suitable formats for characterizing vehicle mobility for many purposes, such as operational planning and effectiveness analysis. It should be pointed out, however, that they are not directly suitable for parametric analysis of vehicle design.

For a fighting vehicle, such as a tank, its mobility may be described in terms of its operational mobility and battlefield mobility when moving under its own power [4.3].

The operational mobility is the ability of the tank to move in the zone of operations. It is related to the power-to-weight ratio, vehicle weight, operating range, and reliability. The higher the power-to-weight ratio of the vehicle, the higher is its potential speed with which it can move from one area to another. Vehicle weight affects tractive performance over soft terrain, as discussed in Chapter 2, and also restricts the type of road bridge that the vehicle can cross. The operating range of the vehicle affects the frequency of refueling stops from the origin to the destination, and hence its average speed. Vehicle reliability also has an effect on its operational mobility, as the higher it is, the greater is the probability that it will arrive at the destination on schedule.

The battlefield mobility is the ability of the tank to move when engaging enemy

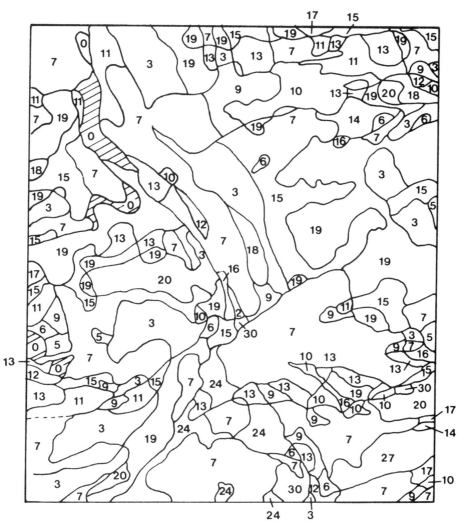

Fig. 4.15 Mobility map of a 2.5 ton truck. Number in the map designates the maximum achievable speed in miles per hour in a given patch; cross-hatched area indicates where the vehicle is immobile. (Reproduced with permission of the Society of Automotive Engineers from reference 4.12.)

forces in the battlefield. This requires that it should be able to move over various types of terrain, ranging from soft soils to hard, rough ground, and to negotiate obstacles at the highest possible speed so as to minimize its exposure to enemy fire. The weight and the design of the track-suspension system of a fighting vehicle greatly affect its performance over soft terrain and its speed over rough ground. The power-to-weight ratio, to a great extent, determines the acceleration and agility of the vehicle, and hence its ability to take evasive maneuvers under battlefield conditions. Figure 4.17 shows the relationships of the acceleration distance and time for two tanks, Leopard 1 and 2, with different power-to-weight ratios. Leop-

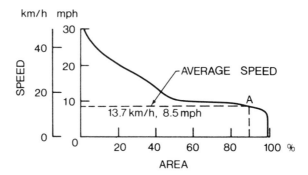

Fig. 4.16 Mobility profile of a 2.5 ton truck. (Reproduced with permission of the Society of Automotive Engineers from reference 4.12.)

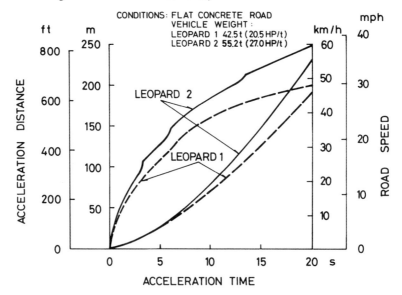

Fig. 4.17 Speed (top curves) and distance (bottom curves) versus acceleration time of two main battle tanks, Leopard 1 and 2. (Reproduced with permission of MTU Motoren-und Turbinen-Union Friedrichshafen GmbH, Germany.)

ard 2, with a power-to-weight ratio of 27 hp/tonne (20 kW/tonne), can attain a given speed or travel a specific distance faster than Leopard 1 with 20.5 hp/tonne (15.3 kW/tonne) [4.3]. Figure 4.18 shows the time taken by a number of tanks with different power-to-weight ratios to accelerate from standstill to 32 or 48 km/h (20 or 30 mph) on hard road surfaces. It can be seen, for instance, that the time required to accelerate the vehicle to a speed of 32 km/h (20 mph) approaches a more or less constant value when the power-to-weight ratio is up to approximately 40 hp/tonne (30 kW/tonne). This indicates that it is not effective to increase the power-to-weight ratio beyond a certain level for a given operating condition. Armor protection also affects the battlefield mobility of a tank. With better armor protection, it can move more freely under battlefield conditions, and it has improved battlefield survivability.

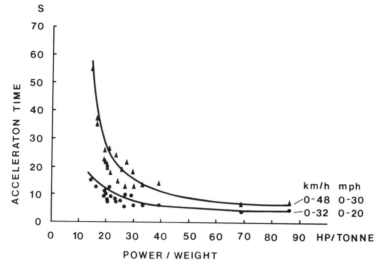

Fig. 4.18 Variation of acceleration time from standstill to a given speed with vehicle power-to-weight ratio. (Reproduced with permission from *Technology of Tanks* by R. M. Ogorkiewicz, Jane's Information Group, 1991.)

4.5 SELECTION OF VEHICLE CONFIGURATIONS FOR OFF-ROAD OPERATIONS

Vehicle configuration can generally be defined in terms of form, size, weight, and power [4.2]. Selection of vehicle configuration is primarily based on mission and operational requirements and on the environment in which the vehicle is expected to operate. In addition, fuel economy, safety, cost, impact on the environment, reliability, maintainability, and other factors have to be taken into consideration. To define an optimum vehicle configuration for a given mission and environment, a system analysis approach should therefore be adopted.

The analysis of terrain–vehicle systems usually begins with defining mission requirements, such as the type of work to be performed, the kind of payload to be transported, and the operational characteristics of the vehicle system, including output rates, cost, and economy. The physical and geometric properties of the terrain over which the vehicle is expected to operate are collected as inputs. Competitive vehicle concepts with probability of accomplishing the specified mission requirements are chosen, based on past experience and future development trends. The operational characteristics and performance of the vehicle candidates are then analyzed and compared. In the evaluations, the methods and techniques discussed in Chapter 2 and in the preceding sections of this chapter may be employed. As a result of the system analysis, an order of merit for the vehicle candidates is established, from which an optimum vehicle configuration is selected [4.2].

Thus, selection of vehicle configuration for a given mission and environment is a complex process, and it is not possible to define the optimum configuration without detailed analysis. However, based on the current state of the art of off-road transport technology, some generalization of the merits and limitations of existing vehicle configurations may be made. Broadly speaking, there are currently four basic types of ground vehicle capable of operating over a specific range of unprepared terrain: wheeled vehicles, tracked vehicles, air cushion vehicles, and hybrid vehicles.

Wheeled Vehicles   Referring to the analysis of the tractive performance of off-road vehicles given in Chapter 2 and in the preceding sections of this chapter, the maximum drawbar-pull-to-weight ratio of a vehicle may be expressed by

$$\frac{F_d}{W} = \frac{F - \Sigma R}{W} = \frac{cA + W \tan \phi - f_r W}{W}$$

$$= \frac{c}{p} + \tan \phi - f_r \tag{4.25}$$

This equation indicates that for a given terrain with specific values of cohesion and angle of internal shearing resistance, c and ϕ, the maximum drawbar-pull-to-weight ratio is a function of the contact pressure p and the coefficient of motion resistance f_r. The lower the contact pressure and the coefficient of motion resistance, the higher is the maximum drawbar-pull-to-weight ratio. Since the contact pressure and the motion resistance are dependent on the design of the vehicle, the proper selection of vehicle configuration is of utmost importance.

For given overall dimensions and gross weight, a tracked vehicle will have a larger contact area than a wheeled vehicle. Consequently, the ground contact pressure, and hence the sinkage and external motion resistance of the tracked vehicle, would generally be lower than that of an equivalent wheeled vehicle. Furthermore, a tracked vehicle has a longer contact length than a wheeled vehicle of the same overall dimensions. Thus, the slip of a tracked vehicle is usually lower than that of an equivalent wheeled vehicle for the same thrust. As a result, the mobility of the tracked vehicle is generally superior to that of the wheeled vehicle in difficult terrain.

The wheeled vehicle is, however, a more suitable choice than the tracked one when frequent on-road travel and high road speeds are required.

Tracked Vehicles   Although the tracked vehicle has the capability of operating over a wide range of unprepared terrain, to fully realize its potential, careful attention must be given to the design of the track system. The nominal ground pressure of the tracked vehicle (i.e., the ratio of the vehicle gross weight to the nominal ground contact area) has been quite widely used as a design parameter of relevance to soft ground performance. However, the shortcomings in its general use are now evident, both in its neglect of the actual pressure variation under the track and in its inability to distinguish between track designs giving different soft ground mobility. It has been shown that the vehicle sinkage, and hence motion resistance, depend on the maximum pressure exerted by the vehicle on the ground and not the nominal pressure. Therefore, it is of prime importance that the design of the track system should give as uniform a contact pressure on the ground as possible under normal operating conditions. For low-speed tracked vehicles, fairly uniform ground contact pressure could be achieved by using a relatively rigid track with a long track pitch and a large number of small diameter roadwheels. For high-speed tracked vehicles, to minimize the vibration of the vehicle and of the track, relatively large diameter roadwheels with considerable suspension travel and short track pitch are required. This would result in a rather nonuniform pressure distribution under the track. The overlapping roadwheel arrangement shown in Fig. 2.53 provides a possible compromise in meeting the conflicting requirements for soft ground mobility and high-speed operations. Pneumatic tracks and pneumatic cushion devices have also been proposed to provide a more uniform pressure distribution on the ground.

Experience and analysis have shown that the method of steering is also of importance to the mobility of tracked vehicles in difficult terrain. Articulated steering provides the vehicle with better mobility and maneuverability than skid-steering over soft terrain. Articulated steering also makes it possible for the vehicle to achieve a more rational form since a long, narrow vehicle encounters less external resistance over soft ground than does a short, wide vehicle with the same contact area. From an environmental point of view, articulated steering causes less damage to the terrain during maneuvering than skid-steering. A detailed analysis of the characteristics of various steering methods for tracked vehicles will be given in Chapter 6.

The characteristics of the transmission also play a significant role in vehicle mobility over soft ground. Generally speaking, automatic transmission is preferred as it allows gear changing without interruption of power flow to the running gear.

Air-Cushion Vehicles A vehicle wholly supported by an air cushion and propelled by a propeller or fan air can operate over level terrain of low bearing capacity at relatively high speeds. It has, however, very limited capabilities in slope climbing, slope traversing, and obstacle crossing. Its maneuverability in confined space is generally poor without a ground contact device. Existing air propulsion devices are relatively inefficient, and could not generate sufficient thrust at low speeds. Over rugged terrain, skirt damage could pose a serious problem, while over snow or sandy terrain, visibility could be considerably reduced by a cloud of small particles formed around the vehicle. With the current state of the art, the potential of the air-cushion vehicle with air propulsion can only be fully exploited over relatively flat and smooth terrain at high speeds. A detailed analysis of the performance of air-cushion vehicles will be given in Chapter 8.

Hybrid Vehicles Hybrid vehicles are those that employ two or more forms of running gear, such as the half-tracked vehicle with front wheel steering, the air-cushion assist-wheeled vehicle, and the air-cushion assist-tracked vehicle.

The tractive performance of a half-tracked vehicle can be predicted using a combination of the methods developed for wheeled and tracked vehicles described in Chapter 2.

The performance and characteristics of the air-cushion assist-wheeled vehicle will be analyzed in detail in Chapter 8. It can be said, however, that the use of the wheel as a directional control device for the air-cushion vehicle in overland operations is quite effective. However, the use of the wheel as a traction device over difficult terrain has severe limitations, as mentioned previously.

Over exceedingly soft and cohesive terrain, such as deep mud or semi-liquid swamp, the air-cushion assist-tracked vehicle may have certain advantages from a technical standpoint. This is because over this type of terrain, the air cushion can be used to carry a high proportion of the vehicle weight, thus minimizing the sinkage and motion resistance of the vehicle. The track could then be used solely as a propulsion device. Since in a cohesive type of terrain, the thrust is mainly a function of the track contact area and the cohesion of the terrain, and is more or less independent of the normal load, a track with suitable dimensions may provide the vehicle with the necessary thrust and mobility. However, the added weight, size, and cost of the air-cushion-assist device must be carefully evaluated against the benefits obtainable, and the decision on the development of this hybrid vehicle configuration should be based on the results of a comprehensive cost-effectiveness analysis.

REFERENCES

4.1   G.V. Cleare, "Factors Affecting the Performance of High-Speed Track Layers," *Proc. Institution of Mechanical Engineers*, vol. 178, part 2A, no. 2, 1963–1964.

4.2   M.G. Bekker, *Introduction to Terrain-Vehicle Systems.*   Ann Arbor, MI: University of Michigan Press, 1969.

4.3   R.M. Ogorkiewicz, *Technology of Tanks.*   London: Jane's Information Group, 1991.

4.4   Z. Kolozsi and T.T. McCarthy, "The Prediction of Tractor Field Performance," *Journal of Agricultural Engineering Research*, vol. 19, pp. 167–172, 1974.

4.5   L.E. Osborne, "Ground-Drive Systems for High-Powered Tractors," *Proc. Institution of Mechanical Engineers*, vol. 184, part 3Q, 1969–1970.

4.6   W. Söhne, "Four-Wheel-Drive or Rear-Wheel-Drive for High Power Farm Tractors," *Journal of Terramechanics*, vol. 5, no. 3, 1968.

4.7   J.Y. Wong, "Optimization of the Tractive Performance of Four-Wheel-Drive Off-Road Vehicles," *SAE Transactions*, vol. 79, paper 700723, 1970.

4.8   P.A. Dudzinski, "The Problems of Multi-Axle Vehicle Drives," *Journal of Terramechanics*, vol. 23, no. 2, 1986.

4.9   A.R. Reece, "The Shape of the Farm Tractor," *Proc. Institution of Mechanical Engineers*, vol. 184, part 3Q, 1969–1970.

4.10   J.Y. Wong, "On the Application of Air Cushion Technology to Overland Transport," *High Speed Ground Transportation Journal*, vol. 6, no. 3, 1972.

4.11   J.Y. Wong, "System Energy in High Speed Ground Transportation," *High Speed Ground Transportation Journal*, vol. 9, no. 1, 1975.

4.12 C.J. Nuttall, Jr., A.A. Rula, and H.J. Dugoff, "Computer Model for Comprehensive Evaluation of Cross-Country Vehicle Mobility," *SAE Transactions*, paper 740426, 1974.

4.13 M.P. Jurkat, C.J. Nuttall, and P.W. Haley, "The U.S. Army Mobility Model (AMM-75)," in *Proc. 5th Int. Conf. of the International Society for Terrain-Vehicle Systems*, vol. IV, Detroit, MI, 1975.

4.14 J.Y. Wong, *Terramechanics and Off-Road Vehicles*. Amsterdam, The Netherlands: Elsevier Science Publishers B.V., 1989.

PROBLEMS

4.1 Calculate the drawbar power and tractive efficiency of the off-road vehicle described in Example 4.1 at various operating speeds when the third gear with a total reduction ratio of 33.8 is engaged.

4.2 An off-road vehicle pulls an implement that has a resistance of 17.792 kN (4000 lb). The motion resistance of the vehicle is 6.672 kN (1500 lb). Under these circumstances, the slip of the running gear is 35%. The transmission efficiency is 0.80. What percentage of the power is lost in converting engine power into drawbar power?

4.3 A four-wheel-drive off-road vehicle has a rigid coupling between the front and rear drive axles. The thrust–slip characteristics of the front and rear axles are assumed to be identical, and are given in the following table. Owing to unequal tire inflation pressure and uneven wear of tires, the theoretical speed of the front tires is 6% higher than that of the rear tires. The motion resistance of the vehicle is 1.67 kN (375 lb). The vehicle is to pull an implement that has a resistance of 16.51 kN (3712 lb). Determine whether or not torsional wind-up in the transmission will occur. Also determine the thrust distribution between the front and rear axles and the slip efficiency of the vehicle.

Thrust-Slip Relationship for the Drive-Axle (Front or Rear)

Slip (%)	5	10	15	20	25	30	40
Thrust, kN	5.12	8.0	10.23	12.0	13.34	14.23	16.01

4.4 If the four-wheel-drive off-road vehicle described in Problem 4.3 is equipped with an overrunning clutch, instead of a rigid coupling, between the front and rear drive axles, so that the front axle will not be driven until the slip of the rear tires is up to 10%, determine the thrust distribution between the drive axles and the slip efficiency of the vehicle when it pulls an implement that has a resistance of 14.06 kN (3160 lb). The motion resistance of the vehicle is 1.67 kN (375 lb).

4.5 A two-wheel-drive tractor with a weight utilization factor of 75% is to be designed mainly for operation in the speed range 10–15 km/h (6.2–9.3 mph).

Both the transmission efficiency and the slip efficiency are assumed to be 85%. The average value of the coefficient of motion resistance is 0.1, and that of the traction coefficient is 0.4. Determine the appropriate range of the power-to-weight ratio for the tractor.

4.6 An off-road transporter with a gross weight of 44.48 kN (10,000 lb) carries a payload of 17.79 kN (4000 lb). The coefficient of motion resistance of the vehicle is 0.15. Both the transmission efficiency and the slip efficiency are 0.85. If the transporter travels at a speed of 15 km/h (9.3 mph) and the average specific fuel consumption of the engine is 0.25 kg/kW · h (0.41 lb/hp · h), determine the fuel consumed in transporting 1 tonne of payload for 1 km. Also calculate the transport productivity, the power consumption per unit productivity, and the transport efficiency of the vehicle system.

CHAPTER 5

HANDLING CHARACTERISTICS OF ROAD VEHICLES

The handling characteristics of a road vehicle are concerned with its response to steering commands and to environmental inputs, such as wind gust and road disturbances, that affect its direction of motion. There are two basic issues in vehicle handling: one is the control of the direction of motion of the vehicle; the other is its ability to stabilize its direction of motion against external disturbances.

The vehicle as a rigid body has six degrees of freedom, translations along the x, y, and z axes, and rotations about these axes, as shown in Fig. 5.1. The primary motions associated with the handling behavior of a vehicle are longitudinal, lateral, and yaw motions (i.e., translation along the x axis, translation along the y axis, and rotation about the z axis, respectively). In practice, during a turning maneuver, the vehicle body rolls (i.e., rotating about the x axis). This roll motion may cause the wheels to steer, thus affecting the handling behavior of the vehicle. Furthermore, bounce and pitch motions of the vehicle body (i.e., translation along the z axis and rotation about the y axis, respectively) may also affect the steering response of the vehicle. However, the inclusion of these motions in the analysis only becomes necessary when considering the limits of handling characteristics.

This chapter is intended to serve as an introduction to the study of the handling characteristics of road vehicles. Simplified linear models for the handling behavior of passenger cars and tractor–semitrailers in which suspension characteristics are not taken into account will be presented. The models demonstrate the effects on handling behavior of major vehicle design and operational parameters, such as tire properties, location of the center of gravity, and forward speed, and lead to conclusions of practical significance concerning directional control and stability. The response of the vehicle to steering input and its directional stability associated with a fixed steering wheel, which are usually referred to as fixed-control characteristics, will be analyzed.

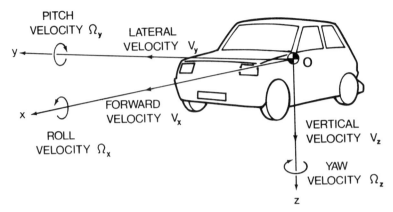

Fig. 5.1 Vehicle axis system.

5.1 STEERING GEOMETRY

In examining the handling characteristics of a road vehicle, it is convenient to begin with a discussion of the cornering behavior of the vehicle at low speeds, with the effect of the centrifugal force being neglected. For road vehicles, steering is normally effected by changing the heading of the front wheels through the steering system, although four-wheel steering has been introduced to passenger cars. At low speeds, there is a simple relation between the direction of motion of the vehicle and the steering wheel angle. The prime consideration in the design of the steering system is minimum tire scrub during cornering. This requires that during the turn, all tires should be in pure rolling without lateral sliding. To satisfy this requirement, the wheels should follow curved paths with different radii originating from a common center, as shown in Fig. 5.2. This establishes the proper relationship between the steer angle of the inside front wheel δ_i and that of the outside front wheel δ_o. From Fig. 5.2, it can be readily seen that the steer angles δ_i and

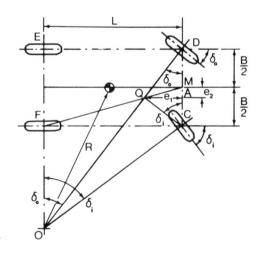

Fig. 5.2 Steering geometry.

δ_o should satisfy the following relationship:

$$\cot \delta_o - \cot \delta_i = B/L \tag{5.1}$$

where B and L are the track (or tread) and wheelbase of the vehicle, respectively.

The steering geometry that satisfies Eq. 5.1 is usually referred to as the Ackerman steering geometry.

The relationship between δ_i and δ_o that satisfies Eq. 5.1 can be illustrated graphically. Referring to Fig. 5.2, first connect the midpoint of the front axle M with the center of the inside rear wheel F. Then lay out the steer angle of the outside front wheel δ_o from the front axle. Line DO intersects line MF at Q. Connect point Q with the center of the inside front wheel C; then angle $\angle QCM$ is the steer angle of the inside front wheel δ_i that satisfies Eq. 5.1. This can be proved from the geometric relations shown in Fig 5.2:

$$\cot \delta_o = (B/2 + e_2)/e_1$$

$$\cot \delta_i = (B/2 - e_2)/e_1$$

and

$$\cot \delta_o - \cot \delta_i = 2e_2/e_1 \tag{5.2}$$

Since triangle ΔMAQ is similar to triangle ΔMCF,

$$\frac{e_2}{e_1} = \frac{B/2}{L}$$

Eq. 5.2 can then be rewritten as

$$\cot \delta_o - \cot \delta_i = B/L$$

The results of the above analysis indicate that if the steer angles of the front wheels δ_i and δ_o satisfy Eq. 5.1, then by laying out the steer angles δ_i and δ_o from the front axle, the intersection of the noncommon sides of δ_i and δ_o (i.e., point Q in Fig. 5.2) will lie on the straight line connecting the midpoint of the front axle and the center of the inside rear wheel (i.e., line MF in Fig. 5.2).

Figure 5.3 shows the relationship between δ_o and δ_i that satisfies Eq. 5.1 for a vehicle with $B/L = 0.56$, as compared to a parallel steer curve ($\delta_i = \delta_o$) and a typical steering geometry used in practice [5.1].

To evaluate the characteristics of a particular steering linkage with respect to the Ackerman steering geometry, a graphic method may be employed. First, the steer angles of the inside front wheel δ_i with suitable increment are laid out from the initial position of the steer arm CH, as shown in Fig. 5.4. Then, from the pivot of the inside steer arm H, an arc is struck with a radius equal to the length of the tie rod HI. This intersects the arc generated by the steer arm of the outside front

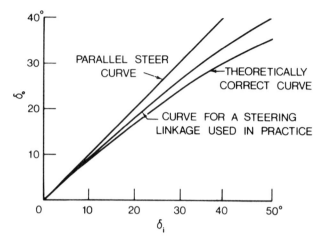

Fig. 5.3 Characteristics of various types of steering linkage. (Reproduced with permission from reference 5.1.)

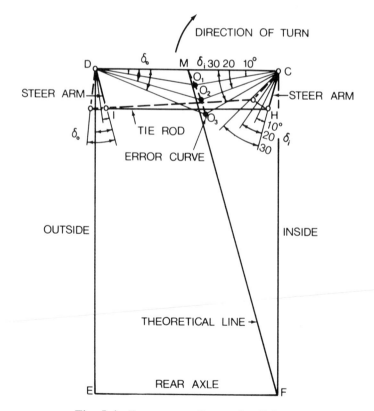

Fig. 5.4 Error curve of a steering linkage.

wheel *DI*. The intersection then defines the corresponding steer angle of the outside front wheel δ_o. By laying out the steer angles of the inside front wheel δ_i and the corresponding steer angles of the outside front wheel δ_o from the front axle, the noncommon sides of δ_i and δ_0 will intersect at points 0_1, 0_2, and 0_3, as shown in Fig. 5.4. If the steering geometry satisfies Eq. 5.1, the intersections of the non-common sides of δ_i and δ_o will lie on the straight line *MF*, as mentioned previously. The deviation of the curve connecting 0_1, 0_2, and 0_3 from line *MF* is therefore an indication of the error of the steering geometry with respect to the Ackerman criterion. Steering geometry with an error curve that deviates excessively from line *MF* shown in Fig. 5.4 will exhibit considerable tire scrub during cornering. This results in excessive tire wear and increased steering effort.

It should be mentioned that the graphic method described above is only applicable to the type of coplanar steering linkage shown in Fig. 5.4, which is commonly used in vehicles with a front beam axle. For vehicles with front independent suspensions, the steering linkage will be more complex. Dependent on the type of independent suspension used, the front wheels may be steered via a three-piece tie rod or by a rack and pinion with outer tie rods. The approach for constructing steering error curves for these linkages is similar to that described above. The procedure, however, is more involved.

5.2 STEADY-STATE HANDLING CHARACTERISTICS OF A TWO-AXLE VEHICLE

Steady-state handling performance is concerned with the directional behavior of a vehicle during a turn under nontime-varying conditions. An example of a steady-state turn is a vehicle negotiating a curve with constant radius at a constant forward speed. In the analysis of steady-state handling behavior, the inertia properties of the vehicle are not involved.

When a vehicle is negotiating a turn at moderate or higher speeds, the effect of the centrifugal force (an inertia force arising from the normal component of acceleration towards the center of the turn) acting at the center of gravity can no longer be neglected. To balance the centrifugal force, the tires must develop appropriate cornering forces. As discussed in Chapter 1, a side force acting on a tire produces a side slip angle. Thus, when a vehicle is negotiating a turn at moderate or higher speeds, the four tires will develop appropriate slip angles. To simplify the analysis, the pair of tires on an axle are represented by a single tire with double the cornering stiffness, as shown in Fig. 5.5. The handling characteristics of the vehicle depend, to a great extent, on the relationship between the slip angles of the front and rear tires, α_f and α_r.

The steady-state response to steering input of a vehicle at moderate and higher speeds is more complex than that at low speeds. From the geometry shown in Fig. 5.5, the relationship among the steer angle of the front tire δ_f, the turning radius R, the wheel base L, and the slip angles of the front and rear tires α_f and α_r is given by [5.2]

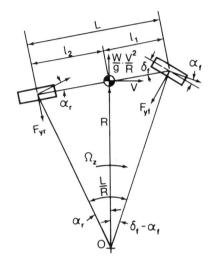

Fig. 5.5 Simplified steady-state handling model for a two-axle vehicle.

$$\delta_f - \alpha_f + \alpha_r = L/R$$

or

$$\delta_f = L/R + \alpha_f - \alpha_r \qquad (5.3)$$

This indicates that the steer angle δ_f required to negotiate a given curve is a function of not only the turning radius R, but also the front and rear slip angles α_f and α_r. The slip angles α_f and α_r are dependent on the side forces acting on the tires and their cornering stiffness. The cornering forces on the front and rear tires F_{yf} and F_{yr} can be determined from the dynamic equilibrium of the vehicle in the lateral direction. For small steer angles, the cornering forces acting at the front and rear tires are approximately given by

$$F_{yf} = \frac{W}{g}\frac{V^2}{R}\frac{l_2}{L} \qquad (5.4)$$

$$F_{yr} = \frac{W}{g}\frac{V^2}{R}\frac{l_1}{L} \qquad (5.5)$$

where W is the total weight of the vehicle, g is the acceleration due to gravity, V is the vehicle forward speed, and other parameters are shown in Fig. 5.5.

The normal load on each of the front tires W_f and that on each of the rear tires W_r under static conditions are expressed by

$$W_f = Wl_2/2L$$
$$W_r = Wl_1/2L$$

Equations 5.4 and 5.5 can be rewritten as

$$F_{yf} = 2W_f \frac{V^2}{gR}$$ (5.6)

$$F_{yr} = 2W_r \frac{V^2}{gR}$$ (5.7)

The slip angles α_f and α_r therefore are given by

$$\alpha_f = \frac{F_{yf}}{2C_{\alpha f}} = \frac{W_f}{C_{\alpha f}} \frac{V^2}{gR}$$ (5.8)

$$\alpha_r = \frac{F_{yr}}{2C_{\alpha r}} = \frac{W_r}{C_{\alpha r}} \frac{V^2}{gR}$$ (5.9)

where $C_{\alpha f}$ and $C_{\alpha r}$ are the cornering stiffness of each of the front and rear tires, respectively. As described in Chapter 1, the cornering stiffness of a given tire varies with a number of operational parameters, including inflation pressure, normal load, tractive (or braking) effort, and lateral force. It may be regarded as a constant only within a limited range of operating conditions.

Substituting Eqs. 5.8 and 5.9 into Eq. 5.3, the expression for the steer angle δ_f required to negotiate a given curve becomes [5.2]

$$\delta_f = \frac{L}{R} + \left(\frac{W_f}{C_{\alpha f}} - \frac{W_r}{C_{\alpha r}} \right) \frac{V^2}{gR}$$

$$= \frac{L}{R} + K_{us} \frac{V^2}{gR}$$

$$= \frac{L}{R} + K_{us} \frac{a_y}{g}$$ (5.10)

where K_{us} is usually referred to as the understeer coefficient and is expressed in radians, and a_y is the lateral acceleration. Equation 5.10 is the fundamental equation governing the steady-state handling behavior of a road vehicle. It indicates that the steer angle required to negotiate a given curve depends on the wheelbase, turning radius, forward speed (or lateral acceleration), and understeer coefficient of the vehicle, which is a function of the weight distribution and tire cornering stiffness.

Dependent on the values of the understeer coefficient K_{us} or the relationship between the slip angles of the front and rear tires, the steady-state handling characteristics may be classified into three categories: neutral steer, understeer, and oversteer [5.2].

5.2.1 Neutral Steer

When the understeer coefficient $K_{us} = 0$, which is equivalent to the slip angles of the front and rear tires being equal (i.e., $\alpha_f = \alpha_r$ and $W_f/C_{\alpha f} = W_r/C_{\alpha r}$), the steer angle δ_f required to negotiate a given curve is independent of forward speed and is given by

$$\delta_f = L/R \qquad (5.11)$$

A vehicle having this handling property is said to be "neutral steer." Its handling characteristics for a constant radius turn are represented by a horizontal line in the steer angle–speed diagram shown in Fig. 5.6.

For a neutral steer vehicle, when it is accelerated in a constant radius turn, the driver should maintain the same steering wheel position. In other words, when it is accelerated with the steering wheel fixed, the turning radius remains the same, as illustrated in Fig. 5.7. When a neutral steer vehicle originally moving along a straight line is subjected to a side force acting at the center of gravity, equal slip angles will be developed at the front and rear tires (i.e., $\alpha_f = \alpha_r$). As a result, the vehicle follows a straight line path at an angle to the original, as shown in Fig. 5.8.

5.2.2 Understeer

When the understeer coefficient $K_{us} > 0$, which is equivalent to the slip angle of the front tire α_f being greater than that of the rear tire α_r (i.e., $\alpha_f > \alpha_r$ and $W_f/C_{\alpha f} > W_r/C_{\alpha r}$), the steer angle δ_f required to negotiate a given curve increases with

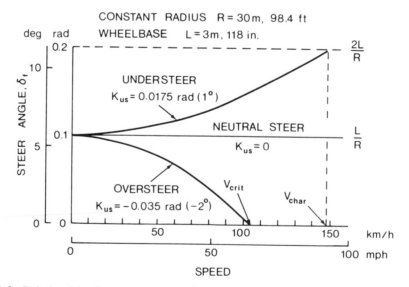

Fig. 5.6 Relationships between steer angle and speed of neutral steer, understeer, and oversteer vehicles.

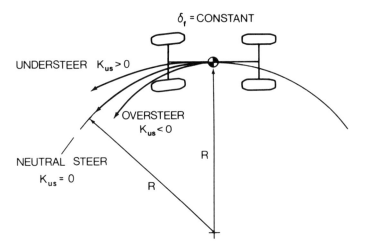

Fig. 5.7 Curvature responses of neutral steer, understeer, and oversteer vehicles at a fixed steer angle.

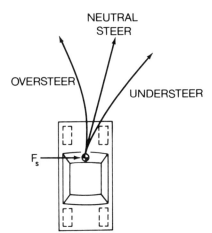

Fig. 5.8 Directional responses of neutral steer, understeer, and oversteer vehicles subject to a side force at the center of gravity.

the square of vehicle forward speed (or lateral acceleration). A vehicle with this handling property is said to be "understeer." Its handling characteristics for a constant radius turn are represented by a parabola in the steer angle–speed diagram shown in Fig. 5.6.

For an understeer vehicle, when it is accelerated in a constant radius turn, the driver must increase the steer angle. In other words, when it is accelerated with the steering wheel fixed, the turning radius increases, as illustrated in Fig. 5.7. When a side force acts at the center of gravity of an understeer vehicle originally moving along a straight line, the front tires will develop a slip angle greater than that of the rear tires (i.e., $\alpha_f > \alpha_r$). As a result, a yaw motion is initiated, and the vehicle turns away from the side force, as shown in Fig. 5.8.

For an understeer vehicle, a characteristic speed V_{char} may be identified. It is the speed at which the steer angle required to negotiate a turn is equal to $2L/R$, as shown in Fig. 5.6. From Eq. 5.10,

$$V_{\text{char}} = \sqrt{\frac{gL}{K_{us}}} \tag{5.12}$$

5.2.3 Oversteer

When the understeer coefficient $K_{us} < 0$, which is equivalent to the slip angle of the front tire α_f being less than that of the rear tire α_r (i.e., $\alpha_f < \alpha_r$ and $W_f/C_{\alpha f} < W_r/C_{\alpha r}$), the steer angle δ_f required to negotiate a given curve decreases with an increase of vehicle forward speed (or lateral acceleration). A vehicle with this handling property is said to be "oversteer." The relationship between the required steer angle and forward speed for this kind of vehicle at a constant radius turn is illustrated in Fig. 5.6.

For an oversteer vehicle, when it is accelerated in a constant radius turn, the driver must decrease the steer angle. In other words, when it is accelerated with the steering wheel fixed, the turning radius decreases, as illustrated in Fig. 5.7. When a side force acts at the center of gravity of an oversteer vehicle originally moving along a straight line, the front tires will develop a slip angle less than that of the rear tires (i.e., $\alpha_f < \alpha_r$). As a result, a yaw motion is initiated, and the vehicle turns into the side force, as illustrated in Fig. 5.8.

For an oversteer vehicle, a critical speed V_{crit} can be identified. It is the speed at which the steer angle required to negotiate any turn is zero, as shown in Fig. 5.6. From Eq. 5.10,

$$V_{\text{crit}} = \sqrt{\frac{gL}{-K_{us}}} \tag{5.13}$$

It should be noted that for an oversteer vehicle, the understeer coefficient K_{us} in the above equation has a negative sign. It will be shown later that the critical speed also represents the speed above which an oversteer vehicle exhibits directional instability.

The prime factors controlling the steady-state handling characteristics of a vehicle are the weight distribution of the vehicle and the cornering stiffness of the tires. A front-engined, front-wheel-drive vehicle with a large proportion of the vehicle weight on the front tires may tend to exhibit understeer behavior. A rear-engined, rear-wheel-drive car with a large proportion of the vehicle weight on the rear tires, on the other hand, may tend to have oversteer characteristics [5.1]. Changes of weight distribution will alter the handling behavior of a vehicle.

A number of design and operational parameters affect the cornering stiffness of the tires, and thus the handling performance of the vehicle. Mixing of radial-ply with bias-ply tires in a vehicle may have serious consequences in its handling characteristics. Installing laterally stiff radial-ply tires on the front and relatively flexible bias-ply tires on the rear may change an otherwise understeer vehicle to an oversteer one. Lowering the inflation pressure in the rear tires can have similar effects, as the cornering stiffness of a tire usually decreases with a decrease of inflation pressure. The lateral load transfer from the inside tire to the outside on an axle during a turn will increase the slip angle required to generate a given cornering force, as discussed in Chapter 1. Thus, lateral load transfer will affect the handling behavior of the vehicle. The application of a driving or braking torque to the tire during a turn will also affect the cornering behavior of the vehicle, as a driving or braking torque modifies the cornering properties of the tire, as mentioned in Chapter 1. For a rear-wheel-drive vehicle, the application of tractive effort during a turn reduces the cornering stiffness of the rear tires, producing an oversteering effect. On the other hand, for a front-wheel-drive car, the application of tractive effort during a turn reduces the cornering stiffness of the front tires, thus introducing an understeering effect.

It should also be mentioned that the effects of roll steer (the steering motion of the front or rear wheels due to the relative roll motion of the sprung mass with respect to the unsprung mass), roll camber (the change in camber of the wheels due to the relative motion of the sprung mass with respect to the unsprung mass), and compliance steer (the steering motion of the wheels with respect to the sprung mass resulting from compliance in, and forces on, the suspension and steering linkages) would be significant under certain circumstances, and that they should be taken into account in a more comprehensive analysis of vehicle handling. The effect of these factors can, however, be included in a modified form of the understeer coefficient K_{us}, and Eq. 5.10, which describes the steady-state handling performance, still holds.

In summary, there are a number of design and operational factors that would affect the understeer coefficient of a vehicle, and hence its handling characteristics. For a practical vehicle, the understeer coefficient would vary with operating conditions. Figure 5.9 shows the changes in the understeer coefficient, expressed in degrees, with lateral acceleration for four different types of passenger car [5.3].

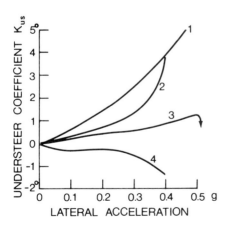

Fig. 5.9 Variation of understeer coefficient with lateral acceleration of various types of car. 1—a conventional front engine/rear-wheel-drive car; 2—a European front engine/front-wheel-drive car; 3—a European rear engine/rear-wheel-drive car; 4—an American rear engine/rear-wheel-drive car. (Reproduced with permission from reference 5.3.)

Curve 1 represents the characteristics of a conventional front-engine/rear-wheel-drive car. It shows that the understeer coefficient increases sharply with an increase of lateral acceleration. Curve 2 represents the behavior of a European front-engine/front-wheel-drive car. It exhibits similar characteristics. The characteristics of a European rear-engine/rear-wheel-drive car are represented by curve 3. It indicates that the vehicle exhibits understeer behavior up to lateral acceleration of approximately 0.5 g, above which it tends to become oversteer. The behavior of an American rear-engine/rear-wheel-drive compact car is represented by curve 4. It shows that the vehicle exhibits oversteer characteristics in the operating range shown.

Among the three types of steady-state handling behavior, oversteer is not desirable from a directional stability point of view, which will be discussed later in this chapter. It is considered desirable for a road vehicle to have a small degree of understeer up to a certain level of lateral acceleration, such as 0.4 g, with increasing understeer beyond this point [5.3]. This would have the advantages of sensitive steering response associated with a small degree of understeer during the majority of turning maneuvers. The increased understeer at higher lateral accelerations, on the other hand, would provide the required stability during tight turns.

To illustrate the changes in the handling behavior of road vehicles with operating conditions, a handling diagram is often used. In this diagram, the vehicle lateral acceleration in g-units, a_y/g (V^2/gR), is plotted as a function of the parameter ($L/R - \delta_f$), where L is the wheelbase, R is the turning radius, and δ_f is the average front tire steer angle. During a turning maneuver, the turning radius R may be difficult to measure directly. However, it can be readily determined from the yaw velocity Ω_z (measured using a rate-gyro) and the forward speed V of the vehicle ($R = V/\Omega_z$). Therefore, in the handling diagram, the lateral acceleration in g-units, a_y/g, is often plotted as a function of ($\Omega_z L/V - \delta_f$), as shown in Fig. 5.10. From Eq. 5.10, the relationship between a_y/g and ($\Omega_z L/V - \delta_f$) is expressed by

$$K_{us} \frac{V^2}{gR} = K_{us} \frac{a_y}{g} = -(L/R - \delta_f) = -(\Omega_z L/V - \delta_f)$$

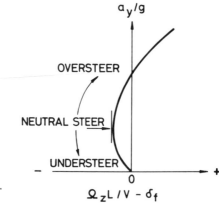

Fig. 5.10 Handling diagram.

The slope of the curve shown in the handling diagram (Fig. 5.10) is given by

$$\frac{d\,(a_y/g)}{d\,(\Omega_z L/V - \delta_f)} = -\frac{1}{K_{us}} \tag{5.14}$$

This indicates that the handling behavior of a road vehicle can be identified by the slope of the curve shown in the handling diagram. If the slope is negative, then it implies that the understeer coefficient K_{us} is positive. Consequently, the vehicle exhibits understeer behavior. If the slope is infinite, then it indicates that the understeer coefficient K_{us} is zero and that the vehicle is neutral steer. On the other hand, if the slope is positive, then it implies that the understeer coefficient K_{us} is negative and that the vehicle is oversteer.

It should be noted that the value of the parameter $(\Omega_z L/V - \delta_f)$ is sensitive to the errors in the measurements of Ω_z, V, and δ_f. A small error in the values of Ω_z, V, and δ_f may result in a significant error in the value of the parameter $(\Omega_z L/V - \delta_f)$. For instance, if the wheelbase L of a vehicle is 2.7 m (8 ft, 10 in.), and the nominal values of Ω_z, V, and δ_f are 0.1389 rad/s (7.96 deg/s), 50 km/h (31 mph), and 0.0427 rad (2.45 deg), respectively, then an error of $\pm\,1\%$ in these values will result in an error of approximately $\pm\,6\%$ in the value of $(\Omega_z L/V - \delta_f)$. An error of $\pm\,5\%$ in these values will result in an error in the value of $(\Omega_z L/V - \delta_f)$ ranging from -29.9% to $+31.7\%$.

Example 5.1. A passenger car has a weight of 20.105 kN (4520 lb) and a wheelbase of 2.8 m (9 ft, 2 in.). The weight distribution on the front axle is 53.5%, and that on the rear axle is 46.5% under static conditions.

a) If the cornering stiffness of each of the front tires is 38.92 kN/rad (8750 lb/rad) and that of the rear tires is 38.25 kN/rad (8600 lb/rad), determine the steady-state handling behavior of the vehicle.

b) If the front tires are replaced by a pair of radial-ply tires, each of which has a cornering stiffness of 47.82 kN/rad (10,750 lb/rad), and the rear tires remain unchanged, determine the steady-state handling behavior of the vehicle under these circumstances.

Solution. **a)** The understeer coefficient of the vehicle is

$$K_{us} = \frac{W_f}{C_{\alpha f}} - \frac{W_r}{C_{\alpha r}} = \frac{20,105 \times 0.535}{2 \times 38,920} - \frac{20,105 \times 0.465}{2 \times 38,250}$$

$$= 0.016 \text{ rad } (0.92°).$$

The vehicle is understeer, and the characteristic speed is

$$V_{\text{char}} = \sqrt{\frac{gL}{K_{us}}} = 41.5 \text{ m/s} = 149 \text{ km/h (93 mph)}$$

b) When a pair of radial-ply tires with higher cornering stiffness are installed in the front axle, the understeer coefficient of the vehicle is

$$K_{us} = \frac{20{,}105 \times 0.535}{2 \times 47{,}820} - \frac{20{,}105 \times 0.465}{2 \times 38{,}250} = -0.0097 \text{ rad } (-0.56°)$$

The vehicle is oversteer, and the critical speed is

$$V_{crit} = \sqrt{\frac{gL}{-K_{us}}} = 53.1 \text{ m/s} = 191 \text{ km/h} (119 \text{ mph})$$

5.3 STEADY-STATE RESPONSE TO STEERING INPUT

A vehicle may be regarded as a control system upon which various inputs are imposed. During a turning maneuver, the steer angle induced by the driver can be considered as an input to the system, and the motion variables of the vehicle, such as yaw velocity, lateral acceleration, and curvature, may be regarded as outputs. The ratio of the yaw velocity, lateral acceleration, or curvature to the steering input can then be used for comparing the response characteristics of different vehicles [5.2].

5.3.1 Yaw Velocity Response

Yaw velocity gain is an often used parameter for comparing the steering response of road vehicles. It is defined as the ratio of the steady-state yaw velocity to the steer angle. Yaw velocity Ω_z of the vehicle under steady-state conditions is the ratio of the forward speed V to the turning radius R. From Eq. 5.10, the yaw velocity gain G_{yaw} is given by

$$G_{yaw} = \frac{\Omega_z}{\delta_f} = \frac{V}{L + K_{us}V^2/g} \tag{5.15}$$

Equation 5.15 gives the yaw velocity gain with respect to the steer angle of the front wheel. If the yaw velocity gain with respect to the steering wheel angle is desired, the value obtained from Eq. 5.15 should be divided by the steering gear ratio.

For a neutral steer vehicle, the understeer coefficient K_{us} is zero; the yaw velocity gain increases linearly with an increase of forward speed, as shown in Fig. 5.11. For an understeer vehicle, the understeer coefficient K_{us} is positive. The yaw velocity gain first increases with an increase of forward speed, and reaches a maximum at a particular speed, as shown in Fig. 5.11. It can be proved that the max-

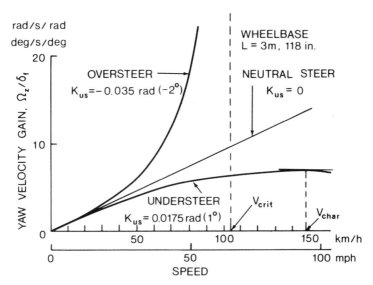

Fig. 5.11 Yaw velocity gain characteristics of neutral steer, understeer, and oversteer vehicles.

imum yaw velocity gain occurs at the characteristic speed V_{char} mentioned previously.

For an oversteer vehicle, the understeer coefficient K_{us} is negative; the yaw velocity gain increases with the forward speed at an increasing rate, as shown in Fig. 5.11. Since K_{us} is negative, at a particular speed, the denominator of Eq. 5.15 is zero, and the yaw velocity gain approaches infinity. This speed is the critical speed V_{crit} of an oversteer vehicle discussed previously.

The results of the above analysis indicate that from the point of view of handling response to steering input, an oversteer vehicle is more sensitive than a neutral steer one, and in turn, a vehicle with neutral steer characteristics is more responsive than an understeer one. Since the yaw velocity of a vehicle is an easily measured parameter, the yaw velocity gain–speed characteristics can be obtained from tests. The handling behavior of a vehicle can then be evaluated from the yaw velocity gain characteristics. For instance, if the yaw velocity gain of a vehicle is found to be greater than the forward speed divided by the wheel base (i.e., neutral steer response), the vehicle is oversteer, and if it is less, it is understeer.

5.3.2 Lateral Acceleration Response

Lateral acceleration gain, defined as the ratio of the steady-state lateral acceleration to the steer angle, is another commonly used parameter for evaluating the steering response of a vehicle. By rearranging Eq. 5.10, the lateral acceleration gain G_{acc} is given by

$$G_{acc} = \frac{V^2/gR}{\delta_f} = \frac{a_y/g}{\delta_f} = \frac{V^2}{gL + K_{us}V^2} \tag{5.16}$$

where a_y is the lateral acceleration.

Equation 5.16 gives the lateral acceleration gain with respect to the steer angle of the front wheel. If the acceleration gain with respect to the steering wheel angle is desired, the value obtained from Eq. 5.16 should be divided by the steering gear ratio.

For a neutral steer vehicle, the value of the understeer coefficient K_{us} is zero; the lateral acceleration gain is proportional to the square of forward speed, as shown in Fig. 5.12(a). For an understeer vehicle, the value of the understeer coefficient K_{us} is positive; the lateral acceleration gain increases with speed, as shown in Fig. 5.12(a). At very high speeds, the first term in the denominator of Eq. 5.16 is much smaller than the second term, and the lateral acceleration gain approaches a value of $1/K_{us}$ asymptotically.

For an oversteer vehicle, the value of the understeer coefficient K_{us} is negative. The lateral acceleration gain increases with an increase of forward speed at an increasing rate, as the denominator of Eq. 5.16 decreases with an increase of speed. At a particular speed, the denominator of Eq. 5.16 becomes zero, and the lateral acceleration gain approaches infinity. It can be shown that this speed is the critical speed of an oversteer vehicle.

5.3.3 Curvature Response

The ratio of the steady-state curvature $1/R$ to the steer angle is another parameter commonly used for evaluating the response characteristics of a vehicle. From Eq. 5.10, this parameter is expressed by

$$\frac{1/R}{\delta_f} = \frac{1}{L + K_{us}V^2/g} \tag{5.17}$$

Equation 5.17 gives the curvature response with respect to the steer angle of the front wheel. If the curvature response with respect to the steering wheel angle is desired, the value obtained from Eq. 5.17 should be divided by the steering gear ratio.

For a neutral steer vehicle, the understeer coefficient K_{us} is zero; the curvature response is independent of forward speed, as shown in Fig. 5.12(b). For an understeer vehicle, the understeer coefficient K_{us} is positive; the curvature response decreases as the forward speed increases, as shown in Fig. 5.12(b).

For an oversteer vehicle, the understeer coefficient K_{us} is negative; the curvature response increases with the forward speed. At a particular speed, the curvature response approaches infinity, as shown in Fig. 5.12(b). This means that the turning

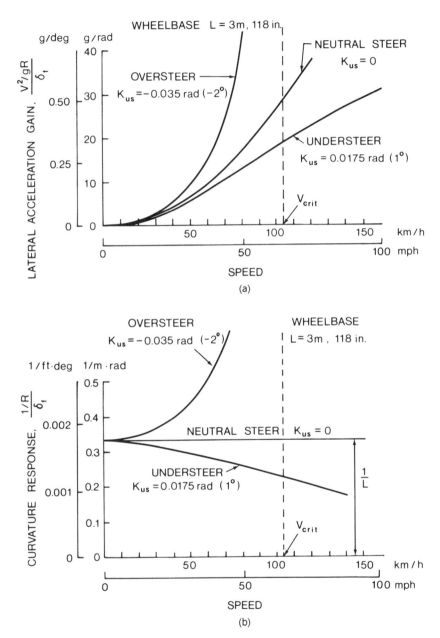

Fig. 5.12 (a) Lateral acceleration gain characteristics of neutral steer, understeer, and oversteer vehicles. (b) Curvature responses of neutral steer, understeer, and oversteer vehicles.

radius approaches zero and the vehicle spins out of control. This speed is, in fact, the critical speed V_{crit} of an oversteer vehicle discussed previously.

The results of the above analysis illustrate that from the steering response point of view, the oversteer vehicle has the most sensitive handling characteristics, while the understeer vehicle is the least responsive.

Example 5.2. A vehicle has a weight of 20.105 kN (4520 lb) and a wheelbase of 3.2 m (10.5 ft). The ratio of the distance between the center of gravity of the vehicle and the front axle to the wheelbase is 0.465. The cornering stiffness of each of the front tires is 38.92 kN/rad (8750 lb/rad) and that of the rear tires is 38.25 kN/rad (8600 lb/rad). The average steering gear ratio is 25. Determine the yaw velocity gain and the lateral acceleration gain of the vehicle with respect to the steering wheel angle.

Solution. The understeer coefficient of the vehicle is

$$K_{us} = \frac{W_f}{C_{\alpha f}} - \frac{W_r}{C_{\alpha r}} = \frac{20,105 \times 0.535}{2 \times 38,920} - \frac{20,105 \times 0.465}{2 \times 38,250} = 0.016 \text{ rad } (0.92°)$$

From Eq. 5.15, the yaw velocity gain with respect to the steering wheel angle is

$$G_{yaw} = \frac{\Omega_z}{\delta_f \xi_s} = \frac{V}{(L + K_{us}V^2/g)\, \xi_s}$$

where ξ_s is the steering gear ratio. The yaw velocity gain of the vehicle as a function of forward speed is shown in Fig. 5.13. From Eq. 5.16, the lateral acceleration gain with respect to the steering wheel angle is

$$G_{acc} = \frac{a_y/g}{\delta_f \xi_s} = \frac{V^2}{(gL + K_{us}V^2)\, \xi_s}$$

The lateral acceleration gain of the vehicle as a function of forward speed is also shown in Fig. 5.13.

5.4 TESTING OF HANDLING CHARACTERISTICS

To measure the handling behavior of a road vehicle under steady-state conditions, various types of test can be conducted on a skid pad, which in essence is a large, flat, paved area. Three types of test can be distinguished: the constant radius test, the constant forward speed test, and the constant steer angle test. During the tests, the steer angle, forward speed, and yaw velocity (or lateral acceleration) of the vehicle are usually measured. Yaw velocity can be measured by a rate-gyro or

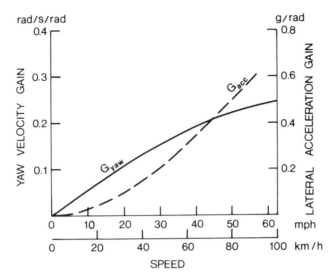

Fig. 5.13 Yaw velocity gain and lateral acceleration gain characteristics of a passenger car.

determined by the lateral acceleration divided by vehicle forward speed. Lateral acceleration can be measured by an accelerometer or determined by the yaw velocity multiplied by vehicle forward speed. Based on the relationship between the steer angle and the lateral acceleration or yaw velocity obtained from tests, the handling characteristics of the vehicle can be evaluated.

5.4.1 Constant Radius Test

In this test, the vehicle is driven along a curve with a constant radius at various speeds. The steer angle δ_f or the angle of the steering wheel required to maintain the vehicle on course at various forward speeds together with the corresponding lateral acceleration are measured. The steady-state lateral acceleration can also be deduced from the vehicle forward speed and the known turning radius. The results can be plotted as shown in Fig. 5.14 [5.4]. The handling behavior of the vehicle can then be determined from the slope of the steer angle–lateral acceleration curve. From Eq. 5.10, for a constant turning radius, the slope of the curve is given by

$$\frac{d\delta_f}{d(a_y/g)} = K_{us} \qquad (5.18)$$

This indicates that the slope of the curve represents the value of the understeer coefficient.

If the steer angle required to maintain the vehicle on a constant radius turn is the same for all forward speeds (i.e., the slope of the steer angle–lateral acceleration curve is zero), as shown in Fig. 5.14, the vehicle is neutral steer. The vehicle

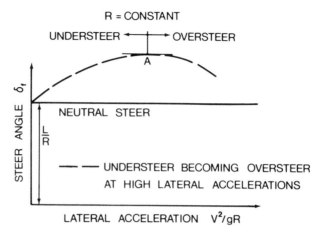

Fig. 5.14 Assessment of handling characteristics by constant radius test. (Reproduced with permission from *Vehicle Dynamics* by J.R. Ellis, Business Books, 1969.)

is considered to be understeer when the slope of the steer angle–lateral acceleration curve is positive, which indicates the value of the understeer coefficient K_{us} being greater than zero, as shown in Fig. 5.14. The vehicle is considered to be oversteer when the slope of the curve is negative, which indicates the value of the understeer coefficient K_{us} being less than zero, as illustrated in Fig. 5.14.

For a practical vehicle, owing to the nonlinear behavior of tires and suspensions, load transfer, and the effects of tractive (or braking) effort, the value of the understeer coefficient K_{us} varies with operating codnitions. A curve rather than a straight line to represent the steer angle–lateral acceleration relationship is usually obtained. It is possible for a vehicle to have understeer characteristics at low lateral accelerations and oversteer characteristics at high lateral accelerations, as shown in Fig. 5.14.

5.4.2 Constant Speed Test

In this test, the vehicle is driven at constant forward speed at various turning radii. The steer angle and the lateral acceleration are measured. The results can be plotted as shown in Fig. 5.15 [5.4]. The handling behavior of the vehicle can then be determined from the slope of the steer angle–lateral acceleration curve. From Eq. 5.10, for a constant speed turn, the slope of the curve is given by

$$\frac{d\delta_f}{d(a_y/g)} = \frac{gL}{V^2} + K_{us} \tag{5.19}$$

If the vehicle is neutral steer, the value of the understeer coefficient K_{us} will be zero and the slope of the steer angle–lateral acceleration line will be a constant of gL/V^2, as shown in Fig. 5.15 [5.4].

The vehicle is considered to be understeer when the slope of the steer angle–

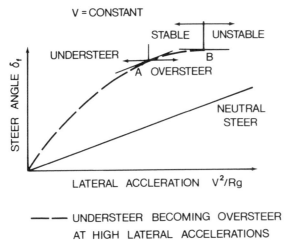

Fig. 5.15 Assessment of handling characteristics by constant speed test. (Reproduced with permission from *Vehicle Dynamics* by J.R. Ellis, Business Books, 1969.)

lateral acceleration curve is greater than that for the neutral steer response at a given forward speed (i.e., gL/V^2), which indicates that the value of the understeer coefficient K_{us} is positive, as shown in Fig. 5.15. The vehicle is considered to be oversteer when the slope of the curve is less than that for the neutral steer response at a given forward speed (i.e., gL/V^2), which indicates that the value of the understeer coefficient K_{us} is negative, as shown in Fig. 5.15.

When the slope of the curve is zero

$$\frac{gL}{V^2} + K_{us} = 0$$

and

$$V^2 = \frac{gL}{(-K_{us})} = V^2_{crit}$$

This indicates that the oversteer vehicle is operating at the critical speed, and that the vehicle is at the onset of directional instability.

If, during the tests, the steer angle and yaw velocity are measured, then the slope of the steer angle–yaw velocity curve can also be used to evaluate the steady-state handling behavior of the vehicle in a similar way.

5.4.3 Constant Steer Angle Test

In this test, the vehicle is driven with a fixed steering wheel angle at various forward speeds. The lateral accelerations at various speeds are measured. From the test results, the curvature $1/R$, which can be calculated from the measured lateral acceleration and forward speed by $1/R = a_y/V^2$, is plotted against lateral acceleration, as shown in Fig. 5.16. The handling behavior can then be determined by the slope of the curvature–lateral acceleration curve. From Eq. 5.10, for a constant steering wheel angle, the slope of the curve is given by

$$\frac{d(1/R)}{d(a_y/g)} = -\frac{K_{us}}{L} \qquad (5.20)$$

If the vehicle is neutral steer, the value of the understeer coefficient K_{us} will be zero, and the slope of the curvature–lateral acceleration curve is zero. The characteristics of a neutral steer vehicle are therefore represented by a horizontal line, as shown in Fig. 5.16.

The vehicle is considered to be understeer when the slope of the curvature–lateral acceleration curve is negative, which indicates that the value of the understeer coefficient K_{us} is positive, as shown in Fig. 5.16. The vehicle is considered to be oversteer when the slope of the curvature–lateral acceleration curve is positive, which indicates that the value of the understeer coefficient K_{us} is negative.

In general, the constant radius test is the simplest and requires little instrumentation. The steer angle of the front tire (or the steering wheel angle) and forward speed are the only essential parameters to be measured during the test, as the steady-state lateral acceleration can be deduced from vehicle forward speed and the given turning radius. The constant speed test is more representative of the actual road behavior of a vehicle than the constant radius test, as the driver usually maintains a more or less constant speed in a turn and turns the steering wheel by the required amount to negotiate the curve. The constant steer angle test, on the other hand, is easy to execute. Both the constant speed and constant steer angle tests would require, however, the measurement of the lateral acceleration or yaw velocity.

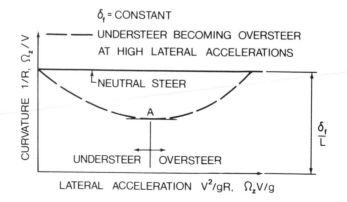

Fig. 5.16 Assessment of handling characteristics by fixed steer angle test.

5.5 TRANSIENT RESPONSE CHARACTERISTICS

Between the application of steering input and the attainment of steady-state motion, the vehicle is in a transient state. The behavior of the vehicle in this period is usually referred to as "transient response characteristics." The overall handling quality of a vehicle depends, to a great extent, on its transient behavior. The optimum transient response of a vehicle is that which has the fastest response with a minimum of oscillation in the process of approaching the steady-state motion.

In analyzing the transient response, the inertia properties of the vehicle must be taken into consideration. During a turning maneuver, the vehicle is in translation as well as in rotation. To describe its motion, it is convenient to use a set of axes fixed to and moving with the vehicle body because, with respect to these axes, the mass moments of inertia of the vehicle are constant, whereas with respect to axes fixed in space, the mass moments of inertia vary as the vehicle changes its orientation.

To formulate the equations of transient motion for a vehicle during a turning maneuver, it is necessary to express the absolute acceleration of the center of gravity of the vehicle (i.e., the acceleration with respect to axes fixed in space) using the reference frame attached to the vehicle body [5.5].

Let ox and oy be the longitudinal and lateral axes fixed to the vehicle body with origin at the center of gravity, and let V_x and V_y be the components of the velocity V of the center of gravity along the axes ox and oy, respectively, at time t, as shown in Fig. 5.17. As the vehicle is in both translation and rotation during a turn, at time $t + \Delta t$, the direction and magnitude of the velocity of the center of gravity as well as the orientation of the longitudinal and lateral axes of the vehicle change, as shown in Fig. 5.17. The change of the velocity component parallel to the ox axis is

$$(V_x + \Delta V_x) \cos \Delta\theta - V_x - (V_y + \Delta V_y) \sin \Delta\theta$$

$$= V_x \cos \Delta\theta + \Delta V_x \cos \Delta\theta - V_x - V_y \sin \Delta\theta - \Delta V_y \sin \Delta\theta \quad (5.21)$$

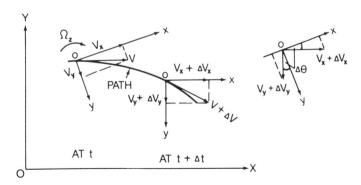

Fig. 5.17 Analysis of plane motions of a vehicle using axes fixed to vehicle body.

Consider that $\Delta\theta$ is small, and neglect second-order terms; the above expression becomes

$$\Delta V_x - V_y \Delta\theta \qquad (5.22)$$

The component along the longitudinal axis of the absolute acceleration of the center of gravity of the vehicle can be obtained by dividing the above expression by Δt. In the limit, this gives

$$a_x = \frac{dV_x}{dt} - V_y \frac{d\theta}{dt} = \dot{V}_x - V_y \Omega_z \qquad (5.23)$$

The component dV_x/dt (or $\dot{V}_x$) is due to the change in magnitude of the velocity component V_x and is directed along the ox axis, and the component $V_y d\theta/dt$ (or $V_y\Omega_z$) is due to the rotation of the velocity component V_y. Following a similar approach, the component along the lateral axis of the absolute acceleration of the center of gravity of the vehicle a_y is

$$a_y = \frac{dV_y}{dt} + V_x \frac{d\theta}{dt} = \dot{V}_y + V_x \Omega_z \qquad (5.24)$$

Referring to Fig. 5.18, for a vehicle having plane motion, the equations of motion using axes fixed to the vehicle body are given by

$$m \left(\dot{V}_x - V_y \Omega_z \right) = F_{xf} \cos \delta_f + F_{xr} - F_{yf} \sin \delta_f \qquad (5.25)$$

$$m \left(\dot{V}_y + V_x \Omega_z \right) = F_{yr} + F_{yf} \cos \delta_f + F_{xf} \sin \delta_f \qquad (5.26)$$

$$I_z \dot{\Omega}_z = l_1 F_{yf} \cos \delta_f - l_2 F_{yr} + l_1 F_{xf} \sin \delta_f \qquad (5.27)$$

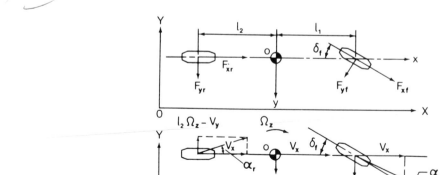

Fig. 5.18 Simplified vehicle model for analysis of transient motions.

where I_z is the mass moment of inertia of the vehicle about the z axis (see Fig. 5.1).

In deriving the above equations, it is assumed that the vehicle body is symmetric about the longitudinal plane (i.e., the xoz plane in Fig. 5.1), and that roll motion of the vehicle body is neglected.

If the vehicle is not accelerating or decelerating along the ox axis, Eq. 5.25 may be neglected, and the lateral and yaw motions of the vehicle are governed by Eqs. 5.26 and 5.27.

The slip angles α_f and α_r can be defined in terms of the vehicle motion variables Ω_z and V_y. Referring to Fig. 5.18, and using the usual small angle assumptions,

$$\alpha_f = \delta_f - \frac{l_1\Omega_z + V_y}{V_x} \tag{5.28}$$

$$\alpha_r = \frac{l_2\Omega_z - V_y}{V_x} \tag{5.29}$$

The lateral forces acting on the front and rear tires are a function of the corresponding slip angle and cornering stiffness, and are expressed by

$$F_{yf} = 2C_{\alpha f}\alpha_f \tag{5.30}$$

$$F_{yr} = 2C_{\alpha r}\alpha_r \tag{5.31}$$

Combining Eqs. 5.26–5.31, and assuming that the steer angle is small and F_{xf} is zero, the equations of lateral and yaw motions of a vehicle with steer angle as the only input variable become

$$m\dot{V}_y + \left[mV_x + \frac{2l_1C_{\alpha f} - 2l_2C_{\alpha r}}{V_x}\right]\Omega_z$$

$$+ \left[\frac{2C_{\alpha f} + 2C_{\alpha r}}{V_x}\right]V_y = 2C_{\alpha f}\delta_f(t) \tag{5.32}$$

$$I_z\dot{\Omega}_z + \left[\frac{2l_1^2C_{\alpha f} + 2l_2^2C_{\alpha r}}{V_x}\right]\Omega_z + \left[\frac{2l_1C_{\alpha f} - 2l_2C_{\alpha r}}{V_x}\right]V_y$$

$$= 2l_1C_{\alpha f}\delta_f(t) \tag{5.33}$$

In the above equations, $\delta_f(t)$ represents the steer angle of the front wheel as a function of time. If, in addition to the steer angle, external forces or moments, such as aerodynamic forces and moments, are acting on the vehicle, they should be added to the right-hand side of Eqs. 5.32 and 5.33 as input variables.

When the input variables, such as the steer angle and external disturbing forces, and the initial conditions are known, the response of the vehicle, expressed in terms of yaw velocity Ω_z and lateral velocity V_y as functions of time, can be determined by solving the differential equations. As an example, Fig. 5.19 shows the yaw velocity responses to a step input of steering angle of 0.01 rad (0.57°) for a station wagon with different types of tire traveling at 96 km/h (60 mph) [5.6]. Figure 5.20 shows the yaw velocity responses to a step input of aerodynamic side force of 890 N (200 lb) for the same vehicle.

5.6 DIRECTIONAL STABILITY

The directional stability of a vehicle is concerned with its ability to stabilize its direction of motion against disturbances. A vehicle is considered to be directionally stable if, following a disturbance, it returns to a steady-state regime within a finite time. A directionally unstable vehicle diverges more and more from the original path, even after the disturbance is removed. The disturbance may arise from crosswind, momentary forces acting on the tires from the road, slight movements of the steering wheel, and a variety of other causes.

With a small perturbation about an equilibrium position, a vehicle may be regarded as a linear dynamic system. The equations of lateral and yaw motions are a set of linear differential equations with constant coefficients, as shown in Eqs. 5.32 and 5.33. Following a disturbance, the lateral and yaw velocities, V_y and Ω_z,

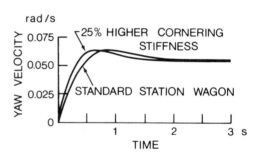

Fig. 5.19 Yaw velocity response of a station wagon to a step input of steer angle of 0.01 rad at 96 km/h (60 mph). (Reproduced with permission of the Society of Automotive Engineers from reference 5.6.)

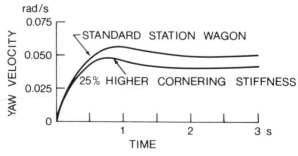

Fig. 5.20 Yaw velocity response of a station wagon to a step input of lateral force of 890 N (200 lb) at 96 km/h (60 mph). (Reproduced with permission of the Society of Automotive Engineers from reference 5.6.)

will vary with time exponentially, $V_y = A_1 e^{\psi t}$ and $\Omega_z = A_2 e^{\psi t}$. The stability of the vehicle is determined by the value of ψ. If ψ is a real number and positive, the values of lateral and yaw velocities will increase exponentially with time, and the vehicle will be directionally unstable. A real and negative value of ψ indicates that motions of the vehicle converge to a steady state in a finite time, and that the vehicle is directionally stable. If ψ is a complex number with a positive real part, the motions will be oscillatory with increasing amplitudes, and thus the system will be directionally unstable. A complex value of ψ with a negative real part indicates that the motions are oscillatory with decreasing amplitudes, and thus the vehicle is directionally stable.

To evaluate the directional stability of a vehicle, it is, therefore, necessary to determine the values of ψ. Since only the motions of the vehicle following a disturbance are of interest in the evaluation of stability, the steering input and the like are taken to be zero. This is equivalent to the examination of the free vibrations of the vehicle in the lateral direction and in yaw following the initial disturbance. To obtain the values of ψ, the following solutions to the differential equations for lateral and yaw motions (i.e., Eqs. 5.32 and 5.33) are assumed:

$$V_y = A_1 e^{\psi t} \tag{5.34}$$

$$\Omega_z = A_2 e^{\psi t} \tag{5.35}$$

Then

$$\dot{V}_y = A_1 \psi e^{\psi t} \tag{5.36}$$

$$\dot{\Omega}_z = A_2 \psi e^{\psi t} \tag{5.37}$$

On substituting these values into Eqs. 5.32 and 5.33, and setting the right-hand sides of the equations to zero, the equations become

$$mA_1\psi + \left[\frac{2C_{\alpha f} + 2C_{\alpha r}}{V_x}\right] A_1 + \left[\frac{mV_x^2 + 2l_1 C_{\alpha f} - 2l_2 C_{\alpha r}}{V_x}\right] A_2 = 0 \tag{5.38}$$

$$I_z A_2\psi + \left[\frac{2l_1 C_{\alpha f} - 2l_2 C_{\alpha r}}{V_x}\right] A_1 + \left[\frac{2l_1^2 C_{\alpha f} + 2l_2^2 C_{\alpha r}}{V_x}\right] A_2 = 0 \tag{5.39}$$

The above equations can be rewritten as

$$mA_1\psi + a_1 A_1 + a_2 A_2 = 0 \tag{5.40}$$

$$I_z A_2\psi + a_3 A_1 + a_4 A_2 = 0 \tag{5.41}$$

where

$$a_1 = \frac{2C_{\alpha f} + 2C_{\alpha r}}{V_x}$$

$$a_2 = \frac{mV_x^2 + 2l_1 C_{\alpha f} - 2l_2 C_{\alpha r}}{V_x}$$

$$a_3 = \frac{2l_1 C_{\alpha f} - 2l_2 C_{\alpha r}}{V_x}$$

$$a_4 = \frac{2l_1^2 C_{\alpha f} + 2l_2^2 C_{\alpha r}}{V_x}$$

Equations 5.40 and 5.41 are known as the amplitude equations, which are linear, homogeneous, algebraic equations. It can be shown that to obtain a nontrivial solution for ψ, the determinant of the amplitudes must be equal to zero. Thus,

$$\begin{vmatrix} m\psi + a_1 & a_2 \\ a_3 & I_z\psi + a_4 \end{vmatrix} = 0 \tag{5.42}$$

Expanding the determinant yields the characteristic equation

$$mI_z\psi^2 + (I_z a_1 + ma_4)\,\psi + (a_1 a_4 - a_2 a_3) = 0 \tag{5.43}$$

It can be shown that if $(I_z a_1 + ma_4)$ and $(a_1 a_4 - a_2 a_3)$ are both positive, then ψ must be either a negative real number or a complex number having a negative real part. The terms $I_z a_1$ and ma_4 are clearly always positive; hence, it follows that the vehicle is directionally stable if $a_1 a_4 - a_2 a_3$ is positive. It can be shown that the condition for $a_1 a_4 - a_2 a_3 > 0$ is

$$L + \frac{V_x^2}{g}\left(\frac{W_f}{C_{\alpha f}} - \frac{W_r}{C_{\alpha r}}\right) > 0$$

or

$$L + \frac{V_x^2}{g} K_{us} > 0 \tag{5.44}$$

where K_{us} is the understeer coefficient defined previously. This indicates that the examination of the directional stability of a vehicle is now reduced to determining the conditions under which Eq. 5.44 is satisfied. When the understeer coefficient K_{us} is positive, Eq. 5.44 is always satisfied. This implies that when a vehicle is understeer, it is always directionally stable. When the understeer coefficient K_{us} is negative, which indicates that the vehicle is oversteer, the vehicle is directionally stable only if the speed of the vehicle is below a specific value:

$$V_x < \sqrt{\frac{gL}{-K_{us}}}$$
(5.45)

This specific speed is, in fact, the critical speed V_{crit} of an oversteer vehicle discussed previously. This indicates that an oversteer vehicle will be directionally stable only if it operates at a speed lower than the critical speed.

The analysis of vehicle handling presented in this chapter is based on a simplified vehicle model. For a practical vehicle, the lateral and yaw motions are coupled with the motions in fore and aft (translation along the x axis shown in Fig. 5.1), roll (rotation about the x axis), pitch (rotation about the y axis), and bounce (translation along the z axis). The coupling is through mechanisms such as changes in cornering properties of tires with the application of tractive or braking effort, longitudinal and lateral load transfer during a turning maneuver, and changes in the steering characteristics of the vehicle due to motions of the vehicle body relative to the unsprung parts. More complete evaluations of the handling behavior of road vehicles, in which the interactions of lateral and yaw motions with those in the other directions are taken into consideration, have been made [5.4, 5.7, 5.9].

It should also be pointed out that, in practice, the handling of a vehicle involves the continuous interaction of the driver with the vehicle. To perform a comprehensive examination of vehicle handling qualities, the characteristics of the human driver therefore should be included. This topic is, however, beyond the scope of the present text.

5.7 STEADY-STATE HANDLING CHARACTERISTICS OF A TRACTOR–SEMITRAILER

An approach similar to that for the analysis of a two-axle vehicle described in Section 5.2 can be followed to evaluate the steady-state handling characteristics of a tractor–semitrailer with three axles, as shown in Fig. 5.21. For the tractor, the equation governing its steady-state handling behavior is similar to Eq. 5.10 and is expressed by

$$\delta_f = \frac{L_t}{R} + \left(\frac{W_f}{C_{\alpha f}} - \frac{W_r}{C_{\alpha r}}\right)\frac{V^2}{gR}$$

$$= \frac{L_t}{R} + K_{us.t}\frac{V^2}{gR}$$
(5.46)

where L_t is the wheelbase of the tractor and $K_{us.t}$ is the understeer coefficient of the tractor.

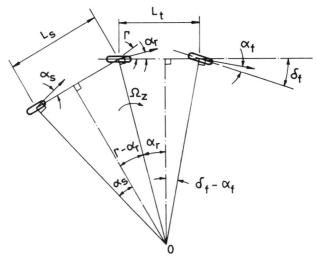

Fig. 5.21 Simplified steady-state handling model for a tractor-semitrailer.

For most of the tractor–semitrailers, the fifth wheel is located slightly ahead of the center of the tractor rear axle. In the following simplified analysis, the fifth wheel, however, is assumed to be located above the center of the tractor rear axle. With this assumption, the tractor rear tire may be considered as the "steered tire" for the semitrailer, and the articulation angle Γ between the tractor and the semitrailer may be expressed by

$$\Gamma = \frac{L_s}{R} + \left(\frac{W_r}{C_{\alpha r}} - \frac{W_s}{C_{\alpha s}}\right)\frac{V^2}{gR}$$

$$= \frac{L_s}{R} + K_{us.s}\frac{V^2}{gR} \tag{5.47}$$

where L_s is the wheelbase of the semitrailer, W_s and $C_{\alpha s}$ are the load and cornering stiffness of each of the tires on the semitrailer axle, respectively, and $K_{us.s}$ is the understeer coefficient for the semitrailer.

The ratio of the articulation angle Γ to the steer angle of the tractor front tire δ_f is usually referred to as the articulation angle gain, and is given by

$$\frac{\Gamma}{\delta_f} = \frac{L_s/R + K_{us.s}\,(V^2/gR)}{L_t/R + K_{us.t}\,(V^2/gR)} \tag{5.48}$$

An examination of the above equation reveals that five different types of steady-state handling behavior of a tractor–semitrailer are possible [5.11].

1. Both the tractor and semitrailer are understeer. In this case, both $K_{us.t}$ and $K_{us.s}$ are positive, and the articulation angle gain is finite and positive for all values of forward speed, as shown in Fig. 5.22. Consequently, the tractor–semitrailer is directionally stable.

2. The tractor is understeer, while the semitrailer is oversteer. In this case, $K_{us.t}$ is positive, whereas $K_{us.s}$ is negative, and the articulation angle gain remains finite for all values of forward speed, as shown in Fig. 5.23. However, when the forward speed V is greater than V_{ct} described below, the articulation angle gain changes from positive to negative:

$$V_{ct} = \sqrt{\frac{gL_s}{-K_{us.s}}}\qquad(5.49)$$

This indicates that when the forward speed V approaches V_{ct}, the articulation angle Γ approaches zero, and when $V > V_{ct}$, the orientation of the semitrailer with respect to the tractor will be opposite that shown in Fig. 5.21.

3. The tractor is oversteer, while the semitrailer is understeer. In this case, $K_{us.t}$ is negative and $K_{us.s}$ is positive. It can be seen that when the forward speed approaches the critical speed V_{crit} described below, the denominator in Eq. 5.48 approaches zero and the articulation angle gain approaches infinity, as

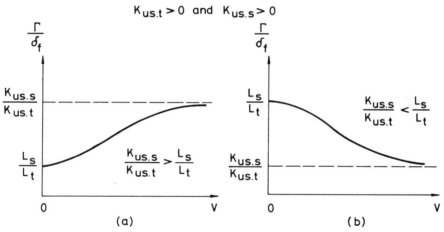

Fig. 5.22   Steady-state handling characteristics of a tractor-semitrailer with $K_{us.t} > 0$ and $K_{us.s} > 0$.

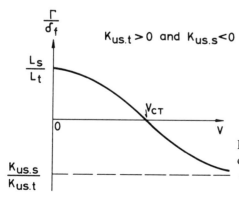

Fig. 5.23   Steady-state handling characteristics of a tractor–semitrailer with $K_{us.t} > 0$ and $K_{us.s} < 0$.

shown in Fig. 5.24:

$$V_{\text{crit}} = \sqrt{\frac{gL_t}{-K_{us.t}}} \tag{5.50}$$

This indicates that when the forward speed V approaches V_{crit}, the tractor longitudinal axis becomes increasingly oriented towards the center of the turn, resulting in jackknifing.

4. Both the tractor and semitrailer are oversteer, and the ratio of the understeer coefficient of the semitrailer to that of the tractor is less than the ratio of the semitrailer wheelbase to the tractor wheelbase. In this case, $K_{us.s} < 0$, $K_{us.t} < 0$, and $(K_{us.s}/K_{us.t}) < (L_s/L_t)$; the variation of the articulation angle gain with forward speed is shown in Fig. 5.25. Similar to case 3, when the for-

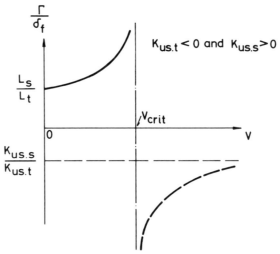

Fig. 5.24 Steady-state handling characteristics of a tractor–semitrailer with $K_{us.t} < 0$ and $K_{us.s} > 0$.

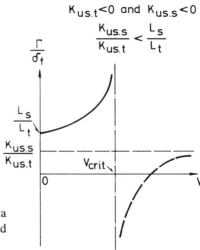

Fig. 5.25 Steady-state handling characteristics of a tractor–semitrailer with $K_{us.t} < 0$, $K_{us.s} < 0$, and $K_{us.s}/K_{us.t} < L_s/L_t$.

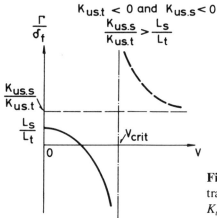

Fig. 5.26 Steady-state handling characteristics of a tractor–semitrailer with $K_{us.t} < 0$, $K_{us.s} < 0$, and $K_{us.s}/K_{us.t} > L_s/L_t$.

ward speed approaches the critical value defined by Eq. 5.50, jackknifing will occur.

5. Both the tractor and semitrailer are oversteer, and the ratio of the understeer coefficient of the semitrailer to that of the tractor is greater than the ratio of the semitrailer wheelbase to the tractor wheelbase. In this case, $K_{us.s} < 0$, $K_{us.t} < 0$, and $(K_{us.s}/K_{us.t}) > (L_s/L_t)$; the variation of the articulation angle gain with forward speed is shown in Fig. 5.26. It can be seen that the articulation angle gain decreases with increasing forward speed. When the forward speed V approaches V_{ct} defined by Eq. 5.49, the gain approaches zero. With a further increase in the forward speed, the gain becomes negative and approaches minus infinity as the forward speed approaches V_{crit}, defined by Eq. 5.50. In this case, the semitrailer longitudinal axis becomes increasingly oriented towards the center of the turn, resulting in trailer swing.

The results of the above analysis indicate that for any form of directional instability (jackknifing or trailer swing) to occur, the tractor must be oversteer. Jackknifing can occur when the semitrailer is either understeer or oversteer. However, for trailer swing to occur, in addition to the condition that the semitrailer must be oversteer, it is required that the ratio of the understeer coefficient of the semitrailer to that of the tractor be greater than the ratio of the semitrailer wheelbase to the tractor wheelbase. Further analysis of the steering response of articulated vehicles, including truck–trailers, may be found in references [5.12, 5.13].

5.8 SIMULATION MODELS FOR THE DIRECTIONAL BEHAVIOR OF ARTICULATED ROAD VEHICLES

With the increasing use in road transport of heavy articulated vehicles or road trains, which consist of a tractor unit and one or more semitrailers or full trailers, concerns for their safety in operation have been growing. This has stimulated intensive theoretical and experimental studies of the directional control and stability of this type of vehicle. A number of computer simulation models have been developed. A brief description of the basic features of some of the better known models is given below [5.14–5.18].

1. The Linear Yaw Plane Model   This model is a linear mathematical model for studying the directional behavior of multiple articulated vehicles. It was developed at the University of Michigan Transportation Research Institute (UMTRI), originally for the purpose of analyzing the directional behavior of double-bottom tankers.

In developing the equations of motion for the model, the roll dynamics of the vehicle is neglected. Furthermore, the vehicle is assumed to travel at a constant forward velocity. The degrees of freedom considered in the model are limited to the lateral and yaw motions of the tractor and articulation in the horizontal plane of the other sprung masses of a multiple articulated vehicle.

The following are the major assumptions made in the process of deriving the equations of motion.

a. The cornering (lateral) force and aligning moment (torque) generated at the tire–road interface are assumed to be linear functions of the slip angle of the tire.

b. Articulation angles made by the various units of the vehicle train are small.

c. The motion of the vehicle takes place on a horizontal surface.

d. There are no significant tire forces present in the longitudinal direction (either tractive or braking).

e. Pitch and roll motions of the sprung masses are small, and hence neglected.

f. All joints are frictionless, and articulation takes place about vertical axes.

g. Each unit of the articulated vehicle is assumed to be a rigid body, and the unsprung masses are assumed to be rigidly attached to their respective sprung masses.

2. TBS Model   TBS is a simplified nonlinear mathematical model, originally formulated by Leucht [5.19]. An interactive computer program based on Leucht's model was developed by Moncarz et al. [5.15].

In developing the equations of motion for the model, the basic assumptions made are similar to those for the linear yaw plane model. However, the following major improvements have been introduced.

a. A nonlinear tire model is used to represent the cornering force–slip angle relationship of a tire.

b. The dynamic load transfers (both longitudinal and lateral) have been taken into account in determining the normal load on each tire.

3. Yaw/Roll Model   The yaw/roll model was developed at UMTRI for the purpose of predicting the directional and roll responses of articulated vehicles in turning maneuvers which approach the rollover condition.

In the model, the forward velocity of the lead unit is assumed to remain constant during the maneuver. Each sprung mass is treated as a rigid body with up to five degrees of freedom (dependent upon the constraints at the hitch): lateral, vertical, yaw, roll, and pitch. The axles are treated as beam axles which are free to roll and bounce with respect to the sprung mass to which they are attached.

The basic assumptions for this model are as follows.

a. The relative roll motion between the unsprung and sprung masses takes place about roll centers, which are located at fixed distances beneath the sprung masses.

b. Nonlinearities in the force–displacement behavior of a suspension, such as suspension lash, are taken into account.

c. The cornering force and aligning moment produced by a given tire is a nonlinear function of the slip angle and vertical load. The influence of wheel camber on lateral force generation is neglected.

d. The model permits the analysis of articulated vehicles which are equipped with any of the four coupling mechanisms, namely, conventional fifth wheel, inverted fifth wheel, pintlehook, and kingpin.

e. Both closed-loop (defined path input) and open-loop (defined steer angle input) modes of steering input can be accommodated, and the effects of the steering system compliance are taken into account.

The running time of this model is about five times that of the linear yaw plane model, and it requires a large amount of input data.

4. The Phase 4 Model   This model was originally developed at UMTRI in 1980 for simulating the braking and steering dynamics of trucks, tractor–semitrailers, doubles, and triples. It is a comprehensive computer model for simulating the braking and steering response of commercial vehicles.

The Phase 4 model is a time-domain mathematical simulation of a truck/tractor, a semitrailer, and up to two full trailers. The motions of the vehicles are represented by differential equations derived from Newtonian mechanics that are solved for successive time increments by digital integration.

The mathematical model incorporates up to 71 degrees of freedom. The number of degrees of freedom is dependent upon vehicle configuration and is derived from the following:

a. six degrees of freedom (three translational and three rotational) for the truck/tractor sprung mass;

b. three rotational degrees of freedom for the semitrailer (the other three translational degrees of freedom of the semitrailer are effectively eliminated by dynamic constraints at the hitch);

c. five degrees of freedom for each of the two full trailers allowed;

d. two degrees of freedom (bounce and roll) for each of the 13 axles allowed;

e. a wheel rotational degree of freedom for each of the 26 wheels allowed.

For the simulation of lateral dynamic behavior, the model incorporates state-of-the-art representations of truck tire cornering force characteristics and vehicle suspension properties of significance to cornering behavior.

The program can be operated open-loop or closed-loop, and on roads of specified grade or cross-slope.

It can be seen that these models vary greatly in capability, in complexity, in the number of degrees of freedom considered, and in the amount of input data required. For instance, the Phase 4 model incorporates up to 71 degrees of freedom, and requires up to approximately 2300 lines of input data, dependent upon vehicle configuration. On the other hand, the linear yaw plane model only includes the lateral and yaw motions of the tractor and articulation in the horizontal plane of the other sprung masses of the articulated vehicle, and only requires up to 35 lines of input data.

The capabilities and limitations of the simulation models described above have been examined [5.17, 5.18]. The steady-state steering response and the lateral dynamic behavior in a lane-change maneuver of a representative five-axle tractor–semitrailer have been predicted using the four models and compared with available experimental data. Figure 5.27 shows the lateral acceleration responses to steering input of the tractor–semitrailer in steady-state turns at a forward speed of 69 km/h (43 mph) on a dry, smooth asphalt surface predicted using the four models. The measured values are also shown in the figure. Based on the predicted lateral accelerations and yaw rates of the tractor, a handling diagram for the vehicle is drawn, as shown in Fig. 5.28. For comparison, the measured data are also shown.

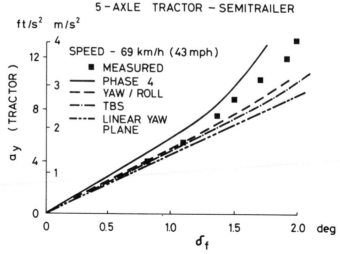

Fig. 5.27 Comparison of steady-state lateral acceleration response to steering input of a tractor–semitrailer predicted by various models.

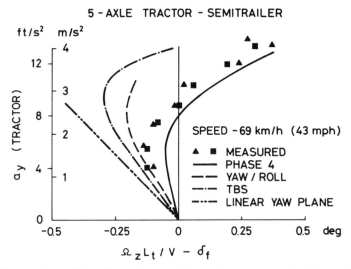

Fig. 5.28 Comparison of handling characteristics of a tractor–semitrailer predicted by various models.

It should be noted that the square symbol in the figure represents the value calculated from the measured yaw rate of the tractor at a forward speed of 69 km/h (43 mph), whereas the triangular symbol represents the value taken from reference [5.20].

It can be seen from Fig. 5.27 that the lateral accelerations of the tractor predicted using the linear yaw plane model, the TBS model, and the yaw/roll model are reasonably close within the range up to 2° of front wheel steering angle (equivalent to a lateral acceleration of approximately 0.3 g). However, there is a significant difference between the lateral accelerations predicted using the Phase 4 model and those predicted using the other three models for front wheel steering angles greater than 1.5° (equivalent to a lateral acceleration of approximately 0.2 g). It can be noted that at an average front wheel steering angle $\delta = 1.0°$, the differences between the measured lateral acceleration and the predicted ones using the Phase 4 model, the yaw/roll model, the TBS model, and the linear yaw plane model are 17.5, 1.2, 2.3, and 7.7%, respectively. At an average front wheel steering angle of $\delta = 1.5°$, the corresponding differences are 10.3, 13.1, 13.8, and 22.3%, respectively. This indicates that the Phase 4 model gives a better prediction of lateral acceleration than the other three models when the lateral acceleration is greater than about 0.2 g.

Based on the data shown in Fig. 5.27, it appears that for lateral accelerations below 0.2 g, the four computer simulation models give similar predictions, and the predicted values agree reasonably well with the measured ones. For lateral accelerations greater than 0.2 g, the Phase 4 model gives a better prediction of the trend of yaw divergence than the other three models in comparison with the measured values. However, the Phase 4 model overestimates the response, while the yaw/roll model and the TBS model underestimate it. For lateral accelerations higher than 0.2 g, the linear yaw plane model gives the highest error of prediction among the four models. This is primarily due to the fact that in the linear yaw plane model, a linear tire model is adopted, and the cornering stiffness of the tire obtained at zero slip angle is used in the predictions. Furthermore, the load transfer and its effects on tire characteristics have been entirely neglected.

It should also be mentioned that the lateral accelerations which cause an inside tire to lift off the ground, predicted using the Phase 4 model, the yaw/roll, and the TBS model, are considerably lower than the measured one reported in reference [5.20].

Figure 5.28 illustrates the steady-state handling characteristics of the vehicle as predicted by the four computer simulation models. It can be seen that the lateral acceleration at which the vehicle changes from understeer to oversteer, referred to as the "transition acceleration," predicted using the Phase 4 model is just under 0.2 g. The transition accelerations predicted using the yaw/roll model and the TBS model are approximately 0.25 g and 0.3 g, respectively, while the measured one is approximately 0.2 g. Below the transition acceleration, the Phase 4 model underestimates the understeer level (or understeer coefficient) as compared with the measured data, whereas the TBS model and the linear yaw plane model overestimate the understeer level to varying degrees. It should be mentioned that since a linear tire model is used, the linear yaw plane model is unable to predict any variation of the handling behavior of the vehicle with lateral acceleration, and the predicted understeer level remains a constant.

In general, among the four models studied, the Phase 4 model gives the best overall prediction of the variation of handling behavior with lateral acceleration for the five-axle tractor–semitrailer examined, although there is still a noticeable difference between the predicted and measured values, as can be seen from Fig. 5.28.

The lateral acceleration, yaw rate, and articulation angle of the tractor–semitrailer in a lane-change maneuver were predicted using the Phase 4 model, the yaw/roll model, the TBS model, and the linear yaw plane model, and are shown in Figs. 5.29–5.33. The simulated results were compared with the measured data reported in reference [5.21].

It can be seen that the responses of the tractor and semitrailer predicted by the four models generally follow the same trend as that measured. However, there are differences between the predicted peak values and the measured ones. For instance, the differences between the measured peak value of tractor lateral acceleration and those predicted using the Phase 4 model, the yaw/roll model, the TBS model, and the linear yaw plane model are approximately 16, 10, 33, and 46%, respectively, as shown in Fig. 5.29. The agreement between the measured peak value of semitrailer lateral acceleration and those predicted is better than that for the tractor lateral acceleration. The differences between the measured peak value of semitrailer lateral acceleration and those predicted using the Phase 4 model, the yaw/roll model, the TBS model, and the linear yaw plane model are approximately 20, 8, 12, and 20%, respectively, as can be seen from Fig. 5.30. The agreement between the measured tractor yaw rate response and those predicted using the four models appears to be reasonable. The differences between the measured peak value of tractor yaw rate and those predicted using the Phase 4 model, the yaw/roll

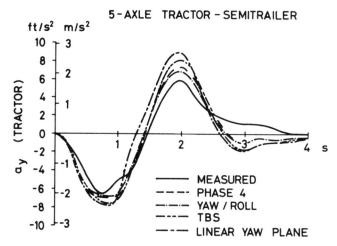

Fig. 5.29 Variation of tractor lateral acceleration with time in a lane-change maneuver predicted by various models.

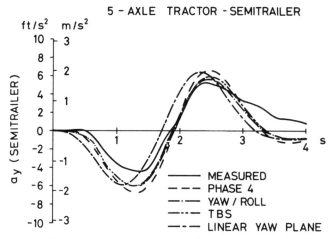

Fig. 5.30 Variation of semitrailer lateral acceleration with time in a lane-change maneuver predicted by various models.

model, the TBS model, and the linear yaw plane model are approximately 9.8, 4.9, 15.8, and 21.9%, respectively, as can be seen from Fig. 5.31. The measured semitrailer yaw rate response and those predicted using the four models again show reasonable agreement. The differences between the measured peak value of the semitrailer yaw rate and those predicted using the Phase 4 model, the yaw/roll model, the TBS model, and the linear yaw plane model are approximately 13.3, 0, 3.3, and 13.3%, respectively, as shown in Fig. 5.32. The articulation angle responses predicted using the four models are reasonably close. The differences between the peak values of articulation angle predicted using the four models are within 10%. However, there is a noticeable difference between the measured and predicted peak values of articulation angle. For instance, the difference between the measured and the predicted peak value of articulation angle using the Phase 4 model is approximately 22%, as can be seen from Fig. 5.33.

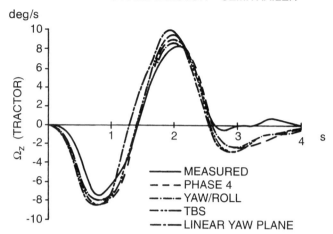

Fig. 5.31 Variation of tractor yaw rate with time in a lane-change maneuver predicted by various models.

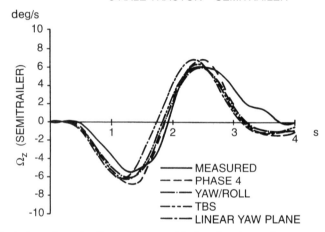

Fig. 5.32 Variation of semitrailer yaw rate with time in a lane-change maneuver predicted by various models.

It should also be noted from the figures that there is a phase shift between the measured and predicted responses, and that there is a significant difference between the measured and predicted responses during the period from 3 to 4 s.

In summary, it appears that in comparison with the measured data, the steady-state steering responses of the representative tractor–semitrailer predicted using the four simulation models all have varying degrees of discrepancy, and that there are no significant differences in the steady-state steering responses predicted using the four models in the lateral acceleration range up to approximately 0.25 g. There are, however, significant differences in the handling characteristics predicted using the four simulation models in most cases, as shown in the handling diagram (Fig. 5.28). Since the linear yaw plane model does not take into account the effects of load transfer and uses a linear tire model, it is not capable of predicting changes

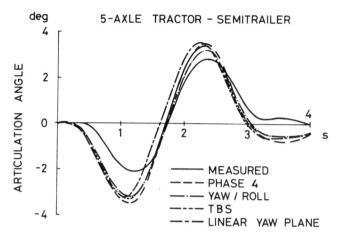

Fig. 5.33 Variation of articulation angle with time in a lane-change maneuver predicted by various models.

in handling behavior with lateral acceleration. On the other hand, the Phase 4 model, the yaw/roll model, and the TBS model take into account the effects of load transfer and the nonlinear behavior of tires to varying degrees. Consequently, these three models can predict changes in handling behavior with lateral acceleration. It should be noted, however, that the predictions made by these three models are still noticeably different from the measured data available. For a lane-change maneuver, the responses of the representative tractor–semitrailer predicted by the four simulation models generally follow the same trend as that measured. However, there are noticeable discrepancies between the measured and predicted ones.

REFERENCES

5.1   K.J. Bunker, "Theoretical and Practical Approaches to Motor Vehicle Steering Mechanisms," in J.G. Giles, Ed., *Steering, Suspension and Tyres*, Automotive Technology Series, Vol. 1.   London, England: Butterworths, 1968.

5.2   R.T. Bundorf, "The Influence of Vehicle Design Parameters on Characteristic Speed and Understeer," *SAE Transactions*, vol. 76, 1968.

5.3   J. Fenton, Ed., *Handbook of Automotive Design Analysis*.   London, England: Butterworths.

5.4   J.R. Ellis, *Vehicle Dynamics*.   London, England: Business Books, 1969.

5.5   W. Steeds, *Mechanics of Road Vehicles*.   London, England: Iliffe & Sons, 1960.

5.6   R.T. Bundorf, D.E. Pollock, and M.C. Hardin, "Vehicle Handling Response to Aerodynamic Inputs," Society of Automotive Engineers, paper 716B, June 1963.

5.7   L. Segel, "Theoretical Prediction and Experimental Substantiation of the Response of the Automobile to Steering Control," *Proc. Institution of Mechanical Engineers*, Automobile Division, 1956–1957.

5.8   D.W. Whitcomb and W.F. Milliken, Jr., "Design Implications of a General Theory of Automobile Stability and Control," *Proc. Institution of Mechanical Engineers*, Automobile Division, 1956–1957.

5.9   H.S. Radt and H.B. Pacejka, "Analysis of the Steady State Turning Behavior of an Automobile," in *Proc. Institution of Mechanical Engineers Symp. on the Control of Vehicles During Braking and Cornering*, June 1963.

5.10   D.E. Cole, *Elementary Vehicle Dynamics*, Department of Mechanical Engineering, University of Michigan, Ann Arbor, 1971.

5.11   R.D. Ervin and C. Mallikarjunarao, "A Study of the Yaw Stability of Tractor-Semi-trailer Combinations," in *Proc. 7th IAVSD Symp. on Dynamics of Vehicles on Roads and Tracks*, Swets and Zeitlinger, 1982.

5.12   M. El-Gindy and J.Y. Wong, "Steering Response of Articulated Vehicles in Steady-State Turns," Society of Automotive Engineers, paper 852335, 1985.

5.13   M. El-Gindy and J.Y. Wong, "Steady-State Steering Response of an Articulated Vehicle with a Multi-Axle Steering Dolly," Society of Automotive Engineers, paper 850537, 1985.

5.14   C.B. Winkler, C. Mallikarjunarao, and C.C. MacAdam, "Analytical Test Plan: Part I—Description of Simulation Models for Parameter Analysis of Heavy Truck Dynamic Stability," Report of the University of Michigan Transportation Research Institute, Apr. 1981.

5.15   H.T. Moncarz, J.E. Bernard, and P.S. Fancher, "A Simplified, Interactive Simulation for Predicting the Braking and Steering Response of Commercial Vehicles," Report UMHSRI-PF-75-8, University of Michigan Highway Safety Research Institute, Aug. 1975.

5.16   J.Y. Wong and M. El-Gindy, "Computer Simulation of Heavy Vehicle Dynamic Behavior, User's Guide to the UMTRI Models," Technical Report 3, Vehicle Weights and Dimensions Study, Roads and Transportation Association of Canada, June 1985.

5.17   J.Y. Wong and M. El-Gindy, "A Comparison of Various Computer Simulation Models for Predicting the Lateral Dynamic Behavior of Articulated Vehicles," Technical Report of Vehicle Weights and Dimensions Study, Vol. 16, Roads and Transportation Association of Canada, July 1986.

5.18   M. El-Gindy and J.Y. Wong, "A Comparison of Various Computer Simulation Models for Predicting the Directional Responses of Articulated Vehicles," *Vehicle System Dynamics*, vol. 16, no. 5-6, 1987.

5.19   P.M. Leucht, "The Directional Dynamics of the Commerical Tractor-Semitrailer Vehicle During Braking," Society of Automotive Engineers, paper 700371, 1970.

5.20   R.D. Ervin, R.L. Nisonger, C. Mallikarjunarao, and T.D. Gillespie, "The Yaw Stability of Tractor-Semitrailers During Cornering," Report DOT HS-805 141, PB80-116775, U.S. Department of Commerce, National Technical Information Service, June 1979.

5.21   P.S. Fancher, C. Mallikarjunarao, and R.L. Nisonger, "Simulation of the Directional Response Characteristics of Tractor-Semitrailer Vehicles," Report UM-HSRI-79-9, PB 80-189632, U.S. Department of Commerce, National Technical Information Service, Mar. 1979.

PROBLEMS

5.1   A passenger car weighs 20.02 kN (4500 lb) and has a wheelbase of 279.4 cm (110 in.). The center of gravity is 127 cm (50 in.) behind the front axle.

If a pair of radial-ply tires, each of which has a cornering stiffness of 45.88 kN/rad (180 lb/deg), are installed in the front, and a pair of bias-ply tires, each of which has a cornering stiffness of 33.13 kN/rad (130 lb/deg), are installed in the rear, determine whether the vehicle is understeer or oversteer. Also calculate the characteristic or critical speed of the vehicle as appropriate. What would happen to the steady-state handling characteristics of the vehicle, if the front and rear tires are interchanged?

5.2 A sports car weighs 9.919 kN (2230 lb) and has a wheelbase of 2.26 m (7.4 ft). The center of gravity is 1.22 m (4 ft) behind the front axle. The cornering stiffness of each front tire is 58.62 kN/rad (230 lb/deg) and that of each rear tire is 71.36 kN/rad (280 lb/deg). The steering gear ratio is 20:1. Determine the steady-state yaw velocity gain and lateral acceleration gain of the vehicle in the forward speed range of 10–160 km/h (6.2–99.4 mph).

5.3 The sports car described in Problem 5.2 has a mass moment of inertia about a vertical axis passing through its center of gravity of 570 kg · m² (420 slug · ft²). If the car is given a step input of steering wheel angle of 30° at a speed of 80.5 km/h (50 mph), determine the rise time for the yaw velocity response.

CHAPTER 6

STEERING OF TRACKED VEHICLES

The handling characteristics of tracked vehicles have certain unique features and are quite different from those of wheeled vehicles. A separate treatment of the steering of tracked vehicles is therefore required. There are a number of possible methods that can accomplish the steering of a tracked vehicle. These include skid-steering, steering by articulation, and curved track steering.

In skid-steering, the thrust of one track is increased and that of the other is reduced, so as to create a turning moment to overcome the moment of turning resistance due to the skidding of the tracks on the ground and the rotational inertia of the vehicle in yaw, as shown in Fig. 6.1. Since the moment of turning resistance is usually considerable, significantly more power may be required during a turn than in a straight line motion. Furthermore, braking of the inside track is often required in making a turn. This results in a reduction of the maximum resultant forward thrust that the vehicle can develop. Over weak terrain, this often leads to immobilization.

For tracked vehicles consisting of two or more units, steering may be accomplished by rotating one unit against the other using a steering joint to make the vehicle follow a prescribed, curved path, as shown in Fig. 6.2 [6.1]. In articulated steering, turning is initiated by activating the steering joint between the two units, and no adjustment of the thrusts of the outside and inside tracks is required. Thus, the resultant forward thrust of the vehicle can be maintained during a turn. Articulated steering can therefore provide tracked vehicles with better mobility during turning maneuvers than skid-steering, particularly over soft ground.

Another method for directional control of tracked vehicles is that of curved track steering. To initiate a turn, the laterally flexible track is laid down on the ground in a curve, as shown in Fig. 6.3 [6.2]. This can be achieved using various kinds of mechanical arrangement, one of which is illustrated in Fig. 6.3. In this partic-

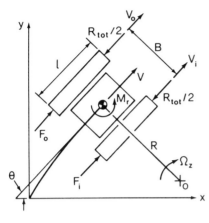

Fig. 6.1 Principles of skid steering. (From *Theory of Land Locomotion* by M.G. Bekker, copyright © by the University of Michigan, 1956, reproduced with permission of the University of Michigan Press.)

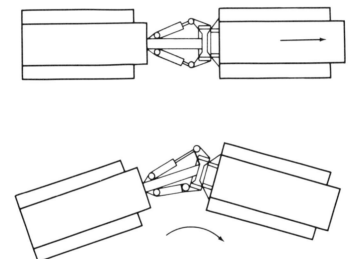

Fig. 6.2 Articulated steering. (Reproduced with permission from reference 6.1.)

ular arrangement, each of the roadwheels of the track is mounted on an axis inclined at a suitable angle from the vertical in a longitudinal plane so that movement around these axes displaces the lower part of the wheels to form a curved track. Steering movement of the roadwheels may be activated by a conventional steering wheel through racks and pinions and individual push rods [6.2]. The main advantage of this steering method is that less power is required in making a turn as compared with skid-steering. However, owing to the limitations of the lateral flexibility of the track, the minimum turning radius of the vehicle is quite large. To achieve a smaller turning radius, a supplementary steering mechanism, such as skid-steering, has to be provided. Thus, not only does the complexity of design of the vehicle increase, but also the potential advantages of curved track steering in power saving may not be fully realized.

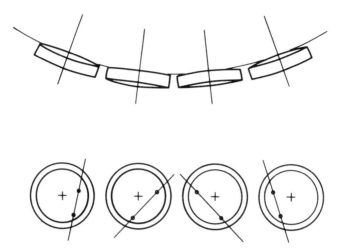

Fig. 6.3 Curved track steering. (Reproduced with permission from reference 6.2.)

Among the various steering methods available for tracked vehicles, the skid-steering and articulated steering are commonly used. The principles of these two steering methods will therefore be discussed in detail in this chapter.

6.1 KINETICS OF SKID-STEERING

The turning behavior of a tracked vehicle using skid-steering depends on the thrusts of the outside and inside tracks F_0 and F_i, the resultant resisting force R_{tot}, the moment of turning resistance M_r exerted on the track by the ground, and vehicle parameters as shown in Fig. 6.1. The simple case of steering at low speeds on a level ground will be examined first. The problem of steering tracked vehicles at high speeds will be discussed later. At low speeds, the centrifugal force may be neglected, and the behavior of the vehicle can be described by the following two equations of motion:

$$m \frac{d^2s}{dt^2} = F_0 + F_i - R_{tot} \tag{6.1}$$

$$I_z \frac{d^2\theta}{dt^2} = \frac{B}{2}(F_0 - F_i) - M_r \tag{6.2}$$

where s is the displacement of the center of gravity of the vehicle, θ is the angular displacement of the vehicle, B is the tread of the vehicle (i.e., the spacing between the centerlines of the two tracks), and I_z and m are the mass moment of inertia of the vehicle about the vertical axis passing through its center of gravity and the mass of the vehicle, respectively. With known initial conditions, the above two differential equations can be integrated, and the trajectory of the center of gravity and the orientation of the vehicle can be determined as discussed by Bekker [6.3].

Under steady-state conditions, there are no linear and angular accelerations:

$$F_0 + F_i - R_{\text{tot}} = 0 \tag{6.3}$$

$$\frac{B}{2}(F_0 - F_i) - M_r = 0 \tag{6.4}$$

The thrusts of the outside and inside tracks required to achieve a steady-state turn are therefore expressed by

$$F_0 = \frac{R_{\text{tot}}}{2} + \frac{M_r}{B} = \frac{f_r W}{2} + \frac{M_r}{B} \tag{6.5}$$

$$F_i = \frac{R_{\text{tot}}}{2} - \frac{M_r}{B} = \frac{f_r W}{2} - \frac{M_r}{B} \tag{6.6}$$

where f_r is the coefficient of motion resistance of the vehicle in the longitudinal direction and W is the vehicle weight.

To determine the values of the thrusts F_0 and F_i, the moment of turning resistance M_r must be known. This can be determined experimentally or analytically. If the normal pressure is uniformly distributed along the track, the lateral resistance per unit length of the track R_l can be expressed by

$$R_l = \frac{\mu_t W}{2l} \tag{6.7}$$

where μ_t is the coefficient of lateral resistance and l is the contact length of the track.

The value of μ_t depends not only on the terrain, but also on the design of the track. Over soft terrain, the vehicle sinks into the ground, and the tracks together with the grousers will be sliding on the surface, as well as displacing the soil laterally during turning maneuvers. The lateral forces acting on the tracks and the grousers due to displacing the soil laterally form part of the lateral resistance. It has been shown that under certain circumstances, the lateral resistance of a track may also depend on the skid of the track in the lateral direction and the turning radius [6.4]. Table 6.1 shows the average values of μ_t for steel and rubber tracks over various types of ground [6.5].

Assuming that the coefficient of lateral resistance μ_t is a constant, the resultant moment of the lateral resistance about the centers of the two tracks M_r (i.e., moment of turning resistance) can be expressed by (Fig. 6.4)

$$M_r = 4\frac{W\mu_t}{2l}\int_0^{l/2} x\, dx = \frac{\mu_t W l}{4} \tag{6.8}$$

TABLE 6.1 Values of Lateral Resistance of Tracks Over Various Surfaces

| Track Material | Coefficient of Lateral Resistance μ_t | | |
	Concrete	Hard Ground (not paved)	Grass
Steel	0.50–0.51	0.55–0.58	0.87–1.11
Rubber	0.90–0.91	0.65–0.66	0.67–1.14

Source: Reference 6.5.

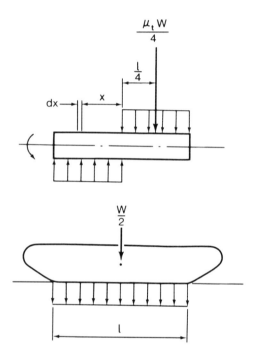

Fig. 6.4 Moment of turning resistance of a track with uniform pressure distribution.

Accordingly, Eqs. 6.5 and 6.6 can be rewritten in the following form:

$$F_0 = \frac{f_r W}{2} + \frac{\mu_t W l}{4B} \tag{6.9}$$

$$F_i = \frac{f_r W}{2} - \frac{\mu_t W l}{4B} \tag{6.10}$$

It should be emphasized that the value of M_r as calculated by Eq. 6.8 is for a vehicle with a uniform normal pressure distribution, turning at low speeds on level ground. Methods for predicting the moment of turning resistance of a track with a trapezoidal or triangular shape of normal pressure distribution or with normal loads concentrated under the roadwheels have been proposed or developed [6.6, 6.7].

Equations 6.9 and 6.10 are of fundamental importance, and they lead to conclusions of practical significance regarding the steerability of a tracked vehicle. As discussed in Chapter 2, the maximum thrust of a track is limited by terrain properties and vehicle parameters. For the outside track,

$$F_0 \le cbl + \frac{W \tan \phi}{2} \tag{6.11}$$

where b is the track width and c and ϕ are the cohesion and angle of internal shearing resistance of the terrain, respectively.

Substituting Eq. 6.9 into Eq. 6.11,

$$\frac{f_r W}{2} + \frac{\mu_t W l}{4B} \le cbl + \frac{W \tan \phi}{2}$$

and

$$\frac{l}{B} \le \frac{1}{\mu_t} \left(\frac{4cA}{W} + 2 \tan \phi - 2f_r \right)$$

where A is the contact area of one track.

This indicates that to enable a tracked vehicle to steer without spinning the outside track, the ratio of track length to tread of the vehicle, l/B, must satisfy the following condition:

$$\frac{l}{B} \le \frac{2}{\mu_t} \left(\frac{c}{p} + \tan \phi - f_r \right) \tag{6.12}$$

where p is the average normal pressure on the track, which is equal to $W/2A$.

On a sandy terrain with $c = 0$, $\phi = 30°$, $\mu_t = 0.5$, and $f_r = 0.1$, the value of l/B should be less than 1.9. In other words, if the ratio of contact length to tread of a tracked vehicle is greater than 1.9, the vehicle will not be able to steer on the terrain specified. On a clayey terrain, with $c = 3.45$ kPa (0.5 psi), $\phi = 10°$, $p = 6.9$ kPa (1 psi), $\mu_t = 0.4$, and $f_r = 0.1$, the value of l/B must be less than 2.88. These examples show the importance of the ratio of contact length to tread of a tracked vehicle to its steerability.

From Eq. 6.10, it can also be seen that if $\mu_t l/2B > f_r$, the thrust of the inside track F_i will be negative. This implies that to achieve a steady-state turn, braking of the inside track is required. For instance, with $\mu_t = 0.5$, $f_r = 0.1$, and $l/B = 1.5$, the value of $\mu_t l/2B$ will be greater than that of f_r, which indicates that a braking force has to be applied to the inside track. Since the forward thrust of the outside track of a given vehicle is limited by terrain properties as shown in Eq. 6.11, the application of a braking force to the inside track during a turn reduces the maximum resultant forward thrust of the vehicle, and thus the mobility of the vehicle over weak terrain will be adversely affected. Figure 6.5 shows the ratio of

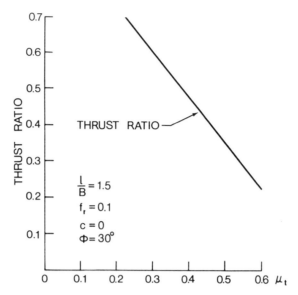

Fig. 6.5 Effect of lateral resistance coefficient on the maximum thrust available during a turn.

the maximum resultant forward thrust as limited by the track–terrain interaction during a turn to that when in a straight line motion as a function of the coefficient of lateral friction μ_t for a tracked vehicle with $l/B = 1.5$ operating over a terrain with $c = 0$, $\phi = 30°$, and $f_r = 0.1$. It can be seen that as the value of μ_t increases from 0.2 to 0.5, the maximum resultant forward thrust available during a steady-state turn decreases from approximately 74 to 35% of that when traveling in a straight line.

On hard grounds, the resultant of the longitudinal and lateral forces acting on a track during a turn may be assumed to obey the law of Coulomb friction. The resultant force is limited by the coefficient of friction and the normal load on the track, and acts in the opposite direction to the relative motion of the track with respect to the ground. Based on these assumptions, the steering characteristics of tracked vehicles have been analyzed in detail by Steeds [6.8].

Example 6.1. A tracked vehicle weighs 155.68 kN (35,000 lb) and has a tread of 203.2 cm (80 in.). Each of the two tracks has a contact length of 304.8 cm (120 in.) and a width of 76.2 cm (30 in.). The contact pressure is assumed to be uniform. The vehicle travels over a terrain with a cohesion $c = 3.45$ kPa (0.5 psi) and an angle of internal shearing resistance $\phi = 25°$. Over this terrain, the coefficient of motion resistance f_r is 0.15 and the average coefficient of lateral resistance μ_t is 0.5.

a) Determine the steerability of the vehicle over the terrain specified if the skid-steering method is employed.

b) Determine the required thrusts of the outside and inside tracks during a steady-state turn.

Solution.

a) From Eq. 6.12, the limiting value for the ratio of track length to tread is

$$\frac{l}{B} = \frac{2}{\mu_t}\left(\frac{c}{p} + \tan\phi - f_r\right) = 1.67$$

Since the ratio of track length to tread of the vehicle l/B is 1.5, which is less than the limiting value of 1.67, the vehicle is steerable over the terrain specified.

b) The thrusts of the outside and inside tracks required during a steady-state turn can be determined using Eqs. 6.9 and 6.10:

$$F_0 = \frac{f_r W}{2} + \frac{\mu_t W l}{4B} = 40.87 \text{ kN (9188 lb)}$$

$$F_i = \frac{f_r W}{2} - \frac{\mu_t W l}{4B} = -17.52 \text{ kN } (-3938 \text{ lb})$$

The results indicate that the brake has to be applied to the inside track during the turn.

6.2 KINEMATICS OF SKID-STEERING

Figure 6.1 shows a tracked vehicle turning about a center O. If the sprocket of the outside track is rotating at an angular speed of ω_0 and that of the inside track is rotating at an angular speed of ω_i and the tracks do not slip (or skid), the turning radius R and the yaw velocity of the vehicle Ω_z can be expressed by

$$R = \frac{B}{2}\frac{(r\omega_0 + r\omega_i)}{(r\omega_0 - r\omega_i)} = \frac{B(K_s + 1)}{2(K_s - 1)} \tag{6.13}$$

$$\Omega_z = \frac{r\omega_0 + r\omega_i}{2R} = \frac{r\omega_i(K_s - 1)}{B} \tag{6.14}$$

where r is the radius of the sprocket and K_s is the angular speed ratio ω_0/ω_i.

It should be pointed out, however, that during a turning maneuver, an appropriate thrust or braking force must be applied to the track, as described previously. As a consequence, the track will either slip or skid, depending on whether a forward thrust or a braking force is applied. The outside track always develops a forward thrust, and therefore it slips. On the other hand, the inside track may develop a forward thrust or a braking force, depending on the magnitude of the turning resistance moment M_r and other factors as defined by Eq. 6.6. When the slip (or skid) of the track is taken into consideration, the turning radius R' and yaw velocity Ω_z' are given by

$$R' = \frac{B[r\omega_0(1 - i_0) + r\omega_i(1 - i_i)]}{2[r\omega_0(1 - i_0) - r\omega_i(1 - i_i)]}$$

$$= \frac{B[K_s(1 - i_0) + (1 - i_i)]}{2[K_s(1 - i_0) - (1 - i_i)]} \qquad (6.15)$$

$$\Omega'_z = \frac{r\omega_0(1 - i_0) + r\omega_i(1 - i_i)}{2R'}$$

$$= \frac{r\omega_i[K_s(1 - i_0) - (1 - i_i)]}{B} \qquad (6.16)$$

where i_0 and i_i are the slip of the outside track and that of the inside track, respectively. For a given vehicle over a particular terrain, the values of i_0 and i_i depend on the thrusts F_0 and F_i. The relationship between thrust and slip (or skid) can be determined using the methods described in Chapter 2. When a braking force is applied to the inside track, the track skids. Equations 6.15 and 6.16 still hold; however, i_i will have a negative value.

To illustrate the effect of track slip on the steering characteristics of a tracked vehicle, the ratio of the turning radius with track slipping R' to that without slipping R is plotted against the speed ratio $K_s = \omega_0/\omega_i$ in Fig. 6.6. Curve 1 shows the relationship between R'/R and K_s when the outside track slips at 20% and the inside track is disconnected from the transmission by declutching. Curve 2 shows the variation of the value of R'/R with K_s when the outside track slips and the inside track skids. This occurs when the outside track develops a forward thrust and a braking force is applied to the inside track.

It is shown that the value of R'/R is always greater than unity. Thus, the effect of track slip (or skid) is to increase the turning radius for a given speed ratio K_s.

6.3 SKID-STEERING AT HIGH SPEEDS

In the above analysis of the mechanics of skid-steering, low-speed operation is assumed, and the effect of the centrifugal force is neglected. When a tracked ve-

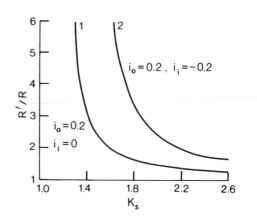

Fig. 6.6 Effect of track slip on turning radius.

hicle is turning at moderate and higher speeds, or with a relatively small turning radius, the centrifugal force may be significant, and its effect should be taken into consideration.

Consider that a tracked vehicle is in a steady-state turn on level ground. To achieve equilibrium in the lateral direction, the resultant lateral force exerted on the track by the ground must be equal to the centrifugal force, as shown in Fig. 6.7. Assume that the normal pressure distribution along the track is uniform, and that the coefficient of lateral resistance μ_t is a constant; then to satisfy the equilibrium condition in the lateral direction, the center of turn must lie at a distance s_0 in front of the transverse centerline of the track–ground contact area AC, as shown in Fig. 6.7. The distance s_0 can be determined by the following equation [6.3]:

$$\left(\frac{l}{2} + s_0\right)\frac{\mu_t W}{l} - \left(\frac{l}{2} - s_0\right)\frac{\mu_t W}{l} = \frac{WV^2}{gR'}\cos\beta$$

$$s_0 = \frac{lV^2}{2\mu_t gR'}\cos\beta = \frac{la_y}{2\mu_t g}\cos\beta \qquad (6.17)$$

where a_y is the lateral acceleration of the center of gravity of the vehicle.

Since the turning radius R' is usually large compared with the contact length of the track l, β would be small, and accordingly, $\cos\beta$ may be assumed to be equal to 1. Equation 6.17 can be rewritten as follows:

$$s_0 = \frac{la_y}{2\mu_t g} \qquad (6.18)$$

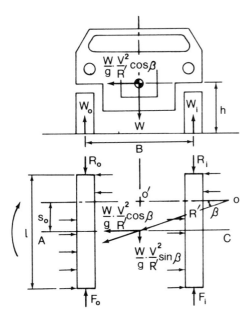

Fig. 6.7 Forces acting on a tracked vehicle during a turn at high speeds. (From *Theory of Land Locomotion* by M.G. Bekker, copyright © by the University of Michigan, 1956, reproduced with permission of the University of Michigan Press.)

As a consequence of the shifting of the center of turn, the equivalent moment of turning resistance M_r will have two components: one is the moment of the lateral resistance exerted on the tracks by the ground about $0'$, and the other is the moment of the centrifugal force about $0'$:

$$M_r = \frac{\mu_t W}{l} \left[\int_0^{l/2 + s_0} x\,dx + \int_0^{-(l/2 - s_0)} x\,dx \right] - \frac{WV^2 s_0}{gR'}$$

$$= \frac{\mu_t W}{2l} \left(\frac{l^2}{2} + 2s_0^2 \right) - \frac{WV^2 s_0}{gR'} \tag{6.19}$$

Substituting Eq. 6.18 into Eq. 6.19, the equivalent moment of turning resistance M_r becomes

$$M_r = \frac{\mu_t W l}{4} \left(1 - \frac{V^4}{g^2 R^2 \mu_t^2} \right)$$

$$= \frac{\mu_t W l}{4} \left(1 - \frac{a_y^2}{g^2 \mu_t^2} \right) \tag{6.20}$$

The above equation indicates that when the centrifugal force is taken into consideration, the equivalent moment of turning resistance is reduced.

The centrifugal force also causes lateral load transfer. Thus, the longitudinal motion resistances of the outside and inside track R_0 and R_i will not be identical:

$$R_0 = \left(\frac{W}{2} + \frac{hWV^2}{BgR'} \right) f_r \tag{6.21}$$

$$R_i = \left(\frac{W}{2} - \frac{hWV^2}{BgR'} \right) f_r \tag{6.22}$$

where h is the height of the center of gravity of the vehicle.

Furthermore, the centrifugal force has a component along the longitudinal axis of the vehicle, $WV^2 s_0 / gR'^2$. This component has to be balanced by the thrusts developed by the tracks. Therefore, when the centrifugal force is taken into account, the thrusts required to maintain the vehicle in a steady-state turn are expressed by [6.3]

$$F_0 = \left(\frac{W}{2} + \frac{hWV^2}{BgR'} \right) f_r + \frac{WV^2 s_0}{2gR'^2} + \frac{\mu_t W l}{4B} \left[1 - \left(\frac{V^2}{gR'\mu_t} \right)^2 \right]$$

$$= \left(\frac{W}{2} + \frac{hWa_y}{Bg} \right) f_r + \frac{Wa_y s_0}{2gR'} + \frac{\mu_t W l}{4B} \left[1 - \left(\frac{a_y}{g\mu_t} \right)^2 \right] \tag{6.23}$$

$$F_i = \left(\frac{W}{2} - \frac{hWV^2}{BgR'}\right)f_r + \frac{WV^2 s_0}{2gR'^2} - \frac{\mu_t W l}{4B}\left[1 - \left(\frac{V^2}{gR'\mu_t}\right)^2\right]$$

$$= \left(\frac{W}{2} - \frac{hWa_y}{Bg}\right)f_r + \frac{Wa_y s_0}{2gR'} - \frac{\mu_t W l}{4B}\left[1 - \left(\frac{a_y}{g\mu_t}\right)^2\right] \qquad (6.24)$$

Figure 6.8 illustrates the required ratios of the thrust to vehicle weight for the outside and inside tracks, F_0/W and F_i/W, as a function of lateral acceleration in g-units, a_y/g, for a given vehicle on a particular terrain. It can be seen that as the lateral acceleration increases, the ratio of the thrust to vehicle weight for the outside track F_0/W decreases. This is mainly due to the fact that the moment of the centrifugal force about the center of turn increases with an increase of lateral acceleration. As a consequence, the equivalent moment of turning resistance decreases with an increase of lateral acceleration. It can also be noted that the ratio of the thrust to vehicle weight for the inside track F_i/W is usually negative, which implies that braking of the inside track is required to maintain a steady-state turn. The magnitude of the braking force of the inside track decreases, however, as the lateral acceleration increases. This is again mainly due to the decrease of the equivalent moment of turning resistance with the increase of lateral acceleration.

Equations 6.23 and 6.24 specify the thrusts of the outside and inside tracks required under a steady-state turn for a given vehicle speed and turning radius. However, to achieve a specific turning radius and vehicle speed, certain kinematic relationships have to be satisfied. These include the relationship among turning radius, vehicle speed, track slips, and sprocket speeds. To determine the required sprocket speeds for a specific turning radius and vehicle speed, the slips of the outside and inside tracks i_0 and i_i should be determined. To do this, the required thrusts F_0 and F_i should first be calculated using Eqs. 6.23 and 6.24. Then from

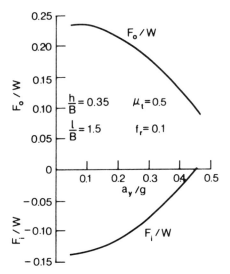

Fig. 6.8 Thrusts on the outside and inside tracks required during a turn as a function of lateral acceleration.

the relationship between thrust and slip discussed in Chapter 2, the values of i_0 and i_i can be obtained. The required angular speed ratio K_s for a given turning radius R' can be determined from Eq. 6.15:

$$K_s = \frac{(2R' + B)(1 - i_i)}{(2R' - B)(1 - i_0)} \tag{6.25}$$

The angular speeds of the sprockets ω_0 and ω_i required to achieve a specific vehicle forward speed V can then be obtained from Eq. 6.16:

$$\omega_i = \frac{2V}{r[K_s(1 - i_0) + (1 - i_i)]} \quad \text{and} \quad \omega_0 = K_s\omega_i \tag{6.26}$$

It can be seen that when the effect of the centrifugal force is taken into consideration, the analysis of the turning maneuver of a tracked vehicle becomes more involved.

6.4 POWER CONSUMPTION OF SKID-STEERING

When a tracked vehicle is traveling in a straight line, the power consumption P_{st} due to the motion resistance R_{tot} is

$$P_{st} = R_{tot}V_{st} = f_r W V_{st} \tag{6.27}$$

where V_{st} is the vehicle speed in a straight line motion.

It should be mentioned that power loss due to slip of the vehicle running gear may also be significant over unprepared terrain. In the following analysis of power consumption during a turning maneuver, the power loss due to slip is, however, neglected in order to simplify the analysis.

When a tracked vehicle is making a steady-state turn, power is consumed by the motion resistance, the moment of turning resistance, and the braking torque in the steering system. The power required during a turn P_t can be expressed by [6.9]

$$P_t = R_{tot}V + M_r\Omega_z + M_b\omega_b \tag{6.28}$$

where V is the speed of the center of gravity of the vehicle during a turn, M_b is the frictional torque of the brake (or clutch) in the steering system, and ω_b is the relative angular velocity of the frictional elements (or the relative velocity of the driving element with respect to the driven element) in the brake (or clutch). When the brake is fully applied (or the clutch is fully engaged) and there is no relative motion between the frictional elements, the power loss in the brake (or clutch) will be zero.

The ratio of the power consumption during a steady-state turn to that in straight line motion can be expressed by

$$\frac{P_t}{P_{st}} = \frac{V}{V_{st}} + \frac{M_r \Omega_z}{f_r W V_{st}} + \frac{M_b \omega_b}{f_r W V_{st}}$$

$$= \frac{V}{V_{st}} \left(1 + \frac{M_r}{f_r W R} + \frac{M_b \omega_b}{f_r W V} \right) \tag{6.29}$$

For a given tracked vehicle on a particular terrain, the power ratio P_t/P_{st} depends on the ratios of V/V_{st}, $M_r/f_r W R$, and $M_b \omega_b/f_r W V$, which in turn are dependent, to a great extent, on the characteristics of the steering system used. The characteristics and the corresponding power ratio P_t/P_{st} of some typical steering systems for tracked vehicles will be discussed in the next section.

6.5 STEERING MECHANISMS FOR TRACKED VEHICLES

There are various types of steering mechanism available for tracked vehicles using the principles of skid-steering.

6.5.1 Clutch/Brake Steering System

This system is shown schematically in Fig. 6.9. To initiate a turn, the inside track is disconnected from the driveline by declutching, and the brake is usually applied. The outside track is driven by the engine and generates a forward thrust. The thrust on the outside track and the braking force on the inside track form a turning moment that steers the vehicle. This steering system is very simple, but the steering brake usually absorbs considerable power during a turn. The clutch/brake steering system is therefore mainly used in low-speed tracked vehicles such as farm tractors and construction vehicles.

It should be mentioned that under certain circumstances, the clutch/brake steering system may cause the so-called "reversed steering" (i.e., the controls are operated so as to initiate an intended right-hand turn, but the vehicle actually turns to the left or vice versa). For instance, if the vehicle is descending a slope with the throttle closed, the disengaging of the steering clutch on one side will free the associated track, while the retarding torque from the engine applies on the other

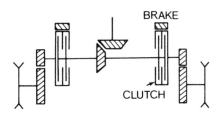

Fig. 6.9 Schematic view of a clutch–brake steering system.

track (if, at the instant of steering, the initial vehicle speed is faster than that corresponding to the engine speed with the throttle closed). If the coefficient of lateral resistance is low, this will cause the vehicle to make a skid turn in the direction opposite that intended. Reversed steering can be eliminated by arranging the disengagement of the steering clutch and the application of the brake to overlap so that the disengaging of the clutch will be immediately followed by a braking action on the sprocket.

Consider a turning maneuver in which the inside track of the vehicle is disconnected from the driveline by declutching and the brake is fully applied. The inside track thus has zero forward speed. The vehicle will be turning about the center of the inside track, and the minimum turning radius R_{min} will be equal to $B/2$. Assume that, during the turn, the engine is running at the same speed as that prior to turning. It is obvious that with the clutch/brake steering system, the forward speed of the center of gravity of the vehicle at the minimum turning radius will be half of that prior to turning, and $V/V_{st} = 0.5$. Since the brake of the inside track is fully applied, there will be no power loss in the brake. The power ratio P_t/P_{st} for a tracked vehicle with a clutch/brake steering system at the minimum turning radius is therefore given by

$$\frac{P_t}{P_{st}} = 0.5 \left(1 + \frac{M_r}{f_r WB/2} \right) \tag{6.30}$$

Assume that the normal pressure under the track is uniformly distributed and the vehicle is turning at low speeds. The moment of turning resistance M_r is given by Eq. 6.8, and Eq. 6.30 can be rewritten as follows:

$$\frac{P_t}{P_{st}} = 0.5 \left(1 + \frac{\mu_t l}{2 f_r B} \right) \tag{6.31}$$

For a tracked vehicle with a clutch/brake steering system, having $l/B = 1.5$ and operating over a terrain with a coefficient of lateral resistance $\mu_t = 0.5$ and a coefficient of motion resistance $f_r = 0.1$, the power consumption during a steady-state turn at the minimum turning radius will be 2.375 times that when the vehicle is traveling in a straight line. This indicates that considerably more power is required during a turning maneuver as compared to that in a straight line motion. If the power loss due to track slip is included, the total power consumption during a turn will be even higher.

6.5.2 Controlled Differential Steering System

This type of steering system is shown schematically in Fig. 6.10. Gear A is driven through a gearbox by the engine. In a straight line motion, brakes B_1 and B_2 are not applied, and gears C_1, C_2, D_1, and D_2 form an ordinary differential. For steering, the brake of the inside track, such as B_2, is applied. This results in a reduction

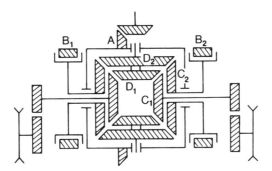

Fig. 6.10 Schematic view of a controlled differential steering system.

of the speed of the inside track and a corresponding increase of the speed of the outside track. Thus, the forward speed of the center of gravity of the vehicle during a turn will be the same as that in a straight line motion for a given engine speed. A kinematic analysis of the controlled differential will show that the relationship between the angular speed of the sprocket of the outside track ω_0 to that of the inside track ω_i can be expressed by

$$K_s = \frac{\omega_0}{\omega_i} = \frac{K_{di} + 1 - K_{di}\omega_{B2}}{K_{di} - 1 + K_{di}\omega_{B2}} \tag{6.32}$$

where K_{di} is the gear ratio of the differential and is equal to $N_{D2}N_{C1}/N_{D1}N_{C2}$, where N_{C1}, N_{C2}, N_{D1}, and N_{D2} are the number of teeth of the gears C_1, C_2, D_1, and D_2 in the differential, respectively, and ω_{B2} is the angular speed of the brake drum B_2. If brake B_2 is fully applied and the drum does not slip, Eq. 6.32 can be rewritten as follows:

$$K_s = \frac{K_{di} + 1}{K_{di} - 1} \tag{6.33}$$

It should be noted that when brake B_2 is fully applied, the minimum turning radius is achieved. From Eq. 6.13, the minimum turning radius of a tracked vehicle with a controlled differential steering system is therefore expressed by

$$R_{\min} = \frac{B}{2}\left(\frac{K_s + 1}{K_s - 1}\right) = \frac{BK_{di}}{2} \tag{6.34}$$

The power ratio P_t/P_{st} for a tracked vehicle with a controlled differential steering system at the minimum turning radius is given by

$$\frac{P_t}{P_{st}} = \frac{V}{V_{st}} \left(1 + \frac{M_r}{f_r W R_{\min}} \right)$$

$$= 1 + \frac{M_r}{f_r W B K_{di}/2} \tag{6.35}$$

where $V/V_{st} = 1$, as mentioned previously.

When the normal pressure under the track is uniformly distributed and the vehicle is turning at low speeds, Eq. 6.35 can be rewritten as

$$\frac{P_t}{P_{st}} = 1 + \frac{\mu_t l}{2 f_r B K_{di}} \tag{6.36}$$

For a vehicle with $l/B = 1.5$ and $K_{di} = 2.0$, and operating over a terrain with $\mu_t/f_r = 5$, the power consumption during a steady-state turn at the minimum turning radius will be 2.875 times that when the vehicle is traveling in a straight line.

6.5.3   Planetary Gear Steering System

One of the simplest forms of planetary gear steering system for tracked vehicles is shown schematically in Fig. 6.11. The input from the engine is through bevel gearing to shaft A, which is connected, through the planetary gear train, to the sprockets of the tracks.

In the system shown, the input to the gear train is through sun gear B and the output is through arm C, which is connected to the sprocket. In a straight line motion, both clutches are engaged and the brakes are released. For steering, the clutch on the inside track is disengaged and the brake is applied to ring gear D. If the brake is fully applied to hold the ring gear fixed, the angular speed of the sprocket of the inside track is determined by

$$\omega_i = \omega_a \left(\frac{N_B}{N_B + N_D} \right) \tag{6.37}$$

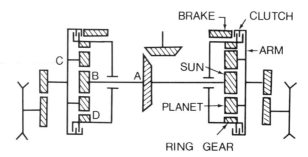

Fig. 6.11   Schematic view of a planetary gear steering system.

where ω_a is the angular speed of shaft A, and N_B and N_D are the number of teeth of the sun gear and the ring gear, respectively. Since the angular speed of the sprocket of the outside track ω_0 is the same as ω_a, the speed ratio K_s can be expressed by

$$K_s = \frac{\omega_0}{\omega_i} = \frac{N_B + N_D}{N_B} \tag{6.38}$$

It should be noted that if the engine speed is kept constant, then the forward speed of the center of gravity of the vehicle will be less during a turn than in a straight line motion. The forward speed of the vehicle V during a turn is determined by

$$V = \frac{(\omega_0 + \omega_i)r}{2} = \frac{\omega_i r(K_s + 1)}{2} \tag{6.39}$$

It should also be mentioned that when the brake is fully applied on one side, the minimum turning radius is achieved. The minimum turning radius $R_{\min}$ is expressed by

$$R_{\min} = \frac{B}{2}\left(\frac{K_s + 1}{K_s - 1}\right) = \frac{B}{2}\left(\frac{2N_B + N_D}{N_D}\right) \tag{6.40}$$

When a tracked vehicle with a planetary gear steering system is turning at the minimum turning radius, the power ratio P_t/P_{st} is expressed by

$$\frac{P_t}{P_{st}} = \frac{V}{V_{st}}\left(1 + \frac{M_r}{f_r W R_{\min}}\right)$$

$$= \frac{(K_s + 1)}{2K_s}\left(1 + \frac{M_r}{f_r W B(K_s + 1)/2(K_s - 1)}\right) \tag{6.41}$$

For a vehicle with a uniform normal pressure distribution and turning at low speeds, Eq. 6.41 can be rewritten as

$$\frac{P_t}{P_{st}} = \frac{1}{2K_s}\left[(K_s + 1) + \frac{\mu_t l(K_s - 1)}{2f_r B}\right] \tag{6.42}$$

For $K_s = 2$, $l/B = 1.5$, and $\mu_t/f_r = 5$, the power consumption during a steady-state turn at the minimum turning radius will be 1.68 times that when the vehicle is in a straight line motion.

The results of the analysis of the characteristics of various steering systems described above indicate that considerably more power is required during a turn than in a straight line motion. To reduce the power requirements during a turn using the skid-steering principle, a number of regenerative steering systems have been developed for high-speed tracked vehicles [6.10].

In a regenerative steering system, the power input to the sprocket from the inside track due to the negative thrust (or braking force) can be transferred through the system to the sprocket of the outside track, which develops a positive thrust. This helps to supply the power required by the sprocket of the outside track. The engine only has to provide the difference between the sprocket powers of the outside and inside tracks.

6.6 ARTICULATED STEERING

For vehicles consisting of two or more units, steering can be effected by rotating one unit against the other to make the vehicle follow a prescribed curved path. This kind of steering method is referred to as "steering by articulation" or "articulated steering." There are two principal configurations of articulated steering. One is usually called wagon steer, as shown in Fig. 6.12. This configuration is for vehicles having a common body frame, but with two separate chassis. Steering is effected by rotating both or one of the two tracked chassis about a vertical axis. Normally, the tracked chassis have freedom in pitch to allow good ground contact over rough surfaces. The wagon steer configuration has been adopted in some heavy tracked transporters, as shown in Fig. 6.13. Another articulated steering configuration uses an articulation joint to connect separate vehicle units, as shown

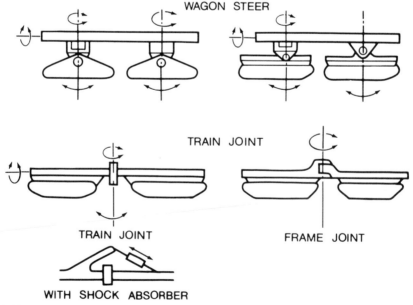

Fig. 6.12 Various configurations of articulated steering. (Reproduced with permission from reference 6.1.)

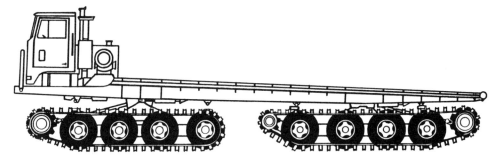

Fig. 6.13 An off-road transporter with wagon steer, Foremost Husky Eight. (Courtesy of Canadian Foremost Ltd.)

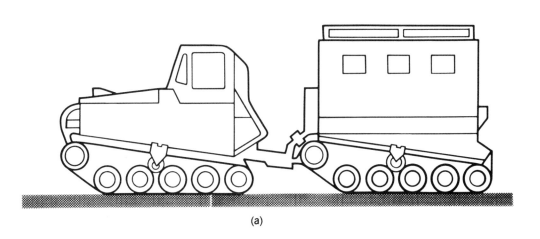

(a)

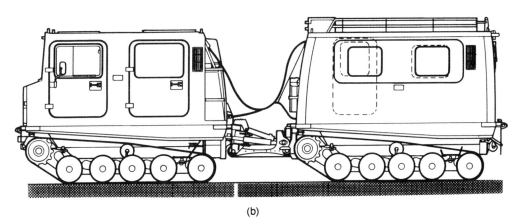

(b)

Fig. 6.14 Articulated vehicles with train joint. (a) Volvo BV 202. (Courtesy of Volvo BM AB.) (b) Hagglunds BV 206. (Courtesy of Hagglunds Vehicle AB.)

in Fig. 6.12. Steering is achieved by rotating one unit against the other. Usually, the design of the joint allows the two units to have freedom in pitch and roll within a certain range. Steering with an articulation joint has been adopted in vehicles for use over marginal terrain, as shown in Fig. 6.14. Articulated steering has also been employed in off-road wheeled vehicles, as shown in Fig. 6.15 [6.11, 6.12].

In comparison with the skid-steering method, articulated steering requires much less power to execute a turn. Furthermore, using articulated steering, the resultant forward thrust of the vehicle can be maintained during a turn, whereas a net reduction in the maximum resultant forward thrust is accompanied by skid-steering. Thus, over marginal terrain, articulated steering can provide the vehicle with better mobility than skid-steering. In addition, to satisfy the steerability criterion, the ratio of contact length to tread of a vehicle must be in a certain range when using skid-steering. For a heavy tracked transporter to meet the required ratio of contact length to tread, the vehicle will be too wide to be practical. This is the basic reason why articulated steering is widely used in heavy tracked transporters. Articulated steering also makes it possible for heavy tracked vehicles to achieve a more rational form since a long, narrow vehicle encounters less obstacle resistance and motion resistance over unprepared terrain than a short, wide vehicle with the same track contact area. Field experience has also shown that the handling quality of articulated vehicles is satisfactory, even at speeds up to 72 km/h (45 mph) in some cases [6.1].

Figure 6.16 shows the variations of the ratios of thrust to vehicle weight for the outside and inside tracks, F_0/W and F_i/W, for the identical front and rear units of an articulated tracked vehicle with the ratio of turning radius to track contact length R/l [6.13]. The drive axles of both the front and rear units of the articulated vehicle have a simple differential which results in equal thrust distribution between the outside and inside tracks. The symbols shown in the figure represent measured data obtained with a model vehicle traveling on a hard, level ground. As a com-

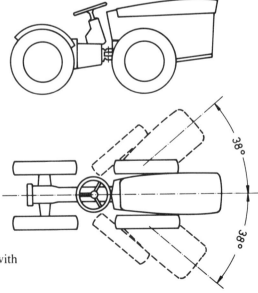

Fig. 6.15 An off-road wheeled vehicle with articulated steering.

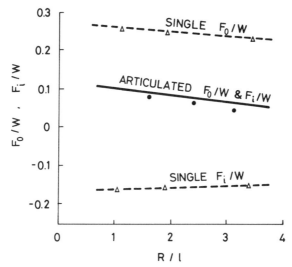

Fig. 6.16 Relationships between thrust-to-weight ratio and turning radius to track length ratio for vehicles with skid steering and articulated steering. (Reproduced with permission from reference 6.13.)

parison, the thrust-to-vehicle-weight ratios for the outside and inside tracks, F_0/W and F_i/W, of a single unit tracked vehicle with skid-steering, as a function of the ratio of turning radius to track contact length R/l, are also shown in the figure. It can be seen that a large thrust and braking force are developed on the outside and inside tracks, respectively, with skid-steering, whereas with articulated steering, the required thrust is much smaller in executing a given turn.

It should be mentioned, however, that the minimum turning radius of an articulated tracked vehicle usually is larger than that of an equivalent vehicle with skid-steering. The first cost of the articulated vehicle is usually higher than that of a similar vehicle with skid-steering, particularly for smaller size vehicles, since the articulated vehicle has at least two separate units of chassis which necessitate the replication of suspension and track systems [6.1].

REFERENCES

6.1 C.J. Nuttall, "Some Notes on the Steering of Tracked Vehicles by Articulation," *Journal of Terramechanics*, vol. 1, no. 1, 1964.

6.2 L.F. Little, "The Alecto Tracklayer," *Journal of Terramechanics*, vol. 1, no. 2, 1964.

6.3 M.G. Bekker, *Theory of Land Locomotion*. Ann Arbor, MI: University of Michigan Press, 1956.

6.4 M.K. Kar, "Prediction of Track Forces in Skid-Steering of Military Tracked Vehicles," *Journal of Terramechanics*, vol. 24, no. 1, 1987.

6.5 I. Hayashi, "Practical Analysis of Tracked Vehicle Steering Depending on Longitudinal Track Slippage," in *Proc. 5th Int. Conf. of the International Society for Terrain-Vehicle Systems*, Vol. II, Detroit–Houghton, MI, 1975.

6.6   J.E. Crosheck, "Skid-Steering of Crawlers," Society of Automotive Engineers, paper 750552, 1975.

6.7   M. Kitano and M. Kuma, "An Analysis of Horizontal Plane Motion of Tracked Vehicles," *Journal of Terramechanics*, vol. 14, no. 4, 1978.

6.8   W. Steeds, "Tracked Vehicles," *Automobile Engineer*, Apr. 1950.

6.9   I.D. Lvov, *Theory of Tractors* (in Russian).   Moscow, Russia: National Scientific and Technical Publishers, 1960.

6.10   W. Steeds, *Mechanics of Road Vehicles*.   London, England: Iliffe and Sons, 1960.

6.11   P.A. Dudzinski, "Problems of Turning Process in Articulated Terrain Vehicles," in *Proc. 7th Int. Conf. of the International Society for Terrain-Vehicle Systems*, Vol. 1, Calgary, Canada, 1981.

6.12   A. Oida, "Turning Behavior of Articulated Frame Steering Tractor, Parts 1 and 2," *Journal of Terramechanics*, vol. 20, no. 3/4, 1983 and vol. 24, no. 1, 1987.

6.13   K. Watanabe and M. Kitano, "Study on Steerability of Articulated Tracked Vehicles—Part I. Theoretical and Experimental Analysis," *Journal of Terramechanics*, vol. 23, no. 2, 1986.

PROBLEMS

6.1   A tracked vehicle with skid-steering is to be designed for operation over various types of terrain ranging from desert sand with $c = 0$ and $\phi = 35°$ to heavy clay with $c = 20.685$ kPa (3 psi) and $\phi = 6°$. The average value of the coefficient of motion resistance is 0.15, and that of the coefficient of lateral resistance is 0.5. The vehicle has a uniform contact pressure of 13.79 kPa (2 psi). Select a suitable value for the ratio of contact length to tread for the vehicle.

6.2   A tracked vehicle weighs 155.68 kN (35,000 lb) and has a contact length of 304.8 cm (120 in.) and a tread of 203.2 cm (80 in.). The vehicle has a uniform contact pressure and is equipped with a clutch/brake steering system. On a sandy terrain, the value of the coefficient of motion resistance is 0.15, and that of the coefficient of lateral resistance is 0.5. The angle of internal shearing resistance of the terrain ϕ is 30°.

a) Determine the thrusts of the outside and inside tracks required to execute a steady-state turn.

b) If, during the turn, the sprocket of the outside track, with a radius of 0.305 m (1 ft), is rotating at 10 rad/s, and the inside track is disconnected from the driveline by declutching and the brake is applied, determine the turning radius and yaw velocity of the vehicle during the turn. The slip of the running gear during the turn may be neglected in the calculations.

6.3   Referring to Problem 6.2, estimate the maximum drawbar pull that the tracked vehicle could develop during a steady-state turn. Also calculate the ratio of the maximum drawbar pull available during a steady-state turn to that in a straight line motion under the conditions specified.

6.4 A tracked vehicle is equipped with a controlled differential steering system having a gear ratio of 3:1. The vehicle weighs 155.68 kN (35,000 lb), and has a tread of 203.2 cm (80 in.) and a contact length of 304.8 cm (120 in.). The contact pressure of the track is assumed to be uniform. On a particular terrain, the value of the coefficient of motion resistance is 0.15, and that of the coefficient of lateral resistance is 0.5. Determine the minimum turning radius of the vehicle. Also calculate the power required to maintain a steady-state turn at the minimum turning radius when the speed of the center of gravity of the vehicle is 10 km/h (6.2 mph).

CHAPTER 7

VEHICLE RIDE CHARACTERISTICS

Ride quality is concerned with the sensation or feel of the passenger in the environment of a moving vehicle. Ride comfort problems mainly arise from vibrations of the vehicle body, which may be induced by a variety of sources, including surface irregularities, aerodynamic forces, vibrations of the engine and driveline, and nonuniformities (imbalances) of the tire/wheel assembly. Usually, surface irregularities, ranging from potholes to random variations of the surface elevation profile, act as a major source that excites the vibration of the vehicle body through the tire/wheel assembly and the suspension system. Excitations by aerodynamic forces are applied directly to the vehicle body, while those due to engine and driveline vibrations are transmitted through engine/transmission mounts. Excitations resulting from mass imbalances and dimensional and stiffness variations of the tire/wheel assembly are transmitted to the vehicle body through the suspension.

The objective of the study of vehicle ride is to provide guiding principles for the control of the vibration of the vehicle so that the passenger's sensation of discomfort does not exceed a certain level. To achieve this objective, it is essential to have a basic understanding of the human response to vibration, the vibrational behavior of the vehicle, and the characteristics of surface irregularities.

7.1 HUMAN RESPONSE TO VIBRATION

In general, passenger ride comfort (or discomfort) boundaries are difficult to determine because of the variations in individual sensitivity to vibration and of a lack of a generally accepted method of approach to the assessment of human response to vibration. Considerable research has, however, been conducted by a number of investigators in an attempt to define ride comfort limits. A variety of methods for

348

assessing human tolerance to vibration have been developed over the years [7.1, 7.2]. They include the following.

1. *Subjective Ride Measurements.* The traditional technique for comparing vehicle ride quality in the automotive industry in the past is to compare vehicles driven over a given road section with a trained ride jury. With a large enough jury and a well-designed evaluation scheme, this method could provide a meaningful comparison of the ride quality of different vehicles. The degree of difference in ride quality, however, cannot be quantitatively determined by this type of subjective evaluation.

2. *Shake Table Tests.* In an attempt to quantitatively study human response to vibration, a large number of shake table experiments have been performed over the years. Most of this research pertains to human response to sinusoidal excitation. It is intended to identify zones of comfort (or discomfort) for humans in terms of vibration amplitude, velocity, or acceleration in a given direction (such as foot-to-head, side-to-side, or back-to-chest) over a specific frequency range.

3. *Ride Simulator Tests.* In these tests, ride simulators are used to replicate the vibration of the vehicle traveling over different road surfaces. In some facilities, an actual vehicle body is mounted on hydraulic actuators, which reproduce vehicle motions in pitch, roll, and bounce (or heave). Road inputs are fed into the actuators. Using the simulator, it is possible to establish a human subjective tolerance limit in terms of vibration parameters.

4. *Ride Measurements in Vehicles.* Shake table tests and ride simulator tests described above are conducted under laboratory conditions. They do not necessarily provide the same vibration environments to which the passenger is subject while driving on the road. Therefore, on-the-road ride measurements, particularly for passenger cars, have been performed. This test method attempts to correlate the response of test subjects in qualitative terms, such as "unpleasant" or "intolerable," with vibration parameters measured at the location where the test subject is situated under actual driving conditions.

The assessment of human response to vibration is complex in that the results are influenced by the variations in individual sensitivity, and by the test methods and sensation levels used by different investigators. Over the years, numerous ride comfort criteria have been proposed. Figure 7.1 shows one of such criteria for vertical vibration described in the *Ride and Vibration Data Manual J6a* of the Society of Automotive Engineers [7.3]. The recommended limits shown in the figure are also referred to as Janeway's comfort criterion. It defines the acceptable amplitude of vibration as a function of frequency. It can be seen that as the frequency increases, the allowable amplitude decreases considerably. The Janeway comfort criterion consists of three simple relationships, each of which covers a certain frequency range, as shown in Fig. 7.1. In the frequency range 1–6 Hz, the

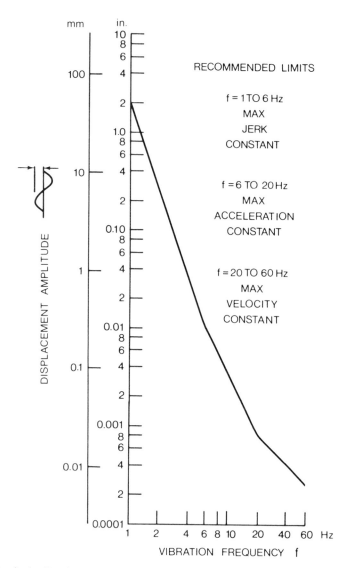

Fig. 7.1 Vertical vibration limits for passenger comfort proposed by Janeway. (Reproduced with permission of the Society of Automotive Engineers from reference 7.3.)

peak value of jerk, which is the product of the amplitude and the cube of the circular frequency, should not exceed 12.6 m/s^3 (496 in./s^3). For instance, at 1 Hz (2π rad/s), the recommended limit for amplitude is 12.6 m $\cdot$ s^{-3}/(2π s^{-1})^3 = 0.0508 m (2 in.). In the frequency range 6–20 Hz, the peak value of acceleration, which is the product of the amplitude and the square of the circular frequency, should be less than 0.33 m/s^2 (13 in./s^2), whereas in the range 20–60 Hz, the peak value of velocity, which is the product of the amplitude and the circular frequency, should not exceed 2.7 mm/s (0.105 in./s). It should be noted that Janeway's comfort criterion is based on data for vertical sinusoidal vibration of a single frequency. When two or more components of different frequencies are present, there is no established basis on which to evaluate the resultant effect. It is probable, however, that the component, which taken alone represents the highest sensation level, will govern the sensation as a whole. Furthermore, all of the data used to establish the ride comfort boundaries were obtained with test subjects standing or sitting on a hard seat.

Recently, a general guide for defining human tolerance to whole-body vibration has been developed and adopted as the International Standard ISO 2631 [7.4, 7.5]. This guide is recommended for the evaluation of vibrational environments in transport vehicles as well as in industry, and it defines three distinct limits for whole-body vibration in the frequency range 1–80 Hz:

1. Exposure limits, which are related to the preservation of safety (or health), and should not be exceeded· without special justification.
2. Fatigue or decreased proficiency boundaries, which are related to the preservation of working efficiency, and which apply to such tasks as driving a road vehicle or a tractor.
3. Reduced comfort boundaries, which are concerned with the preservation of comfort, and which in transport vehicles are related to such functions as reading, writing, and eating in a vehicle.

Figure 7.2(a) shows the fatigue or decreased proficiency boundaries for vertical vibration (foot-to-head or along the z axis in Fig. 7.3), which are defined in terms of root-mean-square values (rms) of acceleration as a function of frequency for various exposure times. It can be seen that as the average daily exposure time increases, the boundary lowers. The fatigue or decreased proficiency boundaries for lateral vibration (side-to-side or along the y axis, and back-to-chest or along the x axis in Fig. 7.3) are shown in Fig. 7.2(b). When vibration takes place in more than one direction simultaneously, corresponding boundaries apply to each vectorial component in the three axes. The exposure limits for safety (or health) reasons are obtained by raising the fatigue or decreased proficiency boundaries shown in Fig. 7.2(a) and (b) by a factor of two (6 dB higher), whereas the reduced comfort boundaries are obtained by lowering the boundaries shown in Fig. 7.2(a) and (b) by a factor of 3.15 (10 dB lower).

It should be pointed out that vibrations in the frequency range below 1 Hz are a special problem, associated with symptoms such as motion sickness, which are of a character different from the effects of higher frequency vibrations. A severe discomfort boundary and a reduced comfort boundary for various exposure times in the frequency range of 0.1–1 Hz have been recommended by the International Organization for Standardization (ISO).

The "absorbed power," which is the product of vibration force and velocity transmitted to the human body, has also been proposed as a parameter of significance in evaluating human response to vibration [7.2]. It is a measure of the rate at which vibrational energy is absorbed by a human, and it has been used to define

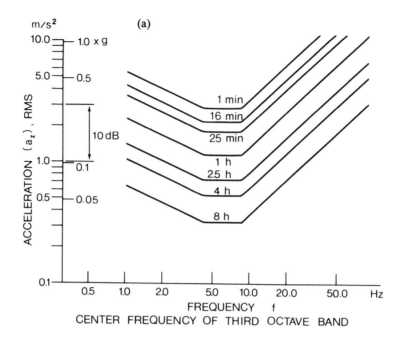

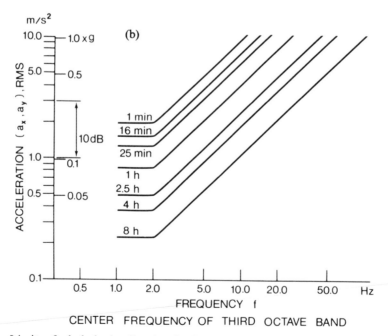

Fig. 7.2 Limits of whole-body vibration for fatigue or decreased proficiency in (a) vertical direction and (b) transverse direction, recommended by the ISO.

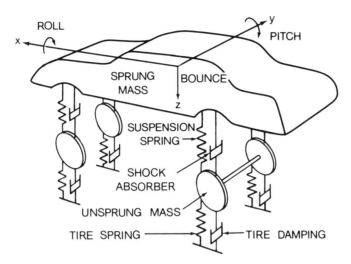

Fig. 7.3   A seven-degree-of-freedom ride model for a passenger car.

human tolerance to vibration for military vehicles negotiating rough terrain [7.2, 7.6]. The concept of "absorbed power" has been adopted by the U.S. Army AMM-75 Ground Mobility Model and subsequently by the NATO Reference Mobility Model for evaluating the ride quality of military vehicles. Presently, the tolerance limit is taken as 6 W absorbed power at the driver's position, and the ride-limiting speed is that speed at which the driver's average absorbed power over the total elapsed time reaches a sustained level of 6 W.

It should be reiterated that most of the data used in establishing the ride comfort criteria described above were obtained using sinusoidal inputs, whereas the actual vehicle vibration is usually of a random nature. Hence, the ride comfort criteria thus far proposed may require revision as new data become available.

Having defined a specific ride comfort criterion, the designer should then select an appropriate suspension system to ensure that the level of vehicle vibration is below the specified limits when operating over a particular range of environments.

7.2   VEHICLE RIDE MODELS

To study the ride quality of ground vehicles, various ride models have been developed. For a passenger car with independent front suspensions, a seven-degree-of-freedom model, as shown in Fig. 7.3, may be used. In this model, the pitch, bounce, and roll of the vehicle body, as well as the bounce of the two front wheels, and the bounce and roll (tramp) of the solid rear axle are taken into consideration. The mass of the vehicle body is usually referred to as the "sprung mass," whereas the mass of the running gear together with the associated components is referred to as the "unsprung mass." For a cross-country military vehicle shown in Fig. 7.4, a fifteen-degree-of-freedom model may be used, which includes the pitch, bounce, and roll of the vehicle body and the bounce of each roadwheel.

To study the vibrational characteristics of the vehicle, equations of motion based on Newton's second law for each mass have to be formulated. Natural frequencies and amplitude ratios can be determined by considering the principal modes (normal modes) of vibration (or the free vibration) of the system. When the excitation of the system is known, the response can, in principle, be determined by solving the equations of motion. However, as the degrees of freedom of the system increase, the analysis becomes increasingly complex. Digital computer simulations are usually employed.

A vehicle represents a complex vibration system with many degrees of freedom. It is possible, however, to simplify the system by considering only some of the major motions of the vehicle. For instance, to obtain a qualitative insight into the functions of the suspension, particularly the effects of the sprung and unsprung mass, spring stiffness, and damping on vehicle vibrations, a linear model with two degrees of freedom, as shown in Figs. 7.5 and 7.6, may be used. On the other hand, to reach a better understanding of the pitch and bounce vibration of the vehicle body, a two-degree-of-freedom model, as shown in Fig. 7.7, may be employed.

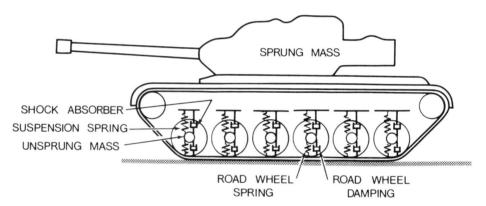

Fig. 7.4 A ride model for a military tracked vehicle.

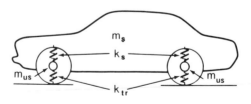

$$m_s \;=\; 1814 \text{ kg,} \quad 4000 \text{ lb}$$
$$m_{us} \;=\; 181 \text{ kg,} \quad 400 \text{ lb, COMBINED}$$
$$k_s \;=\; 88 \text{ kN/m,} \quad 500 \text{ lb/in., COMBINED}$$
$$k_{tr} \;=\; 704 \text{ kN/m,} \quad 4000 \text{ lb/in., COMBINED}$$

Fig. 7.5 A two-degree-of-freedom ride model for the sprung and unsprung mass.

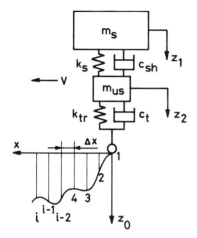

Fig. 7.6 A quarter-car model.

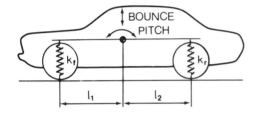

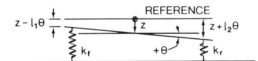

Fig. 7.7 A two-degree-of-freedom ride model for bounce and pitch of the sprung mass.

7.2.1 Two-Degree-of-Freedom Vehicle Model for Sprung and Unsprung Mass

The two-degree-of-freedom model shown in Figs. 7.5 and 7.6 includes an unsprung mass representing the wheels and associated components and a sprung mass representing the vehicle body. Their motions in the vertical direction can be described by two coordinates, z_1 and z_2 (Fig. 7.6), with origins at the static equilibrium positions of the sprung and unsprung mass, respectively. This model can be used to represent a quarter of a car. As a result, it is often referred to as the "quarter-car" model. By applying Newton's second law to the sprung and unsprung mass separately, the equations of motion of the system can be obtained.

For vibrations excited by surface undulation, the equations of motion are as follows:

for the sprung mass,

$$m_s \ddot{z}_1 + c_{sh}(\dot{z}_1 - \dot{z}_2) + k_s(z_1 - z_2) = 0 \qquad (7.1)$$

and for the unsprung mass,

$$m_{us}\ddot{z}_2 + c_{sh}(\dot{z}_2 - \dot{z}_1) + k_s(z_2 - z_1) + c_t\dot{z}_2 + k_{tr}z_2 = F(t) = c_t\dot{z}_0 + k_{tr}z_0 \quad (7.2)$$

where m_s is the sprung mass, m_{us} is the unsprung mass, c_{sh} is the damping coefficient of the shock absorber, c_t is the damping coefficient of the tire, k_s is the stiffness of the suspension spring, k_{tr} is the equivalent spring stiffness of the tire, and $F(t)$ is the excitation acting on the wheels and induced by surface irregularities. If z_0 is the elevation of the surface profile and $\dot{z}_0$ represents the vertical velocity of the tire at the ground contact point, which is the slope of the profile multiplied by the forward speed of the vehicle, then the excitation due to surface undulation may be expressed by $c_t\dot{z}_0 + k_{tr}z_0$, as shown in Eq. 7.2. Excitations due to aerodynamic forces and to vibrations of the engine and driveline are applied to the sprung mass, while those due to nonuniformities of the tire/wheel assembly are applied to the unsprung mass. If the excitation of the system is known, then, in principle, the resulting vibrations of the sprung and unsprung mass can be determined by solving Eqs. 7.1 and 7.2.

To determine the natural frequencies of the two-degree-of-freedom system shown in Fig. 7.6, the free vibration of the system is considered (or the principal modes of vibration are considered). The equations of motion for free vibration are obtained by setting the right-hand sides of both Eqs. 7.1 and 7.2 to zero.

For an undamped system, from Eqs. 7.1 and 7.2, the equations of motion for free vibration are as follows:

$$m_s\ddot{z}_1 + k_sz_1 - k_sz_2 = 0 \quad (7.3)$$

$$m_{us}\ddot{z}_2 + k_sz_2 - k_sz_1 + k_{tr}z_2 = 0 \quad (7.4)$$

The solutions to the above differential equations can be assumed to be in the following form:

$$z_1 = Z_1 \cos \omega_n t \quad (7.5)$$

$$z_2 = Z_2 \cos \omega_n t \quad (7.6)$$

where ω_n is the undamped circular natural frequency and Z_1 and Z_2 are the amplitudes of the sprung and unsprung mass, respectively.

Substituting the assumed solutions into Eqs. 7.3 and 7.4, one obtains the following amplitude equations:

$$(-m_s\omega_n^2 + k_s)Z_1 - k_sZ_2 = 0 \quad (7.7)$$

$$-k_sZ_1 + (-m_{us}\omega_n^2 + k_s + k_{tr})Z_2 = 0 \quad (7.8)$$

These equations are satisfied for any Z_1 and Z_2 if the following determinant is zero:

$$\begin{vmatrix} (-m_s\omega_n^2 + k_s) & -k_s \\ -k_s & (-m_{us}\omega_n^2 + k_s + k_{tr}) \end{vmatrix} = 0 \qquad (7.9)$$

Expanding the determinant leads to the characteristic equation of the system:

$$\omega_n^4(m_s m_{us}) + \omega_n^2(-m_s k_s - m_s k_{tr} - m_{us} k_s) + k_s k_{tr} = 0 \qquad (7.10)$$

The solution of the characteristic equation yields two natural frequencies of the system, ω_{n1}^2 and ω_{n2}^2:

$$\omega_{n_1}^2 = \frac{B_1 - \sqrt{B_1^2 - 4A_1 C_1}}{2A_1} \qquad (7.11)$$

$$\omega_{n_2}^2 = \frac{B_1 + \sqrt{B_1^2 - 4A_1 C_1}}{2A_1} \qquad (7.12)$$

where

$$A_1 = m_s m_{us},$$

$$B_1 = m_s k_s + m_s k_{tr} + m_{us} k_s,$$

$$C_1 = k_s k_{tr}.$$

Although each of these leads to frequencies $\pm\omega_{n1}$ and $\pm\omega_{n2}$, the negative values are discarded as being of no physical significance. The corresponding natural frequencies in Hz (cycles/s) are expressed by

$$f_{n1} = \frac{1}{2\pi}\omega_{n1} \qquad (7.13)$$

$$f_{n2} = \frac{1}{2\pi}\omega_{n2} \qquad (7.14)$$

For a typical passenger car, the sprung mass m_s is an order of magnitude higher than the unsprung mass m_{us}, while the stiffness of the suspension spring k_s is an order of magnitude lower than the equivalent spring stiffness of the tire k_{tr}, as shown in Fig. 7.5. In view of this, an approximate method may be used to determine the two natural frequencies of the system. The approximate values of the natural frequencies in Hz of the sprung and unsprung mass, f_{n-s} and f_{n-us}, can be expressed by

$$f_{n-s} = \frac{1}{2\pi}\sqrt{\frac{k_s k_{tr}/(k_s + k_{tr})}{m_s}} \qquad (7.15)$$

$$f_{n-us} = \frac{1}{2\pi}\sqrt{\frac{k_s + k_{tr}}{m_{us}}} \tag{7.16}$$

With the values of m_s, m_{us}, k_s, and k_{tr} shown in Fig. 7.5, the two natural frequencies calculated using Eqs. 7.13 and 7.14 are 1.04 and 10.5 Hz, respectively, which are found to be practically identical to those obtained using Eqs. 7.15 and 7.16. It is noted that the natural frequency of the unsprung mass is an order of magnitude higher than that of the sprung mass. It should also be mentioned that for passenger cars, the damping ratio provided by shock absorbers is usually in the range of 0.2–0.4, and that the damping of the tire is relatively insignificant. Consequently, there is little difference between the undamped and damped natural frequencies, and undamped natural frequencies are commonly used to characterize the system.

The wide separation of the natural frequencies of the sprung and unsprung mass has a significant implication on the vibration isolation characteristics of the suspension system. For instance, if the wheel hits a bump, the impulse will set the wheel into oscillation. When the wheel passes over the bump, the unsprung mass will be in free oscillation at its own natural frequency f_{n-us}. For the sprung mass, however, the excitation will be the vibration of the unsprung mass. The ratio of the frequency of excitation to the natural frequency of the sprung mass is therefore equal to f_{n-us}/f_{n-s}. Since the value of f_{n-us} is an order of magnitude higher than that of f_{n-s}, the amplitude of oscillation of the sprung mass will be very small. As can be seen from Fig. 7.8 when the ratio of the frequency of excitation to the natural frequency of the system is high, the transmissibility ratio, which is the ratio of output to input of a vibrating system, is very low. Thus, excellent vibration isolation for the sprung mass (i.e., vehicle body) is achieved in this case.

When the vehicle travels over an undulating surface, the excitation will normally consist of a wide range of frequencies. As can be seen from Fig. 7.8, high-frequency inputs can be effectively isolated through the suspension because the natural frequency of the sprung mass is low. Low-frequency excitations can, however, be transmitted to the vehicle body unimpeded, or even amplified, as the transmissibility ratio is high when the frequency of excitation is close to the natural frequency of the sprung mass.

If the road profile is sinusoidal, then the responses of the sprung and unsprung mass can be determined using the classical methods in vibration analysis. For the two-degree-of-freedom system shown in Fig. 7.6, with the damping of the tire neglected, the ratio of the vibration amplitude of the sprung mass Z_1 to that of the surface profile Z_0 is expressed by

$$\frac{Z_1}{Z_0} = \frac{\sqrt{A_2}}{\sqrt{B_2 + C_2}} \tag{7.17}$$

where

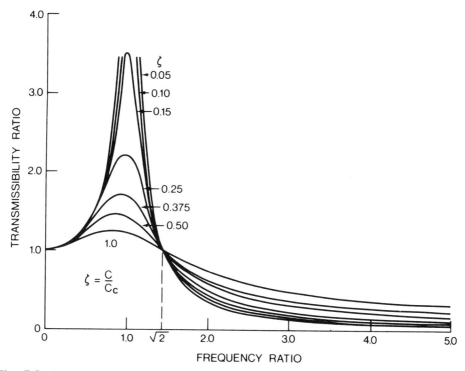

Fig. 7.8 Transmissibility ratio as a function of frequency ratio for a single-degree-of-freedom system.

$$A_2 = (k_s k_{tr})^2 + (c_{sh} k_{tr} \omega)^2,$$

$$B_2 = [(k_s - m_s \omega^2)(k_{tr} - m_{us} \omega^2) - m_s k_s \omega^2]^2,$$

$$C_2 = (c_{sh} \omega)^2 [m_s \omega^2 + m_{us} \omega^2 - k_{tr}]^2.$$

The ratio of the vibration amplitude of the unsprung mass Z_2 to that of the surface profile Z_0 is given by

$$\frac{Z_2}{Z_0} = \frac{\sqrt{A_3}}{\sqrt{B_2 + C_2}} \tag{7.18}$$

where $A_3 = [k_{tr}(k_s - m_s \omega^2)]^2 + (c_{sh} k_{tr} \omega)^2$.

In the equations above, ω is the circular frequency of excitation, which is equal to $2\pi V / l_w$, where V is the vehicle speed and l_w is the wavelength of the road profile.

If the damping of the shock absorber is neglected (i.e., $c_{sh} = 0$), then the expressions for the responses of the sprung and unsprung mass to the excitation of sinusoidal road profile are simplified, and the following relations are obtained:

$$\frac{Z_1}{Z_0} = \frac{k_s k_{tr}}{(k_s - m_s\omega^2)(k_{tr} - m_{us}\omega^2) - m_s k_s\omega^2}$$

$$= \frac{k_s k_{tr}}{m_s m_{us}(\omega_{n1}^2 - \omega^2)(\omega_{n2}^2 - \omega^2)} \tag{7.19}$$

$$\frac{Z_2}{Z_0} = \frac{k_{tr}(k_s - m_s\omega^2)}{m_s m_{us}(\omega_{n1}^2 - \omega^2)(\omega_{n2}^2 - \omega^2)} \tag{7.20}$$

where ω_{n1} and ω_{n2} are the undamped circular natural frequencies of the system.

It is noted that when the frequency of excitation ω coincides with one of the natural frequencies, resonance results. The resonance of the unsprung mass (tire/wheel assembly) is usually referred to as ''wheel hop'' resonance.

In the evaluation of the overall performance of a suspension system, the following three aspects should be considered.

1. *Vibration Isolation.* This can be evaluated by the response of the sprung mass (output) to the excitation from the ground (input). Usually, the transmissibility ratio (or transfer function) can be used as a basis for assessing the vibration isolation characteristics of a linear suspension system.

   Figure 7.9 shows the effect of the ratio of the unsprung mass to the sprung mass m_{us}/m_s on the transmissibility ratio of a two-degree-of-freedom

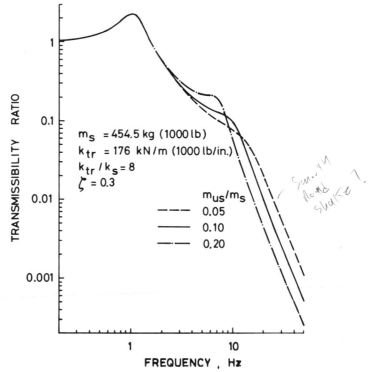

Fig. 7.9 Transmissibility ratio as a function of frequency for the sprung mass of a quarter-car model with different ratios of unsprung to sprung mass.

system with $m_s = 454.5$ kg (1000 lb), $k_{tr} = 176$ kN/m (1000 lb/in.), $k_{tr}/k_s = 8$, and damping ratio $\zeta = 0.3$. It can be seen that in the frequency range below the natural frequency of the sprung mass (around 1 Hz), the mass of the unsprung parts has very little effect on the vibration of the sprung mass. When the frequency of excitation is close to the natural frequency of the unsprung mass (around 10 Hz), the lighter the unsprung mass, the lower the transmissibility ratio will be, which implies that with the same level of excitation, the vibration of the sprung mass is lower with a lighter unsprung mass. However, in the frequency range above the natural frequency of the unsprung mass, a lighter unsprung mass will lead to a slightly higher transmissibility ratio.

Based on the results presented above, it can be said that while the unsprung mass has little influence on the vibration of the sprung mass in the low-frequency range, a lighter unsprung mass does provide better vibration isolation in the midfrequency range. There is a slight penalty, however, in the frequency range higher than the natural frequency of the unsprung mass.

Figure 7.10 shows the effect of the ratio of the equivalent tire stiffness k_{tr} to the suspension spring stiffness k_s on the transmissibility ratio of the system. For a given tire stiffness, a higher ratio of k_{tr}/k_s indicates a lower suspension spring stiffness. It can be seen that in the frequency range below the natural frequency of the sprung mass, the lower the ratio of k_{tr}/k_s, the

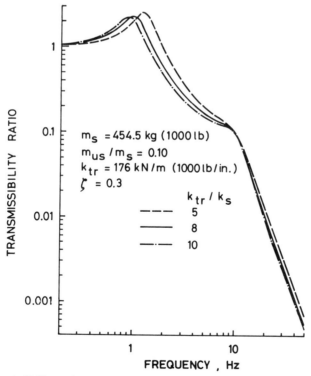

Fig. 7.10 Transmissibility ratio as a function of frequency for the sprung mass of a quarter-car model with different ratios of tire stiffness to suspension spring stiffness.

lower the transmissibility ratio will be. In the frequency range between the natural frequency of the sprung mass and that of the unsprung mass, a softer suspension spring (or higher k_{tr}/k_s ratio) provides better vibration isolation. In the frequency range above the natural frequency of the unsprung mass, the suspension spring stiffness has a relatively insignificant effect on the vibration of the sprung mass, and the transmissibility ratio is more or less independent of the ratio k_{tr}/k_s.

Based on the results presented above, it can be seen that a softer suspension spring provides better vibration isolation in the mid- to high-frequency range, although there is some penalty in the frequency range below the natural frequency of the sprung mass.

Figure 7.11 shows the effect of the damping ratio ζ on the transmissibility ratio of the system. It can be seen that in the frequency range close to the natural frequency of the sprung mass, the higher the damping ratio, the lower the transmissibility ratio will be. In the frequency range between the natural frequency of the sprung mass and that of the unsprung mass, the lower the damping ratio, the lower the transmissibility ratio will be. At a frequency close to the natural frequency of the unsprung mass, the damping ratio has little effect on the response of the sprung mass. However, in the frequency range above the natural frequency of the unsprung mass, the lower the damping ratio, the lower the transmissibility ratio will be.

Based on the results described above, it can be seen that to provide good

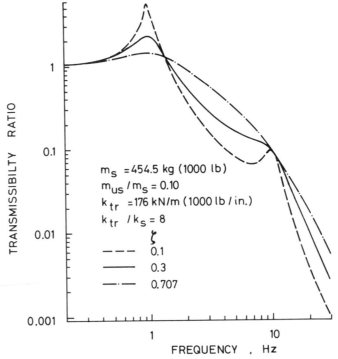

Fig. 7.11 Transmissibility ratio as a function of frequency for the sprung mass of a quarter-car model with different damping ratios.

vibration isolation in the frequency range close to the natural frequency of the sprung mass, a high damping ratio is required. However, in the mid- to high-frequency range, a lower damping ratio is preferred.

2. *Suspension Travel.* This is measured by the deflection of the suspension spring or by the relative displacement between the sprung and unsprung mass $(z_2 - z_1)$. It defines the space required to accommodate the suspension spring movement between bump and rebound stops, commonly known as the "rattle space."

Figure 7.12 shows the effect of the ratio of the unsprung mass to the sprung mass m_{us}/m_s on the suspension travel ratio of the system, which is defined as the ratio of the maximum relative displacement between the sprung and unsprung mass $(z_2 - z_1)_{max}$ to the amplitude of the sinusoidal road profile Z_0. It can be seen that for a given amplitude of the surface profile Z_0, in the frequency range below the natural frequency of the sprung mass, the mass ratio m_{us}/m_s has little effect on suspension travel. In the frequency range between the natural frequency of the sprung mass and that of the unsprung mass, the increase in the mass ratio causes an increase in suspension travel. However, in the frequency range above the natural frequency of the unsprung mass, the higher the mass ratio, the lower the suspension travel will be.

Based on the results shown above, it can be said that while the unsprung

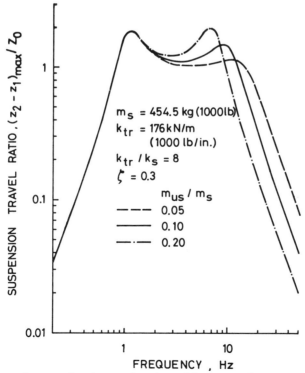

Fig. 7.12 Suspension travel ratio as a function of frequency for a quarter-car model with different ratios of unsprung to sprung mass.

mass has little effect on suspension travel in the low-frequency range, a lighter unsprung mass does reduce suspension travel in the midfrequency range. There is some penalty, however, in the frequency range above the natural frequency of the unsprung mass.

Figure 7.13 shows the effect of the ratio of the equivalent tire stiffness k_{tr} to the suspension spring stiffness k_s on the suspension travel ratio. It can be seen that in the frequency range below the natural frequency of the sprung mass, a softer suspension spring leads to higher suspension travel. In the frequency range above the natural frequency of the unsprung mass, the suspension spring stiffness has little effect on suspension travel. In the midfrequency range between the natural frequency of the sprung mass and that of the unsprung mass, the suspension travel is initially lower with a softer suspension spring, and then higher at a frequency approaching the natural frequency of the unsprung mass. The frequency at which this changeover takes place is called the "crossover" frequency, and is approximately 3 Hz for the system examined.

Based on the results shown above, it can be said that in the low-frequency range, a softer suspension spring often leads to higher suspension travel. In the high-frequency range, the suspension spring stiffness has little effect on suspension travel. In the midfrequency range from the natural frequency of the sprung mass to the "crossover" frequency (i.e., from 1 to 3 Hz for the

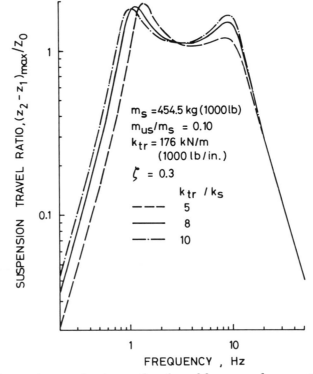

Fig. 7.13 Suspension travel ratio as a function of frequency for a quarter-car model with different ratios of tire stiffness to suspension spring stiffness.

system examined), a softer suspension spring leads to lower suspension travel. In the frequency range from the "crossover" frequency to the natural frequency of the unsprung mass, a softer suspension spring, however, leads to higher suspension travel.

Figure 7.14 shows the effect of the damping ratio ζ on the suspension travel ratio. It is interesting to note that over the entire frequency range from below the natural frequency of the sprung mass to above the natural frequency of the unsprung mass, the higher the damping ratio, the lower the suspension travel will be. This indicates that to reduce the suspension travel, a higher damping ratio is required.

3. *Road Holding.* When the vehicle system vibrates, the normal force acting between the tire and the road fluctuates. Since the cornering force, tractive effort, and braking effort developed by the tire are related to the normal load on the tire, the vibration of the tire affects the road-holding capability and influences the handling and performance of the vehicle. The normal force between the tire and the road during vibration can be represented by the dynamic tire deflection or by the displacement of the unsprung mass relative to the road surface.

Figure 7.15 shows the effect of the ratio of the unsprung mass to the sprung mass m_{us}/m_s on the dynamic tire deflection ratio, which is the ratio of the maximum relative displacement between the unsprung mass and the road surface $(z_0 - z_2)_{max}$ to the amplitude of the sinusoidal road profile Z_0.

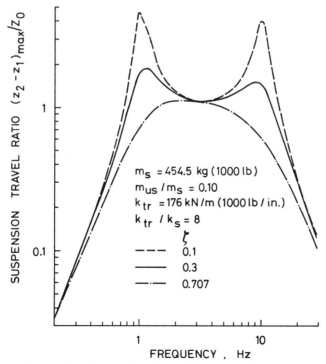

Fig. 7.14 Suspension travel ratio as a function of frequency for a quarter-car model with different damping ratios.

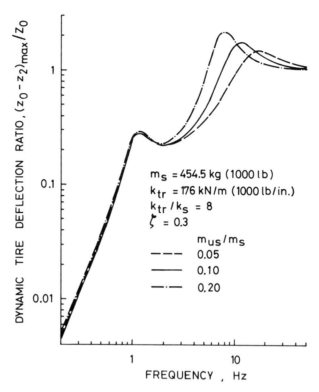

Fig. 7.15 Dynamic tire deflection ratio as a function of frequency for a quarter-car model with different ratios of unsprung to sprung mass.

It can be seen that in the frequency range below the natural frequency of the sprung mass, the mass ratio m_{us}/m_s has little effect on the dynamic tire deflection (or road holding). In the midfrequency range between the natural frequency of the sprung mass and that of the unsprung mass, a lighter unsprung mass leads to lower dynamic tire deflection. In the frequency range above the natural frequency of the unsprung mass, the unsprung mass has a relatively insignificant effect on the dynamic tire deflection. It should be noted that if, during vibration, the relative displacement between the unsprung mass and the road surface is such that it allows the static tire deflection (i.e., the deflection of the tire under static load) to fully recover, the normal force between the tire and the road will be reduced to zero or the tire is at the verge of bouncing off the ground. This is an undesirable situation, as the tire is losing contact with the ground and the road-holding capability of the vehicle is adversely affected. For the system shown in Fig. 7.15, with a sprung mass of 454.4 kg (1000 lb) and a mass ratio $m_{us}/m_s = 0.2$, the static tire deflection is approximately 3 cm (5.345 kN/176 kN/m) or 1.2 in. If the vehicle travels over a sinusoidal road profile at an appropriate speed which generates a frequency of excitation close to the unsprung mass natural frequency (i.e., $f = V/l_w = f_{n-us} = 8$ Hz, where V is the vehicle speed and l_w is the wavelength of the road profile), then from Fig. 7.15, the ratio of the maximum dynamic tire deflection to the amplitude of the road profile is approximately 2. It indicates that if the amplitude of the road profile is 1.5 cm (0.6 in.), the maximum dynamic tire deflection will be 3 cm (1.2 in.). Since the static tire deflection is 3 cm (1.2 in.), this implies that under these circumstances, the tire will lose contact with the ground during part of the vibration cycle.

Figure 7.16 shows the effect of the ratio of the equivalent tire stiffness k_{tr} to the suspension spring stiffness k_s on the dynamic tire deflection ratio. It can be seen that in the low- and high-frequency ranges, the suspension spring stiffness has a relatively insignificant influence on the dynamic tire deflection. In the midfrequency range between the natural frequency of the sprung mass and the "crossover" frequency (i.e., from 1 to 6 Hz for the system shown), a softer suspension spring leads to lower dynamic tire deflection. However, in the frequency range close to the natural frequency of the unsprung mass, a stiffer suspension spring leads to lower dynamic tire deflection, and hence better road-holding capability.

Based on the results described above, it can be seen that a softer suspension spring will generally provide better overall vibration isolation. However, to achieve better road-holding capability at a frequency of excitation close to the natural frequency of the unsprung mass, a stiffer suspension spring is preferred. This is the reason why the suspension spring for performance cars is usually stiffer than that for ordinary passenger cars. Conse-

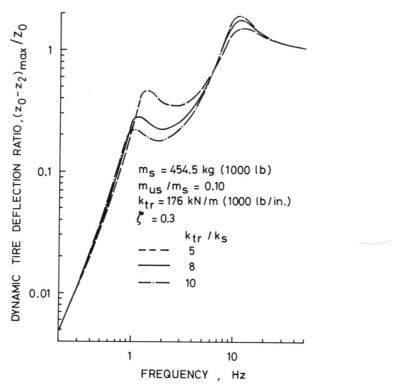

Fig. 7.16 Dynamic tire deflection ratio as a function of frequency for a quarter-car model with different ratios of tire stiffness to suspension spring stiffness.

quently, the natural frequency of the sprung mass for performance cars (up to 2 or 2.5 Hz) is higher than that for ordinary passenger cars (usually in the range from 1 to 1.5 Hz).

Figure 7.17 shows the effect of the damping ratio on the dynamic tire deflection ratio. It can be seen that in the frequency range below the natural frequency of the sprung mass or close to the natural frequency of the unsprung mass, to maintain good road-holding capability, higher damping is required. However, in the midfrequency range between the natural frequency of the sprung mass and that of the unsprung mass, lower damping is preferred.

7.2.2 Numerical Methods for Determining the Response of a Quarter-Car Model to Irregular Surface Profile Excitation

In practice, road profile is usually irregular and is seldom sinusoidal. To determine the response of the two-degree-of-freedom system shown in Fig. 7.6 to the excitation of irregular surface profiles, numerical methods are used.

As noted previously, in Fig. 7.6, z_0 describes the elevation of the surface profile, and $\dot{z}_0$ represents the vertical velocity of the tire at the ground contact point, and is expressed by

$$\dot{z}_0 = V \frac{dz_0}{dx} \qquad (7.21)$$

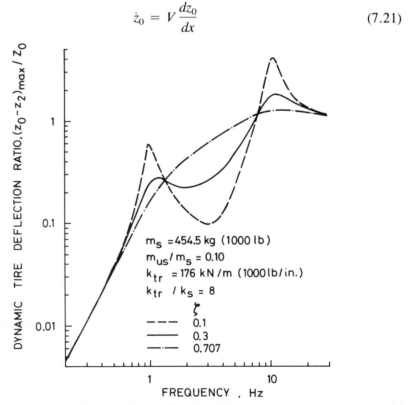

Fig. 7.17 Dynamic tire deflection ratio as a function of frequency for a quarter-car model with different damping ratios.

where V is the forward speed of the vehicle and dz_0/dx is the slope of the surface profile.

When the vehicle is traveling at a constant speed, both z_0 and $\dot{z}_0$ can be considered as functions of time, and are known for a given road profile. The responses of the sprung and unsprung mass, z_1, $\dot{z}_1$, $\ddot{z}_1$, z_2, $\dot{z}_2$, and $\ddot{z}_2$, at different locations (or stations, as shown in Fig. 7.6) can be obtained using the following numerical procedure based on the Taylor series [7.7].

If, at the initial point (station 1 shown in Fig. 7.6), $(z_0)_1$ and $(\dot{z}_0)_1$ are zero, then $(z_1)_1 = (\dot{z}_1)_1 = (\ddot{z}_1)_1 = (z_2)_1 = (\dot{z}_2)_1 = (\ddot{z}_2)_1 = 0$ (the subscript outside the parentheses indicates the station number).

At station 2,

$$(z_1)_2 = (\dot{z}_1)_2 \Delta t/3 = (\ddot{z}_1)_2 (\Delta t)^2/6 \tag{7.22}$$

$$(\dot{z}_1)_2 = (\ddot{z}_1)_2 \Delta t/2 \tag{7.23}$$

$$(z_2)_2 = (\dot{z}_2)_2 \Delta t/3 = (\ddot{z}_2)_2 (\Delta t)^2/6 \tag{7.24}$$

$$(\dot{z}_2)_2 = (\ddot{z}_2)_2 \Delta t/2 \tag{7.25}$$

From Eqs. 7.1 and 7.2 and neglecting the damping of the tire c_t,

$$m_s(\ddot{z}_1)_2 = c_{sh}[(\dot{z}_2)_2 - (\dot{z}_1)_2] + k_s[(z_2)_2 - (z_1)_2] \tag{7.26}$$

$$m_{us}(\ddot{z}_2)_2 = c_{sh}[(\dot{z}_1)_2 - (\dot{z}_2)_2] + k_s[(z_1)_2 - (z_2)_2] + k_{tr}[(z_0)_2 - (z_2)_2] \tag{7.27}$$

Substituting Eqs. 7.22, 7.23, 7.24, and 7.25 into the two equations above and solving them simultaneously, one obtains

$$(\ddot{z}_1)_2 = \frac{k_{tr}(z_0)_2 A_4}{B_4 C_4 - A_4^2}$$

$$(\ddot{z}_2)_2 = \frac{(\ddot{z}_1)_2 B_4}{A_4}$$

where

$$A_4 = [c_{sh}\Delta t/2 + k_s(\Delta t)^2/6]$$

$$B_4 = [m_s + c_{sh}\Delta t/2 + k_s(\Delta t)^2/6]$$

$$C_4 = [m_{us} + c_{sh}\Delta t/2 + (k_s + k_{tr})(\Delta t)^2/6]$$

The set of equations given above enables the values of the parameters at station 2, $(\ddot{z}_1)_2$, $(\dot{z}_1)_2$, $(z_1)_2$, $(\ddot{z}_2)_2$, $(\dot{z}_2)_2$, and $(z_2)_2$, to be determined for a given elevation of road profile at station 2, $(z_0)_2$. It should be noted that the time increment Δt in the above equations is taken as the increment in horizontal distance Δx (Fig. 7.6) divided by vehicle speed V, that is, $\Delta t = \Delta x/V$. The value of Δt selected depends on the accuracy required. In general, Δt should be less than 5% of the period of the free vibration of the unsprung mass τ_{us}, where $\tau_{us} = 1/f_{n-us}$ and f_{n-us} is the undamped natural frequency of the unsprung mass.

At subsequent stations i (≥ 3),

$$(z_1)_i = (\ddot{z}_1)_{i-1}(\Delta t)^2 + 2(z_1)_{i-1} - (z_1)_{i-2} \tag{7.28}$$

$$(\dot{z}_1)_i = [3(z_1)_i - 4(z_1)_{i-1} + (z_1)_{i-2}]/2\Delta t \tag{7.29}$$

$$(\ddot{z}_1)_i = \{c_{sh}[(\dot{z}_2)_i - (\dot{z}_1)_i] + k_s[(z_2)_i - (z_1)_i]\}/m_s \tag{7.30}$$

$$(z_2)_i = (\ddot{z}_2)_{i-1}(\Delta t)^2 + 2(z_2)_{i-1} - (z_2)_{i-2} \tag{7.31}$$

$$(\dot{z}_2)_i = [3(z_2)_i - 4(z_2)_{i-1} + (z_2)_{i-2}]/2\Delta t \tag{7.32}$$

$$(\ddot{z}_2)_i = \{k_{tr}[(z_0)_i - (z_2)_i] - c_{sh}[(\dot{z}_2)_i - (\dot{z}_1)_i] - k_s[(z_2)_i - (z_1)_i]\}/m_{us} \tag{7.33}$$

As an example, Fig. 7.18(a) shows the acceleration response of the sprung mass of a quarter-car model traveling over an irregular road surface shown in Fig. 7.18(b) at a speed $V = 80$ km/h (50 mph), obtained using the numerical procedure described above. The parameters of the quarter-car model used in the simulation are $m_s = 454.5$ kg (1000 lb), $m_{us}/m_s = 0.10$, $k_{tr} = 176$ kN/m (1000 lb/in.), $k_{tr}/k_s = 8$, and $\zeta = 0.3$.

7.2.3 Two-Degree-of-Freedom Vehicle Model for Pitch and Bounce

Because of the wide separation of the natural frequencies of the sprung and unsprung mass, the up and down linear motion (bounce) and the angular motion (pitch) of the vehicle body and the motion of the wheels may be considered to exist almost independently. The bounce and pitch of the vehicle body can therefore be studied using the model shown in Fig. 7.7. In this model, damping is neglected.

By applying Newton's second law and using the static equilibrium position as the origin for both the linear displacement of the center of gravity z and angular displacement of the vehicle body θ, the equations of motion for the system can be formulated.

For free vibrations, the equation of motion for bounce is

$$m_s\ddot{z} + k_f(z - l_1\theta) + k_r(z + l_2\theta) = 0 \tag{7.34}$$

and the equation of motion for pitch is

$$I_y\ddot{\theta} \text{ (or } m_s r_y^2 \ddot{\theta}) - k_f l_1(z - l_1\theta) + k_r l_2(z + l_2\theta) = 0 \tag{7.35}$$

where k_f is the front spring stiffness, k_r is the rear spring stiffness, and I_y and r_y are the mass moment of inertia and radius of gyration of the vehicle body about the y axis (Fig. 7.3), respectively.

By letting

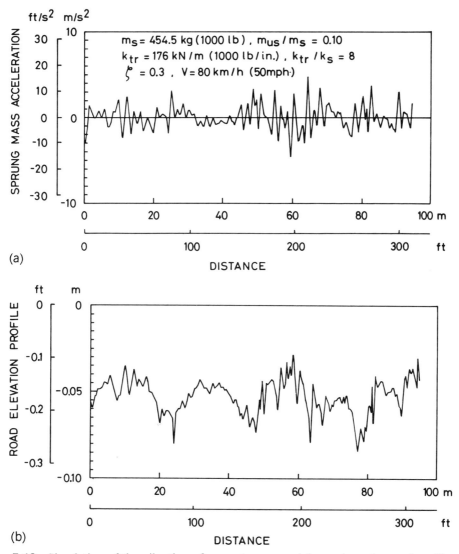

Fig. 7.18 Simulation of the vibration of a quarter-car model over irregular road profiles. (a) Sprung mass acceleration. (b) Road elevation profile.

$$D_1 = \frac{1}{m_s} (k_f + k_r)$$

$$D_2 = \frac{1}{m_s} (k_r l_2 - k_f l_1)$$

$$D_3 = \frac{1}{I_y} (k_f l_1^2 + k_r l_2^2) = \frac{1}{m_s r_y^2} (k_f l_1^2 + k_r l_2^2)$$

Eqs. 7.34 and 7.35 can be rewritten as

$$\ddot{z} + D_1 z + D_2 \theta = 0 \qquad (7.36)$$

$$\ddot{\theta} + D_3\theta + \frac{D_2}{r_y^2} z = 0 \tag{7.37}$$

It is evident that D_2 is the coupling coefficient for the bounce and pitch motions, and that these motions uncouple when $k_f l_1 = k_r l_2$. With $k_f l_1 = k_r l_2$, a force applied to the center of gravity induces only bounce motion, while a moment applied to the body produces only pitch motion. In this case, the natural frequencies for the uncoupled bounce and pitch motions are

$$\omega_{nz} = \sqrt{D_1} \tag{7.38}$$

$$\omega_{n\theta} = \sqrt{D_3} \tag{7.39}$$

It is found that this would result in poor ride.

In general, the pitch and bounce motions are coupled, and an impulse at the front or rear wheel excites both motions. To obtain the natural frequencies for the coupled bounce and pitch motions, the free vibration of the system is considered (or the principal modes of vibration are considered). The solutions to the equations of motion (i.e., Eqs. 7.34 and 7.35) can be expressed in the form of

$$z = Z \cos \omega_n t \tag{7.40}$$

$$\theta = \Theta \cos \omega_n t \tag{7.41}$$

where ω_n is the undamped circular natural frequency, and Z and Θ are the amplitudes of bounce and pitch, respectively.

Substituting the above equations into Eqs. 7.36 and 7.37, one obtains the following amplitude equations:

$$(D_1 - \omega_n^2)Z + D_2\Theta = 0 \tag{7.42}$$

$$\left(\frac{D_2}{r_y^2}\right) Z + (D_3 - \omega_n^2)\Theta = 0 \tag{7.43}$$

Following an approach similar to that described in Section 7.2.1, one obtains the characteristic equation for the system:

$$\omega_n^4 - (D_1 + D_3)\omega_n^2 + \left(D_1 D_3 - \frac{D_2^2}{r_y^2}\right) = 0 \tag{7.44}$$

From Eq. 7.44, two natural frequencies ω_{n_1} and ω_{n_2} can be obtained:

$$\omega_{n_1}^2 = \frac{1}{2} (D_1 + D_3) - \sqrt{\frac{1}{4} (D_1 - D_3)^2 + \frac{D_2^2}{r_y^2}} \tag{7.45}$$

$$\omega_{n_2}^2 = \frac{1}{2}(D_1 + D_3) + \sqrt{\frac{1}{4}(D_1 - D_3)^2 + \frac{D_2^2}{r_y^2}} \qquad (7.46)$$

These frequencies for coupled motions, ω_{n_1} and ω_{n_2}, always lie outside of the frequencies for uncoupled motions, ω_{nz} and $\omega_{n\theta}$.

From Eqs. 7.42 and 7.43, the amplitude ratios of the bounce and pitch oscillations for the two natural frequencies ω_{n_1} and ω_{n_2} can be determined.

For ω_{n_1},

$$\left.\frac{Z}{\Theta}\right|_{\omega_{n_1}} = \frac{D_2}{\omega_{n_1}^2 - D_1} \qquad (7.47)$$

and for ω_{n_2},

$$\left.\frac{Z}{\Theta}\right|_{\omega_{n_2}} = \frac{D_2}{\omega_{n_2}^2 - D_1} \qquad (7.48)$$

It can be shown that the two amplitude ratios will have opposite signs.

To further illustrate the characteristics of the bounce and pitch modes of oscillation, the concept of oscillation center is introduced. The location of the oscillation center is denoted by l_0 measured from the center of gravity, and it can be determined from the amplitude ratios. Thus, one center is associated with ω_{n_1}, and the other with ω_{n_2}.

For ω_{n_1},

$$l_{01} = \frac{D_2}{\omega_{n_1}^2 - D_1} \qquad (7.49)$$

and for ω_{n_2},

$$l_{02} = \frac{D_2}{\omega_{n_2}^2 - D_1} \qquad (7.50)$$

When the value of the amplitude ratio is negative, the oscillation center will be located to the right of the center of gravity of the vehicle body, in accordance with the sign conventions for z and θ shown in Fig. 7.19. On the other hand, when the value of the amplitude ratio is positive, oscillation center will be located to the left of the center of gravity. In general, a road input at the front or rear wheel will cause a moment about each oscillation center, and therefore will excite both bounce and pitch oscillations. In other words, the body motion will be the sum of the oscillations about the two centers.

Usually, the oscillation center that lies outside of the wheelbase is called the

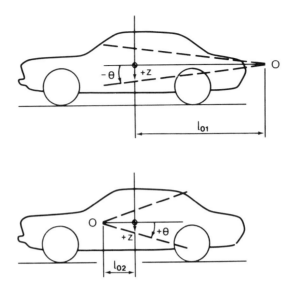

Fig. 7.19   Oscillation centers for bounce and pitch of sprung mass.

bounce center, and the associated natural frequency is called the bounce frequency. On the other hand, the oscillation center that lies inside of the wheelbase is called the pitch center, and the associated natural frequency is called the pitch frequency.

Example 7.1. Determine the pitch and bounce frequencies and the location of oscillation centers of an automobile with the following data:

- sprung mass m_s = 1500 kg (weight 3300 lb)
- radius of gyration r_y = 1.2 m (3.94 ft)
- distance between the front axle and center of gravity l_1 = 1.4 m (4.59 ft)
- distance between the rear axle and center of gravity l_2 = 1.7 m (5.57 ft)
- front spring stiffness k_f = 35 kN/m (2398 lb/ft)
- rear spring stiffness k_r = 38 kN/m (2604 lb/ft).

Solution. The constants D_1, D_2, and D_3 are first calculated as follows:

$$D_1 = \frac{k_f + k_r}{m_s} = \frac{35{,}000 + 38{,}000}{1500} = 48.7 \text{ s}^{-2}$$

$$D_2 = \frac{k_r l_2 - k_f l_1}{m_s} = \frac{38{,}000 \times 1.7 - 35{,}000 \times 1.4}{1500} = 10.4 \text{ m} \cdot \text{s}^{-2}$$

$$D_3 = \frac{k_f l_1^2 + k_r l_2^2}{m_s r_y^2} = \frac{35{,}000 \times 1.4^2 + 38{,}000 \times 1.7^2}{1500 \times 1.2^2} = 82.6 \text{ s}^{-2}$$

$$\left(\frac{D_2}{r_y}\right)^2 = 75.1 \text{ s}^{-4}$$

$$D_3 + D_1 = 131.3 \text{ s}^{-2}$$

$$D_3 - D_1 = 33.9 \text{ s}^{-2}$$

$$\omega_{n_1}^2 = \frac{1}{2}(D_1 + D_3) - \sqrt{\frac{1}{4}(D_1 - D_3)^2 + \left(\frac{D_2}{r_y}\right)^2}$$

$$= 65.65 - \sqrt{287.3 + 75.1} = 46.6 \text{ s}^{-2}$$

$$\omega_{n_1} = 6.83 \text{ s}^{-1} \quad \text{or} \quad f_{n1} = 1.09 \text{ Hz}$$

$$\omega_{n_2}^2 = \frac{1}{2}(D_1 + D_3) + \sqrt{\frac{1}{4}(D_1 - D_3)^2 + \left(\frac{D_2}{r_y}\right)^2}$$

$$= 65.65 + \sqrt{287.3 + 75.1} = 84.7 \text{ s}^{-2}$$

$$\omega_{n_2} = 9.2 \text{ s}^{-1} \quad \text{or} \quad f_{n2} = 1.46 \text{ Hz}$$

The location of the oscillation centers can be determined using Eqs. 7.49 and 7.50.

For ω_{n_1},

$$l_{01} = \left.\frac{Z}{\Theta}\right|_{\omega_{n_1}} = \frac{D_2}{\omega_{n_1}^2 - D_1} = \frac{10.4}{46.6 - 48.7} = -4.95 \text{ m (195 in.)}$$

and for ω_{n_2},

$$l_{02} = \left.\frac{Z}{\Theta}\right|_{w_{n_2}} = \frac{D_2}{\omega_{n_2}^2 - D_1} = \frac{10.4}{84.7\text{-}48.7} = +0.29 \text{ m (11.5 in.)}$$

This indicates that one oscillation center is situated at a distance of 4.95 m (195 in.) to the right of the center of gravity, and the other is located at a distance of 0.29 m (11.5 in.) to the left of the center of gravity, as shown in Fig. 7.19.

For most passenger cars, the natural frequency for bounce is in the range of 1.0–1.5 Hz, and the natural frequency for pitch is slightly higher than that for bounce. For cars with coupled front–rear suspension systems, the natural frequency for pitch may be lower than that for bounce. In roll, the natural frequency is usually higher than those for bounce and pitch because of the limits imposed on roll angles and the effect of antiroll bars. The natural frequency for roll usually varies in the range of 1.5–2.0 Hz for cars.

The location of the oscillation centers has practical significance to ride behavior. One case of interest is that when the motions of bounce and pitch are uncoupled (i.e., $k_f l_1 = k_r l_2$). In this case, one oscillation center will be at the center of gravity, and the other will be at an infinite distance from the center of gravity. The other case of interest is that when $r_y^2 = l_1 l_2$. In this case, one oscillation center will be located at the point of attachment of the front spring to the vehicle body (or its equivalent), and the other at the point of attachment of the rear spring to the body. This can be verified by setting $l_{01} = l_2$ and $l_{02} = l_1$ in Eqs. 7.49 and 7.50, respectively. It should also be noted that under these circumstances, the two-degree-of-freedom model for pitch and bounce shown in Fig. 7.7 can be repre-sented by a dynamically equivalent system with two concentrated masses at the front and rear attachment points (or their equivalents), as shown in Fig. 7.20. The equivalent concentrated mass at the front will be $m_s l_2 / (l_1 + l_2)$, and that at the rear will be $m_s l_1 / (l_1 + l_2)$. The equivalent system is, in fact, two single-degree-of-freedom systems with natural frequency $\omega_{nf} = \sqrt{k_f(l_1 + l_2)/m_s l_2}$ for the front, and natural frequency $\omega_{nr} = \sqrt{k_r(l_1 + l_2)/m_s l_1}$ for the rear. Thus, there is no interaction between the front and rear suspensions, and input at one end (front or rear) causes no motion of the other. This is a desirable condition for a good ride. For practical vehicles, however, this condition often cannot be satisfied. Currently, the ratios of $r_y^2/l_1 l_2$ vary from approximately 0.8 for sports cars through 0.9–1.0 for conventional passenger cars to 1.2 and above for some front-wheel-drive cars.

In considering the natural frequencies for the front and rear ends, it should be noted that excitation from the road to a moving vehicle will affect the front wheels first and the rear wheels later. Consequently, there is a time lag between the ex-citation at the front and that at the rear. This results in a pitching motion of the vehicle body. To minimize this pitching motion, the equivalent spring rate and the natural frequency of the front end should be slightly less than those of the rear end. In other words, the period for the front end $(2\pi/\omega_{nf})$ should be greater than that for the rear end $(2\pi/\omega_{nr})$. This ensures that both ends of the vehicle will move in phase (i.e., the vehicle body is merely bouncing) within a short time after the front end is excited. From the point of view of passenger ride comfort, pitching is more annoying than bouncing. The desirable ratio of the natural frequency of the front end to that of the rear end depends on the wheelbase of the vehicle, the average driving speed, and the wavelengths of the road profile.

7.3   INTRODUCTION TO RANDOM VIBRATION

7.3.1   Surface Elevation Profile as a Random Function

In early attempts to investigate vehicle ride characteristics, excitation from the ground in the form of sine waves, step functions, or triangular waves was used. While these inputs could provide a basis for comparative evaluation of various designs, they could not serve as a valid basis for studying the actual ride behavior of the vehicle since surface profiles are rarely of simple forms. Later, it is found that ground profiles should be more realistically described as a random function, as shown in Fig. 7.21. The characteristic of a random function is that its instan-

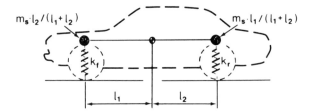

Fig. 7.20 Equivalent system having two concentrated masses for the vehicle body.

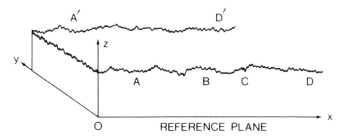

Fig. 7.21 Surface elevation profile as a random function.

taneous value cannot be predicted in a deterministic manner. For instance, the elevation of the surface profile z above a reference plane at any particular point, such as A, is not predictable as a function of the distance x between the point in question and the origin shown in Fig. 7.21 if the surface profile is truly random in the popular sense of the term. However, certain properties of random functions can be described statistically. For instance, the mean or the mean-square value of a random function can be determined by averaging, and the frequency content of the function can be established by methods based on the Fourier transform.

There are certain concepts of random functions that are of practical importance. Referring to the surface profile shown in Fig. 7.21, if the statistical properties of the portion of the road between A and B are the same as those of any other portion such as CD, then in practical terms, the random function representing the surface profile is said to be stationary. This means that under these circumstances, the statistical properties of the surface profile derived from a portion of the road can be used to define the properties of the entire section of the road surface. If the statistical properties of the surface profile on one plane such as AD are the same as those on any parallel plane such as $A'D'$, then in practical terms, the random function representing the surface profile is said to be ergodic. Thus, if the random function is stationary and ergodic, the analysis will be simplified to a great extent.

The frequency composition of a random function is of importance. It may be established by methods based on the Fourier transform. For instance, after obtaining the surface profile shown in Fig. 7.21, one can perform a frequency analysis to make an estimate of the amplitudes for various wavelengths present [7.8]. The amplitude can then be plotted against the wavelength, as shown in Fig. 7.22. In

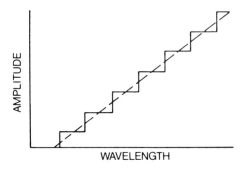

Fig. 7.22 Relationship between amplitude and wavelength of a surface profile.

many cases, there are seldom any distinct wavelengths; therefore, an average value for the amplitude over a certain waveband is determined. Under certain circumstances, the relationship between the amplitude and wavelength may be smoothed, and the amplitude may be expressed as a continuous function of wavelength, as shown by the dotted line in Fig. 7.22.

In random vibrations, the mean-square value of amplitude, and not the value of amplitude, is of prime interest since it is associated with the average energy. For a harmonic component $z_n(x)$ with amplitude Z_n and wavelength l_{wn}, it can be expressed as

$$z_n(x) = Z_n \sin\left(\frac{2\pi x}{l_{wn}}\right) = Z_n \sin \Omega_n x$$

where $\Omega_n = 2\pi/l_{wn}$ is the circular spatial frequency of the harmonic component expressed in rad/m (rad/ft).

The mean-square value of the component $\bar{z}_n^2$ is

$$\bar{z}_n^2 = \frac{1}{l_{wn}} \int_0^{l_{wn}} \left[Z_n \sin\left(\frac{2\pi x}{l_{wn}}\right)\right]^2 dx$$

$$= \frac{Z_n^2}{2} \tag{7.51}$$

For a function containing a number of discrete frequencies, its frequency content can be expressed in terms of the mean-square values of the components, and the result is a discrete spectrum shown in Fig. 7.23. In general, the mean-square contribution in each frequency interval $\Delta\Omega$ is of interest. By letting $S(n\Omega_0)$ be the power spectral density of the mean-square value in the interval $\Delta\Omega$ at frequency $n\Omega_0$, the following relation can be obtained:

$$S(n\Omega_0)\Delta\Omega = \frac{Z_n^2}{2} = \bar{z}_n^2 \tag{7.52}$$

and the discrete power spectral density becomes

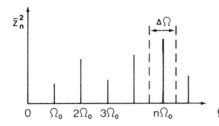

Fig. 7.23 Discrete frequency spectrum of a random function.

$$S(n\Omega_0) = \frac{Z_n^2}{2\Delta\Omega} = \frac{\bar{z}_n^2}{\Delta\Omega} \qquad (7.53)$$

If the function contains a large number of frequencies, the discrete power spectral density function $S(n\Omega_0)$ becomes more or less a continuous power spectral density function $S(\Omega)$, such as that shown in Fig. 7.24. The mean-square value of the function $z(x)$ is then given by

$$\bar{z}^2 = \int_0^\infty S(\Omega)d\Omega \qquad (7.54)$$

It should be noted that the mean-square value of the function in any frequency band of interest, such as $\Omega_1-\Omega_2$ shown in Fig. 7.24, can be calculated as follows:

$$\bar{z}^2_{\Omega_1 \rightarrow \Omega_2} = \int_{\Omega_1}^{\Omega_2} S(\Omega)d\Omega \qquad (7.55)$$

It may be mentioned that the determination of power spectral densities from random data has been greatly facilitated by the availability of digital spectral density analyzers [7.9]. The analyzer performs the filtering operation by heterodyning the random signal through a highly selective narrow bandpass filter with a given center frequency. The instantaneous value of the filtered signal is squared, and the squared instantaneous value over the sampling time is then averaged to obtain the mean-square value. With division of the mean-square value by the bandwidth, the average power spectral density at the given center frequency is obtained. As the center frequency of the narrow bandpass filter is varied, the power spectral densities at a series of selected center frequencies can be determined, and a plot

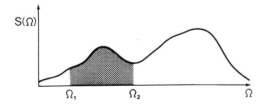

Fig. 7.24 Continuous power spectral density function.

of the power spectral density versus frequency is obtained. Alternatively, an analyzer can be constructed with a collection of contiguous narrow bandpass filters that together cover the frequency range of interest. For this kind of multiple filter analyzer, no frequency scan is needed for obtaining a spectrum. Multiple filter analyzers are widely used in practice.

When the surface profile is regarded as a random function, it can be characterized by a power spectral density function. Figure 7.25 shows the power spectral densities for profile amplitude as a function of spatial frequency for some runways and highways, and Fig. 7.26 shows the power spectral density functions for various types of unprepared terrain [7.10, 7.11]. The spatial frequency Ω is the inverse of the wavelength l_w (i.e., $\Omega = 1/l_w$), and is expressed in cycles per meter (or cycles per foot). The power spectral density for the profile amplitude is expressed in $m^2/cycles/m$ (or $ft^2/cycles/ft$).

It has been found that the relationships between the power spectral density and the spatial frequency for the ground profiles shown in Figs. 7.25 and 7.26 can be approximated by

$$S_g(\Omega) = C_{sp}\Omega^{-N} \tag{7.56}$$

where $S_g(\Omega)$ is the power spectral density function of the elevation of the surface profile, and C_{sp} and N are constants. Fitting this expression to the curves shown

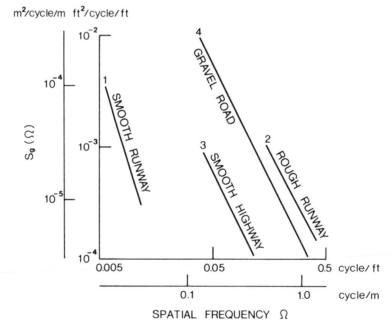

Fig. 7.25 Power spectral density as a function of spatial frequency for various types of road and runway. (Reproduced with permission of the Society of Automotive Engineers from reference 7.10.)

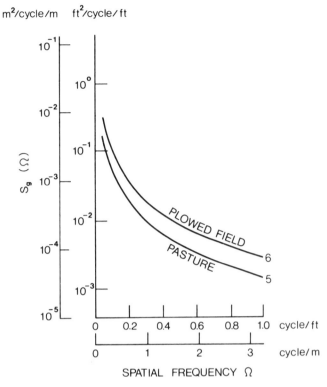

Fig. 7.26 Power spectral density as a function of spatial frequency for two types of unprepared terrain.

TABLE 7.1 Values of C_{sp} and N for Power Spectral Density Functions for Various Surfaces

No.	Description	N	C_{sp}	C'_{sp}
1	Smooth runway	3.8	4.3×10^{-11}	1.6×10^{-11}
2	Rough runway	2.1	8.1×10^{-6}	2.3×10^{-5}
3	Smooth highway	2.1	4.8×10^{-7}	1.2×10^{-6}
4	Highway with gravel	2.1	4.4×10^{-6}	1.1×10^{-5}
5	Pasture	1.6	3.0×10^{-4}	1.6×10^{-3}
6	Plowed field	1.6	6.5×10^{-4}	3.4×10^{-3}

Source: References 7.10 and 7.11.

Note: C_{sp} is the value used for computing $S_g(\Omega)$ in $m^2/\text{cycles}/m$. C'_{sp} is the value used for computing $S_g(\Omega)$ in $ft^2/\text{cycles}/ft$. The numbers in the table refer to the curves shown in Figs. 7.25 and 7.26.

in Figs. 7.25 and 7.26 yields the values of C_{sp} and N as given in Table 7.1. N is a dimensionless constant, while the dimensions of C_{sp} vary with the value of N.

Attempts by various organizations have been made over the years to classify the roughness (irregularities) of road surfaces. The International Organization for Standardization (ISO) has proposed a road roughness classification (Classes A–H) based on the power spectral density [7.12]. Figure 7.27 shows the classification proposed by ISO. In the ISO classification, the relationships between the power spectral density $S_g(\Omega)$ and the spatial frequency Ω for different classes of road roughness may be approximated by two straight lines with different slopes on a log–log scale, as shown in Fig. 7.27. The relationships are as follows:

For $\Omega \le \Omega_0 = 1/2\pi$ cycles/m,

$$S_g(\Omega) = S_g(\Omega_0) (\Omega/\Omega_0)^{-N_1} \tag{7.57}$$

and for $\Omega > \Omega_0 = 1/2\pi$ cycles/m,

$$S_g(\Omega) = S_g(\Omega_0) (\Omega/\Omega_0)^{-N_2} \tag{7.58}$$

The range of values of $S_g(\Omega_0)$ at a spatial freqency $\Omega_0 = 1/2\pi$ cycles/m for different classes of road is given in Table 7.2, and the values of N_1 and N_2 are 2.0 and 1.5, respectively.

For instance, for a Class B road (which is considered to be a "good" road from a surface roughness viewpoint), the value of $S_g(\Omega_0)$ at a spatial frequency $\Omega_0 = 1/2\pi$ cycles/m varies in a range from 8×10^{-6} to 32×10^{-6} m^2/cycles/m, as

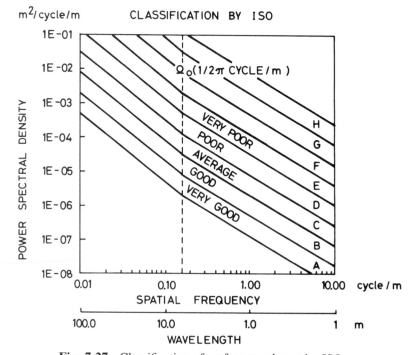

Fig. 7.27 Classification of surface roughness by ISO.

TABLE 7.2 Classification of Road Roughness Proposed by ISO

Road Class	Degree of Roughness $S_g(\Omega_0)$, 10^{-6} m^2/cycles/m	
	Range	Geometric Mean
A (Very Good)	<8	4
B (Good)	8–32	16
C (Average)	32–128	64
D (Poor)	128–512	256
E (Very Poor)	512–2048	1024
F	2048–8192	4096
G	8192–32,768	16384
H	>32,768	

shown in Table 7.2. From Eqs. 7.57 and 7.58, the relationships between the power spectral density $S_g(\Omega)$ and the spatial frequency Ω at the upper and lower bound can be expressed by the following.

For the lower bound,

$$\text{for } \Omega \leq \Omega_0, \ S_g(\Omega) = 8 \times 10^{-6} \, (2\pi\Omega)^{-2} \text{ m}^2/\text{cycles}/\text{m}$$

$$\text{for } \Omega > \Omega_0, \ S_g(\Omega) = 8 \times 10^{-6} \, (2\pi\Omega)^{-1.5} \text{ m}^2/\text{cycles}/\text{m}$$

and for the upper bound,

$$\text{for } \Omega \leq \Omega_0, \ S_g(\Omega) = 32 \times 10^{-6} \, (2\pi\Omega)^{-2} \text{ m}^2/\text{cycles}/\text{m}$$

$$\text{for } \Omega > \Omega_0, \ S_g(\Omega) = 32 \times 10^{-6} \, (2\pi\Omega)^{-1.5} \text{ m}^2/\text{cycles}/\text{m}$$

For vehicle vibration analysis, it is more convenient to express the power spectral density of surface profiles in terms of the temporal frequency in Hz rather than in terms of the spatial frequency since the vehicle vibration is a function of time. The transformation of the spatial frequency Ω in cycles/m (or cycles/ft) to the temporal frequency f in Hz is that of the speed of the vehicle:

$$f \text{ Hz} = \Omega \text{ (cycles/m)} \ V \text{ (m/s)}$$
$$= \Omega \text{ (cycles/ft)} \ V \text{ (ft/s)} \qquad (7.59)$$

The transformation of the power spectral density of the surface profile expressed in terms of the spatial frequency $S_g(\Omega)$ to that in terms of the temporal frequency $S_g(f)$ is that of the speed of the vehicle:

$$S_g(f) = \frac{S_g(\Omega)}{V} \qquad (7.60)$$

7.3.2 Frequency Response Function

For a linear system, a direct linear relationship between input and output exists. This relationship, which also holds for random functions, is shown in the block diagram of Fig. 7.28 for a vehicle system. The vehicle system, characterized by its transfer function, modifies the input representing the surface irregularities to the output representing the vibration of the vehicle. The transfer function or frequency response function is defined as the ratio of the output to input under steady-state conditions. For instance, if the vehicle is simplified to a single-degree-of-freedom system, and both the input due to surface irregularities and the output representing the vibration of the sprung mass are expressed in the same unit (i.e., displacement, velocity, or acceleration), the modulus of the transfer function $H(f)$ is expressed by

$$|H(f)| = \left| \sqrt{\frac{1 + (2\zeta f/f_n)^2}{[1 - (f/f_n)^2]^2 + [2\zeta f/f_n]^2}} \right| \tag{7.61}$$

where f is the frequency of excitation, f_n is the natural frequency of the system, and ζ is the damping ratio. It is noted that in this case, the transfer function $H(f)$ is simply the transmissibility ratio shown in Fig. 7.8.

If, however, the surface irregularity as input is defined in terms of displacement (or elevation of the surface profile) and the vibration of the sprung mass as output is measured in acceleration, then the modulus of the transfer function $H(f)$ will take the following form:

$$|H(f)| = \left| (2\pi f)^2 \sqrt{\frac{1 + (2\zeta f/f_n)^2}{[1 - (f/f_n)^2]^2 + [2\zeta f/f_n]^2}} \right| \tag{7.62}$$

The squared values of the moduli of two transfer functions representing two simplified, single-degree-of-freedom vehicle models, one with a bounce natural frequency of 3.5 Hz and a damping ratio of 0.1 and the other with a bounce natural frequency of 1.0 Hz and a damping ratio of 0.5, are shown in Fig. 7.29 [7.11]. The transfer functions shown are for predicting vehicle response having displacement as input and acceleration as output.

If the transfer function of a system is known or given, then, in general, the relationship between the input of a system $z_g(t)$ and its output $z_v(t)$, both of which are functions of time, can be expressed as

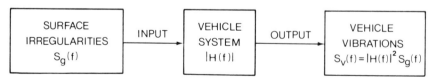

Fig. 7.28 Input and output of a linear vehicle system.

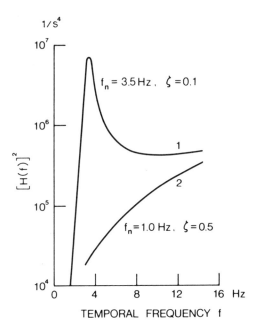

Fig. 7.29 The square of the moduli of the transfer functions of two simplified vehicle models with different natural frequencies and damping ratios.

$$z_v(t) = |H(f)|z_g(t) \tag{7.63}$$

Accordingly, the mean-square values of the input $\overline{z_g^2}$ and output $\overline{z_v^2}$ can be related by

$$\overline{z_v^2} = |H(f)|^2 \, \overline{z_g^2} \tag{7.64}$$

Based on the definition of power spectral density given by Eq. 7.53, and from the equation above, the relationship between the power spectral density of the input $S_g(f)$ and the power spectral density of the output $S_v(f)$ of the system is given by

$$S_v(f) = |H(f)|^2 \, S_g(f) \tag{7.65}$$

This indicates that the power spectral density of the output $S_v(f)$ is related to the power spectral density of the input $S_g(f)$ through the square of the modulus of the transfer function for a linear system.

Equation 7.65 holds regardless of the measure in which the input and output power spectral densities are defined. For instance, if $S_g(f)$ is the power spectral density for the elevation of the surface profile, $S_v(f)$ can be the power spectral density for the acceleration of the sprung mass of the vehicle, provided that an appropriate transfer function is used. In the evaluation of vehicle ride quality, the power spectral density for the acceleration of the sprung mass as a function of frequency is of prime interest.

7.3.3   Evaluation of Vehicle Vibration in Relation to the Ride Comfort Criterion

After the power spectral density function for acceleration of the vehicle has been obtained, further analysis is required to relate it to any ride comfort criterion that may be selected. For instance, if the fatigue or decreased proficiency boundaries for vertical vibration suggested by the International Standard ISO 2631 shown in Fig. 7.2 are adopted, then the transformation of the power spectral density function into root-mean-square values of acceleration as a function of frequency is necessary. As mentioned previously, the mean-square value of acceleration within a certain frequency band can be determined by integrating the corresponding power spectral density function over the same frequency range. In practice, a series of discrete center frequencies within the range of interest is first selected. To determine the mean-square value of acceleration at a given center frequency f_c, the power spectral density function is integrated over a one-third octave band of which the upper cutoff frequency is $\sqrt{2}^3$ times the lower. In other words, by integrating the power spectral density function over a frequency band of 0.89–1.12 f_c, the mean-square value of acceleration at a given center frequency f_c can be obtained. The root-mean-square (rms) value of acceleration at each center frequency f_c can then be calculated by

$$\text{rms acceleration} = \left[\int_{0.89f_c}^{1.12f_c} S_v(f)\,df \right]^{1/2} \tag{7.66}$$

where $S_v(f)$ is the power spectral density function for the acceleration of the vehicle. After obtaining the root-mean-square values of acceleration of the vehicle at a series of center frequencies within the range of interest, one can then evaluate the vibration of the vehicle against the limits specified.

Figure 7.30 shows the measured root-mean-square values of vertical and lateral accelerations at the driver's seat of a North American passenger car traveling at a speed of 80 km/h (50 mph) over a smooth highway as compared with the reduced comfort boundaries recommended by the International Standard ISO 2631 [7.13].

It should be pointed out that the procedure described above is for a simplified vehicle model with a single degree of freedom. A practical vehicle has many degrees of freedom, and between the driver and the vehicle, there is a seat suspension. In addition, more than one random input is imposed on the vehicle. In the case of a passenger car, there are four inputs, one to each wheel. The interaction of the random inputs with each other becomes important in determining the output. The consideration of cross-spectral densities is essential, and the time lag of the input at the rear wheel with respect to the front wheel should also be taken into account. All of these would make the analysis much more complex than that described above. However, analytical techniques based on random vibration theory have been developed into a practical tool to evaluate vehicle ride quality under various operating conditions [7.10].

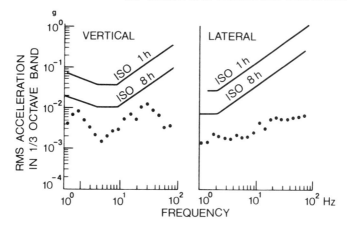

Fig. 7.30 Measured vertical and lateral acceleration of a passenger car traveling at 80 km/h (50 mph) over a smooth road. (Reproduced with permission of the American Society of Mechanical Engineers from reference 7.13.)

7.4 ACTIVE AND SEMI-ACTIVE SUSPENSIONS

As discussed in Section 7.2.1, to achieve good vibration isolation for the sprung mass over a wide range of frequency, a soft suspension spring is generally required, while to provide good road-holding capability at a frequency close to the natural frequency of the unsprung mass ("wheel hop" frequency), a stiff suspension spring is preferred. To reduce the amplitude of vibration of the sprung mass at a frequency close to its natural frequency, a high damping ratio is required, while in the high-frequency range, to provide good vibration isolation for the sprung mass, a low damping ratio is preferred. On the other hand, to achieve good road-holding capability in the high-frequency range, a high damping ratio is required. These conflicting requirements cannot be met by a conventional (passive) suspension system since the characteristics of its spring and shock absorber are fixed and cannot be modulated in accordance with the operating conditions of the vehicle.

To provide the vehicle with improved ride quality, handling, and performance under various operating conditions, the concept of an active suspension has emerged, and various active systems have been proposed or developed [7.15]. The concept of an active suspension system is illustrated in Fig. 7.31. The spring and shock absorber in a conventional system are replaced by a force actuator in an active system. The actuator may also be installed in parallel with a conventional suspension spring. The operating conditions of the vehicle are continuously monitored by sensors. Based on the signals obtained by the sensors and the prescribed control strategy, the force in the actuator is modulated to achieve improved ride, handling, and performance. Generally speaking, the optimum control strategy is defined as the one that minimizes the following:

1. the root-mean-square (rms) value of the sprung mass acceleration
2. the rms value of the suspension travel
3. the rms value of the dynamic tire deflection.

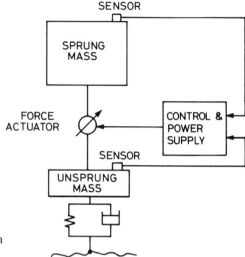

Fig. 7.31 Concept of an active suspension system.

Usually, these quantities are multiplied by weighting factors, and then combined to form an evaluation function. Various control theories have been applied to establishing the optimum control strategy to minimize the evaluation function.

An active suspension can also be used to control the height, roll, dive (forward pitching), and squat (rearward pitching) of the vehicle body. By exercising height control, the ride height of the vehicle body can be kept constant despite changes in load. This ensures adequate suspension travel for negotiating bumps. To reduce aerodynamic resistance and aerodynamic lift at high speeds (see Section 3.2), the ground clearance and the angle of attack of the vehicle body can be conveniently adjusted with an active system. Over rough terrain, the ground clearance and suspension travel can be regulated to suit operating requirements. During cornering, roll control can be achieved by adjusting damping forces or by producing anti-roll forces in the left and right suspensions. With an active system, it is possible to entirely eliminate the roll of the vehicle body and the associated roll–steer (steering action induced by the roll of the vehicle body relative to the tires), thus maintaining the desired handling characteristics during cornering. During acceleration or braking, squat or dive control can be achieved by adjusting damping forces or by producing anti-pitch forces in the front and rear suspensions to maintain the desired attitude of the vehicle body and the required normal load on the tires.

It should be noted, however, that an active suspension system requires significant external power to function, and that there is also a considerable penalty in complexity, reliability, cost, and weight.

With a view to reducing complexity and cost while improving ride, handling, and performance, the concept of a semi-active suspension has emerged. In this kind of system, the conventional suspension spring is usually retained, while the damping force in the shock absorber can be modulated in accordance with operating conditions. Figure 7.32 shows the schematic view of a semi-active system.

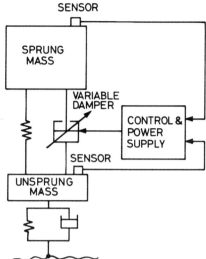

Fig. 7.32   Concept of a semi-active suspension system.

The regulating of the damping force can be achieved by adjusting the orifice area in the shock absorber, thus changing the resistance to fluid flow. More recently, the possible application of the electrorheological fluid to the development of controllable dampers has also attracted considerable interest [7.16, 7.17]. An electrorheological fluid is a mixture of a dielectric base oil and fine semiconducting particles. Its resistance to flow is related to the electrical voltage applied across it. The process is continuous and reversible, and the response is almost instantaneous. By regulating the voltage applied across the flow of the electrorheological fluid in a shock absorber, the damping force can be varied in a convenient way. One of the major challenges facing this novel system is the development of electrorheological fluids that have adequate shear strength and can function effectively over a sufficiently wide temperature range from -40 to $+120°C$.

In comparison with a fully active system, a semi-active suspension requires much less power, and is less complex. It has also been found that when properly designed, the performance of a semi-active system may approach that of a fully active suspension under certain circumstances [7.18].

To successfully develop a semi-active suspension system, in addition to the design of the damper and the properties of the working medium used in the damper, the control strategy for modulating the damping force under various operating conditions is of great importance. Two representative control strategies that have been proposed are outlined below.

1. An on–off control strategy proposed by Krasnicki [7.19] and Margolis and Goshtasbpour [7.20]. This control strategy can be described as follows: a) if $\dot{z}_1(\dot{z}_1 - \dot{z}_2) > 0$, then the maximum (sometimes referred to as "firm") damping is required; b) if $\dot{z}_1(\dot{z}_1 - \dot{z}_2) < 0$, then the minimum (sometimes referred to as "soft") damping is required, where $\dot{z}_1$ and $\dot{z}_2$ are the velocities of the sprung and unsprung mass, respectively.

   This strategy indicates that if the relative velocity of the sprung mass with respect to the unsprung mass is in the same direction as that of the sprung mass absolute velocity, then a maximum damping force should be applied to reduce the acceleration of the sprung mass. On the other hand, if the two velocities are in opposite directions, the damping force should be at a minimum to minimize the acceleration of the sprung mass.

It should be noted that the accurate measurement of the absolute vibration velocity of the sprung mass on a moving vehicle is extremely difficult to achieve. Integrating the signals from an accelerometer to obtain velocity often does not yield sufficiently accurate results, particularly at low frequency. Therefore, this control strategy is difficult to implement in practice.

In some suspension systems, instead of modulating the damping force continuously, the level of damping in the controllable shock absorbers is set by the driver in discrete steps in accordance with driving conditions. For instance, on relatively smooth highways and driving at high speeds, the damping may be set at a low level to provide a good ride. On the other hand, on rough roads and driving at low speeds, the damping may be set at a high level to reduce the vibration amplitude of the vehicle body.

2. A continuous control strategy proposed by Alanoly and Sankar [7.21] and Jolly and Miller [7.22]. This strategy for the continuous adjusting of the damping force can be described as follows: a) if $(\dot{z}_1 - \dot{z}_2)(z_1 - z_2) > 0$, then minimum damping is required; b) if $(\dot{z}_1 - \dot{z}_2)(z_1 - z_2) < 0$, then the desired damping coefficient $c_{sh} = k_s(z_1 - z_2)/(\dot{z}_1 - \dot{z}_2)$, where z_1 and z_2 are the displacements of the sprung and unsprung mass, respectively; $\dot{z}_1$ and $\dot{z}_2$ are velocities of the sprung and unsprung mass, respectively; k_s is the suspension spring stiffness. It should be noted that this control strategy only requires the measurements of the relative displacement and velocity between the sprung and unsprung mass, which can easily be made in practice.

This control strategy indicates that if the spring force and damping force exerted to the sprung mass are in the same direction, to reduce the sprung mass acceleration, the damping force should be a minimum. On the other hand, if the spring force and damping force are in opposite directions, then the damping force should be adjusted in such a way that it will be equal to the spring force in magnitude to produce zero acceleration for the sprung mass.

Figure 7.33 shows the ratio of the rms sprung mass acceleration with an active damper using the continuous control strategy (strategy 2) to that using a passive damper with a fixed damping ratio $\zeta = 0.3$ as a function of vehicle speed over the road profile shown in Fig. 7.18(b), based on simulation results. The damping ratio of the active damper can be continuously varied as required in the range between 0.1 and 1.0. The figure also shows the effect of time delay (from 1 to 5 ms) in modulating the damping force on the response of the sprung mass. It is shown that the semi-active suspension with control strategy 2 offers better vibration isolation than a passive suspension system over a wide range of vehicle speed. It should be noted, how-

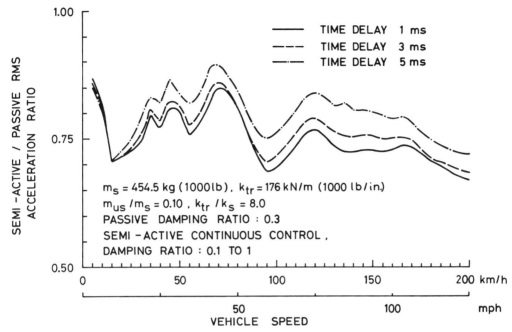

Fig. 7.33 Ratio of the rms value of sprung mass acceleration with a semi-active suspension to that with a passive suspension as a function of vehicle speed over a road with profile shown in Fig. 7.18(b).

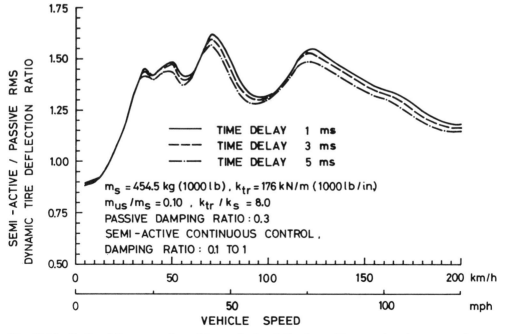

Fig. 7.34 Ratio of the rms value of dynamic tire deflection with a semi-active suspension to that with a passive suspension as a function of vehicle speed over a road with profile shown in Fig. 7.18(b).

ever, that this control strategy does not necessarily offer an optimal road-holding capability. As shown in Fig. 7.34, the ratio of the rms dynamic tire deflection with the active damper to that with the passive damper is greater than one over a wide range of speed, except at speeds lower than 20 km/h (12.5 mph).

It should be mentioned that for the suspension to exert forces to control the unsprung mass motion (or the fluctuation of the normal force between the tire and the road), these forces must be reacted against the sprung mass, thus increasing the vibration of the vehicle body. This imposes a fundamental limit to what an active or semi-active system can realistically achieve in terms of providing optimal vibration isolation and road-holding capability at the same time. It indicates that in the development of the control strategy, a proper compromise has to be struck between ride comfort and road holding.

REFERENCES

7.1   B.D. Van Deusen, "Human Response to Vehicle Vibration," *SAE Transactions*, vol. 77, paper 680090, 1969.

7.2   R.A. Lee and F. Pradko, "Analytical Analysis of Human Vibration," *SAE Transactions*, vol. 77, paper 680091, 1969.

7.3   *Ride and Vibration Data Manual, SAE J6a*, Society of Automotive Engineers, 1965.

7.4   *Guide for the Evaluation of Human Exposure to Whole-Body Vibration*, 2nd ed., International Standard 2631-1978(E), International Organization for Standardization, 1978.

7.5   L.F. Stikeleather, G.O. Hall, and A.O. Radke, "A Study of Vehicle Vibration Spectra as Related to Seating Dynamics," *SAE Transactions*, vol. 81, paper 720001, 1973.

7.6   N.R. Murphy, Jr. and R.B. Ahlvin, "Ride Dynamics Module for AMM-75 Ground Mobility Model," in *Proc. 5th Int. Conf. of the International Society for Terrain-Vehicle Systems*, Vol. IV, Detroit, MI, 1975.

7.7   R.K. Vierck, *Vibration Analysis*, 2nd ed.   New York: Harper and Row, 1979.

7.8   M.A. Macaulay, "Measurement of Road Surfaces," in G.H. Tidbury, Ed., *Advances in Automobile Engineering, Part I*.   Oxford, England: Pergamon Press, 1963.

7.9   J.S. Bendat and A.G. Piersol, *Random Data: Analysis and Measurement Procedures*.   New York: Wiley-Interscience, 1971.

7.10   B.D. Van Deusen, "Analytical Techniques for Design Riding Quality into Automotive Vehicles," *SAE Transactions*, vol. 76, paper 670021, 1968.

7.11   J.Y. Wong, "Effect of Vibration on the Performance of Off-Road Vehicles," *Journal of Terramechanics*, vol. 8, no. 4, 1972.

7.12   ISO/TC108/SC2/WG4 N57, "Reporting Vehicle Road Surface Irregularities," 1982.

7.13   A.J. Healy, "Digital Processing of Measured Random Vibration Data for Automobile Ride Evaluation," ASME Publication, AMD-Vol. 24, 1977.

7.14 D.E. Cole, *Elementary Vehicle Dynamics*, Department of Mechanical Engineering, University of Michigan, Ann Arbor, 1971.

7.15 R.M. Chalasani, "Ride Performance Potential of Active Suspension Systems—Part I and Part II," in *Proc. ASME Symp. on Simulation and Control of Ground Vehicles and Transportation Systems*, L. Segel, J.Y. Wong, E.H. Law, and D. Hrovat, Eds., American Society of Mechanical Engineers, AMD-Vol. 80, DSC-Vol. 2, 1986.

7.16 J.Y. Wong, X.M. Wu, M. Sturk, and C. Bortolotto, "On the Applications of Electro-Rheological Fluids to the Development of Semi-Active Suspension Systems for Ground Vehicles," *Transactions of Canadian Society for Mechanical Engineering*, vol. 17, no. 4B, 1993.

7.17 N.K. Petek, "Shock Absorber Uses Electrorheological Fluid," *Automotive Engineering*, June 1992.

7.18 D.L. Margolis, "Semi-Active Heave and Pitch Control for Ground Vehicles," *Vehicle System Dynamics*, vol. 11, no. 1, 1982.

7.19 E.J. Krasnicki, "The Experimental Performance of an 'On-Off' Active Damper," *Shock and Vibration Bulletin*, vol. 51, part 1, 1981.

7.20 D.L. Margolis and W. Goshtasbpour, "The Chatter of Semi-Active On-Off Suspension and Its Cure," *Vehicle System Dynamics*, vol. 13, no. 3, 1984.

7.21 J. Alanoly and S. Sankar, "A New Concept in Semi-Active Vibration Isolation," *Journal of Mechanisms, Transmissions and Automation in Design, Transactions of the ASME*, June 1987.

7.22 M.R. Jolly and L.R. Miller, "The Control of Semi-Active Dampers Using Relative Feedback Signals," Society of Automotive Engineers, paper 892483, 1989.

7.23 T.D. Gillespie, *Fundamentals of Vehicle Dynamics*, Society of Automotive Engineers, 1992.

PROBLEMS

7.1 The sprung parts of a passenger car weigh 11.12 kN (2500 lb) and the unsprung parts weigh 890 N (200 lb). The combined stiffness of the suspension springs is 45.53 kN/m (260 lb/in.) and that of the tires is 525.35 kN/m (3000 lb/in.). Determine the two natural frequencies of the bounce motions of the sprung and unsprung masses. Calculate the amplitudes of the sprung and unsprung parts if the car travels at a speed of 48 km/h (30 mph) over a road of a sinewave form with a wavelength of 9.15 m (30 ft) and an amplitude of 5 cm (2 in.).

7.2 Owing to the wide separation of the natural frequency of the sprung parts from that of the unsprung parts, the bounce and pitch motions of the vehicle body and the wheel motions exist almost independently. The sprung parts of a vehicle weigh 9.79 kN (2200 lb), its center of gravity is 106.7 cm (42 in.) behind the front axle, and the wheelbase is 228.6 cm (90 in.). The combined stiffness of the springs of the front suspension is 24.52 kN/m (140 lb/in.) and that of the rear suspension is 26.27 kN/m (150 lb/in.). The radius of gyration of the sprung parts about a horizontal transverse axis through the

102.6 cm

center of gravity is 91.5 cm (36 in.). Calculate the natural frequencies of the pitch and bounce motions of the vehicle body. Also determine the locations of the oscillation centers.

7.3 If the vehicle described in Problem 7.2 travels over a concrete highway with expansion joints 15.24 m (50 ft) apart, calculate the speeds at which the bounce motion and pitch motion of the vehicle body are most apt to arise.

7.4 If the radius of gyration of the sprung parts of the vehicle described in Problem 7.2 can be varied, determine the conditions under which the oscillation centers of the vehicle body will be located at the points of attachment of the front and rear springs. Also calculate the natural frequencies of the sprung parts.

7.5 A tractor with a bounce natural frequency of 3.5 Hz and a damping ratio of 0.1 travels at a speed of 5 km/h (3.1 mph) over a plowed field of which the surface roughness characteristics are described in Table 7.1. Determine the root-mean-square value of vertical acceleration of the tractor at a frequency of 1 Hz. Evaluate whether the vibration of the vehicle is acceptable from a fatigue or decreased proficiency viewpoint for an 8 h duration based on the International Standard ISO 2631.

7.6 An independent front suspension of a passenger car carries a mass (sprung mass) of 454.5 kg (or an equivalent weight of 1000 lb). The suspension spring rate is 22 kN/m (125 lb/in.). The mass of the tire/wheel assembly (unsprung mass) is 45.45 kg (or an equivalent weight of 100 lb) and the equivalent tire stiffness is 176 kN/m (1000 lb/in.). The damping ratio ζ of the suspension produced by the shock absorber is 0.3. If the car is traveling on a sinusoidal road profile with a wavelength of 5 m (16.4 ft) and an amplitude of 5 cm (2 in.), estimate the lowest vehicle speed at which the tire may lose contact with the road.

CHAPTER 8

INTRODUCTION TO AIR-CUSHION VEHICLES

An air-cushion vehicle may be defined as a surface vehicle that is supported by a cushion of pressurized air. The cushion performs two basic functions: to separate the vehicle from the supporting surface, thus reducing or eliminating surface contact and the associated resistance, and to provide the vehicle with a suspension system.

Since practical air-cushion concepts emerged in the 1950's, they have found applications in overwater as well as overland transport. In this chapter, the performance of the principal types of air-cushion system will be discussed. The characteristics unique to air-cushion vehicles will also be examined.

8.1 AIR-CUSHION SYSTEMS AND THEIR PERFORMANCE

There are two principal types of air cushion system: the plenum chamber and the peripheral jet.

8.1.1 Plenum Chamber

Figure 8.1 shows the basic features of a simple plenum chamber [8.1]. The majority of current air-cushion vehicles essentially employ a plenum chamber configuration. Pressurized air is pumped into the chamber by a fan or a compressor to form an air cushion that supports the vehicle. Under steady-state conditions, the air being pumped into the chamber is just sufficient to replace the air leaking under the peripheral gap, and the weight of the vehicle W is equal to the lift F_{cu} generated by the cushion pressure p_{cu}:

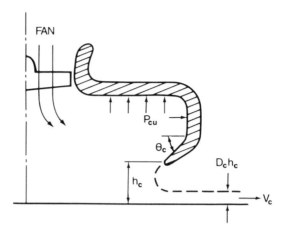

Fig. 8.1 Geometry of a simple plenum chamber. (Reproduced with permission from *Hovercraft Design and Construction* by G.H. Elsley and A.J. Devereux, copyright © by Elsley and Devereux 1968.)

$$F_{cu} = W = p_{cu}A_c \qquad (8.1)$$

where A_c is the effective cushion area.

For most current designs, the cushion pressure varies in the range 1.2–3.3 kPa (25–70 lb/ft^2) for overwater and overland vehicles. For high-speed guided ground transport vehicles, a cushion pressure of 4.2 kPa (87 lb/ft^2) has been used.

Assume that the air inside the chamber is essentially at rest. From Bernoulli's theorem, the velocity of air escaping under the peripheral gap V_c is given by

$$V_c = \sqrt{\frac{2p_{cu}}{\rho}} \qquad (8.2)$$

where ρ is the density of air. The total volume flow of air from the cushion Q is given by

$$Q = h_c l_{cu} D_c V_c = h_c l_{cu} D_c \sqrt{\frac{2p_{cu}}{\rho}} \qquad (8.3)$$

where h_c is the clearance height, l_{cu} is the cushion perimeter, and D_c is the discharge coefficient. The discharge coefficient is primarily a function of the wall angle θ_c shown in Fig. 8.1 and the length of the wall. For a long wall and nonviscous fluid, the values of D_c are as follows:

θ_c	0	45°	90°	135°	180°
D_c	0.50	0.537	0.611	0.746	1.000

In practice, because of the viscosity of the air, the values of D_c tend to be slightly less than those given above.

The power required to sustain the air cushion at the peripheral gap P_a is given by

$$P_a = p_{cu}Q$$

$$= h_c l_{cu} D_c p_{cu}^{3/2} \left(\frac{2}{\rho}\right)^{1/2} \tag{8.4}$$

Substituting Eq. 8.1 into the above equation, one obtains

$$P_a = h_c l_{cu} D_c \left(\frac{W}{A_c}\right)^{3/2} \left(\frac{2}{\rho}\right)^{1/2} \tag{8.5}$$

This equation shows that the power required to sustain the cushion in the plenum chamber varies with the clearance height and the perimeter, and that for a given vehicle, it is proportional to the weight of the vehicle raised to the power of $3/2$. It should be noted that in determining the power required to drive the fan, intake losses, ducting losses, diffusion losses, and fan efficiency should be taken into consideration.

Consider that an air jet with the same amount of volume flow Q and having the same air velocity V_c as those of the air cushion is directly used to generate a lift force. The lift force F_l generated by the change of momentum of the air jet is given by

$$F_l = \rho Q V_c \tag{8.6}$$

An augmentation factor K_a, which is a measure of the effectiveness of an air-cushion system as a lift generating device, can be defined as

$$K_a = \frac{F_{cu}}{F_l} = \frac{p_{cu} A_c}{\rho Q V_c} = \frac{A_c}{2h_c l_{cu} D_c} \tag{8.7}$$

Introducing the concept of hydraulic diameter D_h

$$D_h = \frac{4A_c}{l_{cu}} \tag{8.8}$$

Eq. 8.7 becomes

$$K_a = \frac{D_h}{8h_c D_c} \tag{8.9}$$

This expression shows that the higher the ratio of the hydraulic diameter D_h to the clearance height h_c, the more effective the air-cushion system will be. Useful guidelines for the selection of the configuration and dimensions of air-cushion vehicles can be drawn from this simple equation.

Currently, there are two principal forms of plenum chamber in use: one with a flexible skirt, and the other with a combination of flexible skirt and sidewall, as shown in Fig. 8.2. The prime reason for using the flexible skirt is to allow the vehicle to have relatively large clearance between its hard structure and the supporting surface, while at the same time keeping the clearance height under the skirt sufficiently small to enable the power required for lift to remain within reasonable limits. A combination of flexible skirt and sidewall is used in marine air-cushion vehicles in which the air can only leak through the gaps in the front and rear of the vehicle. The air in the cushion is prevented from leaking along the sides by rigid sidewalls immersed in the water. Thus, the power required to sustain the cushion is reduced. The sidewalls can also contribute to the directional stability of the vehicle.

There are many variants of the plenum chamber configuration with a flexible skirt. Figure 8.3 shows the multiple-cone skirt system used in the Bertin Terraplane BC7 [8.2]. The conical form ensures that the shape of the skirt under pressure is stable. The system can provide the vehicle with sufficient roll and pitch stability. When the vehicle rolls, the air gap of the cone on the downgoing side is reduced. Consequently, the air flow from that side decreases and the cushion pressure increases. This, together with the decrease of cushion pressure in the cone on the upgoing side, provides a restoring moment that tends to bring the vehicle back to its original position. This system is also less sensitive to loss of lift over ditches than the single plenum chamber configuration. The multiple-cone system shown in Fig. 8.3 requires, however, more power to sustain the cushion than an equivalent single plenum chamber because the ratio of the total cushion perimeter l_{cu} to the cushion area A_c is higher than that of a single plenum chamber. In other words,

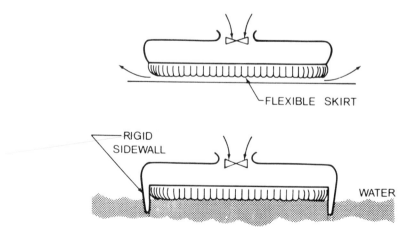

Fig. 8.2 Flexible skirted plenum chamber and rigid sidewall plenum chamber.

the equivalent hydraulic diameter of the multiple-cone skirt system is lower than that of an equivalent single plenum chamber. To reduce the volume flow, a peripheral skirt around the multiple cones may be added, as shown in Fig. 8.4. This also increases the effective cushion area, although the cushion pressure between the cones and the peripheral skirt is lower than that inside the cones.

The performance of the multiple-cone system with a peripheral skirt may be evaluated analytically, as shown by Wong [8.3]. Consider that the cushion pressure inside the cones is p_{cu} and that between the peripheral skirt and the cones is $k_p p_{cu}$, and assume that the air inside the cushion is substantially at rest; then from Bernoulli's theorem, the velocity of the air escaping under the peripheral skirt V_{c2} is given by

$$V_{c2} = \left(\frac{2k_p p_{cu}}{\rho}\right)^{1/2}$$
(8.10)

and the total volume flow from the peripheral skirt Q_2 is given by

$$Q_2 = h_{c2} l_{c2} D_{c2} \left(\frac{2k_p p_{cu}}{\rho}\right)^{1/2}$$
(8.11)

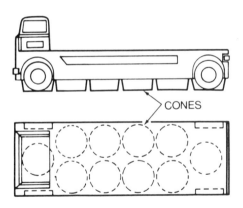

CONES

Fig. 8.3 Multiple-cone skirt system used in the Bertin Terraplane BC7. (Reproduced from reference 8.2.)

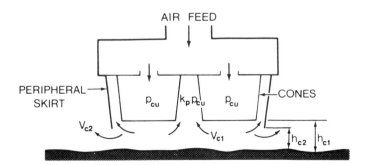

Fig. 8.4 Multiple-cone system with a peripheral skirt.

where h_{c2}, l_{c2}, and D_{c2} are the clearance height, perimeter, and discharge coefficient of the peripheral skirt, respectively.

Under steady-state conditions, the total lift force generated by the system is given by

$$F_{cu} = W = p_{cu}A_{c1} + k_p p_{cu}A_{c2} \qquad (8.12)$$

where A_{c1} is the total cushion area of the cones and A_{c2} is the cushion area between the peripheral skirt and the cones. The cushion pressure p_{cu} required to support the vehicle weight is expressed by

$$p_{cu} = \frac{W}{A_{c1} + k_p A_{c2}} \qquad (8.13)$$

Based on the assumptions of inviscid, incompressible flow, the total volume of air escaping under the cones Q_1 is equal to that escaping under the peripheral skirt Q_2:

$$Q_1 = n_c h_{c1} l_{c1} D_{c1} \left[\frac{2(1 - k_p)\, p_{cu}}{\rho} \right]^{1/2} = Q_2 \qquad (8.14)$$

where n_c is the number of cones, and h_{c1}, l_{c1}, and D_{c1} are the clearance height, perimeter, and discharge coefficient of the cone, respectively.

The power required to sustain the air cushion is given by

$$P_a = p_{cu}Q_1 = p_{cu}Q_2$$

$$= h_{c2} l_{c2} D_{c2} \left[\frac{W}{(A_{c1} + k_p A_{c2})} \right]^{3/2} \left(\frac{2k_p}{\rho} \right)^{1/2} \qquad (8.15)$$

Based on Eqs. 8.11 and 8.14, an expression for the pressure ratio k_p can be derived, and

$$k_p = \frac{n_c^2 h_{c1}^2 l_{c1}^2 D_{c1}^2}{n_c^2 h_{c1}^2 l_{c1}^2 D_{c1}^2 + h_{c2}^2 l_{c2}^2 D_{c2}^2} \qquad (8.16)$$

It is found that the value of k_p calculated from the above equation is very close to that quoted in the literature. It is interesting to note that the difference between the clearance heights h_{c1} and h_{c2} affects the pressure ratio k_p, and hence the characteristics of the cushion system.

The augmentation factor K_a of a multiple-cone system with a peripheral skirt is given by

$$K_a = \frac{A_{c1} + k_p A_{c2}}{2k_p h_{c2} l_{c2} D_{c2}} \tag{8.17}$$

It can be shown that, other conditions being equal, the augmentation factor of the multiple-cone system with a peripheral skirt would be much higher than that of an equivalent system without a peripheral skirt.

Another flexible skirt system of the plenum chamber type is the segmented skirt developed by the Hovercraft Development Ltd. (HDL), as shown in Fig. 8.5(a) [8.4, 8.5]. The unique feature of this type of skirt system is that the segments are unattached to one another. Consequently, when moving over a rough surface, only the segments in contact with the obstacles will deflect. When a segment is damaged

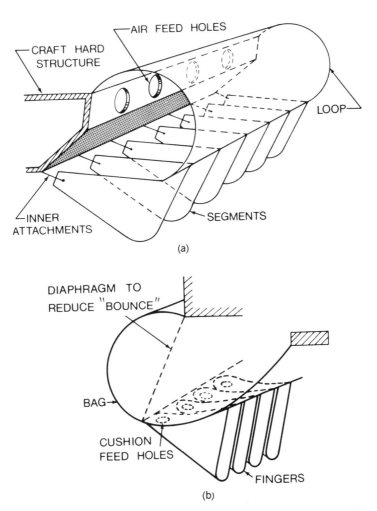

Fig. 8.5 (a) Hovercraft Development Ltd. segmented skirt. (Reproduced with permission of R.L. Trillo from reference 8.5.) (b) British Hovercraft Corporation bag and finger skirt. (Reproduced with permission of the Society of Automotive Engineers from reference 8.4.)

or even removed, adjacent segments expand under cushion pressure and tend to fill the gap. Furthermore, the drag of the segmented skirt is found to be less than that of a continuous skirt because of its higher flexibility. The performance of the segmented skirt system may be predicted using the theory for a simple plenum chamber described previously.

Figure 8.5(b) shows the bag and finger skirt developed by the British Hovercraft Corporation (BHC) [8.4]. The fingers in this skirt system have similar character-istics to those of the segments in the segmented skirt. The cushion air is fed from the bag through holes into the fingers. A diaphragm is installed in the bag to help prevent the vertical oscillation of the skirt system.

Example 8.1. A multiple-cone cushion system with a peripheral skirt similar to that shown in Fig. 8.4 has the following parameters:

- gross vehicle weight, W 48.93 kN (11,000 lb)
- number of cones, n_c 8
- perimeter of each cone, l_{c1} 3.6 m (11.8 ft)
- perimeter of the peripheral skirt, l_{c2} 17.5 m (57.5 ft)
- total cushion area of the cones, A_{c1} 8.2 m² (88.3 ft²)
- cushion area between the cones and the peripheral skirt, A_{c2} 9.6 m² (103.3 ft²)
- clearance heights, h_{c1} and h_{c2} 2.5 cm (1 in.)
- discharge coefficients, D_{c1} and D_{c2} 0.60.

Determine the power required to generate the lift and the augmentation factor.

Solution. From Eq. 8.16, for $D_{c1} = D_{c2}$ and $h_{c1} = h_{c2}$, the pressure ratio k_p is calculated as follows:

$$k_p = \frac{n_c^2 l_{c1}^2}{n_c^2 l_{c1}^2 + l_{c2}^2} = 0.73$$

From Eq. 8.13, the required cushion pressure p_{cu} is determined by

$$p_{cu} = \frac{W}{(A_{c1} + k_p A_{c2})} = 3.22 \text{ kPa } (67 \text{ lb/ft}^2)$$

From Eq. 8.15, the power required to sustain the cushion is obtained by

$$P_a = h_{c2} l_{c2} D_{c2} \left[\frac{W}{(A_{c1} + k_p A_{c2})} \right]^{3/2} \left(\frac{2k_p}{\rho} \right)^{1/2}$$

$$= 52.2 \text{ kW } (70 \text{ hp}).$$

From Eq. 8.17, the augmentation factor K_a is determined as follows:

$$K_a = \frac{A_{c1} + k_p A_{c2}}{2 k_p h_{c2} l_{c2} D_{c2}} = 39$$

8.1.2 Peripheral Jet

In the early days of development of the air-cushion technology, the peripheral jet system was used. This system is schematically shown in Fig. 8.6. In this system, a curtain of air is produced around the periphery by ejecting air downward and inward from a nozzle. This curtain of air helps contain the cushion under the vehicle and reduces air leakage. Thus, it could offer higher operational efficiency than the simple plenum chamber.

In addition to the lift force generated by the cushion pressure, the air jet also provides a small amount of vertical lift. Under steady-state conditions, the weight of the vehicle W is balanced by the lift force F_{cu}:

$$F_{cu} = W = p_{cu} A_c + J_j l_j \sin \theta_j$$

where J_j is the momentum flux of the air jet per unit length of the nozzle, which is the product of the jet velocity and mass flow rate per unit nozzle length, l_j is the nozzle perimeter, and θ_j is the angle of the nozzle from the horizontal.

There are a number of theories for predicting the performance of peripheral jet systems. Among them, the so-called "exponential theory" is one of the most commonly used. In this theory, it is assumed that from the outlet of the nozzle (point A) to the point of ground contact (point B), the jet maintains its thickness as well as its circular path, and that the air is inviscid and incompressible. The total pressure p_j is assumed to be constant across the jet with a static pressure gradient within it. The distribution of static pressure p across the jet must satisfy the boundary conditions, that is, $p = 0$ at the outside and $p = p_{cu}$ at the cushion side.

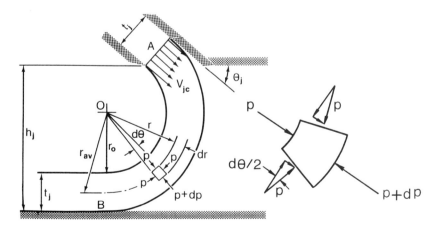

Fig. 8.6 Geometry of a peripheral jet system.

Consider a small element of the jet at a distance r from the center of curvature O. The pressure difference across the element is balanced by the centrifugal force, and the equation of equilibrium for the element is given by

$$(p + dp)\,(r + dr)d\theta - prd\theta - 2p\,\sin(d\theta/2)dr = \frac{\rho V_{jc}^2}{r}\,rdrd\theta$$

where V_{jc} is the velocity of the element.

Neglecting second-order terms and making simplifications, such as $\sin(d\theta/2) \approx d\theta/2$, one can rewrite the equation above as

$$\frac{dp}{dr} = \frac{\rho V_{jc}^2}{r} \tag{8.18}$$

Since the total pressure p_j is assumed to be constant across the jet, from Bernoulli's theorem, the following relation is obtained:

$$p_j = p + \frac{\rho V_{jc}^2}{2} \tag{8.19}$$

Substituting Eq. 8.19 into Eq. 8.18, one obtains

$$\frac{dp}{p_j - p} = \frac{2dr}{r} \tag{8.20}$$

Since the variation of r is limited, the value of r in the above equation may be considered to be constant and equal to the average radius of curvature of the path r_{av}. Integrating Eq. 8.20 and substituting the limits $r = r_0$, $p = 0$; $r = r_0 + t_j$, $p = p_{cu}$, one obtains the following expression relating the cushion pressure p_{cu} and the total pressure of the jet p_j:

$$\frac{p_{cu}}{p_j} = 1 - e^{-2t_j/r_{av}} \tag{8.21}$$

where t_j is the thickness of the jet or nozzle width. Noting that $r_{av} \approx h_j/(1 + \cos\theta_j)$, one obtains

$$\frac{p_{cu}}{p_j} = 1 - e^{-2t_j(1 + \cos\theta_j)/h_j} \tag{8.22}$$

where h_j is the clearance height.

The total volume flow Q_j is given by

$$Q_j = \int_{r_0}^{r_0 + t_j} l_j V_{jc} \, dr$$

$$= \frac{l_j h_j}{1 + \cos \theta_j} \sqrt{\frac{2p_j}{\rho}} [1 - \sqrt{1 - p_{cu}/p_j}] \tag{8.23}$$

and the power required is

$$P_{aj} = p_j Q_j = \frac{l_j h_j (1 - e^{-x}) p_{cu}^{3/2} (2/\rho)^{1/2}}{(1 + \cos \theta_j)(1 - e^{-2x})^{3/2}} \tag{8.24}$$

where $x = t_j (1 + \cos \theta_j)/h_j$.

For given values of h_j, l_j, p_{cu}, and θ_j, the power requirement is a minimum for

$$\frac{\partial P_{aj}}{\partial x} = 0$$

which gives $x = 0.693$. The minimum power $P_{aj\,min}$ is expressed by

$$P_{aj\,min} = \frac{4l_j h_j p_{cu}^{3/2} (2/\rho)^{1/2}}{3\sqrt{3} (1 + \cos \theta_j)} \tag{8.25}$$

Comparing the power requirement of a simple plenum chamber with that of a peripheral jet having the same cushion pressure and similar dimensions ($l_j = l_c$ and $h_j = h_c$), one may obtain the following power ratio:

$$\frac{P_a}{P_{aj\,min}} = \frac{3\sqrt{3} D_c (1 + \cos \theta_j)}{4} \tag{8.26}$$

Assume that $\theta_j = 45°$ and $D_c = 0.6$; the power requirement of a simple plenum chamber will be 33% higher than that of an equivalent peripheral jet system. The augmentation factor K_{aj} for a peripheral jet system is expressed by

$$K_{aj} = \frac{p_{cu} A_c + J_j l_j \sin \theta_j}{J_j l_j}$$

$$= \frac{p_{cu} A_c}{J_j l_j} + \sin \theta_j$$

$$= \frac{p_{cu} D_h}{4 J_j} + \sin \theta_j \tag{8.27}$$

The momentum flux per unit nozzle length J_j can be determined by

$$J_j = \int_{r_0}^{r_0+t_j} \rho V_{jc}^2 dr$$

$$= \int_{r_0}^{r_0+t_j} 2(p_j - p)dr$$

$$= \int_0^{p_{cu}} r dp = r_{av} p_{cu} \tag{8.28}$$

Substituting Eq. 8.28 into Eq. 8.27, one obtains

$$K_{aj} = \frac{D_h}{4r_{av}} + \sin \theta_j$$

$$= \frac{D_h}{4h_j} (1 + \cos \theta_j) + \sin \theta_j \tag{8.29}$$

Comparing the augmentation factor of a simple plenum chamber with that of a peripheral jet system having the same hydraulic diameter and clearance height, one can obtain the following ratio:

$$\frac{K_{aj}}{K_a} = 2D_c \left(1 + \cos \theta_j + 4 \sin \theta_j \frac{h_j}{D_h}\right) \tag{8.30}$$

Assume that $D_c = 0.6$, $\theta_j = 45°$, and $h_j/D_h = 0.001$; the augmentation factor of a peripheral jet system is approximately twice that of an equivalent simple plenum chamber.

Although, in theory, the peripheral jet system appears to be superior to the plenum chamber, in practice it is not necessarily so. It has been found that using flexible nozzles for the peripheral jet system, difficulties arise in maintaining the jet width and angle, and in excessive nozzle wear. Using relatively hard nozzles, on the other hand, would induce high surface drag. Moreover, the advent of the flexible skirt enables the clearance height, and hence the power requirement for lift, to be reduced considerably, while maintaining sufficient clearance between the hard structure of the vehicle and the supporting surface. On some current vehicles, the designed clearance height is only a few millimeters. This renders the power saving aspect of the peripheral jet system rather insignificant. All of these have led to the use of an essentially plenum chamber configuration in almost all of the current air-cushion vehicles.

8.2 RESISTANCE OF AIR-CUSHION VEHICLES

There are drag components unique to air-cushion vehicles which require special attention. For overland operations, in addition to aerodynamic resistance, there are momentum drag, trim drag, and skirt contact drag. For overwater operations, additional wave-making drag, wetting drag, and drag due to waves have to be taken into account.

As mentioned previously, the introduction of flexible skirts permits a considerable reduction of clearance height, and hence power for lift. It should be pointed out, however, that the reduction of clearance height would likely increase the skirt contact drag, thus increasing the power for propulsion. Apparently, a proper balance between the reduction of lift power and the associated increase in propulsion power has to be struck to achieve a minimum total power requirement.

The aerodynamic resistance of an air-cushion vehicle can be evaluated using the methods discussed in Chapter 3. Typical values for the coefficient of aerodynamic resistance C_D obtained from wind-tunnel tests range from 0.25 for SR.N2 to 0.38 for SR.N5 based on frontal area [8.1]. For a surface effect ship, a value of 0.5 for C_D has been reported [8.5].

Momentum Drag   To sustain the cushion, air is continuously drawn into the cushion system. When the vehicle is moving, the air is effectively accelerated to the speed of the vehicle. This generates a resisting force in the direction of the air relative to the vehicle, which is usually referred to as the momentum drag R_m. The momentum drag can be expressed by

$$R_m = \rho Q V_a \tag{8.31}$$

where V_a is the speed of the air relative to the vehicle, and Q is the volume flow of the cushion system. This momentum drag is unique to air-cushion vehicles.

It should be noted that part of the power to overcome momentum drag may be recovered from utilizing the dynamic pressure of the airstream at the inlet of the fan to generate the cushion pressure. The dynamic pressure of the airstream at the intake of the fan p_d is given by

$$p_d = \frac{\rho V_a^2}{2} \tag{8.32}$$

Assume that the efficiency of the cushion system including the fan and ducting is η_{cu}; then the power that can be recovered from generating the cushion pressure is given by

$$P_r = \frac{\eta_{cu} \rho Q V_a^2}{2} \tag{8.33}$$

Since the power required to overcome the momentum drag P_m is equal to $\rho Q V_a^2$, the ratio of P_r to P_m is

$$\frac{P_r}{P_m} = \frac{\eta_{cu} \rho Q V_a^2}{2\rho Q V_a^2} = \frac{\eta_{cu}}{2} \tag{8.34}$$

This indicates that if the efficiency of the cushion system η_{cu} is 100%, half of the power expended in overcoming the momentum drag can be recovered.

Trim Drag   If the cushion base of the vehicle is not horizontal, the lift force that is perpendicular to the cushion base will have a horizontal component. This horizontal component is given by

$$R_{tr} = p_{cu}A_c \sin \theta_t \qquad (8.35)$$

where θ_t is the trim angle (i.e., the angle between the cushion base and the horizontal). R_{tr} may be a drag or a thrust component, dependent upon whether the vehicle is trimmed nose up or down.

Skirt Contact Drag   For overland operations, contact between the skirt and the ground may be inevitable, particularly at low clearance heights. This gives rise to a drag component commonly known as the skirt contact drag R_{sk}. The physical origin of this drag component appears to be derived from the following major sources: friction between the skirt and the ground, and the deformation of the skirt and the terrain, including vegetation due to skirt–ground interaction [8.6]. A reliable method for predicting skirt contact drag is lacking, although from experience it is known that the cushion pressure, clearance height, skirt design and material, and the strength and geometry of the terrain surface have a significant influence on the skirt contact drag. The value of the skirt contact drag is usually obtained from experiments. Table 8.1 gives the values of the coefficient of towing resistance of two air-cushion trailers and a self-propelled air-cushion vehicle over various types of terrain [8.7, 8.8]. One of the air-cushion trailers is equipped with a Bertin-type multiple-cone system with a peripheral skirt and is built by HoverJak; the other is equipped with the Hovercraft Development Ltd. segmented skirt and is built by Terracross [8.7]. The self-propelled air-cushion vehicle is a Bell SK-5 equipped with the type of fingered skirt developed by the British Hovercraft Corporation [8.8]. The coefficient of towing resistance is defined as the ratio of the towing resistance to the total vehicle weight.

It should be mentioned that for the air-cushion trailer built by HoverJak, 2% of the total vehicle weight is carried by the guided wheels, whereas for the one built by Terracross, 7% of the vehicle weight is carried by the guided wheels. The values given in Table 8.1 for the air-cushion trailers include, therefore, both the skirt contact drag and the rolling resistance of the guided wheels. The values given in Table 8.1 for the Bell SK-5 may be considered to be those of the coefficient of skirt contact drag since no guided wheels were used.

In logged-over areas with stumps, the average values of the coefficient of towing resistance range from 0.06 to 0.24 for an air-cushion trailer equipped with a Bertin-type multiple-cone system having a peripheral skirt [8.9].

Knowing the value of the coefficient of skirt contact drag C_{sk}, one can calculate the skirt contact drag R_{sk} from the following equation:

TABLE 8.1 Coefficient of Towing Resistance

Type of Vehicle	Type of Air-Cushion System	Terrain	Coefficient of Towing Resistance	Total Vehicle Weight (kN)
Air-cushion trailer by HoverJak	Multiple-cone system with peripheral skirt	Concrete, dry	0.002–0.005	148.3
		Flat rock, dry	0.014–0.018	(34,000 lb)
		Dry mud	0.011–0.016	130.8
		Sandy road	0.023	(30,000 lb)
Air-cushion trailer by Terracross	H.D.L. type segmented skirt	Wet flat rock	0.018	143.5
				(30,000 lb)
		Water or mud	0.015	
		Wet mud	0.019	206.9
		Dry mud	0.022–0.037	(50,000 lb)
		Churned marsh	0.035	
Self-propelled air-cushion vehicle Bell SK-5	B.H.C. type fingered skirt	Rough hummocky snow, hard-glazed surface	0.002	
		Rock-strewn creek bed, left rough	0.012–0.022	
		Rock-strewn creek bed, graded level	0.020–0.030	58.1 (13,060 lb)
		Swamp grass, tufts in water	0.006–0.034	
		Light brush on rough ground	0.075–0.25	

Source: References 8.7 and 8.8.

$$R_{sk} = C_{sk} W \qquad (8.36)$$

where W is the total vehicle weight.

As mentioned previously, among the various factors, the skirt clearance height has a considerable influence on the skirt contact drag. To establish quantitative relationships between the clearance height of the skirt and the coefficient of skirt contact drag over various surfaces, a series of experiments were carried out by Fowler at the National Research Council of Canada [8.10]. The experiments were performed using segmented skirts at a low speed of approximately 2 m/s (6.6 ft/s) over surfaces ranging from concrete through terrains covered with long grass to rough porous ground with crushed rock. Figure 8.7 shows the variation of the coefficient of skirt contact drag with the product of the clearance height h_c and the coefficient K_{por}, based on measured data. The coefficient K_{por} takes into account the effects of ground porosity on the volume flow of the air cushion system. For instance, over porous ground with crushed rock, the cushion air will escape through not only the clearance between the skirt and the surface, but also the void between rocks under the cushion. This indicates that the total volume flow of the air from the cushion will be higher by a factor of K_{por} than that calculated using Eqs. 8.3, 8.11, 8.14, or 8.23. Accordingly, the power required to sustain the air cushion will also be higher. The approximate values of K_{por} for various types of ground are given in Table 8.2 [8.10]. It can be seen that over a smooth concrete, the value of K_{por} is 1, which indicates that the cushion air only escapes through the clearance between the skirt and the concrete surface. Over crushed rock, the value of K_{por} can be as high as 6, which indicates that the volume of air escaping through the void between rocks is five times that through the clearance between the skirt and the surface.

From Fig. 8.7, it can be seen that the coefficient of skirt contact drag increases significantly when the value of $h_c K_{por}$ falls below a threshold value. For instance, over a smooth concrete, if the value of $h_c K_{por}$ is lower than approximately 0.0035 m (0.14 in.), the value of the coefficient of skirt contact drag will increase

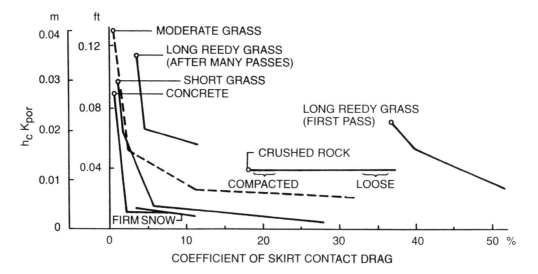

Fig. 8.7 Effect of clearance and ground porosity parameter $h_c K_{por}$ on skirt contact drag coefficient over different surfaces. (Reproduced from reference 8.10.)

TABLE 8.2   Values of Coefficient K_{por} for Various Surfaces

Ground	K_{por}
Smooth concrete	1
Firm snow	1.5
Short grass	6
Moderate grass	6
Long reedy grass (first pass)	6
Long reedy grass (tenth pass)	6
Crushed rock	6

Source: Reference 8.10.

significantly. For long reedy grass (after many passes), the threshold value of $h_c K_{por}$ is approximately, 0.02 m (0.79 in.). It should be noted that the value of $h_c K_{por}$ determines the volume flow and power for lift, while the coefficient of skirt contact drag affects the power for propulsion. To achieve an optimum operating condition for an overland air cushion vehicle, the value of $h_c K_{por}$ must be, therefore, carefully selected so that the total power requirement (including both power for lift and for propulsion) is minimized.

Total Overland Drag For a vehicle wholly supported by an air cushion operating overland, the total drag consists of the aerodynamic resistance, momentum drag, trim drag, and skirt contact drag. It should be pointed out that although wholly air-cushion-supported vehicles can function overland, they are relatively difficult to maneuver and control in constricted space and in the traverse of a slope. The longitudinal slope that this type of vehicle can negotiate is also limited. To solve these problems, surface-contacting devices such as wheels, tracks, and the like may be used. In this type of arrangement, the air cushion is used to carry a proportion of the vehicle weight, while leaving sufficient surface contact for directional control, positioning, and possibly for traction and braking. A vehicle that uses an air cushion together with surface-contacting devices for support is usually referred to as a "hybrid vehicle."

For the hybrid vehicle, the resistance of the surface-contacting device must be taken into consideration in computing the total overland drag. The resistance of the wheels and tracks over unprepared terrain can be predicted using the methods described in Chapter 2. It is found that among the design parameters, the load distribution between the air cushion and the surface-contacting device has a considerable effect on the total power consumption of the hybrid vehicle [8.3]. Figure 8.8 shows the variation of power consumption with the ratio of the load supported by the air cushion W_a to the total vehicle weight W for a particular hybrid vehicle equipped with tires over clay [8.3]. It is shown that for a given hybrid vehicle over a particular type of terrain, there is an optimum load distribution that could minimize the power consumption. Figure 8.9 shows the variation of the optimum load distribution with terrain conditions for a particular hybrid vehicle equipped with tires [8.3].

Another type of overland vehicle system employing air-cushion technology is the air-cushion trailer-towing vehicle system [8.11]. It consists of two separate units: an air-cushion trailer, and a towing vehicle. Figure 8.10 shows schematically an air-cushion trailer built by Terracross [8.7]. The towing vehicle is usually a conventional tracked or wheeled vehicle. The system offers the convenience of an ordinary tractor–trailer unit. It should be mentioned, however, that since the air-cushion trailer is not self-propelled, the mobility of the system depends on the towing vehicle. This restricts the use of this system to areas where the conventional towing vehicle can operate effectively. The towing vehicle has to develop sufficient drawbar pull to overcome the total drag acting on the air-cushion trailer, which includes the skirt contact drag, resistance of guided wheels, and trim drag. This type of system normally operates at low speeds; aerodynamic resistance and mo-

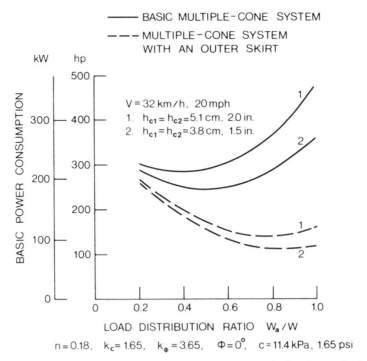

Fig. 8.8 Variation of basic power consumption with load distribution ratio for a hybrid vehicle in clay; the values of k_c and k_ϕ are in U.S. customary units.

mentum drag acting on the air cushion trailer would be insignificant and may be neglected.

As mentioned previously, one of the basic functions of the air-cushion system is to support the vehicle weight. As a consequence, power is required to generate the cushion lift. To compare the relative merits of an air-cushion vehicle with a conventional ground vehicle on a rational basis, the power required to generate the lift by the cushion should be considered equivalent to part of the power required to overcome the motion resistance of a conventional vehicle. The concept of the equivalent coefficient of motion resistance f_{eq} for a vehicle wholly supported by an air cushion is proposed. It is defined as

$$f_{eq} = \frac{P_a}{WV} + \frac{R_m + R_a + R_{sk}}{W} \tag{8.37}$$

where P_a is the power required to sustain the air cushion, W is the total weight of the vehicle, and V is the vehicle speed. It is noted that the equivalent coefficient of motion resistance of an air-cushion vehicle depends on the operating speed.

For a hybrid vehicle partly supported by an air cushion and partly supported by surface-contacting devices, such as tracks and wheels, the equivalent coefficient of motion resistance is defined as

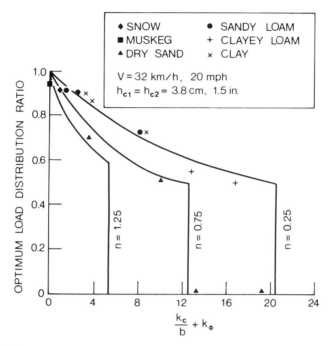

Fig. 8.9 Variation of the optimum load distribution with terrain conditions for a hybrid vehicle equipped with a multiple-cone system having a peripheral skirt; the values of k_c and k_ϕ are in U.S. customary units.

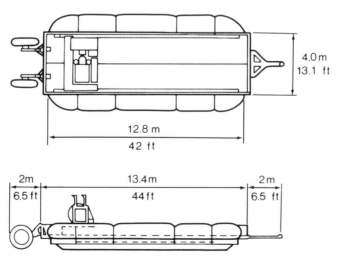

Fig. 8.10 An air-cushion trailer with segmented skirt. (Reproduced with permission from reference 8.7.)

$$f_{eq} = \frac{P_a}{WV} + \frac{R_m + R_a + R_{sk} + R_r}{W} \tag{8.38}$$

where R_r is the motion resistance of the surface contacting device. Figure 8.11 shows the variation of the equivalent coefficient of motion resistance with operating speed for a particular hybrid vehicle equipped with tires over clay, loose sand, and snow [8.11].

Wave-Making Drag   When an air-cushion vehicle travels over water, waves will be generated, as shown in Fig. 8.12. The vehicle tends to align itself with the

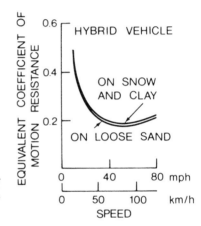

Fig. 8.11 Variation of the equivalent coefficient of motion resistance with speed of a hybrid vehicle over different types of terrain.

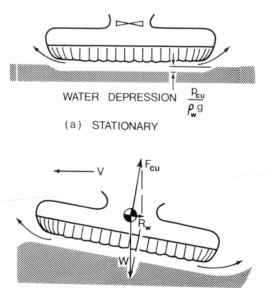

Fig. 8.12 Formation of wave-making drag.

wave, and the cushion base will be inclined. Thus, the lift force produces a rearward component that is commonly known as the wave-making drag.

To reach a better understanding of the mechanism that generates the wave-making drag, it is instructive to consider the nature of the interaction between the air cushion and the water. When the vehicle is on a cushion over water at zero forward speed, the water will be depressed by an amount equal to $p_{cu}/\rho_w g$ where g is the acceleration due to gravity and ρ_w is the mass density of the water, as shown in Fig. 8.12(a). When the vehicle travels forward, the water under the front part of the vehicle is just coming under the action of the cushion pressure, whereas under the rear part of the vehicle, the water surface has been subjected to cushion pressure for a certain period of time. As a consequence, the water surface will be inclined downward towards the rear. As the vehicle tends to align itself with the water surface, the cushion base will take a nose-up attitude, as shown in Fig. 8.12(b). The rearward component of the lift force perpendicular to the cushion base gives rise to the wave-making drag. The magnitude of this drag component increases with speed, and reaches a maximum at a particular speed that is usually referred to as the "hump speed." As the vehicle speed further increases, the time during which the cushion interacts with the water surface becomes shorter. Consequently, the depression of the water becomes less, and the water surface under the vehicle begins to approach level again. The wave-making drag, therefore, decreases accordingly.

The wave-making drag may be predicted with sufficient accuracy by various methods. For a relatively long and narrow air-cushion vehicle, a two-dimensional theory for predicting the wave-making drag R_w based on Lamb's work has been proposed by Crewe and Egginton [8.1, 8.12]:

$$R_w = \frac{2p_{cu}^2 A_c}{l\rho_w g}\left(1 - \cos\frac{gl}{V^2}\right)$$

or

$$\frac{R_w l}{p_{cu}^2 A_c} = \frac{2}{\rho_w g}\left(1 - \cos\frac{gl}{V^2}\right) \tag{8.39}$$

where l is the length of the cushion, p_{cu} is the cushion pressure, A_c is the cushion area, V is the vehicle forward speed, and $V/\sqrt{gl}$ is the Froude number. The variation of $R_w l/p_{cu}^2 A_c$ with the Froude number is shown in Fig. 8.13 [8.1]. It is shown that the wave-making drag is a maximum when the Froude number is 0.56 or $\cos(gl/V^2)$ is equal to -1. This condition is commonly known as the "hump," and the associated drag is called "hump drag." It is interesting to note that the wave-making drag is proportional to the square of the cushion pressure.

A more accurate method for predicting wave-making drag that takes the shape of the planform of the vehicle into account has been developed by Newman and Poole [8.13]. It should be mentioned that the water depth also affects the wave-

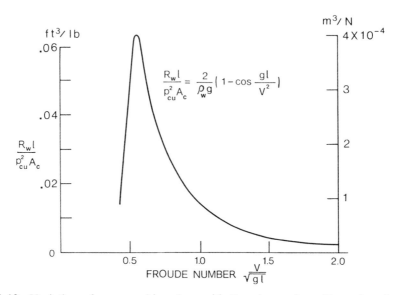

Fig. 8.13 Variation of wave-making drag with Froude number. (Reproduced with permission from *Hovercraft Design and Construction* by G.H. Elsley and A.J. Devereux, copyright © by Elsley and Devereux 1968.)

making drag. Over shallow water, the wave-making drag is higher than that over deep water [8.13].

Wetting Drag   The wetting drag is a drag component due to water spray striking the skirt and skirt–water contact. Although it is known that the clearance height, cushion pressure, vehicle size and shape, and vehicle speed have an influence over the magnitude of the wetting drag, no satisfactory method exists for the prediction of this drag component. A common practice to determine the wetting drag is to measure the total drag over calm water by model or full-scale tests, and then to subtract those drag components that are known or calculable. Thus, the wetting drag R_{wet} is given by [8.1, 8.5]

$$R_{wet} = R_{tot} \text{ (calm water)} - R_a - R_m - R_w - R_{tr} \text{ (if any)} \qquad (8.40)$$

where R_{tot} (calm water) is the total drag measured over calm water.

Drag Due to Waves   So far, no theoretical method is available for the prediction of the drag due to waves. Its value is obtained from model or full-scale tests [8.1, 8.5]. Taking the difference between the total drag over waves, R_{tot} (over waves), and that over calm water, R_{tot} (calm water), at the same speed, one can obtain the drag due to waves R_{wave}:

$$R_{wave} = R_{tot} \text{ (over waves)} - R_{tot} \text{ (calm water)} \qquad (8.41)$$

It has been shown that the wave height, cushion pressure, skirt depth, and vehicle speed have significant effects on the drag due to waves.

Total Overwater Drag   For overwater operations, the total drag of an air-cushion vehicle consists of the aerodynamic resistance, momentum drag, wave-making drag, wetting drag, and drag due to waves. Figure 8.14 shows the relative order of magnitude of various drag components as a function of vehicle speed for overwater operations [8.5]. For vehicles with sidewalls, additional sidewall drag, mainly due to skin friction over the immersed surface, should also be taken into account.

It should be noted that the power consumption of an air-cushion vehicle consists of two major parts: power for lift and power for propulsion. In designing an air-cushion vehicle, power for lift and power for propulsion should, therefore, not be considered in isolation. For instance, increasing the clearance height or volume flow would reduce the skirt contact drag, and hence the power for propulsion.

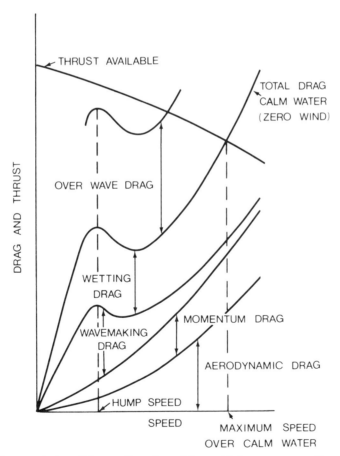

Fig. 8.14 Characteristics of drags of an air-cushion vehicle over water. (Reproduced with permission of R.L. Trillo from reference 8.5.)

However, as discussed previously, the power for lift is proportional to the clearance height. Thus, a compromise has to be made in selecting the clearance height so that the total power requirement would be a minimum, and it should also be compatible with other criteria such as skirt wear and ride comfort.

Example 8.2. The air-cushion vehicle described in Example 8.1 is to be used in overland transport. The frontal area of the vehicle is 6.5 m² (70 ft²) and the aerodynamic drag coefficient is 0.35. The coefficient of the skirt contact drag is estimated to be 0.04. Determine the total drag of the vehicle over level ground at a speed of 20 km/h (12.4 mph).

Solution. The total overland drag includes momentum drag, aerodynamic drag, and skirt contact drag.

  a) The momentum drag R_m is given by Eq. 8.31:

$$R_m = \rho Q V_a = \rho \left[h_{c2} l_{c2} D_{c2} \left(\frac{2k_p p_{cu}}{\rho} \right)^{1/2} \right] V_a$$

Substituting the appropriate values given into the equation above, one obtains

$$R_m = 110.8 \text{ N (24.9 lb)}$$

  b) The aerodynamic drag R_a can be determined using Eq. 3.19:

$$R_a = \frac{\rho}{2} C_D A_f V^2 = 43.2 \text{ N (9.7 lb)}$$

  c) The skirt contact drag R_{sk} can be estimated using Eq. 8.36:

$$R_{sk} = C_{sk} W = 1957 \text{ N (440 lb)}$$

The total overland drag is the sum of the above three drag components:

$$R_{tot} = R_m + R_a + R_{sk} = 2.111 \text{ kN (474.6 lb)}$$

The results indicate that the momentum drag and aerodynamic drag are insignificant at low speeds.

8.3 SUSPENSION CHARACTERISTICS OF AIR-CUSHION SYSTEMS

One of the major functions of an air cushion is to act as a suspension system for the vehicle. To define its characteristics as a suspension, the stiffness and damping in bounce (or heave), roll, and pitch must be determined.

8.3.1 Heave (or Bounce) Stiffness

The heave (or bounce) stiffness can be derived from the relationship between the lift force and vertical displacement. For a simple plenum chamber, this relationship depends, to a great extent, on the fan characteristics. For a practical plenum chamber system, the ducting between the fan and the cushion and the feeding arrangements for the cushion also have a significant influence on its stiffness and damping characteristics. Consider that a simple plenum chamber is in equilibrium at an initial clearance height h_{c0} with initial cushion pressure p_{c0} and volume flow Q_0. Neglecting ducting losses, the fan will operate at point A, as shown in Fig. 8.15. Consider that the cushion system is disturbed from its equilibrium position, and that the clearance height decreases by an amount Δh_c. Accordingly, the volume flow will decrease by an amount ΔQ_0, and the pressure will increase from p_{c0} to $p_{c0} + \Delta p_c$. The operating point of the fan shifts from A to A'. Thus, a restoring force which tends to bring the cushion system back to its original equilibrium position is created, and the system is stable in heave.

If the parameters of the cushion system and the fan characteristics are known, the heave stiffness about an equilibrium position can be predicted [8.14]. An approximate method for predicting the stiffness of a simple plenum chamber is described below to illustrate the procedures involved.

The general relationship between the pressure and volume flow of a fan commonly used in air-cushion vehicles is expressed by

$$p = f(Q)$$

and

$$\frac{dp}{dQ} = f'(Q) \qquad f'(Q) < 0 \tag{8.42}$$

where $f'(Q)$ is the slope of the pressure–flow characteristic curve of the fan.

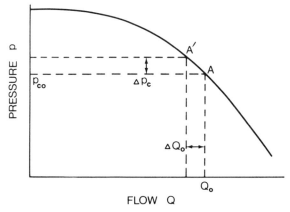

Fig. 8.15 Pressure–flow characteristics of a fan.

The volume flow from the cushion for a simple plenum chamber is governed by Eq. 8.3, and the relationship between the cushion pressure and the air escaping velocity is given by Eq. 8.2. By differentiating Eqs. 8.2 and 8.3, the following relationships can be obtained.

From Eq. 8.2,

$$dV_c = \frac{dp_{cu}}{\rho V_c} \tag{8.43}$$

and from Eq. 8.3,

$$dQ = h_c l_{cu} D_c dV_c + V_c l_{cu} D_c dh_c \tag{8.44}$$

Substituting Eq. 8.43 into Eq. 8.44, one obtains

$$dQ = h_c l_{cu} D_c \frac{dp_{cu}}{\rho V_c} + V_c l_{cu} D_c dh_c \tag{8.45}$$

Neglecting pressure losses between the fan and the cushion (i.e., $p = p_{cu}$) and combining Eqs. 8.42 and 8.45, one obtains

$$dp_{cu} \left[\frac{1}{f'(Q)} - \frac{h_c l_{cu} D_c}{\rho V_c} \right] = V_c l_{cu} D_c dh_c$$

or

$$\frac{dp_{cu}}{\rho V_c^2/2} \left[\frac{\rho V_c}{h_c l_{cu} D_c f'(Q)} - 1 \right] = \frac{2 l_{cu} D_c dh_c}{h_c l_{cu} D_c} \tag{8.46}$$

Since $p_{cu} = \rho V_c^2/2$, the above equation can be written as

$$\frac{dp_{cu}}{p_{cu}} = \left[\frac{2}{\rho V_c/h_c l_{cu} D_c f'(Q) - 1} \right] \frac{dh_c}{h_c} \tag{8.47}$$

The lift force generated by the cushion F_{cu} is equal to $p_{cu} A_c$; the above equation, therefore, can be rewritten as

$$\frac{dF_{cu}}{dh_c} = \left[\frac{2}{\rho V_c/h_c l_{cu} D_c f'(Q) - 1} \right] \frac{F_{cu}}{h_c}$$

$$= K_h \frac{F_{cu}}{h_c} \tag{8.48}$$

Equation 8.48 gives the equivalent heave stiffness of a simple plenum chamber about the equilibrium position. It can be seen that the heave stiffness is strongly dependent on the slope of the pressure–flow characteristic curve of the fan $f'(Q)$. Since the value of $f'(Q)$ varies with the operating point of the fan, bounce stiffness is a function of operating conditions. The general characteristics of the cushion pressure–displacement relationship of a simple plenum chamber under steady-state conditions are shown in Fig. 8.16 [8.5]. It can be seen that the air cushion is essentially a nonlinear system. However, for motions with small amplitudes about an equilibrium position, the system may be linearized.

The damping characteristics of an air-cushion system may be determined experimentally, for instance, using a dynamic heave table [8.5]. The cushion system being tested is mounted above the heave table, which can move up and down relative to the cushion with various amplitudes and frequencies. At a particular amplitude and frequency, the variation of cushion pressure with displacement in a complete cycle is measured. If the system possesses damping, the variation of cushion pressure with displacement will follow different paths during the upward and downward strokes of the table, as shown in Fig. 8.16. The area enclosed by curve $ABCDA$ represents the degree of damping the cushion system possesses. The damping of an air cushion is usually not of a simple viscous type. It is asymmetric and dependent upon the frequency of motion. However, to simplify the analysis, an equivalent viscous damping coefficient c_{eq} for the air cushion may be derived on the basis of equal energy dissipation:

$$c_{eq} = \frac{U}{\pi \omega Z^2} \tag{8.49}$$

where U is the actual energy dissipated in the air cushion during a cycle that is represented by the area enclosed by curve $ABCDA$ in Fig. 8.16, and ω and Z are the circular frequency and amplitude of the heave table, respectively.

Figure 8.17 shows schematically an air-cushion system designed for high-speed guided ground vehicles [8.15]. One of its unique features is the inclusion of a

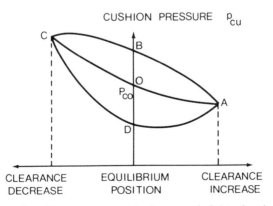

Fig. 8.16 Variation of cushion pressure with clearance height of a simple plenum chamber. (Reproduced with permission of R.L. Trillo from reference 8.5.)

damper to provide the vehicle with sufficient damping to acheive the required ride quality.

8.3.2 Roll Stiffness

Stability in the roll and pitch of air-cushion vehicles may be achieved by two methods: differential pressure and differential area. The multiple-cone system developed by Bertin obtains stability in roll and pitch from the pressure differential between the downgoing side and the upgoing side of the skirt system, as shown in Fig. 8.18. When the vehicle rolls, the clearance height on the downgoing side decreases. From previous analysis, it is known that the volume flow will decrease and the cushion pressure will increase. On the upgoing side, however, the cushion pressure will decrease because of the increase of the clearance height and volume flow. The increase of the lift force on the downgoing side and the decrease of the lift force on the upgoing side form a restoring moment that tends to bring the cushion system back to its equilibrium position.

Consider that the simple cushion system shown in Fig. 8.18 rolls a small angle

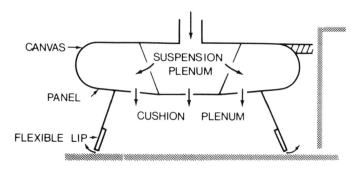

Fig. 8.17 An air-cushion system designed for high-speed guided ground vehicles. (Reproduced with permission from reference 8.15.)

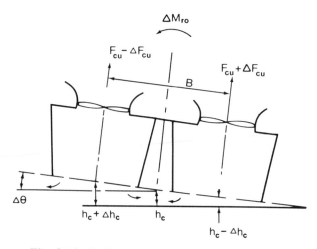

Fig. 8.18 Roll stability by differential pressure.

$\Delta\theta$ with respect to the equilibrium position. The clearance height on the downgoing side will decrease by an average amount Δh_c:

$$\Delta h_c = (B/2)\Delta\theta \qquad (8.50)$$

where B is the beam of the cushion.

On the upgoing side, the clearance height will increase by the same amount. From Eq. 8.48, the restoring moment ΔM_{r0} corresponding to the angular displacement $\Delta\theta$ is expressed by

$$\Delta M_{r0} = B\Delta F_{cu} = \frac{BF_{cu}K_h}{h_c}\Delta h_c$$

$$= \frac{B^2 F_{cu}K_h}{2h_c}\Delta\theta \qquad (8.51)$$

In the limit, the roll stiffness of the system K_r is given by

$$K_r = \frac{dM_{r0}}{d\theta} = \frac{B^2 F_{cu}K_h}{2h_c} \qquad (8.52)$$

Figure 8.19 shows the variation of the restoring moment coefficient C_{r0}, which is equal to $2M_{r0}/WB'$, with roll angle for a $1/5$ scale model of the Bertin BC 8 air cushion vehicle [8.16]. In Fig. 8.19, the effects of the difference in clearance height between the cones and the peripheral skirt on the roll characteristics are illustrated. When the roll angle exceeds a certain range and the downgoing side of the skirt comes into contact with the ground, the roll characteristics of the multiple-

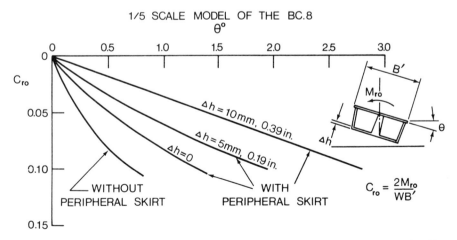

Fig. 8.19 Roll characteristics of the Bertin BC 8 cushion system. (Reproduced with permission from "French Air Cushion Vehicle Developments," by J. Bertin, *Canadian Aeronautics and Space Journal*, January 1968.)

cone system may change significantly, and considerable hysteresis has been observed [8.17].

Roll and pitch stability can also be achieved by using inflated bags (or keels) to divide the cushion into compartments. This method has been used by the British Hovercraft Corporation in their skirt systems, as shown in Fig. 8.20(a) [8.4]. The air pressure in the fan plenum is common to all compartments. However, when the vehicle rolls, on the upgoing side the flow increases, and consequently, the cushion pressure decreases because of increased pressure losses through the cushion feed holes shown in Fig. 8.5(b). On the downgoing side, the flow decreases and the cushion pressure increases accordingly. As a result, a restoring moment is generated, which tends to return the system to its original equilibrium position. This method of achieving roll and pitch stability is essentially based on the principle of differential pressure.

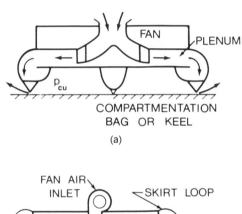

(a)

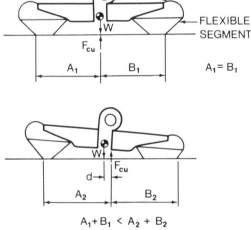

ROLL STABILITY BY DIFFERENTIAL AREA

(b)

Fig. 8.20 (a) Roll stability by compartmentation. (Reproduced with permission of the Society of Automotive Engineers from reference 8.4.) (b) Roll stability by differential area. (Reproduced with permission from reference 8.7.)

The method for obtaining stability in roll and pitch by differential area has been employed by Hovercraft Development Ltd. in the design of their skirt systems. Stability is achieved by the outward movement of the downgoing side of the skirt, thus increasing the cushion area of the downgoing side, as shown in Fig. 8.20(b) [8.7]. Consequently, the lift force on the downgoing side increases, and a restoring moment is generated.

8.4 DIRECTIONAL CONTROL OF AIR-CUSHION VEHICLES

For vehicles wholly supported on an air cushion, their relative freedom from the surface presents unique problems in directional control. The methods for directional control may be divided into four main categories: aerodynamic control surfaces, differential thrust, thrust vectoring, and control ports. These methods are illustrated in Fig. 8.21 [8.2].

Using aerodynamic control surfaces, such as rudders in the slipstream of the air propeller, could provide an effective means for directional control of vehicles wholly supported on an air cushion. However, their effectiveness diminishes with a decrease of the slipstream velocity at low thrust. The control surfaces may also induce adverse rolling moments if the center of pressure of these surfaces is high relative to the center of gravity of the vehicle.

An adequate degree of directional control may be achieved by differential thrust

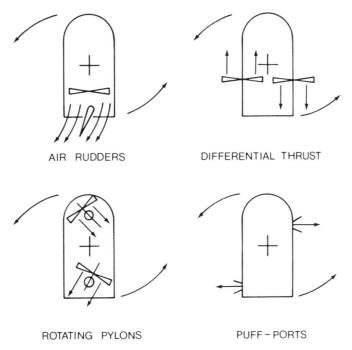

Fig. 8.21 Methods for directional control of air-cushion vehicles. (Reproduced from reference 8.2.)

produced by twin propellers fixed side by side, as shown in Fig. 8.21. The differential thrust may be obtained by controlling the propeller pitch and/or rotating speed. It should be noted, however, that decreasing the thrust on one of the propellers reduces the total forward thrust available, and hence the vehicle speed. In this fixed side-by-side propeller configuration, the thrust is parallel to the longitudinal axis of the vehicle. To provide a lateral force to balance the centrifugal force during a turning maneuver, the vehicle has to operate with a certain yaw angle, as shown in Fig. 8.22 [8.2].

Using fore and aft swiveling pylon-mounted propellers, the yawing moment and side force required for direction control can be generated. For some current designs, the swivel angle is confined to 30° on either side of the longitudinal axis to limit the magnitude of the adverse roll moment. Compared with the fixed side-by-side propeller arrangement, swiveling pylon-mounted propellers can generate a higher yawing moment since the propellers can be mounted further from the center of gravity of the vehicle and less forward thrust is lost for a given yawing moment.

By discharging pressurized air from the so-called "puff-ports" located at each corner of the vehicle, the yawing moment and side force can be provided. They are usually used as an auxiliary device to supplement other control devices.

To further improve the directional control of air-cushion vehicles, surface-contacting devices, such as wheels for overland operations and retractable water rods for overwater operations, have been used. For overland operations, the wheels carry a proportion of the vehicle weight to provide the vehicle with the required cornering force for directional control. The load carried by the wheels ranges from 2 to 30% of the total vehicle weight in existing designs, depending on whether or not the wheels are also used as a propulsive device. It has been found that using the wheel as a directional control device is quite effective [8.3].

The cornering force that a wheel can develop for control purposes consists of two major components: the lateral shearing force on the contact area, and the lateral force resulting from the normal pressure exerted on the sidewall of the wheel, which is similar in nature to that acting on a bulldozer blade or a retaining

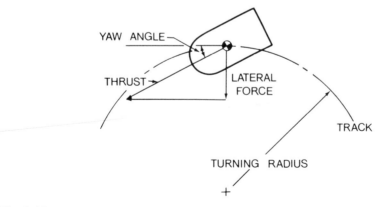

Fig. 8.22 Turning of an air-cushion vehicle with a yaw angle. (Reproduced from reference 8.2.)

wall, as illustrated in Fig. 8.23. The magnitude of this force depends on the sink-age of the wheel and terrain properties, and it may be predicted by the earth pres-sure theory of soil mechanics discussed in Chapter 2.

As an example, Fig. 8.24 shows the variation of the maximum lateral acceler-ation a_y that can be sustained under a steady-state turn with load distribution for a particular hybrid vehicle with tires over clay [8.3]. The lateral acceleration shown is calculated from the maximum cornering force that can be developed by the tires of the vehicle. The possible minimum turning radius of the vehicle at a forward speed of 16 km/h (10 mph) is also plotted as a function of load distribution in Fig. 8.24.

For overwater air-cushion vehicles, methods similar to those for controlling the direction of ships may be employed. For instance, rudders immersed in the water have been used in air-cushion vehicles with rigid sidewalls for purposes of direc-tional control.

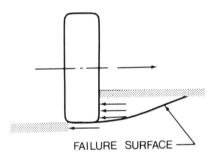

FAILURE SURFACE

Fig. 8.23 Development of cornering force by a tire on deformable terrain.

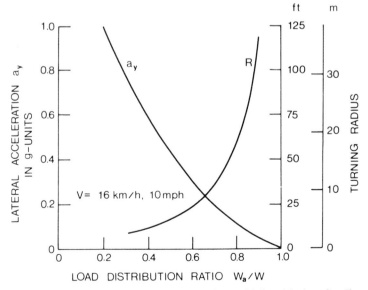

Fig. 8.24 Cornering characteristics of an air-cushion vehicle with tires for directional con-trol in clay.

REFERENCES

8.1 G.H. Elsley and A.J. Devereux, *Hovercraft Design and Construction*. Cornell Maritime Press Inc., 1968.

8.2 National Research Council of Canada, "Air Cushion Vehicles—Their Potential for Canada," Dec. 1969.

8.3 J.Y. Wong, "Performance of the Air-Cushion-Surface-Contacting Hybrid Vehicle for Overland Operation," *Proc. Institution of Mechanical Engineers*, vol. 186, no. 50/72, 1972.

8.4 P.A. Sullivan, "A Review of the Status of the Technology of the Air Cushion Vehicle," *SAE Transactions*, vol. 80, paper 710183, 1971.

8.5 R.L. Trillo, *Marine Hovercraft Technology*. London, England: Leonard Hill, 1971.

8.6 H.S. Fowler, "The Air Cushion Vehicle as a Load Spreading Transport Device," *Journal of Terramechanics*, vol. 12, no. 2, 1975.

8.7 P.L. Eggleton and J. Laframboise, "Field Evaluation of Towed Air Cushion Rafts," Report of Transportation Development Agency, TDA-500-166, Ministry of Transport, Ottawa, Ont., Canada, 1974.

8.8 R.A. Liston, "Operational Evaluation of the SK-5 Air Cushion Vehicle in Alaska," U.S. Army Cold Regions Research and Engineering Laboratory, Report TR 413, 1973.

8.9 C.R. Silversides, T.B. Tsay, and H.M. Mucha, "Effect of Obstacles and Ground Clearance Upon the Movement of an ACV Platform," Forest Management Institute, Information Report FMR-X-62, Department of the Environment, Ottawa, Ont., Canada, 1974.

8.10 H.S. Fowler, "On the Lift-Air Requirement of Air Cushion Vehicles and Its Relation to the Terrain and Operational Mode," Report of the National Research Council of Canada No. 17492 (ME-246), 1979.

8.11 J.Y. Wong, "On the Applications of Air Cushion Technology to Overland Transport," *High Speed Ground Transportation Journal*, vol. 6, no. 3, 1972.

8.12 P.R. Crewe and W.J. Egginton, "The Hovercraft—A New Concept in Maritime Transport," *Quarterly Transactions of Royal Institute of Naval Architects*, no. 3, July 1960.

8.13 J.N. Newman and F.A.P. Poole, "The Wave Resistance of a Moving Pressure Distribution in a Canal," *Schiffstechnik*, vol. 9, no. 45, 1962.

8.14 P. Guienne, "Stability of the Terraplane on the Ground," *Hovering Craft and Hydrofoil*, July 1964.

8.15 J.P. Morel and C. Bonnat, "Air Cushion Suspension for Aerotrain: Theoretical Schemes for Static and Dynamic Operation," in H.B. Pacejka, Ed., *Proc. IUTAM Symp. on the Dynamics of Vehicles on Roads and Railway Tracks*. Amsterdam, The Netherlands: Swets and Zeitlinger B.V., 1975.

8.16 J. Bertin, "French Air Cushion Vehicle Developments," *Canadian Aeronautics and Space Journal*, vol. 14, no. 1, Jan. 1968.

8.17 P.A. Sullivan, M.J. Hinchey, and R.G. Delaney, "An Investigation of the Roll Stiffness Characteristics of Three Flexible Skirted Cushion Systems," Institute for Aerospace Studies, University of Toronto, Toronto, Ont., Canada, Report 213, 1977.

8.18 J.Y. Wong, "On the Application of Air Cushion Technology to Off-Road Transport," *Canadian Aeronautics and Space Journal*, vol. 19, no. 1, Jan. 1973.

PROBLEMS

8.1 An air-cushion vehicle has a gross weight of 80.06 kN (18,000 lb). Its planform is essentially of rectangular shape, 6.09 m (20 ft) wide and 12.19 m (40 ft) long. The cushion system is of the plenum chamber type. The cushion wall angle is 45° with the horizontal. It operates at an average daylight clearance of 2.54 cm (1 in.). Determine the power required to sustain the air cushion. Also calculate the augmentation factor.

8.2 An air-cushion vehicle has the same weight and planform as those of the vehicle described in Problem 8.1, but is equipped with a multiple-cone system with a peripheral skirt. It has eight cones with a diameter of 2.44 m (8 ft). The average daylight clearance of the cones is 2.54 cm (1 in.) and that of the peripheral skirt is 1.9 cm (0.75 in.). The wall angles of the cones and the peripheral skirt are 85° with the horizontal. Determine the power required to generate the cushion lift using a suitable peripheral skirt.

8.3 The air-cushion vehicle described in Problem 8.2 is employed for overland transport. The frontal area of the vehicle is 16.26 m^2 (175 ft^2) and the aerodynamic drag coefficient is 0.38. The value of the coefficient of skirt contact drag over a particular terrain is 0.03. Determine the total overland drag of the vehicle at a speed of 20 km/h (12.4 mph). Also calculate the total power requirements, including both for lift and for propulsion, at that speed.

8.4 Determine the equivalent coefficient of motion resistance of the air-cushion vehicle described in Problem 8.3 at a speed of 20 km/h (12.4 mph).

8.5 The air-cushion vehicle described in Problem 8.1 is employed for overwater transport. The frontal area of the vehicle is 16.26 m^2 (175 ft^2) and the aerodynamic drag coefficient is 0.38. Neglecting the wetting drag, determine the total overwater drag of the vehicle at the hump speed over calm, deep water. Also calculate the total power requirements of the vehicle at the hump speed.

8.6 A proposed tracked air-cushion vehicle weights 195.71 kN (44,000 lb) and has eight lift pads, each of which is 4.27 m (14 ft) long and 1.3 m (4.25 ft) wide. The cushion is of the peripheral jet type with a jet thickness of 6.35 mm (0.25 in.) and the angle of the jet with respect to the horizontal is 50°. The clearance is 6.35 mm (0.25 in.) at equilibrium. If the vehicle is simplified to a single-degree-of-freedom system, estimate the equivalent stiffness of the air-cushion pads and the natural frequency of the vehicle in bounce around the equilibrium position.

INDEX